Slow Fade to Black

Main entrance to the RKO Studio, 780 Gower Street, Hollywood, California. Courtesy of the Academy of Motion Picture Arts and Sciences.

Slow Fade to Black
The Decline of RKO Radio Pictures

RICHARD B. JEWELL

University of California Press

University of California Press, one of the most distinguished university presses in the United States, enriches lives around the world by advancing scholarship in the humanities, social sciences, and natural sciences. Its activities are supported by the UC Press Foundation and by philanthropic contributions from individuals and institutions. For more information, visit www.ucpress.edu.

University of California Press
Oakland, California

© 2016 by Richard B. Jewell

Library of Congress Cataloging-in-Publication Data

Names: Jewell, Richard B., author.
Title: Slow fade to black : the decline of RKO Radio Pictures / Richard B. Jewell.
Description: Oakland, California : University of California Press, [2016] | "2016 | Includes bibliographical references and index.
Identifiers: LCCN 2016004856 | ISBN 9780520289666 (cloth : alk. paper) | ISBN 9780520289673 (pbk. : alk. paper) | ISBN 9780520964242 (ebook)
Subjects: LCSH: RKO Radio Pictures — History.
Classification: LCC PN1999.R3 J484 2016 | DDC 384/.806579494 — dc23
LC record available at http://lccn.loc.gov/2016004856

25 24 23 22 21 20 19 18 17 16
10 9 8 7 6 5 4 3 2 1

For
my parents, Willard and Ann Jewell,
and
my sister, Barbara Jewell Pond

Contents

List of Illustrations	ix
Preface	xi
1. "SHOWMANSHIP IN PLACE OF GENIUS": THE RATHVON-KOERNER REGIME (1942–1945)	1
2. "RKO'S SPIRIT ENCIRCLES GLOBE": THE RATHVON REGIME (1946)	37
3. "THE SCREEN HAS COME OF AGE": THE RATHVON-SCHARY REGIME (1947–1948)	57
4. "THERE IS A LOT OF LIFE IN THE OLD PLACE YET": THE HUGHES-DEPINET-ROGELL REGIME (1948–1950)	86
5. "THE PREDICTABLE UNPREDICTABLE": THE HUGHES-DEPINET REGIME (1950–1952)	107
6. "THE SHORTEST AND MOST BIZARRE PERIOD OF STUDIO OWNERSHIP IN FILM INDUSTRY HISTORY": THE STOLKIN INTERREGNUM (1952)	138
7. "INCOMPETENCE OR INDIFFERENCE": THE HUGHES-GRAINGER REGIME (1953–1955)	151
8. "HE HAD A GREAT SENSE OF ENTITLEMENT, MR. HUGHES": THE SIX-FOOT-FOUR ENIGMA (1948–1955)	180

9. "AN UNTOWARD TURN OF EVENTS":
   THE O'NEIL-O'SHEA-DOZIER REGIME (1955–1957)   188

   EPILOGUE   211

   Notes   217

   Selected Bibliography   249

   Index   255

Illustrations

Main entrance of RKO Studio, Hollywood	*frontispiece*
1. *It's All True*—Orson Welles in Fortaleza, Brazil	6
2. Producer Val Lewton working in his office	19
3. *Tender Comrade*—Charles Koerner celebrating his birthday	26
4. Picketers outside RKO studio	29
5. *Mourning Becomes Electra*—Dudley Nichols and N. Peter Rathvon	46
6. *It's a Wonderful Life*—Frank Capra and James Stewart	52
7. *Notorious*—Alfred Hitchcock, Cary Grant, and Ingrid Bergman	55
8. *Mr. Blandings Builds His Dream House*—H. C. Potter, Myrna Loy, Dore Schary, and Cary Grant	58
9. *Crossfire*—Jean Porter, Edward Dmytryk, Robert Ryan, Robert Young, and Robert Mitchum	70
10. *Out of the Past*—Jacques Tourneur, Jane Greer, and Robert Mitchum	75
11. Floyd Odlum working from home	80
12. *The Big Steal*—Don Siegel, Jack Gross, Robert Mitchum, and Sid Rogell	90
13. RKO Studio at Melrose and Gower in Hollywood	96
14. *Stromboli*—Roberto Rossellini and Ingrid Bergman	97
15. Edgar Bergen and Ned Depinet in Rockefeller Center office	109
16. Jerry Wald and Norman Krasna at RKO	115
17. Howard Hughes in his editing room	117

18. Ralph Stolkin surrounded by four partners — 139
19. *Split Second*—Dick Powell, Jan Sterling, Keith Andes, and Stephen McNally — 147
20. *The French Line*—Jane Russell — 166
21. *The Conqueror*—John Wayne and Dick Powell — 173
22. *Son of Sinbad*—Lili St. Cyr dancing — 177
23. Thomas F. O'Neil presents check to Thomas B. Slack — 189
24. Daniel T. O'Shea with Ginger Rogers — 192
25. *Bundle of Joy*—Norman Taurog, Eddie Fisher, Debbie Reynolds, and Edmund Grainger — 204

Preface

This volume completes my business history of RKO Radio Pictures, one of Hollywood's classical motion picture companies. The first half of the project, *RKO Radio Pictures: A Titan Is Born*, published by the University of California Press in 2012, covers the prehistory of the company through the first half of 1942. This second work picks up the narrative at that historical moment and chronicles the company's most successful era, as well as its decline and eventual death in 1957.

For those who have not read the first volume, a brief overview is in order. RKO came into existence in 1928 because the Radio Corporation of America needed an outlet and showcase for its newly perfected Photophone movie sound recording and reproduction equipment. But David Sarnoff of RCA, one of the pioneers of broadcasting in America, had a grand vision that ranged far beyond sound engineering. He looked forward to a day when radio, the movies, music recordings, theater, vaudeville and even television (then in the planning stages at RCA) would be combined in a symbiotic entertainment conglomerate, each component of which could support and invigorate the others. In short, Sarnoff envisioned the future of global entertainment, though he was unable to bring the dream to fruition during his lifetime.

One reason was the Great Depression, which demolished the dreams of many. Before the Hollywood industry began to suffer the effects of the nation's economic decline, Sarnoff's RKO performed nicely, posting decent profits in 1929 and 1930 despite mediocre early product. But then theater attendance throughout America executed a startling belly flop and, by 1933, RKO was essentially bankrupt. Thanks to the receivership provisions of the U.S. banking codes, the company continued to produce, distribute, and release movies, though it would not be fiscally whole again until 1940. Nevertheless, many of its most famous films came out during this difficult period: *King Kong,* nine Astaire-Rogers musicals including *Top Hat* and *Swing Time,* the multiple award-winning drama *The Informer,* the hilarious screwball comedy *Bringing Up Baby,* the rollicking adventure *Gunga Din,* and a spectacular version of the Victor Hugo classic *The Hunchback of Notre Dame.*

Soon after RKO emerged from receivership in 1940, it began to falter again. The corporate president at that time was George J. Schaefer, a dynamic executive who believed the RKO brand should stand for quality entertainment that would make it the most distinguished and respected of film companies. But the path Schaefer chose to that goal was riddled with potholes. Even Schaefer's greatest triumph, the Orson Welles masterpiece *Citizen Kane,* backfired on him, opening RKO up to the wrath of journalistic tycoon William Randolph Hearst, who interpreted *Kane* as an unflattering portrait of himself. Hearst mounted an effective campaign to stymie the release of the picture, causing Schaefer's finest film to flop at the box office. Most of the other RKO productions released in 1941 and the first half of 1942 also fizzled, bringing the company close to receivership once again. It is at this point, some six months after the United States' entry into World War II, that we pick up the story.

George Schaefer was RKO's fourth corporate president in its fourteen-year history. The company had also employed nine heads of production by that time. RKO's direct competitors—MGM, Paramount, Warner Bros., Twentieth Century–Fox—endured much less turnover in these two crucial executive positions. Those vertically integrated outfits (like RKO, each had production, distribution, and exhibition components) consistently outdistanced RKO in profitability, and one of the primary reasons for their success was executive stability. The absence of continuity at the management level as well as a consistent business philosophy became RKO's Achilles' heel, turning the company into the little kid who constantly chased, but never managed to catch, the big boys.

While a problem at the business level, instability made RKO, in many ways, the most fascinating of all the great American movie companies. It was never business as usual at RKO; the company existed in a perpetual state of reinvention. Consequently, many interesting and talented people were drawn to the organization, and their efforts often produced memorable results, from movies to picture personalities to astounding feats of promotion.

At the risk of redundancy, I will once again emphasize that this book is a *business history* and quote a passage from my introduction to the first volume:

Of course, theatrical motion pictures have always been more than just a business. They are also an art form, a technological phenomenon, a medium of communications, and an influential conveyor of popular culture, and RKO certainly made important contributions in each of these areas. Unfortunately, the scholarship related to Hollywood and its films is often unbalanced, emphasizing artists and artistic achievements while ignoring or even attacking the industrial basis of all production. What many scholars tend to downplay is one simple fact: the films they admire or believe are worth discussing would never have been produced if executives had not believed they would make money for their companies.

Choosing to approach the history of RKO from a business perspective sometimes places me in the awkward position of presenting negative assessments of films and individuals I admire. But just because a movie is aesthetically brilliant and stands the test of time does not mean it was a boon to the company that made it. Many of the greatest cinematic works failed at the box office when first released. From a business perspective, such artists as Howard Hawks and Orson Welles and such films as *Bringing Up Baby* and *Citizen Kane* were bad news for RKO, and the problems they spawned will be detailed in this study. There are plenty of other scholarly works that analyze the excellence of such films; this book will consider them from a different point of view—as commercial products expected to generate substantial revenue.

Now that I have clarified the kind of history I am presenting, I need to offer the following disclaimers. This book focuses on RKO and its principal product: feature-length motion pictures. After years of research, I am convinced that Hollywood companies like RKO rose and fell, thrived, survived, or expired based upon the financial performance of their features. Therefore, certain particularly influential feature motion pictures and the individuals responsible for them will be emphasized. But there were other important components of the organization's business model, especially its world-wide distribution network and its chain of affiliated theaters. The functioning of RKO distribution and exhibition and the people who worked in these areas will play a role in the narrative, but they will not receive as much attention as the feature production end of the corporation.

The company's short films will barely be noted. Over the years, RKO produced hundreds of shorts, mostly comedies starring Leon Errol, Edgar Kennedy, and others. They were licensed to theaters for a nominal price. Directors Mark Sandrich and George Stevens, among others, honed their craft in the shorts unit before graduating to feature filmmaking, but the shorts were always a very small component of RKO's business equation. So was its newsreel, the RKO Pathe News, which the company acquired in the 1931 merger with Pathe. Beginning in 1935, RKO also started distributing the "March of Time," short informational documentaries made by Time, Inc., and, until Walt

Disney partnered with RKO, it offered theater owners cartoons produced by the Van Beuren Corporation. None of these shorts is unimportant, but there will only be room for passing mention of them in this history.[1]

My focus in this volume, as it was in the first, is on the executives with the mandate to propel RKO Radio forward—principally the corporate president and the production chief—and their efforts to make their company the darling of Hollywood, and Wall Street as well. In attempting to present RKO's history from their perspective (and utilizing, whenever possible, their own words), I have had the good fortune of access to primary documents that once resided in the RKO Corporate Archive on Vermont Avenue in Los Angeles. This archive was open to scholars in the 1970s and 1980s, when the late John Hall was in charge. During that time I wrote a dissertation and a coffee-table book *(The RKO Story)* based on those invaluable materials. I also knew that someday I would author a comprehensive history of the corporation, so John allowed me to photocopy many documents from the archive. That permission turned out to be a massive stroke of good luck because most of the RKO Archive was boxed up and shipped to Atlanta in the 1990s, becoming unavailable to researchers. All unsourced references to letters, memoranda, telegrams, reports, and other materials in this study have been culled from the trove of Xerox copies I collected during that period.

The most important item I found in the building on Vermont Avenue was a ledger titled "Statistics of Feature Releases—June 1952," which belonged to C.J. Tevlin, a studio executive who worked at RKO in the late forties and fifties. This ledger contains the production costs, domestic and foreign film rentals, and profits or losses of all RKO feature films up through the end of 1951. Accurate information of this kind is difficult, in many cases impossible, to find for most of Hollywood's classical-era movie companies. Whenever I report financial data related to individual pictures in this study, they are derived from the Tevlin Ledger.

One important RKO leader who left behind few documents in the archive was Howard Hughes, who ran the company between 1948 and 1955, except for a bizarre three-month hiatus in 1952. Though I knew Hughes was odd and secretive, I was still bewildered by his near invisibility in the RKO records until William Fadiman, the studio's story editor during a portion of the Hughes period, cleared up the mystery:

> It is true that there are very few memos in the RKO files from Howard Hughes; there is a reason for that. The memos would come in typed at the bottom, as a signature, H.H. These were pre-Xerox days. About

four, four-thirty, one of his numerous personal secretaries would appear at the office of the man or woman to whom the memo was addressed and ask for the original copy back. He obviously didn't want anyone to know how he was running the company. And the memos may have been trivial, they may have been vital, but the secretary always got the original back.[2]

Nevertheless, I felt I could cover the Hughes period adequately, despite the absence of his personal correspondence. Other primary material from RKO executives and employees was contained in the archive; it often conveyed their reactions or responses to Hughes's directives, and this information, abetted by secondary sources, would suffice. Then another piece of good fortune came my way when one of my graduate students, Eric Hoyt, told me about a cache of Howard Hughes records held by the Texas State Archive. A visit to that repository in Austin helped fill many gaps in my coverage of the Hughes era at RKO and, most important, provided insights into the seemingly inexplicable workings of the famous man's mind. I also had the special benefit of materials discovered in a Hughes Collection at the University of Nevada at Las Vegas, the Dore Schary Collection at the University of Wisconsin, and the Jerry Wald Collection and Richard Fleischer Collection, both at the University of Southern California (USC).

Many wonderful people contributed to this project. I am grateful to Linda Mehr and her staff at the Margaret Herrick Library of the Academy of Motion Picture Arts and Sciences in Beverly Hills. There, Val Almendariz, Barbara Hall, Janet Lorenz, and Faye Thompson were especially helpful. Ned Comstock, the special collections archivist at the USC School of Cinematic Arts Library, deserves a commendation for the enormous number of scholars he has aided, myself included. Steve Hanson and Sandra Garcia-Myers are two other USC stalwarts who aided my efforts. Others who were particularly supportive include Peter Michel of the University of Nevada at Las Vegas Lied Library, Harry Miller of the Wisconsin Center for Film and Theater Research, Dace Taube of the USC Doheny Library Special Collections Department, and Tony Black and the superb staff of the Texas State Archives.

I am indebted to Shawn Guthrie and the Academy of Motion Picture Arts and Sciences for naming me an Academy Scholar and providing a generous grant that helped broaden my research. My own academic home, the USC School of Cinematic Arts, also contributed many different kinds of crucial support. I hope Dean Elizabeth Daley, along with Tara McPherson and Akira Lippit, the chairs of the Critical Studies Department during the period of this book's gestation, understand how much I appreciate their advocacy and help. In addition, I wish to thank Erin Hoge, Jennifer Rosales, and Shipra Gupta, three USC students who located and pulled together important materials for me. And Dr. Kristen Fuhs and Dr. Eric Hoyt—now established academics themselves—contributed to this endeavor in more ways than I could ever adequately recount.

The exceptional staff at University of California Press deserve special commendation for their enthusiastic championing of my work and their outstanding professionalism during every step of the publication process. Mary Francis, Zuha Khan, Rachel Berchten, Aimee Goggins, Bradley Depew, and Susan Silver, in particular, labored to make this a better book. I also appreciate the beneficial suggestions made by two anonymous reviewers engaged by the Press.

In addition, I am beholden to a number of mentors and friends who have had a salutary impact on my work through the years, including Irwin Blacker, Arthur Knight, John Russell Taylor, David Malone, Walter Fisher, E. Russell McGregor, Drew Casper, Frank Rosenfelt, Lisa Majewski, Lawrence Bassoff, Woody Omens, Robert Carringer, John Mueller, Dana Polan, Tom Kemper, and the many students who have kept me on my toes since I taught my first class at USC in the 1970s.

Two others deserve special thanks. I am privileged to hold the Hugh M. Hefner Chair for the Study of American Film at USC. Not only has Hef been an active and enthusiastic participant in my classes during the past twenty years; he is the most passionate advocate of the importance of Hollywood cinema I have ever met. Thank you, Hef, for everything you have done for me, my school, and the movies we both love. I also owe so much to the late Vernon Harbin; his willingness to share his unerring memories of an extraordinary twenty-five-year career at RKO provided keys to understanding the history of this company that were missing in the archive, which he meticulously assembled. I so wish Vernon, who died in 1988, was still around to see this project come to its conclusion.

Finally, those who know me recognize that I have a very special wife and daughter. Lynne and Annie's love and encouragement have always burned brightly, illuminating and warming this man's journey aboard Preston Sturges's "cockeyed caravan." Every word I have written is ultimately a tribute to them.

1. "Showmanship in Place of Genius"
The Rathvon-Koerner Regime (1942–1945)

At the beginning of June 1942 the United States had been at war with Japan, Germany, and Italy for nearly half a year without success. The Japanese military, on the other hand, mounted an extraordinary offensive throughout Asia after bombing Pearl Harbor, "capturing one-sixth of the surface of the planet in only six months."[1] But on June 4 the U.S. Navy scored a resounding victory during the Battle of Midway, sinking four Japanese carriers and effectively short-circuiting the enemy's dominance in the Pacific. Although advancement would be slow, bloody, and intractable from this point forward, the future outcome of battles fought in Europe, Africa, Asia, and the Pacific would generally favor U.S. forces.

In a scenario that eerily mirrored America's early efforts in the global conflict, RKO Radio Pictures, a major American motion picture company, had also been foundering between December 1941 and May 1942. On the day of the Midway confrontation, RKO corporate president George J. Schaefer instructed his new Hollywood production chief Charles W. Koerner to make "no further commitments on the pictures that are to be produced later in the year for 1942–43."[2] This message was issued because it appeared that fiscally challenged RKO might close its studio or fall back into receivership, a state of corporate bankruptcy in which the company had languished throughout most of the 1930s. The order became one of the last formal directives issued by Schaefer, who resigned shortly thereafter.

Charles Koerner obeyed, realizing that even if new funding were found to prop up the company he would likely still be asked to cut his filmmaking budget even further. Nevertheless, perhaps inspired by the confidence that other members of RKO's leadership team seemed to have in his abilities, Koerner showed no signs of despondency. He continued to work resolutely on the films that would comprise the initial portion of the new season's releases. They would be his first pictures as RKO executive producer, and he was determined to turn out successful product.

During the months of financial decline that led to Schaefer's resignation, there had been considerable squabbling among three powerful groups that comprised the leading investors in RKO: RCA, the Rockefeller family, and the Atlas Corporation. Even though the production arm was scheduled to run short of cash and be unable to meet payroll in the middle of June, none would agree to support some sort of stopgap measure to keep the cameras turning.

But as soon as George Schaefer was out of the picture, Floyd Odlum of Atlas, who had never been a supporter of Schaefer, stepped up to protect his investment. Owning some 46 percent of RKO, considerably more than either RCA or the Rockefellers, Odlum arranged to redirect $600,000 from the corporation, which it had to draw from its theater subsidiary, and secured a temporary loan of $800,000 from Manufacturers Trust Company to keep the studio operating throughout June and July. This was only a temporary solution but, by July 10, Odlum had convinced the other owners to accept an arrangement whereby Manufacturers Trust would loan an additional $3 million, with RKO putting up its theaters as collateral.[3] As *Time* magazine reported, Floyd Odlum intended to take a more active interest in RKO than ever before.[4]

Proof of this came in late June with the naming of Odlum subordinate N. Peter Rathvon to replace Schaefer as president of Radio-Keith-Orpheum and chairman of its board of directors.[5] As a reward for ten-plus years of diligent service, Ned Depinet, a veteran executive and the top man in the distribution division, became president of the picture company, RKO Radio Pictures.

This new hierarchy faced enormous challenges, and it is unlikely that anyone in Hollywood expected them to succeed. Indeed, RKO had a dubious history of placing untested, inexperienced executives in key management positions, and the company appeared to be making the same mistake once again. A graduate of the University of Colorado Law School, fifty-one-year-old Peter Rathvon worked for various mining companies, practiced law, and became a member of the New York Stock Exchange before joining the Atlas Corporation in 1933. During his years as one of Floyd Odlum's most important lieutenants, he had applied his fiscal and organizational skills to a number of companies in which Atlas had interests, including RKO. In fact, most of his energies had been focused on the movie concern during the past few years, and he was serving as an RKO vice president and a member of its board of directors when Schaefer submitted his resignation. Still, Rathvon had never functioned as top man of any corporation before, and his knowledge of the motion picture industry was manifestly inferior to that of the executives running the other major Hollywood companies in 1942.

Charlie Koerner, born in 1896, on the other hand, had been working in the business since he started projecting movies at a theater in Havre, Montana, while still a teenager. Following service in World War I, Koerner continued to work in exhibition, catching on with RKO in the early 1930s. Eventually he would be placed in charge of various regional sectors of the RKO theater chain, including those in the Southwest, upstate New York, New England, and the West Coast. Koerner was finally named general manager of all the RKO houses in 1941. But his stay at the company's New York headquarters would be short-lived. In early 1942 he departed for Hollywood, supposedly to pinch-hit for studio production chief Joseph Breen while Breen recuperated from an illness. In fact, this was a ruse to enable Breen, who had been RKO's executive producer for a little over one year, to save face; Schaefer and the company's board of directors had decided Breen could not handle the studio job and were turning it over to Koerner. After his recuperation Breen would head back to his old position running the Production Code Administration, Hollywood's in-house board of censors. Unquestionably, Charles Koerner was a show business veteran, but his long experience was entirely in exhibition, not production; now he was taking on the toughest task of them all, a job that required a daunting matrix of organizational, literary, and personal skills, as well as the instincts of a professional gambler and the foresight of a soothsayer.[6] Many individuals had been named executive producer and failed to deliver the goods (moneymaking pictures) before—at RKO and other companies. But Koerner was undaunted; he summed up his approach by employing an analogy straight from Detroit:

> Successful manufacturing depends on the product produced, is it wanted by the public and if so is it within [the] price range the public is willing to pay. An automobile manufactured with the basic ingredients, appeal and quality of a Packard or Cadillac, and produced at the cost of a Ford will show great profits through sales as a result of demand, but a car produced with the quality of a Ford and at a cost making it imperative to sell at the price of a Packard will not show a profit.[7]

Koerner's goal was to make A pictures that were Packards and Cadillacs, but on Ford budgets.

As if their jobs were not formidable enough, Rathvon and Koerner needed to breathe new life into a company that was very sick—one with a recent track record of disappointing releases, one without any major stars under exclusive contract, one littered with daunting personnel problems, one for whom few creative people in Hollywood wanted to work and from whom few independent exhibitors wanted to lease movies. Nevertheless, this excerpt from a letter written by Rathvon to Koerner in late June suggests that RKO's new corporate president also looked toward the future with considerable enthusiasm:

> My job is tough and vital but no less so is your own. Perhaps the desperate condition in which this company has been allowed to drift leaves no room for optimism but I cannot help feeling that you and Ned [Depinet] and I, with the help of all the good men in this organization, are going to be able to turn the trend and bring the company into black figures before the end of the year.[8]

Inspiring remarks of this type had often been uttered before, usually to be crushed by the harsh reality of RKO's feeble performances. Rathvon's words, however, turned out to be remarkably prophetic.

With the solid backing of Floyd Odlum, Peter Rathvon and Charles Koerner set to work, determined not to make the mistakes their predecessors had made. Sid Rogell, longtime studio manager who resigned toward the end of Schaefer's tenure, was rehired in his former position. He and veteran commitments expert J.J. Nolan would provide Koerner much-needed assistance in running the movie-making plant. The objectives of management included a patriotic component that was personal; it was imperative to restore the company to good health so that the many RKO workers who had already departed, or would soon depart, for the military would have "jobs to return to" when the conflict ended.[9]

One of the first items on the agenda was to clean up various messes left behind by George Schaefer. High on the list was Orson Welles and his two most recent films, *The Magnificent Ambersons* and *It's All True*. Schaefer had hired Welles and was justifiably proud of *Citizen Kane*, but the wunderkind's subsequent films had played a large role in Schaefer's forced resignation. After a disastrous preview of *Ambersons* in Pomona, California, in March 1942, the studio assigned editor Robert Wise to recut the film and, with some forty minutes removed, previewed it several more times. In mid-May a screening at the State Theater in Long Beach went fairly well; many of the preview cards were positive.[10] Still, a number of the respondents complained about the depressing impact of the story, so the studio decided to shoot a different, more upbeat ending.

The picture opened in August, some two months after George Schaefer's departure. It was not handled gently by RKO distribution. In many places

Ambersons played on a double bill with a "Mexican Spitfire" comedy.[11] As expected, it fared poorly. The final deficit on *The Magnificent Ambersons* amounted to $624,000.[12]

Later, Welles would complain bitterly about the emasculation of his masterpiece. The excision of almost one-third of the intended footage plus the new ending galled him, as well as the editing choices made. "They let the studio janitor cut 'The Magnificent Ambersons' in my absence," he wailed.[13] Ever since, cinema scholars have bemoaned the mangling of *Ambersons*, expressing a fervent yearning to view it as Welles intended. Unfortunately, that will never happen. The vital footage is gone forever; on December 10, 1942, Charles Koerner gave instructions to "junk" all the outtakes.[14]

The unanswerable question is why preview audiences reacted so negatively when the picture was first screened. Mark Robson, who assisted Robert Wise with the editing, was mystified by the response:

> That film was heartbreaking. The great things that happened on film. . . . I guess people didn't care. They just left the theatre. I think we must have taken it to dozens of previews. It reached a point when we had to pick up the film at the booth, people were waiting for us as if they were going to beat us up. They were so angered and annoyed.[15]

A version of *The Magnificent Ambersons* at least gained release in 1942. *It's All True* was not so fortunate. An experimental omnibus film designed to foster solidarity between the North and South American continents, the picture's strongest advocate had been RKO investor Nelson Rockefeller, then heading up the government's Office of Inter-American Affairs. Rockefeller understood that the commercial prospects of such a film were limited at best, so an arrangement was concluded guaranteeing that Washington would cover any losses incurred by RKO, up to $300,000. Therefore, George Schaefer could not envision any downside to the arrangement, since he expected Welles to expend no more than a couple of months and $600,000 to complete it. But Welles fooled him. By the time Schaefer quit, Orson Welles had been in Brazil for almost five months and the film's projected final budget, according to studio experts, had climbed well north of a million dollars.[16]

Now that Schaefer had departed, Charles Koerner cast a jaundiced eye on the project. At that time Welles was in Fortaleza shooting material to be used in a section of the film about four fishermen who sailed their raft two thousand miles from northern Brazil to Rio de Janeiro to make the country's president aware of the plight of the starving people in their region. Meanwhile, studio production manager Lynn Shores, who detested Welles

1. Orson Welles on location in Fortaleza, Brazil, during the filming of *It's All True*. Courtesy of the Academy of Motion Picture Arts and Sciences.

and believed the whole adventure had been a colossal waste of time and money, remained in Rio attempting to clear up various loose ends. Among other things, Shores claimed Welles had neglected to secure the proper rights to much of the Brazilian music he planned to include in the picture, forcing the production manager to contend with the problem. In addition, Shores informed the studio that the director had made "all kinds of high, wide and handsome commitments to artists of the Urca [night club] about big rewards they were going to receive for their participation in the picture." According to Shores, these commitments had been promised without proper authorization or approval. Shores, therefore, had to "negotiate" these sensitive matters. On top of all this, Welles threw a temper tantrum just before departing for Fortaleza, tossing china and furniture out of his Rio apartment window to the street below. The resultant newspaper coverage took a scandalous turn until Shores paid hush money to quiet everything down. Shores alleged that the episode cost approximately $2,000.[17]

Rathvon, as well as Koerner, soon became exasperated with Orson Welles. In late June, Shores received instructions to publish a disclaimer in the local papers stating that RKO would no longer be responsible for any commitments or debts incurred by Welles or members of his party.[18] When he returned from Fortaleza, Welles was ordered back to the United States and told no more money for *It's All True* would be forthcoming.

Meanwhile, Charles Koerner and his Hollywood studio associates took further action. Welles's Mercury Production staff were evicted from their offices at the RKO Pathe studio; the footage of *It's All True* was, in effect, impounded; and RKO lawyers began scrutinizing the Welles contracts to determine the studio's rights and potential liabilities should Welles decide to sue.[19] Upon hearing the news in Brazil, he could not resist a good pun. Welles wired his associates, "Don't get excited. We're just passing a rough Koerner on our way to immortality."[20] Officials of the new RKO countered with "All's well that ends Welles."[21]

The ultimate fate of *It's All True* dangled in the breeze for a long time thereafter. At first, the studio planned to finish the picture and distribute it without any further input from the director. To benefit from the U.S. government's $300,000 pledge against losses, the film had to be released. For a time it appeared that Welles might get backing from another distributor, repaying RKO's costs out of the eventual proceeds of the picture. When this failed to materialize, the project entered an uneasy limbo period for more than two years. Finally, RKO sold Welles the footage in late 1944, but he defaulted on his promissory note two years later and the film was returned to the studio's possession.[22] Some of it was later destroyed.

Charlie Koerner quickly garnered a hatchet-man reputation in Hollywood. Besides unceremoniously dumping Mercury Productions and calling a halt to *It's All True*, Koerner also canceled *Name, Age and Occupation*, Pare Lorentz's first Hollywood production, which had been filming for several months. Lorentz was considered America's foremost documentary filmmaker, thanks to two productions made in support of Franklin Roosevelt's New Deal: *The Plow That Broke the Plains* and *The River*. Now he decided to cast his lot with Hollywood and, like Welles, had been given a contract by Schaefer that guaranteed a good deal of autonomy. But Charles Koerner decided the director had abused his privileges unconscionably. *Name, Age and Occupation* had been in production, off and on, since March, yet Lorentz still did not have a finished script in July. The original plan called for a budget between $300,000 and $350,000, most of which Lorentz had spent without coming near to completing the picture. The new studio estimate projected a final cost of $706,317. Lorentz's insistence on the use of Floyd Crosby, a painstaking cameraman; his failure to inform the studio of his production plans, thus making it impossible to anticipate his requirements; and his exposure of an excessive amount of footage at a time when the wartime government demanded film conservation were numbered among Koerner's other grievances. On July 3 Koerner sent Lorentz a strongly worded letter, enumerating the director's abuses, insisting he deliver a complete script "immediately," and setting forth a number of other general production requirements.[23] When Lorentz failed to comply by July 12, Koerner closed down the production. The press were informed that the picture had merely been suspended because of "technical and screen play difficulties," but the new studio chief had no intention of allowing the director ever to shout "Action!" at RKO again.[24] RKO did, at least, gain one valuable asset from the Lorentz fiasco. Fledgling actor Robert Ryan had been placed under contract when Lorentz cast him in *Name, Age and Occupation*. Ryan would soon emerge as one of the studio's leading male performers.

Pare Lorentz sued RKO for $1,619,147 in damages based on "wrongful discharge," but lost in the courts as well as in the studio. The case dragged on for four years before the U.S. Supreme Court refused to review it.[25] The entire episode must have been traumatic for the filmmaker, who appears to have done everything possible to erase it from his life. There is no mention of *Name, Age and Occupation* in Lorentz's memoir or the book-length study of his work.[26] And when Lorentz was honored by the Academy of Motion Picture Arts and Sciences in 1981, he told Aljean Harmetz of the *New York Times* that he had been in Hollywood only once before, "to scrounge some stock footage . . . for one of his movies."[27]

Journalistic accounts of the Welles and Lorentz altercations brought considerable outcry against RKO.[28] The Rathvon-Koerner regime was attacked for its swinish treatment of creative talent and its quintessential Hollywood philistinism. Koerner, however, seemed impervious to these reproaches. Indeed, he abetted the attacks by ruling prestige films and artistic endeavors out of RKO's future plans: "I am thinking commercially. The only people who can afford to experiment are those who have the money to do it. RKO at this point, hasn't."[29] Later in the year Koerner adopted "Showmanship in Place of Genius" as the keynote of the new RKO production philosophy, a direct swipe at the policies of George Schaefer and the cinematic experiments of Orson Welles and Pare Lorentz.[30]

Although one may criticize Charles Koerner for calling attention to past deficiencies, one can hardly fault his actions. He inherited a studio in shambles, only a few paces away from the junkyard. Koerner had to be tough and commercial if RKO was to survive. In late August he announced that he was writing off as a dead loss more than $500,000 worth of story properties acquired by Schaefer.[31] Included in this group were Theodore Dreiser's *Sister Carrie*, H.G. Wells's *The History of Mr. Polly*, Budd Schulberg's

Passage from Bordeaux, Irwin Shaw's *Yankee Fable,* and Edward Anderson's *Thieves Like Us.*

Despite his many difficulties, Koerner began to feel more confident in early fall. As he wrote Odlum's attorney Ed Weisl,

> The place is gradually whipping into shape and I feel exceptionally optimistic. We have completed eight pictures under my so-called regime, namely, "Once Upon a Honeymoon", which looks terrific, "The Navy Comes Through", "Seven Days Leave", "The Falcon's Brother", "Cat People", Seven Miles From Alcatraz", "Ladies Day" and "Mexican Spitfire Sees an Elephant". Peter [Rathvon] saw them all while he was out here and there really isn't a bad picture in the bunch. Naturally, some are better than the others but none of them are "stinkolas" and they are all playable.[32]

There was good news on the financial front as well. The $3 million loan hit company books in late July, thanks to Floyd Odlum's intercession with the bankers.[33] And a last-ditch request by George Schaefer to withdraw some of RKO's frozen funds in Great Britain resulted in $2 million more in August. The negotiations with America's foremost ally on behalf of RKO by the U.S. Treasury Department took too long to save Schaefer's job, but they were ultimately successful, primarily because the money "was urgently needed to remedy the company's financial condition."[34]

In October a sequence of events transpired that clarified the working relationship of RKO's top corporate officers. One of the biggest problems that bedeviled the organization during George Schaefer's presidency was his fondness for micromanagement. This caused particular difficulties in the production arena because Schaefer insisted that he make all important filmmaking decisions. Rather than allow the appropriate personnel to do their jobs, he usurped their authority and pushed through many films that were both critically and commercially disappointing. When Koerner departed New York for Hollywood, he had been promised that final production authority would be his and his alone. Possibly at the insistence of the RKO Board of Directors, even Schaefer could not question or countermand his decisions.

Now Koerner had a new boss and a situation arose that alarmed him. Without consulting the production chief, Peter Rathvon engaged Orson Welles to complete some editing work and film one more scene for *Journey into Fear.* This suspense-thriller had been produced by his Mercury Productions company and shot just before and after Welles departed for Brazil. Welles had acted in it, but its director had been Norman Foster. *Journey into Fear* did not turn out well, and Rathvon hoped Welles could improve it. He was very careful to limit Welles's freedom to make changes, however, as well as the studio's financial commitment for the additional work.

Koerner, being no fan of Orson Welles, was unhappy about the deal and let Rathvon know in a long-distance telephone call, during which he raised the question of his own authority. Rathvon responded,

> I can't begin to tell you how sorry I am that you feel we have made a bad move in letting Welles go to the studio. The angle that disturbs you most, I must admit, never entered my mind. There is nothing in the release that Barret [McCormick, head of publicity] prepared which seemed to me to carry an implication that New York was forcing something on you and that the effect would be a feeling, inside and outside the studio, that the old spectre of domination from New York would be raised. I'm sure you know that is the last thing I want to see happen.[35]

Koerner wrote back, further explaining his reaction:

> The Hollywood scene is of such a nature that every item is eagerly pounced upon by the settlement as a whole. As I anticipated, I had many calls, particularly from the Trade Papers, and of course practically the first question in every instance was along the lines .. "Is New York starting to run the Studio again?" I know that this was certainly not your intent and you and I have seen eye to eye on everything, and my call to you was not so much in the nature of a complaint as one of rather trying to point out the problems with which we are constantly faced.[36]

The important aspect of this exchange is that it establishes Koerner as unquestionable overlord of the production operations of RKO Pictures. The new RKO management believed that George Schaefer's continual interference in studio affairs had contributed to the deterioration of the company. Charles Koerner would not have to worry about upper-echelon meddling; as long as he ran the studio efficiently and turned out successful product, he would have a free hand to buy properties, make commitments to artists, and produce pictures his way. Indeed, the synchrony with which Rathvon and Koerner worked from this point forward would enable RKO to reach hitherto unexplored pinnacles of success.

By the end of the year this synchrony was already paying off. In November the studio had its first profitable month in the previous nine and the December net loss was only $636,371, which included the write-off of $1.1 million more of properties deemed to be worthless.[37] Most important, Koerner was right about his pictures; they quickly began to win the approval of audiences. After years of desultory returns posted by a majority of RKO's releases, nearly every film in the 1942–43 program, which commenced in September 1942, performed well. Among the winners released in the last few months of 1942 were *Seven Days' Leave* ($673,000 profit), *The Navy Comes Through* ($542,000), *Once upon a Honeymoon* ($282,000), *Here We Go Again* ($228,000), and *The Falcon's Brother* ($128,000).

With the exception of *Here We Go Again*, the common denominator of these popular films was the war. Believing audiences would respond to topical films that foregrounded the global conflict in a positive, optimistic fashion, Koerner sponsored movies that soon became tiny blips on the radar screen of film history but exerted a strong pull on contemporary filmgoers.

Koerner understood the public fixation. Most people in the United States, and in many other countries as well, were spending a significant portion of their days reading about the war in the newspapers, listening to the latest updates on the radio, and talking about it with their friends. Given that the hostilities did not go well for the Allies throughout much of 1942, one might have expected spectators to prefer films that avoided the subject, as they generally had during the equally disheartening Depression. But just the opposite was true. Theater patrons sought out movies that reflected the precise moment they were living through, no matter how unrealistic and fanciful those movies happened to be. Koerner's, and RKO's, good fortune was, of course, also attributable to a dramatic upswing in general prosperity that resulted from the increased earning power of millions of war workers, as well as a ravenous demand for screen entertainment.[38] But Charles Koerner deserved considerable credit for recognizing what sorts of stories would be popular in wartime America and producing them. So far, he appeared to have a knack for his job, an instinctive feel for the tastes of the moviegoing public that George Schaefer had lacked.

Koerner also had keen political instincts, which he employed during the making of *Flight for Freedom*. Filmed in the fall of 1942 and released in early 1943, this picture, starring Rosalind Russell and Fred MacMurray, was a speculation on the disappearance of famed aviatrix Amelia Earhart during her around-the-world flight in 1937. It was not a biopic; the fictitious character played by Russell was named Tonie Carter, and the film proposed that she crashed her plane in the Pacific on purpose so the U.S. Navy would have an excuse to search for her and photograph Japanese military fortifications at the same time. Nevertheless, anyone who had followed Earhart's career would recognize that she provided the inspiration for the film's protagonist.

Floyd Odlum, the powerful entrepreneur responsible for the present RKO administration, was married to Jacqueline Cochran, a record-breaking aviatrix in her own right, who had been a friend of Earhart's. Consequently, Odlum did something he had never done before in his seven-year association with RKO—he became very interested in this particular film, asking to read scripts and be kept abreast of production decisions. Initially, Odlum expressed concern that a naval adviser who had been secured for the film would not understand the "woman's angle" crucial to its success. Furthermore, he mentioned a thousand-member organization of women flyers whose first president had been Earhart and whose current president was Cochran. In Odlum's opinion, these women would cast a discerning gaze on the final production: "If the picture is looked upon as portraying women pilots in general, and Amelia in particular, and gets off base in some particular, you [Koerner] will be in Dutch with this group as a whole and they won't hesitate to speak up."[39]

Soon enough, concerns about the reception by the female flyers' collective were forgotten, but in September, after Floyd Odlum read the final script, he sent Koerner a memo that must have shocked him. Odlum claimed that the film's story was based much more on the life of Jacqueline Cochran than the life of Amelia Earhart. After mentioning seven elements that he believed had been lifted from Cochran's life and incorporated into the screenplay, Odlum continued, "This raises a troublesome question or two. Jackie has made it a point not to commercialize her aviation. She has turned down substantial offers for her story. But not caring to sell it is something other than letting others use it without cost." Though he realized that in all likelihood little could be done since production on the film had already commenced, Odlum asked Koerner if he had any "suggestions."[40]

When the man who controls your company asks for suggestions, the typical response is to soft-pedal, placate, or take decisive action, up to and including shutting the production down. But Koerner sensed that Odlum was reading too much into the script, so he asked for a reaction from the producer of *Flight for Freedom*, David Hempstead.

Hempstead was aghast. After stating that "there has never been a book written by or about Miss Cochran, which means that intimate knowledge of her career is scarcely as available as it would be had the facts of her life been more thoroughly documented," he asserted that "neither the three writers who worked on this story, nor I, have incorporated any material which we knew to be from the life of Miss Cochran." Hempstead then pointed out "that certain patterns, scenes and kinds of action are unavoidable whenever you are dealing with a story which involves any highly specialized profession." The rest of Hempstead's memo debunked, point for point, Odlum's contentions, though he did agree to remove one coincidental reference that Hempstead conceded might have bothered Cochran.[41] Koerner relayed the Hempstead information to Odlum and that was the end of it. The production chief recognized that Odlum, a no-nonsense businessman, would most likely appreciate a no-nonsense response. Odlum never again interfered in the RKO production domain, and his respect and fondness for Charlie Koerner only increased with time.

It should be understood that the provocation for movies like *Flight for Freedom* came as much from Washington as Hollywood. One of the remarkable aspects of the World War II–era was the firm and productive partnership that developed between America's political leadership and the movie moguls. President Roosevelt believed the film industry could contribute to the war effort in many positive ways, and he let company leaders know that he expected them to ante up. They responded by making features and shorts that supported the cause, producing documentaries and training films for the troops, emphasizing Allied victories in their newsreels, screening government films and selling war bonds in their theaters, and sending their stars on tours to peddle more bonds and entertain the soldiers. The government repaid these favors by assisting the studios in the making of combat and other pictures, relaxing its investigation of antitrust allegations against the major companies' business practices, and offering deferments to crucial members of the Hollywood labor pool. And the American populace rewarded both entities, becoming the most productive workforce the world had ever seen and patronizing their local movie theaters in record numbers.[42]

RKO pitched in, contributing to the crusade in every way possible. While *Flight for Freedom* continued to take shape under the direction of Lothar Mendes in October 1942, RKO's wholesale commitment to war-oriented product was underlined by the release of "John Smith, Soldier," the first installment of its new documentary series, *This Is America*. The series, produced by the newsreel arm in New York, would replace the *March of Time* two reelers that the studio had been distributing since the mid-1930s. An impasse had arisen between the studio and Henry Luce of Time regarding the handling of the *March of Time*, so the company decided to create its own equivalent.[43]

As the end of 1942 drew near, RKO executives were unusually ebullient. Even veteran distribution chief and new president of the picture company Ned Depinet could hardly believe the turnaround. He sent Charles Koerner a letter on December 21, praising the quality of the films he was delivering and stating that the production chief deserved "the everlasting gratitude of the entire RKO family as well as that of our thousands of exhibitor-customers."[44]

Although Charlie Koerner was still pretty new to the world of film production, he had already developed considerable reverence for the creative abilities of the people who worked inside studio walls. In January he described the picture business as "indestructible" and marveled at the ability of its workers to overcome wartime obstacles. "Despite income ceiling, manpower, raw stock and set construction limitations, the picture industry continues to find ways and means of turning out top product," he said.[45]

Koerner himself continued to crank out pictures in 1943 that were not just successful—they were spectacularly successful—but this did not mean his work became less stressful. Unending headaches were part of the job, and he endured plenty of them in the first half of the new year. The production head attempted to write his boss at least once a week to keep President Rathvon abreast of developments at the studio. His epistles were filled with pain and frustration:

> "Our great difficulty at the present time is in getting scripts ready" (March 5)

> "My 'B' Department is falling apart" (March 24)

> "I do not suppose there will ever come a day that we can call our work completed and without the usual crop of disappointments and annoyances" (March 26)

> "The past week has been full of aggravations and troubles" (May 6)

> "I did not want to write you last week as all the news was bad" (June 10)

Although Koerner may seem like a chronic complainer, he was simply reporting the facts to his boss; he and his staff faced plenty of challenges, many related to the war. For example, the ongoing transition of so many Americans into uniform meant there was a shortage of qualified workers at every level of the motion picture industry. Koerner's problem with scripts for his pictures derived from the fact that many of the best screenwriters were now working for Uncle Sam. He told Rathvon, "there is a terrific scarcity of Writers and regardless of money it is practically impossible to keep up our writing assignments with our requirements."[46]

The scope of Koerner's personnel problems, in fact, ranged far beyond screenwriting. By the end of 1943 more than eight hundred people had traded RKO jobs for military uniforms. All the studios had to scramble to replace their missing employees, so to impose some order on the seller's market for available studio talent, a gentleman's agreement was reached among the executives that they would not raid one another's remaining workforces. But in the Darwinian world of Hollywood, some were more gentlemanly than others. In February Koerner was forced to write Harry Warner, complaining about three "steady employees" of his Camera Effects Department who had departed for Warner Bros. between July and December 1942—Chesley Bonestell and John and Mario Larrinaga. The Larrinaga brothers cited ill health in their resignations, but both were toiling for the Warners, at higher salaries, within two weeks after leaving RKO.[47] These men would not be the only RKO workers to migrate to "greener" pastures during the war years.

Government-imposed rationing of gasoline, rubber, and other materials crucial to the production process proved to be considerable annoyances, but there was special fear about motion picture raw stock. This precious commodity had been rationed since shortly after Pearl Harbor. The quantity of celluloid allotted to RKO was adequate to meet the studio's needs and those of the distribution arm of the company. But Koerner and the other executives were privy to never-ending rumors about an inevitable reduction in raw stock allocations, causing continual dialogue about what they would do if (when) this crisis occurred. Like its competitors, the studio cut back on the number of feature films it produced each year as well as the number of prints manufactured for each release and, fortunately, never ran short of its minimum needs.[48] Indeed, the distribution of fewer pictures in the face of an increasing public appetite for Hollywood product meant that movie runs often lasted longer, leading to higher profits.

Charlie Koerner's other difficulties came with the territory and were not significantly different from those that often plagued his predecessors. Early in 1943 he decided the hiring of Lou Ostrow to head up the B unit had been a mistake. In March Peter Rathvon wrote Koerner that he was very disappointed with one of the recent B pictures, *Petticoat Larceny*. He called it an "all around bad job of writing, direction and production."[49] Koerner was not upset by this. Rathvon rarely criticized the product, and, besides, Koerner understood that the poor quality of the picture was indicative of a larger problem. As he explained in his reply, "I am having a lot of trouble with Mr. Ostrow and some of his producers, particularly [Bert] Gilroy. They are unable to come up with any ideas, they are not ingenious and inclined to make too many excuses. I ... believe very shortly it will be necessary to make rather drastic changes in the entire set-up."[50] Two weeks later Ostrow was gone. Koerner supervised all studio production for a few months before placing veteran studio manager Sid Rogell in charge of B films in September. By the end of that month Bert Gilroy had also been excised from the payroll.

In addition to his B troubles, Charles Koerner had to wrestle with several problematic A productions. One of the most nettlesome was *Government Girl*, a comedy that brought him into conflict, at various times, with original producer David Hempstead, writer-director-producer Dudley Nichols and star Olivia de Havilland (borrowed from Warner Bros.). *China Sky, Higher and Higher, Days of Glory,* and *Tender Comrade* also gave him various degrees of heartburn.

Despite his travails, Charles Koerner managed to ramrod an extraordinary year of releases. Hit after hit poured out of the Gower Street studio. The most important of these was *Hitler's Children*. Independent producer Edward Golden purchased the rights to a book titled *Education for Death* by Gregor Ziemer and brought the project to RKO. Koerner sparked to its potential and set the project up as one of the company's B productions. This was smart because even though Golden would enjoy a nice profit participation, the picture would be financed by RKO and under the ultimate control of Koerner. That became important early in the shooting when director Irving Reis developed, according to Koerner, "an extreme case of the jitters."[51] Koerner sensed there might be trouble and had another director, Edward Dmytryk, ready to take over. Dmytryk was a former editor who had cut *Love Affair* (1939) for the studio and directed several B pictures for Paramount, Columbia, and RKO before this. He did a respectable job, working from a script by Emmet Lavery that damned the Nazis by emphasizing their inhuman treatment of Germany's youth.

The film contained a number of sensationalistic elements—for example, the flogging of an Aryan woman (Bonita Granville) who refuses to embrace Nazism or bear children who will become members of the Hitler Youth and the compulsory sterilization of non-Aryans and other females who defy the führer. Somewhat surprisingly, the industry's censorship arm, the Production Code Administration, allowed these questionable scenes, presumably because they demonstrated the barbarism of America's enemy and provided emotional evidence why it was imperative to defeat the Third Reich. When the film was finished, Koerner, Depinet, and the other executives were so enthusiastic they decided to release the $205,000 production as an A. It became a giant hit, ultimately generating more than $3.3 million in total film rentals and $1,210,000 in profits for RKO.

Recognizing that audiences were hungry for this sort of topical potboiler, Koerner quickly assigned Lavery and Dmytryk to a project that would attack the Japanese in similar fashion. Toward the end of August *Behind the Rising Sun* debuted in theaters. Although it was one of the few World War II–era Hollywood films to contain sympathetic Japanese characters (Reo Seki, played by J. Carroll Naish; and Tama, played by Margo), *Time* magazine still called it an "88-minute jag of ferocious anti-Japanese propaganda."[52] This was precisely what American moviegoers wanted to see; on a final budget of $239,000, *Behind the Rising Sun* siphoned even more revenue into company coffers—a profit of $1,480,000.

But these two films were simply the most spectacular successes in a year that would have been extraordinary without them. A less surprising blockbuster was the Cary Grant vehicle *Mr. Lucky*, about a mendacious gambler transformed into a patriot by a woman (Laraine Day) and the wartime emergency. Ulric Bell, newly installed in Hollywood as overseas representative for the government's Office of War Information, hated the movie. He felt it emphasized the "sordid side of American life" and contained an "inaccurate representation" of the United States that would be harmful when viewed by foreign audiences.[53] Domestic consumers, on the other hand, found the movie's heavy-handed propaganda altogether delicious, resulting in an RKO profit of $1,603,000. Indeed, Hedda Hopper claimed that *Mr. Lucky* attracted more money in its seven-week run at Radio City Music Hall in New York than the picture cost to make.[54]

Other winners in Koerner's first full program included Fred Astaire's return to his old home studio, *The Sky's the Limit* ($625,000 profit); long-delayed combat movie *Bombardier* ($565,000); suspense-thriller *The Fallen Sparrow* ($710,000); and romantic comedies *A Lady Takes a Chance*, starring Jean Arthur ($582,000), and *Government Girl*, starring Olivia de Havilland ($700,000). Of the forty-eight films that made up the 1942–43 program, all but seven made money. These few disappointments included the two Welles pictures, *The Magnificent Ambersons* ($620,000 in losses) and *Journey into Fear* ($193,000), plus *Pride of the Yankees* ($213,000) and *They Got Me Covered* ($150,000), two highly popular releases from independent producer Samuel Goldwyn. The company had been marketing his product since the early forties, even though Goldwyn negotiated such a small distribution fee that every picture produced a loss for RKO, no matter how much money it brought in. RKO executives felt these losses were acceptable, since Goldwyn's pictures lent prestige to RKO and helped the organization sell its own movies.

When all the calculations were complete, the magical 1942–43 program boasted a final profit of $9,008,000. It contained two films—*Behind the Rising Sun* and *Mr. Lucky*—that each made more money than any other film in the fourteen-year history of the company. And it resuscitated RKO's reputation. Overnight, RKO became a Wall Street darling, its stock having quadrupled in value in little more than a year. No one was more delighted than Floyd Odlum; his decision to place a heavy bet on RKO had come at just the right time. And now he was in full command. The Rockefeller family and RCA, whose leader David Sarnoff had been RKO's founding father, both sold their substantial stock holdings in the corporation in 1943, leaving Odlum's Atlas Corporation with clear controlling interest.[55] The days in which the three powerful entities squabbled over RKO priorities and personnel, which began in the mid-1930s, were now past.

In Hollywood, successful product meant Koerner was having a much easier time casting his A films, despite the fact that RKO still did not have any major stars under exclusive contract. Realizing that more actors were moving into the freelance realm, Koerner made arrangements, some for more than one picture, with Cary Grant, Jean Arthur, Rosalind Russell, and Pat O'Brien, and he was successful in borrowing John Garfield, Laraine Day, Fred MacMurray, Olivia de Havilland, and John Wayne from other companies. He also began to pull together a stock company of youthful performers, including Robert Ryan, Robert Mitchum, and Frank Sinatra, some of whom would be able to carry A pictures in later years.

Although Charlie Koerner had not, as yet, deviated from his commercial orientation, his administration did make a surprising but genuine contribution to film art with its horror films produced by Val Lewton. Made quickly on small budgets, these pictures (*Cat People, I Walked with a Zombie, The Leopard Man,* and *The Seventh Victim,* all released in 1943) actually fit the company's new production philosophy to perfection. Indeed, Koerner's experience in the theater business convinced him that there was a dependable audience for scary movies, and he had encouraged George Schaefer to begin producing some back in 1941. Schaefer expressed no interest, but now Koerner was calling the shots, and he made Lewton one of his first hires. No one (except Lewton) expected these pictures to be anything special, but they would eventually gain recognition as the first truly original horror formula since Frankenstein, a formula that eschewed cheap sensationalism, building suspense through suggestion and "brooding anticipation."[56]

Lewton was a unique talent, a Russian émigré and former author of pulp fiction who worked as David Selznick's story editor for several years before Charles Koerner brought him aboard to be RKO's maestro of horror. Known familiarly as the "snake pit," the Lewton unit, for the most part, remained below the studio radar.[57] Fanatically antiauthoritarian, Lewton initially wanted little more than to be left alone. The unit's isolation also enabled its impresario, who turned out to be an outstanding writer and

2. Producer Val Lewton working in his RKO office. Courtesy of the USC Cinematic Arts Library.

producer, to develop into an exceptional mentor of young filmmakers. Editors Mark Robson and Robert Wise were both given opportunities to direct films by Lewton, then went on to long and distinguished Hollywood careers. And director Jacques Tourneur's status rose abruptly after he made *Cat People, I Walked with a Zombie,* and *The Leopard Man* in the snake pit.

A few contemporary critics grasped the value of the producer's exercises in the macabre, but their importance has now grown to such an extent that there are more book-length studies of Val Lewton than of any other filmmaker who worked for RKO, with the possible exception of Orson Welles. Unfortunately, some of these books make outrageous assertions about the financial performance of his pictures. For example, authors Edmund Bansak, Chris Fugiwara, and Joel Siegel all claim his films were so successful that they saved RKO from bankruptcy.[58] In truth, the most profitable of the Lewton productions was *Cat People*, which earned $183,000. Bansak also states that the total gross of *Cat People* exceeded $4 million; in actuality, it totaled $535,000.[59] For comparative purposes, *Tarzan Triumphs*, a picture made independently by producer Sol Lesser and distributed by the company around the same time as *Cat People*, grossed almost five times as much and earned a larger profit for RKO ($208,000).

This effort to correct the historical record is not intended to diminish Lewton's achievements. Val Lewton's major intervention in the development of the horror genre as well as his contributions to a more psychologically complex and compelling cinema are more than enough to earn him an important spot among the masters of cinematic expression. At the same time, Lewton should not be portrayed as something he wasn't—a financial powerhouse—to burnish his importance.

High spirits reigned at the company sales convention, held in mid-July at the Waldorf Astoria Hotel in New York. After describing several of the forty features that would make up the 1943–44 program, Ned Depinet turned over the microphone to Floyd Odlum, the new chairman of the RKO Board of Directors.[60] Odlum had agreed to function as director of the Division of Contract Distribution in the government's Office of Production Management even before Pearl Harbor, so he was particularly concerned with the role the film industry could play in aiding the war effort. The diminutive tycoon told the attendees he believed that motion pictures were not only highly popular; they were also "helping morale, helping build up production, helping the men at the front." In addition, he predicted that the "motion picture industry will have greater opportunities after the war than in the past."[61]

Later in the year Charles Koerner was not so sure. Alarmed by budgets that were beginning to balloon throughout Hollywood, he wrote Rathvon, "it is a continual fight to keep costs down; and while present markets can absorb excessive costs the other Studios are now putting into pictures, I am always fearful of the bubble bursting and again the company being in trouble."[62] Charlie Koerner reckoned that the costs of making movies had risen 25 percent since the war began.[63] Although it's unlikely he foresaw how much more they would increase in the near future, Koerner proved to be more prescient than Floyd Odlum on this subject.

Nevertheless, the war-fueled love affair with the movies grew even stronger, and the film business continued to post extraordinary returns. RKO smashed all previous records with a corporate profit of $6,964,005 in 1943. Domestic film rentals alone increased by approximately 45 percent.[64] Even before these remarkable figures were announced, President Rathvon felt euphoric. Like many others, he believed Charlie Koerner was mainly responsible for the company's success, as evidenced by this excerpt from a letter written to his production chief on December 30:

> I cannot think of a better time to tell you how happy I am over our 1943 record and how proud I am of you and all the great gang at the studio who made the record possible by furnishing an essential ingredient—good pictures. The pictures themselves will go through the process of distribution and amortization leaving a nice residuum of net profit ... but in the making of the pictures there have developed other less tangible but more important assets which will continue to enhance in value and carry over into the years ahead. First of all is the high morale compounded of real leadership and organizational teamwork. Second is the growing sense among talented people that our studio is a decent and happy place to work. Third is the fact that the operation continues to be realistically planned and controlled and will not get out of hand when times are less propitious and grosses less easy to obtain.[65]

Indeed, Rathvon and Floyd Odlum so appreciated Charles Koerner's performance that, earlier in the year, they had signed him to an unprecedented seven-year contract.[66]

The New Year's Eve celebrations that took place one day after Rathvon penned his letter were considerably more festive than they had been a year earlier. During 1943 the global conflict tipped in favor of the Allies, with crucial victories occurring in Russia, North Africa, Romania, Italy (which ousted Mussolini, changed sides, and declared war on Germany), and various islands in the Pacific. Americans began to breathe easier and think about what their lives would be like after the war was over.

Although studio heads surely also looked forward to the end of hostilities, they now clearly understood the beneficial impact that World War II was having on their businesses. All of RKO's principal rivals except Warner Bros. posted higher profits in 1943 than they had in 1942. Paramount led the way with $14.5 million, followed by MGM with $13.4 million and Twentieth Century–Fox with $10.9 million. Warners took a small step backward, finishing "only" $8.2 million in the black after posting an $8.6 million profit in 1942. Though RKO's earnings fell short of these robust figures, they were clearly the most spectacular of the bunch. After losing money in 1942, the company had roared back to profitability.

Charles Koerner moved in several new directions in 1944. He began turning out updated versions of old company productions, such as *Room Service* (new title: *Step Lively*, a musical version of the story, starring Frank Sinatra); *Are These Our Children?* (*Youth Runs Wild*, produced by Val Lewton); and *The Richest Girl in the World* (*Bride by Mistake*, with Laraine

Day and Alan Marshal). He also reintroduced Westerns to the studio output, offering John Wayne in *Tall in the Saddle,* plus new contract actor Robert Mitchum in *Nevada.* And, in the most surprising component of Koerner's game plan, he decided to begin developing a few prestige properties, films that were not likely to generate huge returns at the box office but might win some awards and upgrade the studio's reputation among film critics and the artistically inclined.

The first of these would be *None but the Lonely Heart,* based on a novel by Richard Llewellyn (*How Green Was My Valley*) and written and directed for the screen by playwright Clifford Odets.[67] The studio recreated a portion of London's East End in the largest set ever built inside the RKO-Pathe plant, paired Cary Grant with Ethel Barrymore in the downbeat story, and spent more than $1.3 million (the largest budget in the 1944–45 program) to bring *Lonely Heart* to the screen.[68] As expected, the film lost money, though not much ($72,000). It was hoped the picture might win an Academy Award for RKO stalwart Grant, who was nominated as Best Actor, but he did not take home the coveted statue.[69] Perhaps Charlie Koerner wasn't a philistine after all.

Despite public opinion polls indicating that audience members were tiring of motion pictures dealing with the war and wanted escapist entertainment, RKO kept releasing pictures set in the present that contained plenty of references to the ongoing conflict. *Tender Comrade, Action in Arabia, Passport to Destiny, Days of Glory, Seven Days Ashore, Marine Raiders, The Master Race, Music in Manhattan, My Pal Wolf,* and *Heavenly Days* all fit the profile, though it would be hard to label any of them, with the exception of *Days of Glory,* as nonescapist. None approached *Hitler's Children* or *Behind the Rising Sun* in earnings, but most fared well at the ticket booth.

The continuing popularity of his product and the momentum generated by the corporation's success meant Charles Koerner had an easier time of it in 1944, but not by much. He still encountered periods of choppiness during a year that provided more smooth sailing than his first eighteen months at the studio helm.

In January he was coping with "illness, scripts not coming out according to expectation, inability to secure directors and fully rounded casts." Still, he informed Rathvon that "the mental strain has been rather terrific but all in all the problems are not too serious." By March Koerner was singing a different tune: "I have never taken so much punishment in all my life as during the past several months." In first position among his difficulties was the development of one of his prestige pictures, *Sister Kenny.* A biography of the famous Australian nurse who pioneered a new treatment for polio, the film was designed as a vehicle for Rosalind Russell. But Elizabeth Kenny was still alive, had considerable input into the production, and did not like Russell. Although they had never met, the feud between them escalated, thanks to various gossip columnists. Koerner finally managed to get the two ladies together in his office, a meeting he described as "certainly something that would make a wonderful scenario in itself. Kenny came in with fire in her eyes and was going to tear the whole Studio apart. It finally ended up in a love feast and everyone seems to be happy."[70] Nevertheless, the picture would not go into production for many months.

Koerner endured even more grief related to the casting of *I Married the Navy* (release title: *Bride by Mistake*). The studio head borrowed Dorothy McGuire and Alan Marshal from David Selznick to top the cast of this romantic comedy, but at the eleventh hour McGuire refused to appear in the picture. "Here we were stuck with the director, crew, sets already built, and no leading lady," moaned Koerner. He quickly managed to secure Laraine Day from MGM as a replacement, whereupon Alan Marshal decided he did not want to make the movie either. Frantic negotiations ensued, ending when Koerner talked Marshal into reporting for work.

Other difficulties included the "'Gibson Girl' fiasco" (this planned Ginger Rogers vehicle had story problems and would never be made), "Frank Sinatra acting up," "Anne Shirley coming down with an infected eye on the second day of her picture," and so on.[71] Koerner was also forced to postpone *Mama's Bank Account*, another highly anticipated production, because its screenplay had not come together.[72]

The turmoil calmed down soon after this. On April 7 Koerner wrote Rathvon that he was "feeling better mentally than I have for sometime [sic]." But in September Koerner found himself embarking on a new profession: marriage counselor to the stars. Topping the list was Cary Grant, whose union with Barbara Hutton was on the rocks. Koerner managed to arrange a romantic getaway to a special apartment in San Francisco, where the couple would attempt to patch things up, though the production chief did not feel optimistic about the outcome. Still, Koerner hoped for the best because he knew Grant would be unable to work until he got through this difficult emotional patch. Then one day Koerner was called to the set of *Experiment Perilous*, where Hedy Lamarr was distraught over the breakup of her relationship with John Loder. "I acted as an emissary and finally got the two of them back together," he reported. In addition, at the urging of Rudy Vallee, Koerner interceded in the crooner's rocky marriage to RKO contract starlet Bettejane (later Jane) Greer. The twosome soon reconciled. Obviously feeling quite proud of his efforts, the jocular studio head told Peter Rathvon, "I imagine they will start calling me 'Cupid Koerner.'"[73]

Although Charles Koerner coped with plenty of other problems during 1944, he was feeling upbeat at the end of the year. One of his accomplishments made him particularly proud. He had accepted the leadership of the film industry's nine-hundred volunteer War Chest workers and coordinated their fundraising efforts during the fall. The War Chest, an offshoot of Community Chest, solicited gifts throughout the United States in support of home-front health and welfare agencies and Allied war-relief causes. The hope was to raise more than $7,600,000 in the Los Angeles area, with a significant portion expected to come from the Hollywood community. When the results were tallied in November, the goal had been surpassed and "the motion-picture industry had contributed $1,170, 349.33, the largest amount in its history."[74]

Charles Koerner had to devote many hours to the War Chest campaign, but by that time he had put together a staff in which he had solid confidence, and they had taken a good deal of the burden of running the studio off his shoulders. Koerner restructured the executive producer function into three units, headed by Jack Gross, Sid Rogell, and the team of Robert Fellows and Warren Duff. Gross, Rogell, and Fellows-Duff would monitor the efforts of several of the company's producers, as well as produce some pictures themselves. The company's most respected filmmakers—Leo McCarey, David Hempstead, and Dudley Nichols—continued to report directly to Koerner.[75] The head man was also pleased to have the "largest number of writers on our payroll that I believe the Company has ever had" and a new executive assistant named William Dozier, who was working out very well.[76]

Not everyone appreciated the revised setup. Val Lewton and Sid Rogell had battled constantly, so Koerner placed Lewton under the supervision of Jack Gross after Gross joined RKO. The hypersensitive Lewton quickly developed a hatred for Gross that far surpassed his ill feelings toward Rogell. "I now find myself working for an abysmally ignorant and stupid gentleman called Jack Gross," Lewton wrote his mother and sister on August 20, 1944.[77] Nevertheless, Gross, who came to RKO after working for the industry's foremost horror-film factory, Universal Pictures, did contribute one significant element to the Lewton releases. Believing some star power was needed to pump up the grosses of the Lewton chillers, Gross forced the producer to feature one of the genre's most famous personalities, Boris Karloff, in his films. Val Lewton fought this decision bitterly at first, but he soon developed a special friendship with Karloff and stopped complaining about the mandate.

Although few people noticed, the RKO release schedule in 1944 turned a very significant corner. For the first time in its history the company released more A pictures than Bs. The A output was bolstered by a distribution agreement to handle the product of International Pictures, a new company formed by former RKO corporate president Leo Spitz and longtime Twentieth Century–Fox executive William Goetz. *Casanova Brown, Belle of the Yukon,* and *The Woman in the Window* were the first International productions offered to RKO's theater customers. Thanks to the new deal with International, the ongoing relationships with Samuel Goldwyn and Walt Disney, and Koerner's rapport with freelance talent and other studios, particularly MGM, from whom he borrowed several actors during the year, the stars featured in RKO's 1944 releases were formidable. They included Ginger Rogers, Gary Cooper, Danny Kaye, Eddie Cantor, Frank Sinatra, Pat O'Brien, Bob Hope, Cary Grant, Edward G. Robinson, John Wayne, and Hedy Lamarr.

The B pictures were fewer in number but holding their own. Val Lewton began to work in genres besides horror, producing *Mademoiselle Fifi* and *Youth Runs Wild,* as well as *Curse of the Cat People,* for 1944 release. The Falcon series, launched in 1942 and now featuring Tom Conway as a suave detective, had developed a solid coterie of fans, as had other inexpensive pictures featuring radio personalities "Lum and Abner" and "The Great Gildersleeve." The only misfire was Koerner's attempt to transform the comedy team of Alan Carney and Wally Brown into the RKO equivalent of Universal's dynamic twosome, Bud Abbott and Lou Costello. Carney and Brown's appearances in *Seven Days Ashore* and *Girl Rush* were profitable but failed to generate much enthusiasm among movie customers.

Charlie Koerner's efforts did not match the extraordinary results of his 1942–43 program (1943–44 came up about $3 million shy of the previous release year's profits), but there was still plenty of good news when the results were tallied. Topping the list was *Tender Comrade.* This contemporary weeper about a group of women living together while working in a Douglas Aircraft plant earned a profit of $843,000 and proved that Ginger Rogers still had plenty of box-office moxie. Ulric Bell of the Office of War Information, who had been so hostile to *Mr. Lucky,* felt differently about this heavy-handed slice of celluloid propaganda. "All cheers and hosannas," was his reaction.[78] The movie also demonstrated that director Edward Dmytryk could handle A productions and showed that Robert Ryan, cast opposite Rogers, could hold his own with a top female star.[79]

3. Charles Koerner celebrates his forty-seventh birthday with the cast and crew of *Tender Comrade*. Courtesy of the Academy of Motion Picture Arts and Sciences.

Other happy results were posted by the Eddie Cantor musical *Show Business* ($805,000 profit), the Koerner tribulation *Bride by Mistake* ($600,000), and Frank Sinatra's first RKO production, *Higher and Higher* ($499,000). The John Wayne Western, *Tall in the Saddle*, one of the early 1944–45 releases, also scored nicely, bringing home a profit of $780,000.

Days of Glory, a paean to the courage of America's Russian allies, represented the biggest disappointment of 1944. Produced and written by respected screenwriter Casey Robinson and directed by Jacques Tourneur, whose fine work for Val Lewton had boosted him to the A-picture realm, this picture encountered strong resistance from moviegoers and ended up $593,000 in the hole. To achieve a high level of realism, Robinson and Tourneur cast unknowns in all the roles, making its final budget of $958,000 hard to fathom. Perhaps its inflated cost, absence of box-office names, realistic approach, and subject matter turned off audiences; whatever the reason, the resultant loss outdistanced all of the year's other box-office busts by almost $400,000.

Days of Glory still might have represented a highlight in the company's history if one of the neophytes in the cast had made future RKO pictures. RKO owned half of the original contract that Gregory Peck signed with Casey Robinson—a four-picture commitment. But Koerner botched the opportunity to bring the actor on board, though he recognized Peck's potential even before filming began.[80] After *Days of Glory* turned out to be a flop, Koerner sold RKO's portion of the contract to David O. Selznick, and Peck soon found his talents split among three companies: Selznick, MGM, and Twentieth Century–Fox.[81] This fumble was one of the biggest mistakes of Charles Koerner's Hollywood career.

In December 1944 Koerner preempted his boss's usual year-end encomium, writing Rathvon that he not only was a "great president for the Company" but had "brought to RKO a dignity and a great quality of understanding."[82] Clearly, these two men had now forged a supple partnership based on shared vision, superior communication skills, and mutual respect. The future of their company had never seemed brighter. Year-end corporate profits amounted to $5,206,378, down a bit from 1943. But RKO stockholders were delighted with the progress of the corporation; at a special meeting held on March 14, 1944, they approved a pension trust plan covering more than two thousand members of the company workforce.[83]

By the early months of 1945 most Americans felt confident the end of World War II was imminent and the Allied side would be victorious. In Europe the D-day invasion of June 1944 opened up a crucial second front, and, despite a temporary setback at the Battle of the Bulge, American, British, and Russian forces were moving inexorably toward Berlin. The U.S. Navy continued to defeat the Japanese soundly in the Pacific, reducing their naval operations almost to a nonfactor, and American military men had conquered enough islands to begin bombing Tokyo and other Japanese cities with regularity. On May 7 (V-E day) the Germans surrendered, and on August 14 (V-J day) the Japanese followed suit. The carnage and insanity of war were finally over.

Sadly, President Franklin D. Roosevelt was not able to celebrate either victory. In April 1945 the man who had steered America through the two greatest crises of the twentieth century died while on vacation in Warm Springs, Georgia. Millions would mourn his passing, including many members of the Hollywood community. He had been a good friend to the motion picture industry, especially during World War II, and his support would be sorely missed in the years to come. Vice President Harry S. Truman succeeded Roosevelt in the White House.

Ironically, in the year that the war ended, serious hostilities broke out in Hollywood. After a long period of relative tranquility between producers and the town's labor force, the so-called interior decorators strike began in March 1945, picked up support from members of other unions in subsequent months, and peaked in the fall with production shutdowns and bloody skirmishes outside studio gates. The conflict evolved from a power struggle between the International Alliance of Theatrical Stage Employees (IATSE), which had represented a majority of Hollywood workers for many years but been weakened by the disclosure of corrupt management and mob control of the union, and the Conference of Studio Unions (CSU), a new organization that had taken advantage of the shocking IATSE revelations to add some ten thousand company workers to its membership roster. The CSU, headed by Herbert Sorrell, represented the workers who decided to strike in 1945 despite a no-strike pledge that unions had adopted because of the war.[84] Conditions became so bad in late October that many RKO employees were spending their nights at the studio so they would not have to cross picket lines.[85] Finally, new Motion Picture Association president Eric Johnston, who replaced Will Hays in September, brokered a settlement to what Ralph Roddy of *Variety* would later call "the most disastrous strike in the film industry's history," and a welcome equilibrium returned in November.[86] But this state of equilibrium was tremulous at best, for the violence that accompanied the strike had stained Hollywood's image, there were rumblings of more labor trouble in the near future, and the enmity between the two competitive unions had not been resolved.

The strike affected RKO less than it did most of the company's competitors. Some of its films took longer to shoot than they should have, and the starting dates of a few were pushed back, but no productions were forced to shut down, even temporarily, and the studio remained open throughout the turmoil.

Charles Koerner, who was touring Europe during the worst weeks of the strike, was updated regularly by his assistant Bill Dozier and others at the studio. During the months that led up to this trip, Koerner made some of the best decisions of his career. He encouraged Leo McCarey, whose Rainbow Productions company had a coproduction deal with RKO, to mount a sequel to *Going My Way*, the Academy Award–winning movie of 1944 that McCarey had directed for Paramount release. Two weeks before *The Bells of St. Mary's* was finished, Koerner took a look at ninety minutes of cut footage and predicted the Bing Crosby–Ingrid Bergman vehicle was "destined for one of the all-time box-office highs."[87] He was correct.

Another major coup involved a special arrangement with David O. Selznick. Koerner had endured many frustrations in his previous dealings

4. Picketers mass outside RKO's Gower Street studio in 1945. Courtesy of the Academy of Motion Picture Arts and Sciences.

with both the man who had occupied his office the early 1930s and Selznick's adjutant Daniel T. O'Shea, a lawyer who also worked for RKO during the previous decade. But Koerner recognized that Selznick still had one of the sharpest minds in the business and would make a terrific addition to company operations. The new deal was complicated, entailing a number of future pictures that Selznick's Vanguard Films company and RKO intended to coproduce. In each case the two entities would furnish different elements (story, writers, director, actors, crew members, etc.) to the project and share the costs as well as the revenues. The arrangement proved to be advantageous to both parties, particularly RKO; some of the company's best releases of the 1940s would come from this partnership. It more than substituted for the loss of International Pictures, which merged with Universal during the year. Koerner also entered into an arrangement to partially finance and distribute films made by a new powerhouse independent, Liberty Films. Composed of directors Frank Capra, William Wyler, and George Stevens—all of whom had served in the military during the war— this company would be fronted by former RKO production chief Sam

Briskin. Even before Stevens joined Liberty, it was estimated that the arrangement would yield nine pictures with production costs of approximately $15 million.[88]

Arguably, Charlie Koerner's most audacious gamble was to suggest the casting of Dick Powell as hard-boiled detective Philip Marlowe in *Murder, My Sweet*, a new film version of Raymond Chandler's novel, *Farewell, My Lovely*.[89] Powell, known primarily for his roles as a pleasant but innocuous song-and-dance man in such Warner Bros. musicals as *Gold Diggers of 1933*, *Footlight Parade*, and *Dames*, had left that studio and was suffering through a fallow period in his career. He knew he needed a complete overhaul of his screen persona, and Koerner provided it with special assistance from director Edward Dmytryk and his new partner, producer Adrian Scott. *Murder, My Sweet* would become one of several important building blocks RKO contributed to a new cinematic edifice eventually known as film noir. But more important, at least in the short term, audience members seemed to buy Powell's radical transformation into a tough guy. Koerner and RKO had come up with not only another hit but a rather unlikely new star.[90] Powell was quickly cast in a second he-man role in *Cornered*, to be made by the same team.

At midyear Koerner felt exceedingly chipper. In July he wrote Rathvon that he and the independents had "twenty-six 'A' and Double 'A' pictures set up for RKO product," constituting "the greatest backlog in the history of RKO and the assurance of an uninterrupted flow of definitely fine pictures."[91] He was also justifiably proud of the legitimate stars who would be showcased in the movies: Bing Crosby, Ingrid Bergman, Cary Grant, Ginger Rogers, Paul Henreid, Maureen O'Hara, George Raft, Joan Fontaine, Robert Young, Shirley Temple, Eddie Cantor, Joan Bennett, Dorothy McGuire, Susan Hayward, Rosalind Russell, John Wayne, and Myrna Loy, among others. The era when RKO distribution strained to convince theater owners that films featuring Parkyakarkus, Edward Arnold, and Lily Pons were truly As was now a fast-fading memory.

In August Koerner called his producers together for a combination pep talk and seminar on the practicalities of picture making. After regaling them with good news about past and present product and the studio's financial performance, he encouraged the producers to dig harder for good stories. In particular, he wanted them to be on the lookout for "exploitation ideas." "I'm anxious to make pictures as timely as 'Hitler's Children' and 'Behind the Rising Sun'," he said.[92] One idea that occurred to him was the "Atomic Bomb"; the first two nuclear devices had been dropped on Hiroshima and Nagasaki within the past five days. Although considerable cinematic fallout from the devastating blasts followed, the RKO production head would not manage to contribute to it.

Koerner also emphasized the importance of getting good work out of contract writers and editors and made sure each of the attendees realized that the production chief was anxious to lend assistance. "My door is always open," he emphasized. "I'd much rather take the time and help you straighten out a story point, or casting problem, or music or anything else than have you spend time and money trying to solve something you are not sure of. Bring it in here and we'll kick it around."[93]

Shortly after the war's end, Koerner told Rathvon that the "studio is humming and everyone tremendously happy and optimistic."[94] Therefore, he felt confident he could leave operations in the hands of his assistant Bill Dozier and studio manager Leon Goldberg and embark on his most extensive trip since becoming studio head. The journey took him first to New York and then to Europe, where he would evaluate postwar conditions and their probable impact on company business. In London he met with British film mogul J. Arthur Rank and worked out a coproduction arrangement for *So Well Remembered*, a property that Koerner had been anxious to mount in England for several years.[95] Koerner intended this to be the first of several films that RKO and Rank would make together.

After spending a couple of weeks in London, the production chief headed north for a golfing vacation at the famous Scottish courses before leaving for Paris. Dozier sent him regular cables covering all the activities at the studio, including the worsening strike. On October 23, when key personnel were hunkered down on the lot expecting six hundred–plus picketers to blockade 780 Gower Street the following day, Dozier signed his communique, "Best regards from Stalingrad."[96] Thankfully, the strike was settled on October 24.

Charlie Koerner journeyed on to Germany and then Belgium, returning to Hollywood in early November. He felt optimistic about the reopening of European theaters to American product and the possibility of making future RKO films in Britain and on the Continent. He also missed the worst weeks of the strike; thus, his journey could not have been better timed.

Koerner had barely settled into his old routine when Peter Rathvon asked him to embark on another trip. On November 26 he flew to Mexico City to inspect Churubusco, a new film studio RKO was building nearby.[97] This studio was Rathvon's baby. Taking advantage of the corporation's recent financial success, Rathvon convinced Floyd Odlum that the complex would be a good investment.[98] The press was told that it would be a state-of-the-art rental facility for Mexican filmmakers, but both Rathvon and

Koerner, well aware of the escalating costs of pictures in Hollywood, hoped that RKO might also be able to shoot a few pictures there to take advantage of lower labor costs.

Koerner liked what he saw. Following the excursion, which included a side trip to Acapulco for some relaxation, Koerner wrote Rathvon, raving about the "thoroughly enjoyable trip" and adding that he was "greatly impressed by the entire Mexican situation and the whole set-up looks like a welcome and profitable addition to RKO's operations as a whole. I know that when Floyd [Odlum] gets out here he will be curious as to my reactions and I am going to be most happy in telling him what I think." He then detailed the latest news from the studio and concluded, "All in all our current crop looks good and our plans for the future are progressing in the most gratifying manner." This letter, written on December 19, would be the last he ever sent to his partner in New York.[99]

The 1945 holiday season was particularly joyful throughout America. Now that the war was over, many families came together for the first time in years. Those RKO employees who had gone into the service returned to a much happier company than the one they had left. Once again, RKO distributed more hits than misses in 1945, with its first true Technicolor production *The Spanish Main* (profit: $1,485,000) leading the way, followed by the George Raft vehicle *Johnny Angel* ($1,192,000); the romantic fantasy *The Enchanted Cottage* ($881,000); the romantic comedy *Those Endearing Young Charms* ($644,000); and *Murder, My Sweet* ($597,000). But these impressive figures were dwarfed by the screen entertainment that opened at Radio City Music Hall during the holidays: *The Bells of St. Mary's*. As Koerner anticipated, the film quickly turned into a bonanza. Even though it had to share revenues with Leo McCarey's Rainbow Productions, the company ended up with a profit of $3,715,000. It would be the most successful film in RKO history.

Because *Bells* and several of the other big hits debuted toward the end of the year and banked most of their income in 1946, the Radio-Keith-Orpheum profit for 1945 was only $6 million. Still, morale among company employees had never been higher because nearly all of Koerner's predictions were coming true. The studio finally had a leader who seemed to know his business, and he was telling them the future was bright.

Then, suddenly, Charlie Koerner fell ill. Early in the new year, he was hospitalized. Although Koerner's family and company officials did not release any information about his sickness, everyone expected him to recover and be back at his post in a short time. During January he received regular correspondence from employees in the New York office, some of whom apparently did not even know he was bedridden in Cedars of Lebanon Hospital. In late January his condition worsened, and, to the shock of the entire Hollywood community as well as RKO's worldwide personnel, Charles Koerner died on February 2, 1946. He had contracted a particularly virulent strain of leukemia, which his doctors were unable to suppress. Floyd Odlum, Peter Rathvon, and Ned Depinet issued a joint statement describing Koerner as "one of the best liked and respected executives in Hollywood." They also lauded his basic decency as well as his leadership: "his fairness, kindness and willingness to share with others the honor of achievement enabled him to build a capable and loyal organization—to all of whom his death means not only the loss of an able leader but the passing of a true friend."[100]

Koerner's performance as RKO production head is not as easy to evaluate as it might appear. He became head of the studio at a most opportune moment, just as the Depression was ending and the industrial boom that accompanied U.S. entry into World War II was commencing. In the three-plus years he held the position, good jobs were plentiful throughout America, potential audience members had excess cash in their pockets, and the movies metamorphosed from a pleasant pastime into an important component of the patriotic crusade. Never before and never again would Americans support Hollywood films with such unrestrained zeal.

Also, when compared to the financial performances of the company's vertically integrated competitors, RKO's success during Koerner's tenure does not seem so impressive. Between 1942 and 1945 the average yearly corporate profit of Paramount was approximately $14.4 million; MGM, $13.2 million; Twentieth Century–Fox, $11.7 million; and Warner Bros., $8.4 million. RKO's profit averaged $4.7 million during those four years. But if one examines these figures carefully, a more nuanced picture emerges. None of its competitors had a losing year during the period, while RKO's corporate loss in 1942 pulled its average down considerably. In addition, unlike the early years of the Depression, this was a great time to own theaters. Most of the Big Five profits were derived from their houses, a partial explanation why Paramount, which owned or controlled more than twice as many venues as any other company, topped the industry and would break the bank with an extraordinary profit of $39.2 million in 1946. RKO had the smallest number of theaters and thus, logically, should have finished fifth in the box-office derby. Nevertheless, those theaters gave it a clear advantage over the Little Three—Universal made an average of $3.5 million during the same period and Columbia, $1.8 million, while poorly managed United Artists lagged far behind, posting an average profit of only $350,000 per year.

It is also important to recall the alarming conditions that prevailed at RKO when Koerner took charge. A few months after he moved to Hollywood, there was talk of shuttering the studio or filing for receivership once again. By the end of that first year he and his producers were turning out moneymaking films, and the momentum produced by these hits only accelerated from that time onward. Independent theater owners noticed and began to book more RKO blocks of product; customers noticed and began to flock to RKO movies; even the competition noticed, as Rathvon wrote Koerner in October 1943: "For the first time in its history RKO is on the march and do not think the other companies fail to realize it. The interesting thing is that while there may be some jealousy there is also a surprising amount of good will."[101]

One of the most significant changes wrought by Charles Koerner involved the casting of RKO pictures. Although he was not able to pull together a stable of stars that could rival the actors under contract to the more successful studios, he still managed to stud RKO's A releases with meaningful box-office personalities. Koerner did this by taking advantage of the growing desire of some performers to gain more control over their careers by freelancing and through the development of strong relations with other company leaders, who became more willing than ever before to lend talent to RKO. MGM topped the list, furnishing Koerner with Laraine Day, George Murphy, Robert Young, Hedy Lamarr, Alan Marshal, and Marsha Hunt, among others. Day and Murphy made as many films for RKO as they did for their home studio during the war years. Koerner also managed to borrow actors from every other major studio, plus Republic Pictures and the independent companies run by David O. Selznick and Samuel Goldwyn. He knew how to ingratiate himself with stars as well; it made a favorable impression when his office delivered gifts on the day each new movie began—Pat O'Brien would receive a box of cigars, Joan Fontaine a bouquet of roses.[102]

Most important, Koerner completed his ascent to the upper echelon of Hollywood executives without success going to his head; he remained open and approachable, taking special pride in the harmonious working atmosphere he had cultivated at the studio. Arthur Ungar, the editor of *Daily Variety*, called him "a man without enemies—a man who had taken an organization reeking with dust and grime, reconstructed it, polished it, and made it stand out in a short span of years."[103]

Director Edward Dmytryk, whose career flourished under the production chief, remembered this about Koerner:

> He was the best executive I have ever known. He made decisions quickly and firmly, he could be convinced, and he had the one truly great executive talent—once he delegated authority, he never interfered. Also,

like all truly competent executives I have known, he always seemed to have plenty of time. Whenever I called his secretary with a request to see Koerner, the answer was either "Come right up" or "He's got someone with him—you come up in fifteen minutes." How rare that is.[104]

The renowned French director Jean Renoir, who made *This Land Is Mine* and *Woman on the Beach* for Koerner, felt great affection and respect for him:

> During that period, R.K.O. was run by an extraordinary man, Charlie Koerner. I deeply regretted his unfortunate death. Had he not died, I believe I should have made twenty films for R.K.O.; I would have worked all my life at R.K.O. He was a man who knew the business and the exploitation of cinema, but at the same time conceded that one must experiment.[105]

Pat O'Brien was also a fan:

> He was endowed with more warmth, charm and generosity than anyone who had ever headed a studio during my time. Irving Thalberg would be in second place; he was a charmer, but he never had any close feeling for the people around him, or warmed so fully into life as Charlie Koerner. Charlie not only mingled with the artists, but was a pal to the technicians, the back-lot people as well. If the electricians, grips and gaffers appeared to be having a card game during a coffee break, Koerner if he happened by, would always stop a moment, kibitz a little and proceed on his way.
>   When he died, so did RKO. It's hard to know why a personality could keep a studio afloat—yet often the lack of one destroys it.[106]

RKO did not die after Charlie Koerner's untimely passing—at least not right away. But because he ran the studio for only a short time, he is barely remembered in histories of Hollywood. When he is mentioned in accounts of the "golden era," Koerner is generally portrayed as the "butcher," the man who ruined Orson Welles's *The Magnificent Ambersons*, evicted the Mercury Theatre company from their offices, and prevented Welles from completing *It's All True*. But it can certainly be argued that Welles was the architect of his own sad fate, and, given the precarious state of the company when Koerner made those decisions, he had little choice in the matter.

Viewed in a broader context, Charlie Koerner was, without question, one of the best studio heads of the 1940s. He repaired RKO's broken production machinery in astoundingly short order; contributed to film art through the Val Lewton productions and important early examples of film noir such as *Murder, My Sweet*; developed relationships that would continue to pay tangible dividends for years to come; and boosted RKO's reputation to a level not seen since the heyday of the Astaire-Rogers pictures, if then. It is plausible that RKO's future would have been quite different if Charles Koerner had been around to pilot the studio through the challenging days that lay ahead. Instead, Koerner's death in early 1946 at the age of forty nine turned out to be another major turning point in the chronicle of RKO Radio Pictures.

2. "RKO's Spirit Encircles Globe"
The Rathvon Regime (1946)

On February 5, 1946, four hundred people, among them the elite of Hollywood, gathered at Forest Lawn Cemetery to mourn the death of Charles Koerner. Among the honorary pallbearers were Sam Briskin, Harry Cohn, Walt Disney, Samuel Goldwyn, Will Hays, B.B. Kahane, Eric Johnston, Louis B. Mayer, Joseph Schenck, David O. Selznick, Leo Spitz, Harry and Jack Warner, and Darryl Zanuck. RKO's studios were closed that day; the company contingent was led by Floyd Odlum, Peter Rathvon, and Ned Depinet and included many of the producers, writers, directors, actors, and staff who had worked for the production chief. Most were still trying to make sense of the tragedy, which had come so swiftly and unexpectedly.

The leadership vacuum created by Koerner's passing was addressed two days later, when Floyd Odlum announced that Peter Rathvon would move to Hollywood and take "permanent charge of RKO production."[1] Ned Depinet was made "chief executive in New York" with the new title of executive vice president of the parent company. Other executive shifts included the naming of Malcolm Kingsberg as president of the RKO Theatre Corporation (Rathvon had formerly been in charge of that subsidiary), and Sol Schwartz as vice-president in charge of theater operations under Kingsberg.

Members of the industry were surprised by the news, not so much that Rathvon was taking over the studio but that the move was intended to be permanent. Only one other corporate president (Harry Cohn of Columbia) ran the Hollywood studio rather than the New York headquarters of his company, and most insiders had expected either Rathvon or Koerner's assistant William Dozier to babysit production while a search for a new studio chief took place. Almost a week after the announcement, a writer for *Daily Variety* still apparently could not believe Rathvon intended to become

37

a Hollywood fixture. The trade-paper reported that he planned to "hold down studio production post at RKO until the late Charles W. Koerner's successor is named."[2] This, in fact, would be the ultimate outcome, but it was not what RKO's president had in mind. Perhaps the most compelling evidence of his intentions was the beautiful home purchased for him and his wife in the western section of Los Angeles by RKO during the year; an executive on temporary assignment would almost certainly have rented or resided in a hotel.

At the time Rathvon set up shop on Gower Street, both the industry and RKO were in excellent shape. A late 1945 article by John L. Scott forecast that 1946 would be a banner year for Hollywood: "The once-despised 'flicker' business anticipates an unparalleled boom in 1946, according to facts, figures and predictions offered by major plants. Every large film concern has earmarked huge sums for new sound stages and rebuilding of old ones, which will add considerably to the total investment, which is now more than $2,000,000,000."[3]

RKO's expansion activities turned out to be mostly in New York and Mexico rather than California, but it did boast an impressive celluloid inventory. Among the films completed or in postproduction were *The Spiral Staircase*, starring Dorothy McGuire and George Brent; *From This Day Forward*, starring Joan Fontaine; *Heartbeat*, starring Ginger Rogers; *Without Reservations*, starring Claudette Colbert and John Wayne; *Till the End of Time*, starring Dorothy McGuire, Bill Williams, and Robert Mitchum; *Crack-Up*, starring Pat O'Brien and Claire Trevor; *Sister Kenny*, starring Rosalind Russell; and *Notorious*, starring Cary Grant and Ingrid Bergman. Koerner's team also had some promising pictures either shooting or almost ready for production, such as a Joan Bennett vehicle to be directed by Jean Renoir (final title: *Woman on the Beach*); *Nocturne*, with George Raft; and another Technicolor swashbuckler, *Sinbad the Sailor*, to star Douglas Fairbanks Jr. and Maureen O'Hara. In addition, RKO held commitments (some for more than one picture) from John Garfield, Cary Grant, Paul Henreid, Pat O'Brien, Dick Powell, Randolph Scott, Frank Sinatra, John Wayne, and Robert Young. This was, in fact, quite remarkable, because many actors were now refusing to make more than one or two pictures a year due to the heavy income-tax bite affecting individuals in the upper brackets.

Rathvon imported his executive assistant from New York, Norman Freeman, to fill the same role in Hollywood. Like Rathvon, Freeman had roots in Odlum's Atlas Corporation. He had served in the military during World War II and then been immediately hired by Rathvon following his discharge. Freeman's arrival at the studio created an awkward situation because William Dozier, who played the same role for Koerner, held a contract with almost two years left to run. Rathvon tried to take advantage of the abilities of both men for a few months, but Dozier soon became disenchanted. Perhaps upset that he had not inherited Koerner's position, perhaps frustrated because he was a seasoned production executive now working with two men who had no experience running a studio, Bill Dozier eventually negotiated his release in May. He would land a new job as a vice-president of Universal-International before the end of the year.[4]

Peter Rathvon's personality was quite different from Charles Koerner's. He was more cultured, thoughtful, and reserved, but less approachable and voluble than his predecessor had been. Indeed, he appeared better suited to the corporate presidency than the rough-and-tumble world of the studio. Of former RKO leaders, he most resembled the elegant Merlin Aylesworth, who had served as RKO's chief executive for several years in the 1930s. To his chagrin, Aylesworth never gained admittance into the inner circle of Hollywood moguls because most of his peers felt he was more interested in promoting radio (he was also president of the NBC radio networks at the time) than furthering the interests of the movies.

Rathvon, however, was soon accepted by workers at the studio and respected by members of the Hollywood community. After only two months on the job, he received an invitation to become president of the West Coast Producers Association. Unsure how to respond, he asked Floyd Odlum for his views on the subject. Odlum recommended, by telegram, that he decline the offer: "I doubt that this industry service will help company furthermore these things have a way of taking more time and lasting longer than originally supposed."[5] Rathvon did say no, though he must have been flattered by the invitation. Y. Frank Freeman of Paramount ended up in the position.

N. Peter Rathvon had no illusions about the job he was taking on. He had worked very closely with Charlie Koerner, and the two men discussed the complexities of running a studio more extensively than any other president–executive producer combination in company history. It was also his good fortune to have assumed control in a magical year; rentals from RKO releases poured in at unprecedented levels. Yet before long Rathvon began to appreciate the wisdom of an old Spanish proverb: "It is not the same thing to talk of bulls as to be in the bullring." Occupying the hot seat at the studio was all-consuming; despite plenty of good news, the challenges and problems never seemed to diminish.

One issue that quickly became apparent was the gender imbalance in the actors available for forthcoming productions. When one added together studio-developed talent and commitments from other companies and freelance artists, RKO now had a very strong group of male performers queued up for its coming pictures. But nearly all Hollywood movies, including most of the ones RKO intended to produce, required actresses of equal stature to counterpoint the men. RKO had been grooming several young women for stardom, including Jane Greer, Anne Jeffries, and Barbara Hale, but none had advanced as quickly as their male counterparts, Robert Mitchum, Robert Ryan, and Lawrence Tierney. Nor did the studio have enough borrowing or freelance arrangements with female stars to populate the important roles in the contemplated films. Ironically, just the opposite difficulty had impacted studio production during the 1930s, when RKO's female talent, including Katharine Hepburn, Ginger Rogers, Irene Dunne, and Ann Harding, outnumbered and outclassed its male performers. Rathvon would spend a good deal of time trying to solve this dilemma.

Studio facilities represented another concern. The Gower Street plant was small, especially compared to the spacious lots that MGM, Twentieth Century–Fox, Warner Bros., and Universal-International occupied. The company still owned RKO Pathe in Culver City and occasionally used that lot to film portions of its pictures, but most activity at Pathe came from independents, such as David Selznick and Sol Lesser, who rented space and shot movies there.

Over time there had been many discussions concerning the company's inadequate facilities. At one point a few years earlier, Paramount made overtures about purchasing the Gower Street facility and merging it with its studio to expand its own cramped footage on Melrose Avenue.[6] Rathvon and Koerner had considered the idea of selling to Paramount, buying additional land close by RKO Pathe and moving all California operations to Culver City. Nothing came of the idea at the time but William Pereira, one of the company's young producers *(Johnny Angel)* also happened to be a trained industrial architect; he was now asked to study the situation. According to Norman Freeman, Pereira concluded that there was "insufficient space at our Gower Street studio to expand the facilities and to arrange a layout that would be efficient" and that "while the acreage at the Pathe Studio in Culver City might be sufficiently large, that acreage is laid out wrong for the construction of an efficient studio." Therefore, Pereira recommended, "the best approach would be a sale of both the Gower Street and Culver City studios and the construction of a modern plant at some new location."[7] But after considering the probable price that would be realized for the two lots (perhaps throwing in the ranch in Encino where the company's B Westerns and other "outdoor" pictures were made), the tax implications of such sales, as well as the potential disruption to production activities, it made no sense to act on Pereira's suggestion. Rathvon and RKO would be stuck with their thirteen-acre studio on Gower Street for the foreseeable future.

The dilemma appeared particularly acute at this time because the company had committed to producing one of the most challenging pictures in Hollywood history—*The Robe*. Koerner made a deal to share the costs with producer Frank Ross, who purchased the rights to Lloyd C. Douglas's biblical epic even before the novel was published. It sold three million copies and remained on bestseller lists from 1942 to 1945.[8] Ross headed an independent company that usually made movies starring his wife, Jean Arthur. He and RKO had partnered on *The Devil and Miss Jones* and *A Lady Takes a Chance*, and both pictures had performed nicely. Now Ross was the possessor of a very hot property, and Koerner and the other executives recognized the material's blockbuster potential. They had tried to bring it before the cameras during the war years, but script and logistical problems delayed production.

The screenplay for *The Robe* was finally shaping up and shooting was scheduled to commence in 1947, forcing Rathvon and his associates to face a thorny problem. Not only did this mammoth movie sport the largest preliminary budget in RKO history ($5 million was the staggering figure), but its production would, according to Norman Freeman, "consume our facilities to such a degree that over the course of about six or seven months a total of only four pictures could be produced, other than THE ROBE."[9] Unless some solution was found, RKO could not hope to deliver a full program to its theater customers in 1947–48 and possibly 1948–49.

One obvious answer emerged—make some pictures far from Hollywood. The company was already gearing up to shoot *So Well Remembered* in England in collaboration with J. Arthur Rank. During the rest of the year RKO also made arrangements to fund a film ultimately titled *Man about Town*. It would be made in France, directed by Rene Clair, and represent the first Franco-American coproduction following the end of World War II. In addition, Rathvon set up *Berlin Express*, the first American picture to be filmed (in part) inside Germany since before the war began. And preliminary work aimed at producing *The White Tower* in the French Alps also commenced. By September Rathvon felt uncertain that, while *The Robe* was shooting, any films could be made "on our stages" and was thinking of boosting "next year's production with several features to be made in Mexico."[10] Producing movies in foreign countries was an uncomfortable proposition, as Peter Rathvon understood from the ill-fated Orson Welles excursion to South America, but he seemed to believe RKO had no other viable options.

As Rathvon spent more time within the studio walls, he became increasingly alarmed about another reality ushered in by the changing times. He, along with the other movie moguls, recognized that the costs of production, which had risen steadily during the war, were now accelerating at an even faster clip. With respect to A product, this did not appear to be overly problematic. A concomitant rise in ticket prices, an enthusiastic domestic audience bolstered by many recently demobilized veterans, plus the reopening of thousands of foreign theaters that had been off-limits to American product for years added up to exceptional returns from the top pictures.[11] But B movies were a different story.

While A pictures returned a percentage of box-office revenue, the Bs were leased to theaters for a flat fee, and this film rental had remained steady for years. Rathvon acknowledged that B-unit head Sid Rogell had been turning out better product and doing a "careful, cost-conscious job," but Rogell could not hold back the rising budget tide affecting all the Hollywood companies. Consequently, the Bs were making less and less and, in some cases, not breaking even. In May Rathvon wrote Ned Depinet to ask if there was "any likelihood of getting any *real* increase in flat rental rates on 'B' pictures generally."[12]

Unfortunately, according to Depinet, the answer was "emphatically *no*. We can *not* secure any *real* increase in flat rental rates generally. The best to be expected is about what we are getting now for so long as business holds its present pace."[13] He felt the B program should be continued but had no suggestions about how to make it more economically viable.

Other studios had already cut their program picture output considerably and some announced they intended to stop making them altogether, so Peter Rathvon began to consider that option. If RKO canceled its B program, this could also provide a partial solution to the coming facilities' crunch. Still, before making a decision Rathvon decided he had better ask Norman Freeman to conduct a thorough analysis of the situation.

Freeman presented his report to Rathvon in October. It confirmed that "the profit [of B films] has virtually disappeared as a result of the increased costs and the small remaining profit is not worth the investment and risk unless there are other considerations." Freeman then argued that several important "other considerations" did, in fact, exist. They included the development of actors with star potential like Robert Mitchum, plus the absorption of a significant portion of studio overhead and the indirect costs of distribution by B pictures. He also pointed out that the company was benefiting from the emergence of behind-the-camera talent now moving from B to A pictures, such as producers Adrian Scott and Bert Granet and directors Edward Dmytryk and Robert Wise. Finally, the pictures often came in handy for absorbing commitments to performers whose original projects had not come together. The studio had recently cast Boris Karloff in *Dick Tracy Meets Gruesome* for this very reason. In conclusion, Freeman stated, "Essentially the program picture unit should be operated with the broad view of aiding the company as a whole, as has been the case for the past few years. It should be measured from that standpoint rather than a mere look at the final net profits of the program pictures as they are reported. Those final net profit figures do not begin to tell the whole story."[14] Peter Rathvon read the report and recognized its wisdom. It would be foolhardy to eliminate B pictures, even though their days of small but reliable profits were over. He could only hope that the A films would continue on their record-setting financial pace.[15]

During RKO's history, none of its B films had received more recognition and praise than the Val Lewton–produced horror films, but the executives decided to phase them out in 1946 and release Lewton from his contract. The reasons were complicated. Lewton was a difficult man who constantly fought with his studio superiors. He had gotten along with Koerner pretty well, but Sid Rogell and Jack Gross brought out the worst in him. As Mark Robson said, Lewton "was a man who needed an enemy." The producer also felt that his accomplishments entitled him to bigger budgets and better casts and had finally convinced Koerner to boost him up to A films. But Koerner's death and the indifferent quality of a script Lewton developed about the famous pirate Blackbeard caused the studio to lose its enthusiasm for his advancement. In addition, RKO had been sued for plagiarism on his picture, *The Ghost Ship*. Lewton was outraged by the claim and insisted the case go to trial, even though the matter could have been settled for a few hundred dollars. The plaintiffs prevailed, costing the studio $25,000 and resulting in RKO's loss of ownership in the picture.[16] Perhaps the final straw concerned his last picture with Boris Karloff, *Bedlam*, which lost $40,000, though this was not an unusual outcome for a B film, as already stated.

Most important, Rathvon and other company leaders were no longer impressed by praise for Lewton's work from James Agee, Manny Farber, and other critics; they paid more attention to complaints from customers and theater owners alike, many of whom felt his fright pictures disturbed and adversely affected the minds of young moviegoers. In a letter to Rathvon, Ned Depinet referred to "considerable agitation throughout the land about so called horror and shock pictures" and to "smoldering resistance to such pictures."[17] Both Val Lewton and his productions were now considered an unnecessary nuisance, and he was discharged in May. Subsequently, Lewton would find work at Paramount, MGM, and Universal, though the pictures he made for those companies satisfied neither the producer nor his employers. Sadly, Val Lewton died in 1951 at the age of forty-six. His not-inconsiderable legacy would always be the nine groundbreaking horror films with macabre titles that he made for RKO between 1943 and 1946.

Lewton's career at RKO received no help from Joseph Breen, who made a special trip to the studio in April 1946 to address the company's producers. Breen had served as the company's production chief in 1941 and early 1942, then returned to his former job as the industry's chief censor after the RKO job did not work out. He now expressed his concerns about a number of new trends making it more difficult to enforce the Production Code and causing increased criticism of Hollywood throughout the country. Clearly, Joe Breen, like RKO's executives, must have also been receiving letters condemning the Lewton pictures. Toward the end of his speech, he pointed out the producer in the audience and said, "Now, here's a young man—If I had a dollar for every time he's batted my ears down—and he goes ahead and makes this 'Bedlam' stuff!"[18]

Breen also railed about excessive drinking in pictures, "open-mouthed kissing," the inappropriate treatment of sexuality in independent producer Howard Hughes's *The Outlaw,* and a new sort of picture that he described as presenting "unpleasant people, set down in squalid or sordid surroundings and engaged not only in criminal but in brutal activity. Low tone pictures in which unpleasant people figure importantly."[19] Breen was describing, in his own awkward manner, *Double Indemnity, The Postman Always Rings Twice,* and a number of other dark cinematic tales—he was grappling with the rise of film noir. The head of the Production Code Administration had to admit these pictures were acceptable from the code point of view (because the sinners were punished or killed in the end), but they had still upset members of state and municipal censor boards as well as a number of vocal U.S. filmgoers. Though he could not prevent their production, Joe Breen was convinced they were bad for the film industry and did his utmost to discourage their production.

Peter Rathvon, who introduced Breen that day and listened intently to his speech, was disturbed by the remarks. RKO had already produced several of these films, such as *Murder, My Sweet;* had completed others that would soon be released, such as *Crack-Up;* and planned to make more in the near future. In a subsequent letter to Ned Depinet, Rathvon mentioned the following properties: "If This Be Known," "Build My Gallows High," "Riff-Raff," and "They Wouldn't Believe Me." He continued, "I have given this problem a lot of thought and I assure you we will call a halt to this type of pictures for the time being but the ones I have mentioned are too far along to abandon at this time."[20]

Clearly upset by the negative reaction of some members of the public to this new kind of thriller (even classy examples like *The Spiral Staircase* were garnering complaints), Peter Rathvon decided that his studio should concentrate on prestige product, movies that would be applauded rather than denigrated by the more serious and cosmopolitan members of the audience. He was particularly enthusiastic about *Sister Kenny*. Koerner had set up this uplifting biopic back in 1944 but script problems and other delays prevented it from going into production until late 1945. A series of previews were held in San Francisco and Los Angeles during the first half of 1946; most went well and the film was scheduled for release in the fall.

Rathvon felt so convinced that the picture would become a critical and commercial success that he bought the epic psychological drama "Mourning Becomes Electra" before *Sister Kenny* was released. The team responsible for *Kenny*, composed of producer-writer-director Dudley Nichols and star Rosalind Russell, believed they could make an outstanding film based on the Eugene O'Neill play, and Rathvon viewed them as a crucial component of RKO's future. Of Nichols's ability to write, produce, and direct the mammoth picture, he said, "No other film creator is so well equipped . . . and Mr. O'Neill himself concurs with us in this opinion."[21]

Unfortunately, RKO's president was soon forced to recognize that he had badly misjudged the public's appetite for a cinematic account of Elizabeth Kenny's determined battle against polio. Even though star Rosalind Russell would earn an Oscar nomination for her portrayal of the eponymous heroine, *Sister Kenny* became the biggest loser ($660,000) in a sea of winners. By the time the picture's disappointing box-office performance became apparent, however, it was too late to pull the plug on *Mourning Becomes Electra*. By comparison, this second "high brow" production from Nichols and Russell would make *Sister Kenny* seem like a minor tremor on the Richter scale of cinematic disasters.

Rathvon's quest for "quality" evoked memories of a similar strategy launched by George J. Schaefer after he became RKO corporate president in 1938. Like Schaefer, Rathvon decided the most promising route to his goal of transforming RKO into an industry leader was to sign independent companies that could be counted on to make pictures of substance for RKO

5. Writer-director Dudley Nichols and RKO president N. Peter Rathvon chat on the set of *Mourning Becomes Electra*. Courtesy of the Academy of Motion Picture Arts and Sciences.

release. No shortage of such companies existed in Hollywood in 1946. The government's lofty income-tax rates on high-salaried individuals encouraged many movie veterans to form their own independent outfits. These new companies not only enabled their principals to pay taxes at lower capital gains rates but also afforded greater freedom from studio interference.[22] In addition to Nichols, Russell, and Russell's husband, Frederick Brisson, who banded together and formed Independent Artists, Rathvon happily finalized Koerner's deal with Liberty Films, composed of directors Frank Capra, William Wyler, and George Stevens (with former RKO executive producer Sam Briskin providing administrative oversight), and Argosy Pictures, led by another former RKO production chief, Merian C. Cooper, and his partner, director John Ford. Robert Riskin, who wrote several of Capra's famous pictures, including *It Happened One Night* and *Mr. Deeds*

Goes to Town, also decided to become an independent writer-producer-director and joined the RKO team.

One of George Schaefer's biggest mistakes in the late 1930s and early 1940s had been hiring a number of independents with no Hollywood experience. Rathvon knew better; his arrangements brought some of the industry's most respected talent under the RKO umbrella. But there was a problem—just like many of Schaefer's moves, the new pacts required RKO to supply at least some company funding or to guarantee bank loans taken out by the indies. They were unlike the affiliations with Walt Disney and Samuel Goldwyn, whose productions did not generate significant profits for their distributor but were totally financed by these truly independent producers. The potential rewards of the 1946 deals were much greater, but so were the risks; if the subsequent films did not do well commercially, RKO would be on the hook for a significant portion of the losses.

Peter Rathvon's company was also vulnerable to the Department of Justice's renewed interest in toppling vertical integration. Despite the consent decree of 1940 in the Paramount case, which was designed to remedy the most serious exhibitor complaints against the alleged monopolistic practices of the major studios, independent theater owners claimed they still operated at a terrible disadvantage so long as the Big Five controlled the best theaters in America. The government heeded their criticism and reopened the antitrust case in 1944.[23] In June 1946 a new ruling was issued that, just like the 1940 outcome, satisfied neither side. The decision allowed the big companies to retain their exhibition chains but ordered them to end "all 'sweetheart' arrangements between the studios and unaffiliated circuits," "to either assume full ownership or to sell off any theaters in which their holdings were between 5 and 95 percent," and, most significant, to establish "a system of competitive bidding ... to ensure that films were sold on a strict film-by-film, theater-by-theater basis."[24] Block booking—even marketing small blocks containing only five pictures—was now illegal. Soon, even B films would have to be sold on their own merits, rather than on the coattails of the A pictures, as they had been for many years.[25]

Cleaning up the many theater-sharing arrangements with other members of the Big Five and with independent exhibitors offered additional challenges. Malcolm Kingsberg, head of RKO Theatres, wrote Rathvon on June 14, indicating that he anticipated little difficulty in terminating the theater affiliations between RKO and "Paramount, Loew, Twentieth Century and Warners." The outcome "should not seriously affect our operation," he reported. But Kingsberg did expect problems with "Skouras in New York" and "major difficulties [in] working out partnerships with non-defendant exhibitors, such as Pantages in Los Angeles, Reade-Storrs in Trenton and New Brunswick, New Jersey, and some five or six theatres in New York."[26] Soon, however, both Kingsberg and Rathvon would realize that this was only chapter one of RKO's theater tribulations.

It's not possible to say what ultimately drove Rathvon to abandon the driver's seat at the Hollywood studio, but the strikes of fall 1946 must have played a role in his ultimate decision. In September labor discord pitted set erectors affiliated with the International Alliance of Theatrical Stage Employees (IATSE) against carpenters affiliated with the Conference of Studio Unions (CSU). Soon picketers began to appear at studios and other film-related companies throughout the Los Angeles area. One of the strategies of the Herbert Sorrell–led CSU, whose continuing battle for union supremacy with the IATSE ignited the strike, involved shutting down or curtailing the operations of local film laboratories. If studios could not get their footage processed and printed, they would be unable to deliver their pictures on time, thus disrupting their carefully planned release schedules.

On October 13 lab workers held a meeting and voted to honor the picket lines. The following day the only lab able to operate was the one at Paramount.[27] Eventually most of the labs reopened and caught up, but this was not the case at Technicolor, which was supposed to finish work on *Sinbad the Sailor* and ship prints for the picture's opening in New York on November 5. Consequently, the New York premiere had to be postponed.

Pickets did not disturb operations at the Gower Street studio, but they did show up at RKO Pathe in Culver City on October 24, where three companies were scheduled to shoot. By late morning the situation calmed down enough for work to return to normal.[28] But the strike would linger on, resulting in more disruptions and, ultimately, higher wages for many Hollywood workers. It also led to the eradication of the CSU. Sorrell was attacked as a communist, and his "red-tinged" union discredited by Roy Brewer, the leader of IATSE. These accusations found support with the large and influential Screen Actors Guild, plus powerful Hollywood executives sick of Sorrell's tactics. The CSU faded away in the late 1940s.

President Rathvon was in Mexico and New York during the worst days of the strike. Studio manager Leon Goldberg wrote his boss regularly to keep him apprised of the labor developments, just as Bill Dozier had kept Charles Koerner informed about similar troubles the year before. By the time Rathvon came back to Hollywood, he was exhausted and coping with an ulcer attack that landed him in the same hospital where Koerner had died (Cedars of Lebanon).[29] No wonder he was now committed to hiring a new studio chief so that he could devote all his energies to running the corporation.

Peter Rathvon had originally planned a trip to Europe for September but had to cancel because of the many complications affecting studio operations. Ned Depinet went instead, meeting first with J. Arthur Rank in England. Rank expressed interest in coproducing *The White Tower* and helping RKO land Laurence Olivier and Vivien Leigh for important roles in *The Robe*.[30]

Depinet also reported that Rank had nice things to say about producer Adrian Scott and director Edward Dmytryk, who were then completing the first Rank-RKO coproduction, *So Well Remembered*, and were scheduled to take the reins on *The White Tower*. Dmyryk had written Peter Rathvon several times concerning the progress of *So Well Remembered*, so Rathvon sent him a letter complimenting the director for the solid job he and Scott had done and mentioning the possibility of their working with the Rank organization again.[31]

Dmytryk was not enthused. He did not savor the idea of partnering with Rank, or any other British producer, again. After reminding Rathvon of previous comments he had made about the difficulties of making a film in England and calling the local grip and prop crews "fantastically inefficient," Dmytryk asserted that "the prospect of spending a year in this slow-moving, obstinate country would make it very difficult to persuade me to make the picture here." He ended the letter: "The only positive benefit [of working in England] has been to make me a 110% rather than a 100% American."[32]

Depinet's travels next took him to Paris, where he was impressed with Rene Clair and enthusiastic about the possibilities of *Man about Town*. He also seemed pleased by the quality of the company employees and the receptions he received in Paris and Rome. "Apparently RKO's spirit encircles globe," he wired Rathvon.[33] Ned Depinet continued on to Switzerland, Holland, and Belgium before returning home on October 16.

During the following month Depinet learned that Rathvon had found a promising candidate to run the studio. Dore Schary worked as a publicist, acted on Broadway with Paul Muni, and wrote and directed plays before heading for Hollywood in the mid-1930s. After spending a year as a junior writer at Columbia, he began freelancing scripts and caught on with MGM, where he won a 1938 Academy Award for Best Original Story *(Boys Town)*. Eventually promoted to producer, Schary supervised such MGM hits as *Journey for Margaret*, *Lassie Come Home*, and *Bataan*. Charles Koerner had tried to hire Schary as his second-in-command in 1943, but David

Selznick made Schary a better offer. Nonetheless, Koerner speculated that Schary would not be too happy working for Selznick and that "perhaps at some time in the future we will have a chance to get him." He described Schary as a "fine writer, cost conscious and has a fine standing in the Industry."[34]

In the three years since then, Schary had produced four of the partnership pictures between RKO and Selznick: *The Spiral Staircase, Till the End of Time, The Farmer's Daughter,* and *The Bachelor and the Bobby-Soxer.* These films were made primarily on the RKO lot, giving studio personnel, including Rathvon, ample opportunity to interact with him and form an opinion. The fact that each film turned out well impressed studio workers and executives alike.

On November 11 Rathvon wrote Ned Depinet a "confidential" letter, stating that he and Dore Schary had had a "most satisfactory talk without getting down to details."[35] Still, he anticipated making a "final arrangement" with his new executive producer before the end of 1946, even though there was one significant impediment. Schary had a year to run on his contract with David Selznick, and Rathvon did not expect Selznick would allow Schary to leave early. Nevertheless, Rathvon felt so convinced that Dore Schary was the answer that he was prepared to wait until 1948 for him to begin work at RKO.

Shortly after this Schary traveled to New York for a two-week vacation. In addition to seeing the latest Broadway plays, he met with Depinet and the most important members of the New York staff, all of whom were suitably impressed. A special dinner was arranged at Floyd Odlum's apartment, where Schary became acquainted with the man who controlled the company as well as several members of the RKO Board of Directors. That evening also went well.[36]

By the time Dore Schary returned to Los Angeles, a general consensus prevailed—the company needed to engage his services right away rather than wait another year. And Schary was anxious to make the move. Rathvon knew that Selznick would not let Schary go without exacting a heavy toll on RKO, so he commenced negotiations with considerable trepidation. As expected, the talks did not go well, but near the end of the year the two sides were close enough that members of the media learned Dore Schary would be taking charge of filmmaking at RKO in early 1947.

Actually, two statements were released. Rathvon's brief announcement claimed that since moving to Hollywood he had been "searching for a man of wide production experience and great creative talent to become my associate and supervise the creative aspects of our business," and Dore Schary was "eminently qualified for the post."³⁷ Schary's longer release indicated he was signing on for five years and hoped his regime would "set new patterns and break some old molds." He ended with these stirring words: "I pledge to this new job my own endeavor and ask the works [sic] at RKO to join me in the new years ahead so that between us we can accomplish something that we can be proud of as picture people and as human beings."³⁸

Peter Rathvon's terse statement could be read in two different ways. On the one hand, it may have indicated that he was too exhausted to prepare something more lengthy and eloquent. On the other, it possibly suggested that he was feeling a bit of remorse about giving up the studio post. Despite all the tribulations Rathvon had endured in Hollywood, RKO was enjoying the best year in its history. Final corporate profit for 1946 would amount to $12,187,805, more than double the previous year.³⁹ In addition to *The Spanish Main* and *The Bells of St. Mary's*, both of which brought in most of their revenue in 1946, the company derived sizable profits from *The Spiral Staircase* ($885,000), *Badman's Territory* ($557,000), *Till the End of Time* ($490,000), *Cornered* ($413,000), *From This Day Forward* ($362,000), and *Without Reservations* ($342,000).

RKO also released two films whose quality was, and has remained, unquestioned, though neither would help the corporate bottom line. *The Best Years of Our Lives*, Samuel Goldwyn's stirring account of the difficulties of reintegration into postwar society for three combat veterans of World War II, dominated the Academy Awards, winning seven Oscars, including Best Picture and Best Director for William Wyler. It also prospered at the box office, piling up $7,675,000 in domestic film rentals alone. But RKO had never made a dime on a Goldwyn film because of the inadequate distribution fee charged to market his product, and the "red" figures on *Best Years* added up to $660,000.⁴⁰

Even more disconcerting was the performance of the first Liberty production, Frank Capra's *It's a Wonderful Life*. The picture was based on a short story by Philip Van Doren Stern called "The Greatest Gift," which had originally been sent to Stern's friends in his 1943 Christmas cards. RKO acquired the rights during Charles Koerner's tenure at the suggestion of Cary Grant, but when Capra read it he decided it would be the perfect material for his return to Hollywood production. Neither he nor star James Stewart had made a studio feature since they entered military service in the early 1940s.

Shooting began in the spring at the RKO ranch, where most of the exterior sets were constructed, with the picture's debut planned for the first half of 1947. In May Sam Briskin, the administrative head of Liberty Films,

6. Frank Capra and James Stewart, back from service and ready to work on *It's a Wonderful Life*. Courtesy of the USC Cinematic Arts Library.

wrote Peter Rathvon to request the release of *It's a Wonderful Life* be moved forward to December 1946; this would be perfect timing, in Briskin's opinion, since "the [film's] principal action takes place on Christmas Eve and Christmas Day."[41] Rathvon knew this was not possible but asked Ned Depinet to respond because "I am the fellow who has to live with Briskin."[42] Depinet expected to see Briskin in New York shortly after this. But the former RKO production head was forced to postpone his trip, so Depinet wrote Rathvon a letter, presumably to be shown to the prickly Briskin, explaining why *It's a Wonderful Life* would have to be held for release until 1947. "In all our planning at this end, we have never expected to have Mr. Capra's film until the early part of next year, and the entire list of this season's releases has been scheduled ever since I was at the studio [earlier in the year]," he stated.[43] RKO's planned Christmas release was *Sinbad the Sailor*.

As mentioned previously, the effects of the Hollywood strike on the Technicolor laboratory in Hollywood forced a delay in the striking of *Sinbad* release prints. This opened up the choice slot for *It's a Wonderful Life,* and Briskin grabbed it despite warnings from Depinet that RKO distribution would not have enough time to implement a proper prerelease campaign. Most likely, Depinet and Rathvon decided to allow the move because both loved the film and there were important indicators it could become a blockbuster. George Gallup's organization, Audience Research, examined the results of the film's initial preview and informed Rathvon that "the analysis shows the picture to be among the top pictures in enjoyment of all those ever previewed by Audience Research."[44] Subsequent previews also went through the roof.

Consequently, panic soon reigned after the film performed poorly upon its initial release. On January 13, 1947, Briskin sent Ned Depinet a long, bitter telegram, blaming RKO's New York office for "lack of cooperation and understanding" related to the film's bookings in a number of cities, its "very poor" advertising and exploitation, and the fact that *It's a Wonderful Life* was "rushed into release."[45] Depinet was infuriated. He shot back a heated wire, reminding Briskin that he had been the one who insisted the picture be rushed into theaters "contrary to our earnest advice and pleading that you wait until advertising and publicity could penetrate through to public." Depinet claimed that the many decisions about advertising and theater bookings that made Briskin so angry were finalized "after full consultation and approval of your authorized representative." He also stated that Briskin did not have "the slightest conception of what we have been doing here" but ended his response with a conciliatory request to "relax and have courage as no damage has been done and outlook looks brighter every day."[46] Depinet was wrong about that; the film ended up losing $525,000 for RKO. Moreover, it became the solitary RKO release of one of the most promising independent companies in Hollywood history, Liberty Films; the disappointing box-office performance of *It's a Wonderful Life* played a key role in the partners' decision to sell the company to Paramount, which, in effect, disbanded it. Depinet was right concerning the rash decision to fling the movie into the marketplace at the end of 1946. Although one can only speculate about the reasons for the picture's original failure, its poorly primed release surely contributed to the shocking reception that greeted one of the most beloved motion pictures of all time.[47]

The biggest all-around winner on RKO's 1946–47 program was *Notorious,* a film that generated worldwide gross film income of $7,150,000 and could hold its own with the Goldwyn and Capra pictures in terms of quality. Indeed, it would soon be recognized as the outstanding title to emanate from the coproduction arrangement between RKO and David Selznick and ultimately be viewed as one of the best films RKO ever released. RKO's profit totaled $1,010,000, even though the studio was required to split income with Selznick's Vanguard company.

Each of the pictures made in concert by the two companies involved separate negotiations, but the deal for *Notorious* was representative of most of the arrangements. The narrative, based very loosely on a story titled "Song of the Dragon" by John Taintor Foote, had been developed by David Selznick, who hired Ben Hecht to write the screenplay. Selznick also furnished the services of director Alfred Hitchcock and stars Cary Grant and Ingrid Bergman. RKO contributed most of the production financing; the film was shot on the RKO lot; and a majority of the technical staff, including composer Roy Webb, were company employees.

Although filming went relatively smoothly on the $2,376,000 production, plenty of conflict took place behind the scenes between its makers and the censors. The script focused on cynical playgirl Alicia Huberman (Bergman) who is recruited by American agent Devlin (Grant) to help expose a nest of clandestine Nazis plotting away in Rio de Janeiro. She eventually falls in love with her handler but is forced to marry a key member of the Nazi contingent (Claude Rains). Although she accomplishes her mission, her duplicity is discovered by her husband and his mother. They slowly poison Alicia before Devlin saves the heroine from her captors.

After getting their first look at the screenplay, members of the Production Code Administration (PCA) expressed serious reservations about Alicia's behavior, particularly during the initial portion of the tale that takes place in Miami. Crushed by the conviction of her father as a Nazi traitor to the United States, she adopts a lifestyle marked by excessive drinking and sexual promiscuity before she accepts the role of American operative. In a letter to Selznick written on May 25, 1945, Joseph Breen deemed the material "to be definitely unacceptable" because of "the characterization of your lead, Alicia, as a grossly immoral woman, whose immorality is accepted 'in stride.'"[48] The fact that Alicia later has an affair with Devlin and then marries (and presumably sleeps with) a man she does not love to infiltrate the villains' inner circle did not seem to bother Breen too much, but he found her devil-may-care behavior early in the story to be intolerable.

Promises were made that Alicia's characterization "would be changed in such a way as to avoid any direct inference that she is a woman of loose sex morals," but Hitchcock and company forgot about them before shooting the problematic scenes.[49] When Joe Breen and his cohorts first projected the

7. Director Alfred Hitchcock, Cary Grant, and Ingrid Bergman pose for *Notorious* publicity. Courtesy of the Academy of Motion Picture Arts and Sciences.

picture, they were horrified to discover that Alicia was not only a playgirl but also unmistakably a "kept woman," the mistress of a rich man named Ernest (played by Gavin Gordon), in the Miami sequence.[50] During the next few days the PCA staff screened the film several more times and demanded a number of deletions, but Hitchcock and Selznick, as well as William Gordon, RKO's liaison with the PCA; and Peter Rathvon, who also ended up in the middle of the fray, held firm for more than two months. The ultimate compromise entailed the elimination of one scene between Alicia and Ernest and the reduction of a few shots of drinking and drunkenness at a party in Miami.[51] Consequently, the important plot point concerning Alicia's hedonistic response to the devastating revelation about her father was retained along with other crucial story elements that helped make *Notorious* one of the most sophisticated adult dramas of the 1940s. The power of the Production Code Administration had begun to ebb, freeing filmmakers to grapple with serious subject matter that had been off-limits for many years.

Notorious, It's a Wonderful Life, The Best Years of Our Lives, plus *The Spiral Staircase, Till the End of Time, Cornered,* and others—Peter Rathvon had run the studio during the best and most profitable release year in RKO's history. It was also a golden year for the industry, with total company profits of $119.9 million, which dramatically surpassed any other year in motion picture history. Perhaps Rathvon did have regrets about surrendering the production reins to Dore Schary. But he also knew that all the top pictures of 1946 (except Goldwyn's *Best Years*) had been kick-started by Charlie Koerner before his death. Although he did not realize it at the time, Rathvon's green lighting of product that would emerge from 780 Gower Street in 1947 soon made it apparent that he was, indeed, much more talented as RKO's chief executive than its production chief. N. Peter Rathvon had chosen the right path; it was in his best interest, as well as the best interests of RKO's thousands of employees and stockholders, for him to devote full attention to the demands of the corporate presidency.

3. "The Screen Has Come of Age"
The Rathvon-Schary Regime (1947–1948)

RKO's new production chief offered quite a contrast to his predecessors, who were, for the most part, apolitical individuals. An outspoken progressive, tall, bespectacled, forty-one-year-old Isadore "Dore" Schary embraced the principles of his hero Franklin Roosevelt and the liberal wing of the Democratic Party. This ideology influenced and informed his work. As he stated on numerous occasions: "A picture should be entertaining but it should also have something to say." He fervently believed that the cinema could be a force for the betterment of humanity, had already been creatively involved with a number of social-issue films (e.g., *Boys Town, I'll Be Seeing You, Till the End of Time, The Farmer's Daughter*), and intended to make more now that he held green light power at RKO. He was pleased to discover that a coterie of political lefties was already ensconced at RKO (producers Adrian Scott and John Houseman; writers John Paxton, John Wexley, and Paul Jarrico; director Edward Dmytryk; and actor Robert Ryan), and Schary would hire more individuals of the same political persuasion, such as directors Nicholas Ray and Joseph Losey. He did not realize, however, that some of these men resided well to the left of him politically; they were, in fact, members of the Communist Party. At the time, this fact would probably not have mattered very much to him, but, soon enough, it would matter a great deal.

Schary also sought out and enjoyed the limelight. He loved to give speeches and happily accepted most of the speaking engagements offered him. He took full advantage of media opportunities, quickly becoming the face of RKO and the subject of numerous newspaper and magazine profiles. As his first year at the studio helm evolved, Schary perhaps began to wish he had adopted a lower profile, for he would become a lightning rod of controversy and the object of scathing attacks from conservatives throughout the nation.

8. On the set of *Mr. Blandings Builds His Dream House*—director H. C. Potter, Myrna Loy, producer Dore Schary, and Cary Grant. Courtesy of the Academy of Motion Picture Arts and Sciences.

In actuality, Schary's official RKO tenure didn't commence on the first day of the year and might have been postponed until November if not for the dogged persistence of N. Peter Rathvon. Even though Hollywood had learned of Schary's move to RKO in late 1946, and he had actually started working there, at least part-time, in January, securing his release from the contract with David Selznick and Selznick's second-in-command and chief counsel, Dan O'Shea, took longer than expected. "It has been a tough negotiation as the boys started by asking for the moon," Rathvon wrote Ned Depinet in February. "There were several break-offs when I told them to take Schary back until November, but finally we have agreed on principal terms."[1] The arrangement required Schary to supervise two more coproductions between RKO and Selznick, with the financial elements of the partnership clearly stacked in Selznick's favor. The first film would be *Mr. Blandings Builds His Dream House,* starring Cary Grant and Myrna Loy. When the deal was finally cemented, Dore Schary assumed full charge of RKO production.

Schary would have a powerful partner at the studio: Peter Rathvon himself. Rathvon and his wife enjoyed living in Southern California, so he decided to run the corporation from Hollywood rather than New York. From all indications, Rathvon and Schary got along well. Rathvon had learned that proper functioning of the organization required him to defer to the studio chief regarding all production decisions, though he was not shy about offering opinions. Schary was also not shy about rejecting them.

Ned Depinet would continue to function as head of the New York office as well as the company's distribution leader. He journeyed west later in February 1947 for meetings at the studio. By then Schary had realigned studio operations, with producers Bert Granet, William Pereira, and Adrian Scott reporting directly to him instead of Jack Gross, who would oversee the efforts of Richard Berger, Nat Holt, Harriet Parsons, and Phil Ryan. Robert Sparks, who had served as executive producer on *Honeymoon* and *Out of the Past,* returned to straight producing.[2] Sid Rogell remained in charge of the B unit. During the preceding year Peter Rathvon and his cohorts had made Schary's job a bit easier by eliminating the gender imbalance among the thespians. Newcomer Barbara Bel Geddes; former RKO players Irene Dunne, Myrna Loy, and Ann Sothern; and contract talent Jane Greer, Anne Jeffries, and Barbara Hale were now available for casting opposite Cary Grant, Robert Mitchum, Robert Ryan, Dick Powell, and the other leading male performers. In addition, arrangements to secure the services of Merle Oberon, Loretta Young, Alida Valli, and Cathy O'Donnell for a minimum of one picture each had been completed.

At the late February meetings the top men discussed the forthcoming production program with emphasis on properties scheduled to begin shooting in the near future. Dore Schary had already decided that the company should adopt a new approach to B pictures. Rather than making films of questionable value, such as the Dick Tracy vehicles, he felt RKO could "combine showmanship and also get pictures of distinction in the 'B' category." Therefore, the Tracy series would be abandoned after making "those on which we have already bought the story rights."[3] Although Schary's philosophy sounded pretty similar to Rathvon's abortive Operation Pegasus, Ned Depinet supported the idea. At the end of the meetings Depinet expressed the belief that RKO should never make a picture "for any reason except that we feel it will be a good picture and that for each picture we should ask ourselves ... why we are making it." Consequently, it was resolved that "it would be better to absorb or settle commitments rather than to make a picture merely because we are faced with contract commitments."[4]

Interestingly, nothing was said about *The Robe*, the mammoth movie supposed to tie up filming at both the Gower Street and Culver City studios during the year. It seems the executives' enthusiasm for this Frank Ross project had dampened considerably. Negotiations were now underway for possible production to take place in Great Britain with the participation of J. Arthur Rank.[5]

The decision not to make *The Robe* in Hollywood, at least in 1947, placed the company in an unusual position. Anticipating the huge undertaking's disruption of studio activities, Rathvon had pushed through a large number of films in the last half of 1946 that were now either finished or close to completion. This inventory included *The Devil Thumbs a Ride, The Farmer's Daughter, Trail Street, The Bachelor and the Bobby-Soxer, They Won't Believe Me, Woman on the Beach, Honeymoon, The Long Night, Out of the Past,* and seven other titles. Thus, RKO had more money than ever before tied up in inventory, with most releases planned for many months later to avoid a distribution logjam and give each film proper lead time for advertising and exploitation. In addition, work at the studio continued to churn at a fast clip because Dore Schary's initial productions were gearing up for filming.

The excessive inventory would not have been cause for alarm if business continued to rumble happily along as it had for the past several years. But by spring everyone in Hollywood began to notice disturbing signs. Box-office attendance had started to decline, thanks to the onset of the baby boom era.[6] Young couples celebrated the end of the war by marrying, moving to the suburbs, and starting families. With budgets stretched as they carved out their own small piece of the American dream, these young Americans cut back on moviegoing. If they did decide to catch a picture, they most likely watched it at a neighborhood theater or a drive-in—venues that were more convenient and featured lower admission prices than the picture palaces in urban downtown areas. For many years these first-run theaters had often been packed, bringing in the lion's share of major film-company earnings. Now, they had plenty of vacant seats.

In addition, the costs of making movies had shot up to "frightening" levels (according to Norman Freeman), while box-office returns, foreign as well as domestic, were contracting.[7] Indeed, a laissez-faire attitude toward budgets that took hold during the bountiful war years, plus the high costs of settling the various strikes of 1945 and 1946, had elevated production outlays to hitherto unimagined levels. From its initial program in 1929–30 through the 1941–42 release year, RKO made hundreds of features, but only eleven had budgets that exceeded $1 million and none cost $2 million or more. Of thirty-one RKO films in the 1946–47 program (excluding the independent product), five were budgeted above $1 million and four above $2 million. Even more disturbing was cost escalation at the B level. The company's low-budget Westerns had always been its most inexpensive pictures. RKO released six of them starring Tim Holt in 1941–42 at an average cost of $48,000. Holt entered the military during the war, then came back to RKO in 1947, where he starred in *Thunder Mountain* on a budget of $177,000. He would saddle up for five more "oaters" in 1947–48, each made for approximately the same outlay as *Thunder Mountain*. One might expect the production values and script quality of these later Westerns to be much superior to those of the earlier ones. They were not.

RKO's leaders recognized the difficulties created by the rising costs of the Bs and decided to live with them in 1946 because, as Norman Freeman had demonstrated, these pictures provided a number of supplementary benefits. It was easier to do that when the A product was producing abundant results, but now, suddenly, the "important" pictures were starting to falter. Floyd Odlum, who always viewed matters through a financial prism, noticed and wrote Rathvon in April suggesting a solution:

> I have never been in the center of the production industry in Hollywood, but I have been around the fringes for many years and it is my confirmed belief that no industry has more of a chance to reduce costs than the motion picture industry. It has been built on wastefulness, and that is its very asset now if taken advantage of. There must be ways to cut the number of days necessary before the camera. Some outstanding directors have proved that it isn't necessary to retake and retake and shoot scores of thousands of feet of film in order to get six or seven thousand feet of finished product. I believe you can make a great name for yourself and do an outstanding job for the industry in general and RKO in particular if you will address yourself to this problem. The attack on this problem needs a man of your disposition and experience, and particularly one who is not immersed so much in the day to day affairs of the industry as to lose sight of the forest for the trees.[8]

No record of Rathvon's reply has been found, but he did make Dore Schary aware of Odlum's suggestion. However, the new studio head proved unable to reduce picture costs by a significant amount.

RKO's growing financial problems were exacerbated by earlier decisions unrelated to the rising costs of production. When the company was flush with cash, Rathvon and the board of directors made a number of investments that were now beginning to sour. The Mexican studio, Churubusco, was one of the sore points. It was not generating the requisite rental income, and RKO had managed to set up only one B film to be shot there, *Mystery in Mexico*, directed by Robert Wise.[9]

The corporation also committed a substantial amount of money to lease a twelve-story building at Park Avenue and 106th Street in New York and then convert it into the "world's most modern studio."[10] This brand new RKO Pathe facility contained sound stages, an orchestra and choral-recording studio, a theater, five sound-recording rooms, five dressing and makeup rooms, six editing rooms, and six production offices, plus a carpentry shop, a paint shop, and film vaults. Here, RKO intended to produce the Pathe newsreel, as well as such short subjects as "This Is America," "Sportscopes," and "Flicker Flashbacks." In addition, company leaders envisioned the building as a base to turn out industrial films, merchandising films, educational films, and institutional films for various clients. It would also be available for rental purposes, and the executives were particularly excited when David Selznick leased space there to film *Portrait of Jenny*, starring Jennifer Jones—"the first modern feature picture to be made entirely in New York."[11] Dore Schary scheduled *The Window*, a B thriller starring Bobby Driscoll, Barbara Hale, and Arthur Kennedy, to shoot at the studio after the Selznick picture was finished.

But in July RKO sold the Pathe newsreel to Warner Bros. for $4 million, eliminating one of the main reasons for the new studio's existence.[12] And despite the abundant hype that accompanied its opening in 1946 and early operations in 1947, the studio soon turned into a bigger boondoggle than Churubusco. In October Harry Michalson sent Ned Depinet a memo stating that "the studio was at no time necessary in carrying on all of the . . . RKO Pathe activities. As a matter of fact, . . . we cannot afford to use [the] studio except for scoring and recording to produce the ordinary commercial picture or any of our short subjects." The problem was the overhead charge—then 51 percent—because the studio was not attracting enough business to reduce this excessive figure to a more reasonable number. Michalson calculated that the "success of the whole venture appears to rest in the need for keeping the stages occupied at least 70% of the time because only in this manner are certain normal operating expenses taken up and become rebillable. To accomplish this we would need about four complete feature pictures a year, or one every quarter."[13] This level of activity did not appear likely. One month later Floyd Odlum and other members of the board of directors began looking for an escape route. At a meeting of the board's executive committee, its members "determined to attempt to sublease or assign the present lease upon said premises to others, either for television or other purposes."[14]

Other previous expenditures also began to appear ill-advised. To prepare for a possible move of West Coast–production operations to Culver City, the company purchased real estate adjacent to the studio there and then had producer-architect William Pereira take another look at the replacement cost and present value of the Gower Street lot. According to Pereira, "everything has increased in value in terms of numbers of dollars," including the cost of replacing RKO's venerable studio. His evaluation placed this cost at $9.2 million, as compared to a figure of $6.2 million for its "present worth."[15] Given these numbers, it did not make sense to proceed with a sale of the Gower Street property, at least not at that time. Therefore, the executive committee decided the best course of action would be "to entertain offers to purchase the [Culver City land] and that final determination whether or not to sell be based upon the amount of the offer received."[16] No acceptable offers were presented.

Another troubling issue was recent escalation in expenditures for advertising, publicity, and exploitation. Advertising, in particular, had rocketed out of control. During the war years RKO had ramped up its advertising in national magazines, radio, and newspapers, and the trend continued following the end of the conflict. In 1945 total direct advertising costs for the A pictures amounted to $3,361,000, or 13 percent of estimated domestic gross revenue. The direct costs for 1947 (including *The Best Years of Our Lives*) were projected to be $9,237,000, or 18.2 percent of estimated domestic gross revenue.[17] In November David Goldman wrote Peter Rathvon, "I do not think it will take much argument to convince anyone that we cannot continue to spend an average of 17.1489 [cents] out of each dollar for advertising, . . . especially with negative costs in inventory as high as they are now."[18] Significant reduction in these costs became a priority.

While the aforementioned problems were certainly significant, they would eventually pale compared to other horrors visited upon the motion picture industry in 1947. These included a 20 percent decline in domestic box office and the totally unexpected imposition of a 75 percent ad valorem tax on the earnings of American movie companies in Great Britain, first announced on August. One expert stated that the English market was "almost as important to Hollywood as all other foreign distribution outlets combined."[19] Thus, to have to make due with a quarter of the previous revenue from the British Isles represented a staggering blow to the companies' bottom lines. Other countries soon followed the British lead, setting up their own protectionist measures that limited cash flow to American movie outfits. But it could be argued that even these shocking developments did not throw the industry offtrack as much as the House Un-American Activities Committee (HUAC) investigation into communist influence on Hollywood motion pictures. This inquisition not only sucker punched all the studios; it landed a mighty wallop to the solar plexus of RKO.

While geopolitical tensions between the United States and the USSR had begun to build during the period when the two nations were allies in the world war, historians often cite Winston Churchill's "Iron Curtain" speech, delivered on March 5, 1946, in Fulton, Missouri, as the beginning of the Cold War. The relationship between Russia and the western countries deteriorated rapidly after that. By 1947 many Americans had grown fearful of Soviet espionage inside the United States, as well as the potential for war between the two powerful nations. Numerous politicians, most famously Sen. Joseph McCarthy of Wisconsin, then embarked on a crusade to root out communist activity within the fabric of American life; in October they focused their attention on a high-profile target—Hollywood.

Emissaries of HUAC had begun to interview members of the movie community months before the hearings of October 1947, but it appears most insiders continued to nourish the gross misapprehension that there was little to worry about. On June 9 producer Adrian Scott sent Dore Schary an innocuous memo containing the following humorous PS: "The fact that this memo is written in red is purely coincidental owing to the fact that the Kremlin ran out of black."[20] Four months later the situation was no laughing matter.

First, a group of "friendly" witnesses took the stand in Washington, including former RKO employees Adolphe Menjou and Lela Rogers, mother of Ginger. They testified that advocates of Russian ideology had skillfully infiltrated the motion picture industry and were injecting communist propaganda into American movies. Lela Rogers believed that the popular RKO production *Tender Comrade*, starring her daughter, contained communist propaganda. Her conclusion was based on its title and the fact that the principal female characters agree to live together in communal fashion. She took particular exception to one line of dialogue from the film: "Share and share alike—that's democracy."[21] The picture had been directed by Edward Dmytryk and scripted by Dalton Trumbo. Ms. Rogers also considered RKO's *None but the Lonely Heart*, written for the screen and directed by Clifford Odets, to be similarly subversive.

Then the "unfriendlies" were called by the committee; among the men who soon came to be known as the "Hollywood Ten" were Trumbo plus

Dmytryk and Adrian Scott, then considered RKO's top director-producer team. Their most recent picture, *Crossfire*, was controversial, but it had earned plaudits from many critics and intellectuals and was doing excellent business at the box office—more on this film later in the chapter.

Like the other members of the Ten, Scott and Dmytryk refused to answer questions posed by the Un-American Activities Committee, choosing instead to attack the right of the politicians to interrogate them concerning their political beliefs. Their belligerent response, however principled, was a tactical mistake, robbing them of most of the support they had garnered before the hearings.[22] The Ten would soon be declared "in contempt of Congress" and eventually incarcerated for taking their stand. But right after the hearings concluded no one was sure how the individuals or the studios should respond to the public relations nightmare that immediately engulfed the industry. The major companies had already agreed they would not fire any of their employees because of their political beliefs. Dmytryk later claimed that Dore Schary assured him during the hearings that his job at RKO was protected by an "ironclad contract."[23]

But Schary was only one voice at RKO, though his certainly carried a lot of weight. On November 12, 1947, a meeting of the executive committee of the board of directors took place at the Town House in Los Angeles, a hotel only a few miles from the studio. Chairman Floyd Odlum presided and the other directors present were Rathvon, L. Lawrence Green, and Frederick L. Ehrman. The only absent member was Ned Depinet. Although not members of the board, Dore Schary and attorney Mendel Silberberg also attended, at least for a portion of the meeting. Much of the discussion related to Scott and Dmytryk. If Schary defended the two men as he later claimed, this is not reflected in the minutes of the meeting.[24] In fact, the consensus of those in attendance was "that both Dmytryk and Scott by their actions, attitude, associations, public statements and general conduct before, at and since they appeared before the Committee of the House of Representatives have brought themselves into disrepute with a large section of the public, have offended the community and have prejudiced RKO Radio Pictures, Inc."[25] Furthermore, Silberberg, a highly respected lawyer who often represented the film industry as well as individual companies like RKO, "stated that it was his offhand opinion that said Dmytryk and Scott have by their conduct and actions violated the provisions of their respective contracts." And thus the groundwork was laid for firing two of RKO's most valuable filmmakers.

One day later the board members met again and learned that, in the opinion of company lawyers, RKO "had the legal right to terminate the employment of ... Dmytryk and Scott by the terms of their respective agreements." It was concluded "that such action be taken." But the directors decided to postpone a final decision because more meetings were scheduled to take place at Floyd Odlum's ranch in Indio, California, during the following week. Then, a more definitive "legal opinion would be available." During the first meeting in Indio, held on November 22, it was "RESOLVED, that it is recommended to RKO Radio Pictures, Inc. that said Edward Dmytryk and Adrian Scott be discharged from their employment under the 'moral' clauses of their respective contracts with the said Picture Company and authorize the President and the studio head to take such steps."[26]

Although their fates were sealed, Scott and Dmytryk did not learn the outcome right away. Instead, RKO's executives once again waited to act. They knew that an industry conclave hastily pulled together by the president of the Motion Picture Association of America, Eric Johnston, and to be attended by Schary and Depinet, as well as representatives of all the other important companies, was scheduled to take place at the Waldorf Astoria Hotel in New York two days later.[27] This assembly had been called specifically to discuss the "Communist problem" and how best to defuse it. For two days the top executives debated. Then, despite impassioned resistance from Dore Schary with support from independent producer Walter Wanger, MGM manager Eddie Mannix, Columbia president Harry Cohn, and Samuel Goldwyn, they released one of the most famous (or infamous, depending on one's political persuasion) policy statements in the history of American cinema. It was aimed at the Hollywood Ten, but its purview encompassed a wider swath of the film community. The Waldorf Declaration read, in part,

> We will forthwith discharge or suspend without compensation those in our employ and we will not re-employ any of the ten until such time as he is acquitted or has purged himself of contempt and declares under oath that he is not a Communist.
>
> On the broader issue of alleged subversive and disloyal elements in Hollywood, our members are likewise prepared to take positive action.
>
> We will not knowingly employ a Communist or a member of any party or group which advocates the overthrow of the Government of the United States by force or by any illegal or unconstitutional methods.[28]

With this statement, the era of the blacklist in American film commenced. Now RKO could move in concert with the entire industry, and the studio moved quickly. Scott and Dmytryk were both terminated on November 26. Schary evidently refused to fire them himself, so it was left to Rathvon to hand the two men their notices.²⁹ Scott and Dmytryk responded, issuing a statement that declared, "we believe that the courts will uphold our stand on principle which we now affirm."³⁰ They were wrong; the years of litigation that followed would not result in either exoneration or financial compensation.³¹

Dore Schary's appeals for sanity during this chaotic period did not go unnoticed. He had been called to testify during the October hearings and, naturally, questioned about RKO's employment of Scott and Dmytryk. Schary defended them, stating that he never heard either "make any remarks or attempt to get anything subversive into the films I have worked on with them." This displeased committee chairman J. Parnell Thomas, who lectured Schary about the dangers of a "Rip Van Winkle" attitude toward communism, prompting the RKO studio chief to make his feelings about the doctrine crystal clear:

> I am not a Communist. I have never been a Communist. I never contemplated becoming a Communist, and I am opposed to Communists. I have fought the Communist line at any time that I have seen it become apparent. I fought it in 1940 when it was very apparent, and I have fought it in any possible way I can, and I shall continue to fight it but I believe, along with most American citizens . . . that it is not as great a danger as some people believe it is. I think the American people resent it. I don't think Communism has anything to offer the American people, and that is why I don't think it is as dangerous as some people do.³²

Thomas was not impressed. At the end of Schary's testimony, he again reminded him about Rip Van Winkle.

Schary's appearance before HUAC and his efforts on behalf of Scott and Dmytryk upset a number of the country's conservative writers. He was soon branded a "pinko" by newspaper columnists Hedda Hopper, George Sokolsky, Westbrook Pegler, and others. Even before the meeting at the Waldorf Astoria, the attacks became so disturbing that Schary brought them up at the RKO executive board meeting on November 12. He stated that his testimony before HUAC "was in complete accordance with the policy theretofore established by the Motion Picture Producers Association," that "such unfair criticism was harmful to him," and that "he believed it advisable for the Company to issue a statement clarifying his position on the matter."³³

Although Floyd Odlum's demarcation point on the political spectrum placed him well to the right of Schary, he agreed that something should be done, and the other board members concurred. One day later a letter signed by Odlum and Rathvon to an unnamed stockholder who had criticized Schary's actions was released to the press. It stated that RKO was "unalterably opposed to Communism," then continued,

> This policy does not mean that the management will be carried away by hysteria or words. Calling a man a Communist does not make him one. Unwarranted attacks on Mr. Dore Schary, the executive producer at our studio in Hollywood, are a clear example of what is meant by this last statement. Your company employed Mr. Schary in this top position on account of his outstanding abilities and after careful investigation. At that time we gave him our confidence and he still has our confidence.

The release went on to quote Schary's "I am not a Communist" testimony before HUAC and to make the point that his remarks were in conformity "with the position accepted by all the producing companies."[34]

The supreme irony of the dreadful predicament now affecting Dmytryk, Scott, and Schary as well is that, only a couple of months before, the threesome were on top of the world, thanks to their picture about the importance of tolerance: *Crossfire*. Based on Richard Brooks's novel *The Brick Foxhole*, the film was in preparation before Schary joined RKO. Initially, the production head did not view the project as anything special; in February he ventured the opinion that it could make a "good exploitation picture."[35] Rathvon was not a fan of the story about a deeply prejudiced man who kills someone simply because he is Jewish. He had already informed Schary, "I doubt that it has the least value as a document against racial intolerance and I think there is a chance it might backfire and have an effect opposite to that intended."[36]

But Dore Schary came to a different conclusion. At some point, he recognized that *Crossfire* had the potential to be much more than just an exploitation picture. With the proper emphasis, it could be precisely the sort of movie he favored—a serious feature containing a progressive social message. Around the time *Crossfire* went into production in March, word began to leak out that RKO was making a hard-hitting, realistic picture about anti-Semitism. On March 18 *Crossfire* and its producers became the subject of Cecil Brown's radio broadcast on the Mutual network. Brown described Schary as "one of the brightest executives in Hollywood" and applauded him and Adrian Scott because both "men have told me that pictures can be top-notch entertainment and still convey the issues of the day, the business of getting along better with people, of fighting for more democracy, and upholding the democratic principle."[37]

Now that the film's subject matter was common knowledge, letters of protest began to arrive on the RKO doorstep, many from a surprising source—members of the Jewish community. One of the first, and strongest, came from Judge Joseph M. Proskauer, president of the American Jewish Committee. He had gotten hold of the screenplay and given it a cursory examination. "I want to make clear at the outset that I think your people think there is nothing anti-Semitic in this film. Our people think it is shot with dynamite," he stated. Referring to a speech in the script delivered by police captain Finlay (played in the film by Robert Young), he seemed especially disturbed by the effort "to make [the story] pro-Semitic by some mealy-mouthed statement that a Catholic could be murdered in the same way; but the apologia is like pouring rose water on a cancer."[38] Agreeing with Peter Rathvon's earlier assessment, Judge Proskauer felt the film would probably add to anti-Semitism in the United States rather than subtract from it.

A confident Dore Schary was undeterred. He believed in the picture's value, tirelessly defended it, and reveled in the controversy that continued to build in anticipation of its fall release and would not subside for some months thereafter. Schary took a presentation credit and even appeared on camera to introduce the film's trailer. Debates about its positive or negative impact certainly boosted the box-office response to *Crossfire*, which would eventually rise to the top of all the 1947–48 RKO pictures with a profit of $1,270,000. The fact that the film featured a fine screenplay by John Paxton, solid direction from Dmytryk, exemplary performances by three Roberts—Young, Mitchum, and Ryan—and worked nicely as a noir murder mystery as well as a social message drama added to its luster. It would be nominated for five Academy Awards, including Best Picture.[39]

In the months leading up to the crushing blow that HUAC delivered to the movie capital, Dore Schary rode the *Crossfire* bandwagon to glory. One particularly flattering piece in *PM* magazine was titled, "There's New Hope for Hollywood in Dore Schary of 'Crossfire.'" It suggested that Schary's approach might "give new direction and hope to an industry that has been floundering hopelessly since the end of the war" and quoted him as follows: "the screen isn't a pulpit, but you can still do something that is important and constructive in people's lives and make it entertainment that will sell at the box office."[40]

Even a number of prominent Jews and Jewish organizations embraced the picture, and Schary as well. RKO's studio head received word that Albert Einstein felt *Crossfire* was a "very useful picture and ... would like Hollywood to make more of the kind."[41] After Schary was honored by the Beverly Hills Lodge of B'nai B'rith with an Award for Civic Excellence, he gratefully penned an article for the *National Jewish Monthly*. It ended, "The

9. A coffee break during the production of *Crossfire*—Jean Porter (Mrs. Edward Dmytryk), her husband the director, Robert Ryan, Robert Young, and Robert Mitchum. Courtesy of the Academy of Motion Picture Arts and Sciences.

screen has come of age. Producers must help maintain the mature stature of its adulthood. It can become all-important in bettering the world, while still entertaining. That is my objective and the objective of all of us at RKO."[42]

Whether his coworkers embraced Schary's idealistic approach to cinema was an open question, because most were then grappling with a malady that had not afflicted them in years: cost cutting. In early fall it became clear that RKO's business had executed a startling about-face, and all responsible parties were ordered to pare expenses. The importance of reducing advertising costs has already been mentioned. At the studio Norman Freeman demanded that all department heads slice their budgets significantly. By November it appeared that back-lot expenses would be reduced by a minimum of $700,000 in the following year.[43] RKO also closed down its Story Departments in London and Paris and eliminated personnel and expenses in the New York headquarters. The distribution arm did its part by dismissing twenty-seven members of the force, cutting its special exploitation group by twelve persons, reducing checking expenses, shaving outlays at the exchanges, and instituting economizing measures in the Foreign Department. Ned Depinet expected the savings to amount to some $1.5 million per year.[44] Even the theater company, then the healthiest division in the RKO organization, was not immune. Its mandate was to reduce costs by hundreds of thousands of dollars.

Additional evidence of RKO's tumbling financial fortunes came in October, when the corporation was so desperate to decrease its inventory and pick up some quick cash that it agreed to sell four films to United Artists, which had been suffering throughout the 1940s because of management problems, an inadequate number of appealing pictures to circulate through its distribution channels, and other reasons.[45] During the war UA had purchased several "surplus" films from Paramount, including *I Married a Witch*, starring Fredric March and Veronica Lake, and *The Crystal Ball*, starring Paulette Goddard and Ray Milland. Now facing another shortage of product, UA's executives worked out a similar arrangement with RKO. The studio consented to turn over *Out of the Past, Indian Summer, Station West*, and *Return of the Badmen* to United Artists for approximately $4.5 million. The deal did not contain built-in profit for RKO; the company was essentially unloading the films for their production costs, an indication of how anxious the executives were to slash the bloated inventory. All the legal documents were prepared, but UA could not arrange financing, and the deal fell apart in November.[46]

Perhaps the most surprising target in the cost-cutting effort was Dore Schary himself. To entice him to join RKO, Peter Rathvon and Floyd Odlum had given Schary a contract that paid a weekly salary of $3,800 plus 2.5 percent of the net profits of the corporation during each annual period. After Rathvon negotiated Schary's release from Selznick, the contract was signed and backdated to January 1, 1947.[47] Schary's deal was most generous; during the time Charles Koerner supervised RKO production, he earned a straight $2,000 per week. The compensation was also considerably more than President Rathvon himself made. But toward the end of 1947, Odlum and Rathvon decided Schary's income was excessive given the company's financial troubles and began discussing strategies to convince him to accept a "voluntary reduction in salary."[48]

Schary was well aware of the financial difficulties. Rathvon had sent him an alarming memo in November:

> There have been many indications, world-wide, that our dollar revenue from the foreign market is rapidly declining and well-informed people think we will be lucky if we can maintain a third to a half of it. Meanwhile the domestic market is about twenty percent below last

year. All this means that we are operating at a substantial loss currently, that the inventory we have built has shrunk in value by millions and that unless we make pictures of comparable quality at much less cost we will not survive.[49]

Floyd Odlum then wrote Schary in early December, expressing his concerns about the declining value of RKO stock and his belief that the upcoming program of pictures was crucial. "No program during my association with RKO has been as important as this particular one," he asserted. Odlum ended his letter, "Studio earnings of at least $3,000,000 seem essential. Will this program do it?"[50] Not only did Odlum expect excellent results from RKO's executive producer; he would soon be requesting that Dore Schary give up a significant portion of his compensation as well.

The distressing turnaround in RKO's financial performance was evident when one examined the profit-and-loss figures of the 1947 releases. *Crossfire* did very well (profit: $1,270,000) and *The Bachelor and the Bobby-Soxer* ($700,000), *Nocturne* ($568,000), and *Trail Street* ($365,000) also posted good numbers, but the losers were startling. *Tycoon* ($1,035,000), *The Long Night* ($1,000,000), *Honeymoon* ($675,000), and *Woman on the Beach* ($610,000) caused plenty of consternation, while *Magic Town* ($350,000), *A Likely Story* ($305,000), *Born to Kill* ($243,000), and *Great Day* ($232,000) contributed to the gloom. But the Mount Everest of all catastrophes turned out to be *Mourning Becomes Electra*, which cost the company a record-shattering $2,310,000 in losses, despite a budget that totaled $2,342,000.

This picture, like most of the others released in 1947, had been approved for production by Peter Rathvon, who believed the team of producer-writer-director Dudley Nichols and star Rosalind Russell could transform Eugene O'Neill's grandiloquent, six-hour-long play into a landmark motion picture. Perhaps concerned that audiences would consider *Mourning Becomes Electra* overly "arty," Rosalind Russell told Hedda Hopper before its release that the movie version would actually be a "super-duper thriller with lots of suspense."[51]

Dore Schary was equally enthusiastic about it. In August he wrote Ned Depinet, "I believe it is a great film, and it will not only make money but bring great prestige to the company."[52] Initial road-show engagements handled by the Theatre Guild quickly proved him wrong. Very few spectators showed up during its two-a-day presentations. The picture was then returned to the studio, cut, and rereleased in the normal manner in 1948. This made no difference; it died a rapid, unceremonious death wherever it played.

In her autobiography Rosalind Russell, who somehow scored another Academy Award nomination for her performance, claimed she did not want to make *Mourning Becomes Electra* in the first place and then blamed the catastrophe on nearly everyone but herself: "Katina Paxinou screaming and yelling all over the set; Michael Redgrave, a hell of a good actor, but nervous, taking pills to calm himself; Dudley [Nichols] refusing to change a single line because Eugene O'Neill was his idol. We made a five-hour picture ... and Dudley wouldn't cut an inch, not a frame."[53] In fact, even the road-show version was less than three hours long, though Russell was correct to lay a good deal of blame at Nichols's door. Dudley Nichols deserves a prime spot in the screenwriters' hall of fame, having penned scripts for *The Informer*, *Bringing Up Baby*, and *Stagecoach*, among many others. But his direction of *Mourning Becomes Electra* was positively turgid; how someone who had spent years working with John Ford, Howard Hawks, Fritz Lang, Jean Renoir, and other excellent directors could turn out such a constipated piece of cinema is difficult to understand.[54] A chastened Roz Russell, who had declared in 1946 that she was sick to death of playing "career girls" in romantic comedies, fell back on those very roles after her icy plunge into the deep dramatic waters of *Sister Kenny* and *Mourning Becomes Electra.*[55]

While RKO leaders were wringing their hands over the public rejection of *Mourning Becomes Electra*, another film was released that they had almost completely overlooked—*Out of the Past*. It would eventually be recognized as one of the best RKO movies of them all. Based on the novel *Build My Gallows High* by Geoffrey Homes (a pseudonym for Daniel Mainwaring), the story first came to the attention of studio reader Bill Koenig in September 1945. He loved its intricate tale of love, lust, and deception, describing it to his boss, Manny Wolfe, as a "worthy addition to the rough, tough school of Chandler, Cain and Burnett [that] presents an almost perfect story for an actor like Bogart."[56] Val Lewton also believed a "wonderful picture" could be made from the book.[57] Wolfe, William Dozier (Koerner was in Europe at the time), and Rathvon agreed; five days after submission of the reader's report RKO paid $20,000 for the novel and hired Mainwaring to work on the adaptation.[58] In his April 1946 speech to studio producers, Joseph Breen had discouraged the production of such pictures, but this story was too far along the preproduction track by then for Rathvon to derail it. When the estimating script hit Breen's desk at the PCA in June, he sent one letter to the studio stating that the material was "unacceptable from the standpoint of the Production Code" and another in which he tried his best to bury the project:

This general overall story appears to us to be, definitely, the kind of a story which we should not attempt to make. It has the same, general disagreeable flavor which two or three of your pictures, now in production, have, and I am sure that a picture of this kind will do a definite disservice to this industry.

Because of this, I most earnestly recommend that you find some way to shelve it.[59]

The company declined to follow Breen's advice, leading to many rounds of negotiation over subsequent script drafts and, of course, the shape of the final picture. But other problems cropped up along the way as well. Since RKO had no chance of getting Humphrey Bogart to star, the studio turned to Bogart's former Warner Bros. cohort, John Garfield, for the main role. He was set to play protagonist Jeff Bailey, then suddenly decided he didn't want to do it. RKO's new hard-boiled hero, Dick Powell, circled the part for months before coming to a similar conclusion. Thus, producer Warren Duff and Robert Sparks, who served as executive producer on the movie, were forced to give the part to one of the company's up-and-comers, Robert Mitchum.[60] It would be Mitchum's first starring role in an A picture and one of his best. Support was provided by two other newcomers, Jane Greer as femme fatale Kathie Moffat and Kirk Douglas in the smaller role of gangster Whit Sterling. Each was perfect; in retrospect, it's hard to imagine anyone else embodying these characters. The picture was directed by that former stalwart of the Lewton unit, Jacques Tourneur, and photographed by one of RKO's unsung heroes, the brilliant cinematographer Nicholas Musuraca.

When it was finished, no one at RKO considered *Out of the Past* to be anything special. Indeed, as already mentioned, company leaders would have been happy to offload it to United Artists as part of the four-picture deal that ultimately fell apart. Thus, they were pleasantly surprised when, unlike most of the other films released on the 1947–48 program, it received good notices and actually made a profit, albeit a small one ($90,000). It also opened their eyes to the star potential of Mitchum. Nevertheless, *Out of the Past* remained underappreciated for many years, until a revival of interest in the film noir movement of the 1940s caused critics, cineastes, and academics to take a second look. They elevated this twisting travelogue of the dark corners of the human psyche to well-deserved classic stature.

Dore Schary felt no particular enthusiasm for *Out of the Past*, but the same cannot be said for most other aspects of his RKO job.[61] Despite the year's many setbacks, the continuation of disappointing revenues from company releases, the ongoing shelling from right-wingers convinced he was "soft" on communism, and the pressure from Floyd Odlum to turn the

10. Director Jacques Tourneur, Jane Greer, and Robert Mitchum converse on the set of *Out of the Past*. Courtesy of the Academy of Motion Picture Arts and Sciences.

company around, the ebullient Schary maintained his upbeat demeanor and continued to run the studio "his way."

And, despite the problems that HUAC had visited upon him, Schary remained positively messianic about the potential of the movies to improve humanity. In December he delivered speeches in Philadelphia, Boston, and New York. Indeed, he was so busy during the last month of the year that he prevailed on Robert Ryan to substitute for him in Chicago on December 15. There, Ryan read a speech Schary had prepared for the American Jewish Congress, which was honoring him with an award for "courageous pioneering efforts in combating the racial and religious hatred and bigotry through the medium of the motion picture." In the speech Schary pledged he would never back away from pictures like *Crossfire*, despite opposition from HUAC and other organizations that viewed such films as unseemly and pernicious:

I do not believe that the makers of forward-thinking, courageous films will ever be intimidated. We will make our pictures as we have always made them, and at no time has any subversive material ever reached the American screen, and we will see that none ever does. At the same time, we will not retreat to the making of a program of gingerbread and taffy motion pictures. The American public, our customer, is ready for films that reflect the world we live in, and if we do not make these kinds of films, the public will find other means of entertainment.[62]

Dore Schary was not only feisty but preternaturally optimistic. No previous RKO studio head had ever been so passionate about the company's product, not just his own pictures but some made by the previous regime. In November he wrote Ned Depinet a letter gushing about *The Miracle of the Bells* ("one of the biggest pictures we have ever had") and *I Remember Mama* ("NUMBER ONE for us and a very good chance NUMBER ONE for the entire industry").[63] In January 1948 he amped up the hyperbole for pictures he had sponsored, including *The Boy with Green Hair* ("it will be one of the most talked about of films during the next twelve months"); "The Long Denial" (release title: *A Woman's Secret;* "going to be 1 1/2 hours of the best entertainment we will have"); *Blood on the Moon* ("if we can't make a buck on this we better quit"); and "Your Red Wagon" (release title: *They Live by Night;* "[will be] to our 1948 program what 'Crossfire' was to our 1947"). "Take a look around and see if any company can top [this] list," he told Depinet. "I think we are all in for a good year in which we are going to prove there is nothing wrong with this business that good pictures can't cure."[64]

If Dore Schary really believed this last statement, he must have been a direct descendant of Pollyanna. The business was sickly, and everyone else in Hollywood knew it. The excessive costs of production, the declining domestic audience, the British "confiscatory" tax (which had caused the major studios to place an embargo on film exports to England), the blocked funds and other protectionist measures imposed by other countries, and the defiling effects of HUAC all portended dark days in Hollywood, possibly for years to come.[65] And then there was the rise of television. Back in early 1944 Ralph Austrian, a radio and television consultant, had warned RKO sound director Stephen Dunn that television "will be with us so fast that it will sweep us off our feet if we do not make ready for it."[66] Dunn shared the letter with studio executives, but they, along with most other movie-company leaders, were still unprepared for the rapid ascendance of this new entertainment medium.

Even the Los Angeles County tax assessor added to RKO's woes, raising the Hollywood studio's land assessment by 180 percent over the previous year's.[67] In addition, the Truman administration appeared to be much more committed to trust busting than Roosevelt's New Dealers had ever been, and the ominous Paramount case, which threatened to end vertical integration in the American motion picture business, had now made its way to the U.S. Supreme Court.[68] Sam Goldwyn was one of many who felt uncomfortable about the current state of the business: "Inefficiency must be rooted out of high places as well as all other ranks. It is a startling indictment of our industry that with employment throughout the United States at its highest peak in history, box office receipts have been going down. Unless a thorough and honest housekeeping takes place, the difficulties our industry has experienced of late will fade into insignificance by comparison with those ahead."[69]

Even Dore Schary sounded sober about the state of the industry in a short piece he wrote for *Variety* in early 1948. Schary admitted that the world market for motion pictures had collapsed, thanks to the British tax and the geopolitical uncertainties of the times; consequently, "the cost of films must come down." While he believed that belt tightening would eventually result in better-quality pictures, he insisted that residents of the movie colony should view the business in a much broader context:

> These are tough, angry days we are living at the moment, and Hollywood is not an island unto itself. It reflects the world in which it lives. If things get tougher in the world, they will be tougher in our industry. But if statesmen and international leaders create a pattern of hope for the future, there will be great hope for us in the industry.
>
> So, while I am generally optimistic about our ability to adjust ourselves to the economic circumstances we face, I recognize that our final hope rests only in a world of peace, and a world free of tension and fear. I hope that we will begin to see this kind of a world beginning with the new year.[70]

The RKO Corporation would later report net profit of $5,085,848 for 1947, less than half of its 1946 earnings. And much of the "gravy" came from theater operations, the sale of the RKO Pathe newsreel, and the sale of three theaters. As Peter Rathvon noted in a news release that accompanied the corporation's annual report, the "recession in 1947 consolidated earnings ... was attributable to a substantial loss by RKO Radio Pictures, Inc., the picture producing and distributing subsidiary."[71] In fact, the precise amount lost by the studio arm of the company was $3,556,140.[72] But RKO was not alone in this reversal; all the companies had to cope with the unpleasant jolts of 1947. When the year ended industry profits had fallen nearly $33 million from the year before.

Shrewd and unsentimental Floyd Odlum was aware of these developments, as well as the dwindling value of RKO stock, which had plunged from a high of $28 in 1946 to under $10 a share in December 1947. Consequently, he stepped up a process that had been ongoing for months—seeking the right buyer for the controlling interest in RKO held by his Atlas Corporation. Rathvon certainly knew his mentor's disposition; back in July he had tried to pull together a Wall Street syndicate to purchase the Atlas stock. He failed, but another group, headed by William Paley of the Columbia Broadcasting System, nearly came to an agreement with Odlum. *Daily Variety* reported that Rathvon "stymied" the deal because he would have been replaced had it gone through.[73]

In April 1948 all of RKO's employees became aware that Odlum was thinking of exiting the movie business, when the trade papers carried a story that he and Howard Hughes had reached an impasse in discussions related to the purchase of the stock.[74] Some were pleased that the eccentric Hughes would not be assuming control. Peter Rathvon certainly felt that way; he wrote Odlum that he was "greatly relieved that it is not Hughes who is to take over. I am not really going to be happy with anyone else in your position but I think Hughes would have been probably more difficult than one would anticipate from hearing him talk about his intentions."[75]

Rathvon and company had enough to worry about already. The "economy program" remained top priority, forcing all workers to do more with less. In January the executive committee of the board learned that "reduction in expense for 1948 . . . should total approximately $6,000,000."[76] Still, this was not enough. The pressure to cut costs continued, resulting in the elimination of the home office Christmas party, the company golf tournament, even the annual sales convention.[77] No item was too small for consideration; it was resolved, for example, to have "payroll checks bear the facsimile signature of one officer and the manual signature of another, in lieu of two manual signatures."[78]

Efforts to minimize the damage caused by the company's ill-advised investments in two studios—Churubusco and RKO Pathe in New York—also continued. In January the directors considered closing the Mexican plant but decided it would be more sensible to keep it operating while the corporation looked for some entity to purchase its 49 percent ownership position. Peter Rathvon emphasized, however, that "under no circumstances should additional dollars be sent to Mexico to support the Studio operation."[79] Better news related to the 106th Street operation in New York. Though it took several months of difficult negotiations, much of the building was eventually leased to NBC for television purposes.[80] The lease would last five years.

Despite the gloom, company production hummed along. During the first half of 1948, Schary's studio completed principal photography on *Roughshod, Berlin Express, Rachel and the Stranger, Race Street, The Velvet Touch, Mr. Blandings Builds His Dream House, The Boy with Green Hair, A Woman's Secret, Blood on the Moon, Walk Softly, Stranger,* and *Bodyguard.* The production chief also had *Every Girl Should Be Married, Adventure in Baltimore, Bed of Roses, Easy Living,* and *Battleground* nearly ready to go before the cameras. *Battleground* was the most uncertain of these titles.

Combat movies had been a staple during the war years, but all the major companies abruptly stopped producing them even before the Japanese surrendered. RKO had not made one since *Back to Bataan* in 1945. The accepted wisdom was that the public had grown sick of war and would not support any more pictures about men in arms. Shortly after assuming the top studio job at RKO, Dore Schary announced that "in 18 months or two years from now we should make a war picture and try to best the field." Film history, according to Schary, showed that it had taken several years after the end of World War I before the great silent films about that conflict were produced and embraced by the public. Schary even had a particular subject in mind—the Battle of the Bulge—because most of the previous Hollywood films had dealt with the war in the Pacific.[81] Despite resistance from Ned Depinet and a number of RKO employees polled about the idea, Schary stayed on course. He hired Robert Pirosh, a veteran of the Battle of the Bulge, to write the screenplay and was preparing the film for shooting in late summer or fall 1948.

Floyd Odlum's opinion of the *Battleground* project is unknown, though it seems clear he was not overly impressed with Schary's performance as RKO production chief. The fact that Schary had never agreed to any proposal that would reduce or restructure his salary probably also rankled him. But the bottom line was Schary's score card as studio head. He had managed no turnaround; in fact, RKO was continuing to toss out eye-popping losers, among them the very films about which Schary had waxed so enthusiastically. *I Remember Mama,* for example, was well on its way to a final loss of $1,040,000, while *The Miracle of the Bells* would add $640,000 to the deficit. Other clunkers distributed during the first four months of 1948 included *Night Song* ($1,040,000 loss), *If You Knew Susie* ($490,000) and *So Well Remembered* ($378,000). Not a single picture released between January and April 1948 earned a profit.

Thus, it came as no surprise when Floyd Odlum sold out in May, though the new owner did cause perturbation throughout the motion picture industry. Undeterred by his initial failure to strike a deal, Howard Hughes

11. Financier Floyd Odlum working from home in Indio, California. Courtesy of University of Southern California, on behalf of the USC Specialized Libraries and Archival Collections.

continued to pursue Odlum relentlessly until the two magnates came to an agreement.[82] Hughes purchased 929,000 shares for $9.50 per share from Atlas, a cash outlay of $8,825,500. He now owned approximately 24 percent of RKO's stock, which gave him controlling interest in the corporation.[83] According to Hedda Hopper, the final details were hammered out in a telephone conversation that lasted almost five hours.[84]

Texas-born millionaire Howard Robard Hughes Jr., whose principal businesses were oil drilling, defense, aviation, and air travel, had lived in Los Angeles for many years. He was as famous as any Hollywood star, thanks to his efforts as an aviator in the 1930s. He also had a track record as a film producer, though it was an erratic one.

Hughes's movie career began with such famous films as *Hell's Angels, The Front Page,* and *Scarface,* made in the late 1920s and early 1930s. He then seemingly lost interest in Hollywood production, focusing his efforts instead on aircraft design and flight-speed records, a number of which he established in the late 1930s. Just before America entered the war, Hughes got back in the game, producing the controversial Western, *The Outlaw.* After another idle period dictated by his national-defense efforts, Hughes returned to producing, partnering with celebrated writer-director Preston Sturges in a new independent company, California Pictures. The outfit had completed only one film—*The Sin of Harold Diddlebock,* starring Harold Lloyd—when Hughes bought control of RKO. *Diddlebock* was released in three cities before Hughes, unsatisfied by the initial response, pulled it back for further editing. The final version would later be distributed by RKO under the title, *Mad Wednesday.*

Everyone knew that Howard Hughes was an odd individual and unconventional businessman, but it was his reputation as a meddler that worried RKO's top brass. He had fired Howard Hawks and taken over the direction of *The Outlaw* himself, and rumors were rife that his interference with the work of Max Ophuls, Harold Lloyd, and Sturges in the California Pictures venture had caused all manner of difficulties.

Dore Schary fully expected that he and Howard Hughes would not be able to work together. For one thing, Hughes was a zealous anticommunist who must have been aware of Schary's left-wing politics and attempts to prevent the imposition of the blacklist in Hollywood. And Schary had no intention of becoming a stooge executive producer whose every decision could be overridden by his boss. Thus, when he learned that Floyd Odlum was seriously considering the sale, Schary drove down to the ranch in Indio and did his best to convince Odlum not to pull the trigger on the deal. But, according to Schary, "Odlum was an engineer and a financial giant and had no affection for films. RKO had been an investment designed to earn him a profit, and the sale to Hughes was one way for him to leave with a profit and rid himself of what he termed an 'uneasy relationship' with top motion picture executives whose erratic behavior confused him."[85] The production head evidently did not realize it, but Odlum likely considered Schary to be among those very executives.

Odlum apparently convinced himself that Hughes's stewardship of RKO would have a beneficial impact on the company. In a press release concerning the sale, he stated,

> The tentative contract that Howard Hughes and I entered into several days ago permitted me to withdraw if within a period of time I should obtain a higher cash offer from others. I have received such an offer but

not withstanding this I have today made the purchase agreement with Howard Hughes firm and final. . . .

I accepted the Hughes deal in preference to the alternate bid having in mind Mr. Hughes' indicated plans with respect to the future of the company. These plans are important to Atlas Corporation not only because it has been the sponsor for RKO during more than twelve years past but because Atlas Corporation eliminated from the sale to Hughes, and will continue to hold, a large block of RKO option warrants and is therefore maintaining a direct and heavy financial interest in the company's progress and future.[86]

Odlum would soon be eating (and perhaps choking on) these words.

Peter Rathvon also felt it necessary to issue a statement designed to calm company employees. Like Odlum's, it was turned over to the press for publication:

The protracted negotiations between Mr. Hughes and Mr. Odlum have given rise to many groundless rumors and the circulation of much misinformation.

I have had numerous conversations with Mr. Hughes and we seem to be in agreement on all matters of policy and there is no reason to assume that it will be otherwise in the future.

Mr. Hughes has no hungry army of relatives looking for your jobs or substitutes waiting to step into the RKO management.

Mr. Hughes has many and wide business interests and much experience in our industry. I believe he will be a valuable and constructive influence in our company.

Now that the excitement is over let's all settle back to work.[87]

Dore Schary had the right to opt out of his contract because of the change of ownership and remained unconvinced that Hughes would give him the free hand he required at the studio. Rathvon felt differently and arranged a meeting between the two tall men. According to Schary, Hughes said, "he had no intention of taking over. He wanted me to stay and wanted everything to go on as before. He spoke quietly and sincerely. I agreed to remain on the job."[88] In a statement released at the time, Schary also attempted to quell the rumors concerning his future: "I have had a number of talks with Mr. Howard Hughes and we are in complete accord on present policy and on the projected program for RKO. We have a big schedule of pictures planned and all of us at RKO must now stop listening to rumors and bend all of our energies to making as many good pictures as we possibly can."[89]

And so, per Rathvon's and Schary's instructions, everyone at RKO settled back to work. Although no one expected Hughes to be the sort of hands-off owner that Odlum had been, it seemed probable that he would not be overbearing, given the multifaceted business interests that would limit the amount of time he could devote to his new movie company. Ned Depinet certainly felt RKO was in good hands. After ten days of conferences in Hollywood with Hughes, Rathvon, and Schary, he "radiated optimism over the new set-up": "I am very favorably impressed by Mr. Hughes' ideas and intentions. Mr. Hughes reveals high ambitions for our company and I am convinced he is the type of man who will not be content until RKO is the undisputed champion."[90]

Relative tranquility on Gower Street lasted about six weeks, and then pandemonium suddenly erupted. Veteran studio executive J.J. Nolan was about to return from his summer holiday when Ross Hastings, assistant secretary of the picture company, wrote Nolan that he hoped he and his wife had had a "swell vacation" because "from the looks of things around here you will need the rest":

> Everything was going along on schedule when suddenly on Wednesday, June 23rd, it was announced that BED OF ROSES and BATTLEGROUND were being indefinitely postponed, which I think means abandoned. The following day THE SET UP was added to the list.... Since then Dore has been working entirely at home, and he cancelled his New York trip on Thursday.
>
> No general announcement has been made, and no reason has been stated, although naturally everything is being rumored.[91]

This time the rumors of Dore Schary's departure were soon confirmed. Hughes had broken his word to his production chief, canceling production of the two pictures. Like Ned Depinet, among others, Hughes reckoned *Battleground* would lose money because he doubted the public would have any enthusiasm for it. *Bed of Roses* was a different matter; Hughes rather liked the story—it was the star who met his disapproval.

First Rathvon and then Schary had been excited about the potential of Barbara Bel Geddes. The young stage actress had already appeared in major roles in *I Remember Mama*, *The Long Night*, and *Blood on the Moon* and been cast as the protagonist of *Bed of Roses*. But Hughes, who considered himself a connoisseur of women, found her unappealing and insisted she be replaced. Schary refused and began preparing his resignation. It became official on July 7.[92] No successor was named immediately, though it was rumored that William Dozier would return to his old company as head of production.[93]

Peter Rathvon soon emptied out his office as well.[94] As his last official act, he released a statement on July 26, appointing "Mr. Bicknell Lockhart, Mr. Sid Rogell and Mr. C.J. Tevlin as a studio executive committee to govern the modified program of studio operation pending the forthcoming stockholders meeting at which time a new president will be named in my place."[95] The "modified program of studio operation" meant production was grinding to a halt, with ripple effects throughout the entire organization. Suddenly, the economizing measures of the past year looked positively benign as pink slips hit many RKO desks. In an exchange of memos about the cuts, William Fadiman, head of the Story Department in Hollywood, called the situation "tragic," while his counterpart in New York, Leda Bauer, referred to it as "staggering."[96]

According to one trade paper, Rathvon quit, "following sharp differences of opinion with owner Howard Hughes regarding operational policies at the studio," but it was also whispered that he had been a marked man from the moment the company changed hands.[97] Evidently, Hughes felt that anyone who would approve *Mourning Becomes Electra* for production and sink company money into a Mexican studio was not executive material. At least his successor turned out to be a veteran familiar to all RKO workers. Baronial Ned Depinet accepted the corporate presidency offered by the board of directors on September 8.

Howard Hughes's decision to send Peter Rathvon packing was both short-sighted and unfair. Rathvon had been the most successful president in RKO history, lasting longer in the job than any of his predecessors. He understood the proper relationship between a corporate leader and other company executives, particularly and crucially the studio head. Certainly Rathvon had made mistakes, the largest being his decision to assume the role of executive producer after Charlie Koerner's death. But he soon recognized this error and handed the job over to Dore Schary less than a year later. The fact that Rathvon did not foresee the shocking reversal in the film business placed him shoulder to shoulder with his counterparts. All the Hollywood moguls were blindsided by the crises that suddenly overwhelmed them in 1947. Peter Rathvon had developed into a seasoned industry leader, respected by other company heads and admired by members of the RKO family. Leda Bauer described his resignation as "a great blow to the entire organization here [in New York] and we are still reeling under it."[98] Howard Hughes would have been well served to allow him to carry on.

In his autobiography Dore Schary mentions that he regretted his time at RKO had come to an end, because "I was leaving a studio I had put back on a stronger footing."[99] Even though he did not attend college, Schary was an articulate, highly intelligent, and well-read person who had become an excellent producer of individual pictures, as his work on *The Spiral Staircase*, *The Farmer's Daughter*, and *Mr. Blandings Builds His Dream House* demonstrated. He was also a thoughtful man of principle, whose efforts to swim upstream against the red tide loosed on Hollywood in 1947 deserve plaudits. Robert Wise described him as "very straight, very honest."[100]

But was RKO "on a stronger footing" when Schary left? Not really. Naturally, any evaluation of Dore Schary's performance as RKO studio topper must be provisional, since he occupied the post for only a year and a half. And, as already mentioned, during that time the industry went into a tailspin. Still, by any measure, his accomplishments were unimpressive. For example, when one totes up the profits and losses of the RKO pictures on which Schary's screen credit appears (presumably the titles he was most proud of), the final number is minus $4,871,000. Nor are any of these pictures now considered artistically important or historically significant, with the exception of *Crossfire*, which was largely prepared before Schary took over. One might also question Schary's fondness for moralistic message pictures designed to transform moviegoers into better human beings. Not only did the paying public prove allergic to most heavy-handed "educational" efforts, but some of Schary's favorites, such as *The Boy with Green Hair*, turned out to be embarrassingly poor. Dore Schary deserved many awards for his humanitarian efforts, but none for his oversight of RKO production.[101]

Howard Hughes rid himself of Rathvon and Schary and placed a temporary moratorium on studio production, which, as controlling owner, he had every right to do. It was the way he went about it that was disturbing. After offering assurances to both men, as well as Floyd Odlum, that it would be "business as usual" at RKO, he reneged on those promises. And only two months after pledging that the jobs of company employees were safe, he ordered the firing squad into action. How could anyone believe or trust this man after such behavior?

Around the time Dore Schary departed, an unsigned, undated memo circulated to key people in the studio. If there was a single document that sealed the fate of RKO, this was it. The memo read,

Mr. Hughes desires to retain personal control of the following:

1. Approval of stories and cast.
2. Approval of all important contracts and commitments.
3. Approval of any change in policy with respect to increases in costs or expenditures.
4. Approval of any new personnel in upper echelons or higher salary brackets.[102]

4. "There Is a Lot of Life in the Old Place Yet"

The Hughes-Depinet-Rogell Regime (1948–1950)

Common sense dictates that sound business practices include a high level of coordination and cooperation among the members of any organization.[1] It also obliges the manufacturer of a product to maintain a thoughtful, cordial, and trustworthy relationship with customers. Disagreements will inevitably arise in these interconnected activities, but they should be addressed and resolved in a fashion that does not negatively impact the partnerships necessary for the healthy functioning of a company's business.

From a commercial standpoint, RKO was never a model entertainment organization. Its leaders had made a multitude of mistakes, mistakes that have been pinpointed throughout this book and *RKO Radio Pictures: A Titan Is Born*, which preceded it. Yet the company also succeeded on many levels, producing some highly successful films, building a loyal and committed staff throughout the world, and nurturing relationships with theater owners and moviegoers that were meaningful and, for the most part, positive. To many people, the beeping tower logo conjured forth pleasant associations—of agreeable working conditions, productive affiliations, and cheerful movie memories.

But, soon enough, the residual good will accumulated by the company throughout its twenty-year existence would disappear, swept away by the mercurial, inscrutable Mr. Hughes, whose thought processes, not to mention business philosophy, are difficult to understand. Hughes created his own reality, unmoored from the workaday world that surrounded him. A true nighthawk, he often conducted business in the dimly lit back alleys of Los Angeles, holding meetings in a nondescript Chevrolet. He also relied a great deal on the telephone, never hesitating to awaken his associates in the middle of the night to deliver his directives. From a business perspective these orders were often as confounding as Hughes's outlandish modus operandi. Although no one realized it in May 1948 when Hughes took control, RKO had been consigned to death row. Like many such inmates, it would remain there for a number of years, most overseen by its personal executioner, who would lead his prisoner down the "last mile" but slip away before the final lethal switch was thrown.

Accounting for RKO's decline and ultimate demise is the primary objective of the rest of this study. But two observations can be offered at this point that may help to make some sense of the bewildering events to follow. First, RKO's previous leaders had attempted to develop a positive corporate culture, one that would have the best chance of making the company financially profitable. Some had succeeded; others failed, but most worked hard to achieve this goal. However, the RKO culture changed under Hughes. It became contentious rather than collaborative, distrustful rather than determined, hostile rather than hopeful. In short order, RKO's top management found itself embroiled in bitter conflicts with a remarkable spectrum of potential partners—actors, producers, writers, independent producers, theater owners, stockholders, moguls, industry representatives, labor unions, below-the-line employees, the U.S. government, even other members of the company staff. Many of these adversarial relationships engendered lawsuits, miring RKO in a giant web of litigation that would have sucked the energy out of any organization.

Second, even though some have done this, it would be ridiculous to suggest that Howard Hughes wanted RKO to fail and actively plotted its destruction. Hughes was a successful businessman; and he fully anticipated that his latest venture would fare just as well commercially as the Hughes Tool Company, the lynchpin of his empire. But when he took control of RKO, Hughes no longer had any sense of the importance of time. There are few commercial enterprises in which the old cliché "time is money" is more meaningful than in the motion picture business. A leader of a movie concern must be decisive, keeping abreast of day-to-day developments in the production arena and responding promptly to his staff. Hughes operated quite differently, often taking months to make up his mind about the smallest details. Deadlines to him were anathema; indeed, he seemed to ignore them with a sort of perverse relish. As a consequence, creativity was stifled and picture budgets inflated. Hughes did not set out to bury RKO, but he could not have done a better job of it if he had.

Shortly after key studio employees were informed that all major production decisions would require the approval of Hughes, they discovered that he would not be joining them on the Gower Street lot.[2] Their new leader had decided to work out of an office and screening room that was part of the Samuel Goldwyn complex, close to Hughes's West Coast command post at 7000 Romaine Street in Hollywood.[3] Although RKO and Goldwyn were only a couple of miles apart, this opened a symbolic gulf between the top man and his workers as wide as the Grand Canyon. In previous times staff members at the intimate RKO facility had bumped into the studio head on a regular basis, and it was fairly easy for the top producers, writers, directors, and actors to set up meetings with their leader. No one ever saw Hughes at RKO, and arranging a meeting with him became more difficult than booking one with the president of the United States.

The new studio hierarchy was also unusual. RKO's West Coast operations had been entrusted to three men: Bicknell Lockhart, C.J. Tevlin and Sid Rogell. The tough, flinty Rogell had been a fixture at 780 Gower Street for years, first as studio manager and then as head of B production after Charles Koerner assigned him the job. He would now be the nominal executive producer of RKO's A films as well, though all major decisions required the approval of Howard Hughes. Both Lockhart and Tevlin were Hughes's men, but Creighton J. "Tev" Tevlin was better known in the Hollywood community. He began working for Fox as a traveling auditor in 1917, then became an independent accountant for various producers, including Hughes, during the latter's most active period as a producer, the late 1920s and early 1930s. In 1940 Tevlin became head of General Studios and three years later joined Hughes Productions as the boss's personal assistant. Lockhart was a management consultant who first met Hughes when he was working for MacDonald Bros., a Boston engineering firm. He had limited experience in the motion picture business.

At first, the precise responsibilities of Tevlin and Lockhart were ill-defined, though everyone knew they had considerable power. Eventually it became difficult for RKO employees—even Ned Depinet and Sid Rogell—to reach Hughes, whereupon Tevlin's function was clarified. He became the autocratic gatekeeper; anyone who wanted to communicate with or gain access to Howard Hughes had to go through Tev.[4] Lockhart was a more low-key, shadowy figure; he thoroughly analyzed studio operations with the goal of increasing efficiency and minimizing waste, completed his work, and departed RKO in August 1950.

Another oddity was that Floyd Odlum continued to serve as chairman of the RKO Board of Directors after he sold the huge block of stock that gave Hughes control of the company. As Odlum said at the time, the Atlas Corporation retained a financial interest in RKO because of stock options and other aspects of the sale contract; thus, he had incentive to remain on the board. The fact that Hughes indicated he would be too busy overseeing his other businesses to devote a lot of time to RKO also provided some credibility to the arrangement. Still, it seemed strange that Odlum retained this important position, along with two other members who had joined the board at his behest—L. Boyd Hatch and Harry M. Durning—while neither Hughes nor any of his associates became board members.

Minimal production activity took place at RKO during the remainder of 1948, as Hughes contemplated the kind of pictures he wished to make. This was not a problem at first, because Rathvon and Schary had left behind a significant number of films that would trickle out to theaters during the next two years. Part of the reason for the trickle effect was Hughes's distaste for most of the product made by his predecessors. Consequently, such movies as *Fighting Father Dunne, They Live by Night, Return of the Badmen, Race Street, Rachel and the Stranger, Station West, Indian Summer, Roughshod, The Window, The Boy with Green Hair, Blood on the Moon, A Woman's Secret,* and *Walk Softly, Stranger* enabled RKO to maintain a reasonable release schedule, though most of the titles would be indifferently promoted and advertised and lose money.[5] Still, this group of films was never destined for major commercial success; even if distributed with more enthusiasm, it seems unlikely any of the pictures could have been big hits.

While the studio languished in a somnambulistic state, the first of the Hughes-era scandals took place. On September 1, 1948, Robert Mitchum and actress Lila Leeds were arrested and charged with marijuana possession. The actor had emerged as RKO's brightest young star, and, as *Time* magazine pointed out, the company had "$5,000,000 riding on three unreleased Mitchum films."[6] Nevertheless, "dope" charges were serious business, and there were rumors that RKO management might evoke the morals clause in Mitchum's contract, as it had with Edward Dmytryk and Adrian Scott, and cut him loose to distance itself from his drug use. But where others saw ignominy, Howard Hughes saw opportunity.

Hughes was supposed to be a shy, withdrawn, extremely private man. In many ways this was true, but he worshipped publicity and understood its power.[7] In this case, he thought there would be more upside to backing Mitchum than denouncing him, and he was right. Hughes retained Jerry Giesler, the defense lawyer who had successfully represented Charlie Chaplin in a paternity suit and Errol Flynn in the first of his rape trials, then sat back and watched the controversial case unfold. In September a trailer for Mitchum's next picture, *Rachel and the Stranger*, hit theater screens.[8] Audiences responded enthusiastically whenever the movies' new "bad boy," who costarred with Loretta Young and William Holden in the

12. Director Don Siegel, producer Jack Gross, Robert Mitchum, and studio chief Sid Rogell discuss the script of *The Big Steal*. Courtesy of the Academy of Motion Picture Arts and Sciences.

film, appeared in the preview. Hughes pushed for a quick release and the picture turned out to be one of RKO's biggest hits of 1948, earning profits of $395,000.

Hughes then decided to fast track a George Raft vehicle, *The Big Steal*, and put it into production early in the 1949, with Mitchum replacing Raft as the protagonist. The gambit was not only intended to cash in on the publicity surrounding Mitchum and his apparently expanding box-office appeal; it was also a ploy to keep Mitchum out of jail. As expected, on January 10 Mitchum was convicted of criminal conspiracy to possess marijuana, but his sentencing was postponed until February. Giesler argued that Judge Clement Nye should be lenient because jail time would force *The Big Steal* company to shut down, thus terminating the jobs of most of the other workers on the production. But the judge saw straight through the stratagem, and Mitchum was soon on his way to the Los Angeles County Prison Farm in Castaic, where he would spend forty-three relatively uneventful days. Robert Mitchum appeared contrite after the sentencing: "This is the last time anything like this will happen to me. It has been a sad lesson. I hope it will save other people from a similar fate."[9]

Despite Mitchum's incarceration, director Don Siegel did not suspend production on *The Big Steal*. He took the crew to Mexico and shot around the lead actor for a time, completing the picture after Mitchum was released from jail. And, just as Howard Hughes had foreseen, the episode harmed neither Mitchum nor RKO—in fact, he became a major star after the marijuana bust and remained in the top strata for years thereafter. Mitchum was always grateful to Hughes, whom he jokingly called the "phantom," for supporting him.[10] He would pay the boss back many times over, appearing in a number of poor RKO films as well as tolerating Hughes's penchant for reshoots that often seemed interminable.

The other movie-company leaders watched the circus that developed around Robert Mitchum's marijuana misstep with trepidation. They knew Howard Hughes was unpredictable and wondered if he would orchestrate other embarrassments that might be beneficial to him and RKO but bad for the industry. For example, Hughes had always adopted a pugnacious stance toward the industry's censorship apparatus, squeezing out considerable publicity for such films as *Scarface, Cock of the Air,* and *The Outlaw* in the process, so they figured he would produce pictures at RKO designed to inflame Joseph Breen of the PCA as well as the many blue-nosed critics of Hollywood. They were correct, but what they didn't expect was that he would immediately betray them in a completely different arena or that his actions would have a more profound impact than any censorship fracas ever had.

While the Mitchum case was unspooling in court during the fall of 1948, the Paramount case was also drawing to a conclusion. Back in May a unanimous Supreme Court handed down a devastating decision that upheld the government's charges against the major studios and then sent the case back to a lower court "with instructions to shape a final decree ending alleged monopolistic practices."[11] Moreover, it ordered the court to "reconsider divestiture of theaters as a remedy."[12] This suggested that vertical integration in the movie business was doomed. Still, there were indications that neither RKO nor the other Big Five companies would be required to give up exhibition entirely.[13]

Handling the litigation for RKO was Ralstone E. Irvine of the law firm of Donovan, Leisure, Newton, Lumbard, and Irvine. Known to his colleagues as "Shorty," Irvine reported to the RKO Board on October 15 that he was making progress in his efforts to negotiate a consent decree with the Department of Justice. This settlement "would be based on a relinquishment by the Corporation of certain theatres but without total divorcement of theatre operations from picture production and distribution." He indicated that "the Department was willing to consider such an arrangement but only upon the understanding that the Corporation should retain only a limited number of show-case theatres and not more than one in each metropolitan area."[14] If RKO could hold on to one flagship house in each of its major cities, this would certainly be advantageous for future business.

On October 25 Irvine and RKO lawyer Gordon Youngman met with Robert Wright in Washington, DC, to refine the details of the consent decree. The meeting lasted more than two hours. Although the three men did not cement a final agreement, it seemed clear that as long as it acceded to certain government demands, RKO would be able to continue owning one theater in each city where it operated a "wholly-owned theater" and one theater in each borough of New York. The latter concession was particularly important because the strength of the company's theater empire had always been the New York City area. On October 29 the RKO Board members expressed the unanimous opinion that "the consent decree as finally negotiated was satisfactory and [it was] in the interest of the Corporation and subsidiaries to enter into the decree and terminate the litigation."[15]

One day later, however, chairman Floyd Odlum, L. Boyd Hatch, and Harry M. Durning resigned from the RKO Board of Directors, for reasons that will be discussed later. They were quickly replaced by Howard Hughes and Noah Dietrich, the president of Hughes Tool Company. Hughes was not present at the meeting, but Thomas Slack, general counsel of Hughes Tool Company, stated that "Mr. Hughes was in favor of the proposed consent decree and in favor of the proposed reorganization plan and that he recommends to the board the entry of the decree and the adoption of the plan in principle, subject to the approval of stockholders."[16]

Nevertheless, only two days later Hughes changed his mind. He shocked his RKO colleagues and the entire industry by accepting a consent decree that called for the divestment of the corporation's entire theater chain.[17] The corporation would have a year to split into two companies: one composed of its production-distribution operations and one of its theaters. Hughes was also given a year to dispose of his 24 percent interest in either the production company or the theater company and indicated he intended to hold on to his controlling interest in production.

Even though the May Supreme Court ruling clearly signaled the government's determination to terminate the vertical business model that had worked well for the Big Five companies since the 1920s, most of the major studio executives believed that a compromise arrangement could be reached, enabling them to remain in exhibition. Indeed, the work of Shorty

Irvine demonstrated this was a strong possibility. But this strategy was based on the Five retaining a united front in negotiations with the Department of Justice. Hughes, however, had little interest in the theater business and recognized an opportunity not only to cash in on his RKO investment but also to eliminate certain loose ends still attached to his initial deal with Floyd Odlum. Being the most independent and egocentric of businessmen, Howard Hughes felt no loyalty to the other moguls and calmly fractured their united front. Paramount soon followed the RKO lead, though the new Big Three, MGM, Twentieth Century–Fox, and Warner Bros., continued to battle, hoping they could somehow avoid total divestiture of their theaters. But thanks to the capitulation of RKO and Paramount, they were no longer in a position to bargain. The end of vertical integration in the American film business was now a foregone conclusion.

The Odlum loose ends involved two items: stock options and a secret arrangement between Odlum and Hughes that gave the Atlas Corporation inside position to acquire the RKO theaters if they were split off from the rest of the RKO organization. The theater clause would later become a particularly contentious issue between the two tycoons, but a disagreement over the stock options caused Odlum and his colleagues to resign from the board. Atlas held thousands of RKO stock options exercisable at $15 per share. Since the arrangement with the government would require RKO to be reorganized into two new companies, whether it retained any theaters or not, Odlum felt the strike price of the options should be halved. If this had been agreed to, Atlas, at some future time, would have been able to acquire more than 300,000 shares of either the production-company stock or the theater-company stock, or both, for $7.50 a share.

Hughes, however, hated stock options because they had the potential to dilute his ownership position in a company. He had always resisted offering them even to his most trusted lieutenants.[18] The Atlas options were already a fait accompli when Hughes bought RKO. Thus, the new owner had been looking for a way to nullify their potential impact since then. The fact that lawyers Irvine and Youngman expressed concerns that "any substantial change in the substance of the rights presently enjoyed by the holders of outstanding option warrants ... would be subject to attack unless such change were made for fair and adequate consideration flowing to the Corporation" bolstered Hughes's position to retain the $15 figure for both of the new RKO entities. Believing this to be manifestly unfair, Odlum and his two colleagues resigned, thus uprooting a powerful figure from RKO who might have questioned, even challenged, Hughes's future management of the corporation. In his departing statement, Odlum emphasized that his resignation was "not to be construed as a release or waiver on the part of Atlas Corporation of any rights that it may have against Mr. Howard R. Hughes, the RKO Company, or others, by reason of contractual arrangements with Mr. Hughes or the adoption of said plan or otherwise."[19] Floyd Odlum was not finished with RKO . . . or with Howard Hughes.

Production began to perk up late in 1948. In November Sid Rogell wrote Ned Depinet that John Ford's *She Wore a Yellow Ribbon* (produced by Argosy Pictures for RKO release) had returned from location filming in Monument Valley and was finishing at the studio. *Sam Wynne* (release title: *Strange Bargain*) was also shooting on the lot with Jeffrey Lynn and Martha Scott, and several other projects were now in their final preproduction stages.[20] Among them were two of Hughes's favorites—*It's Only Money* (release title: *Double Dynamite*), a comedy starring Jane Russell, Frank Sinatra, and Groucho Marx; and a melodramatic piece of agitprop, *I Married a Communist*, whose title would also eventually be changed. In addition, Hughes was particularly intrigued by a project being written by Beirne Lay titled *Jet Pilot*. "This will probably be a very big picture," Sid Rogell stated. Some of the RKO workers laid off in the summer had returned to work, and they, along with other company employees, were pleased to find the filmmaking machinery coming back on line.

As expected, the corporate results for 1948 were disappointing—they showed a net profit of only $500,000. In two short years RKO profits had plunged from $12.2 million to $5.1 to $0.5 million. RKO struggled, but most of its competitors did not do appreciably better. Earnings of the other companies also declined, with Universal posting its first loss ($3.2 million) since 1938, and MGM reporting its smallest profit ($4.2 million) since 1924. Reduction of overhead was now a common goal at all the studios. In January 1949 Darryl Zanuck of Twentieth Century–Fox confirmed what everyone in Hollywood already knew: "The 'easy market' is gone."[21]

Surprisingly, momentum on Gower Street did not flag. The company had seven pictures ready to go before the cameras during the first quarter of 1949, featuring such actors as Mitchum, Claudette Colbert, Robert Ryan, and George Raft. It also had a number of major productions scheduled for subsequent months, though Rogell had to admit that studio plans were "subject to change from day to day." While only about half the films Rogell contemplated making in January were actually produced, some of the non-starters would be replaced by other pictures. Indeed, Rogell felt so enthusiastic in February that he told Depinet, "I really think the doldrums are behind us and from now on we will have a pretty steady flow of activity."[22] He was wrong, though 1949 would become the most active film production year of the Hughes era, with twenty RKO features beginning to shoot before December 31.

Two bizarre productions were among them: *I Married a Communist* and *Stromboli*. Since Howard Hughes vehemently opposed communism and intended to use his power to stifle the spread of the doctrine, it came as no surprise that one of his initial RKO pictures would deal with the subject. And he was not alone—Warner Bros., Twentieth Century–Fox, Paramount, and other companies were also making anticommunist features at this historical moment. Hughes, however, allegedly had an additional agenda; he had decided to use the project as a litmus test of his employees' political sympathies. According to legend, if you were offered the film and turned it down, this meant you were either a communist yourself or soft on communism and assured your quick departure from RKO.[23] The fact that the script was poor and would likely result in a bad picture (which it did) did not constitute sufficient grounds for rejecting the movie. This, however, is another example of the dubious validity of many tales told about Howard Hughes. John Cromwell wriggled out of directing *I Married a Communist* but would later helm *The Racket* for RKO. Nicholas Ray also ducked the assignment, then became one of Hughes's personal favorites, despite his history of left-wing political activity.[24] Further confounding one's efforts to make sense out of Hughes's actions, he chose Robert Ryan to be the leading man in the picture; Ryan was another "lefty" of long standing.[25]

Robert Stevenson ended up directing the movie with a cast that included Laraine Day, Janis Carter, John Agar, and Thomas Gomez. When the picture was almost finished, Sid Rogell waxed enthusiastic, stating that it "looks great."[26] Critics and audience members disagreed. After test runs in San Francisco (where the narrative took place) and New York did not go well, the company was forced to change the title to *The Woman on Pier 13*. Neither the title change nor a rejiggered promotional campaign was of much help; the film finished its run with a loss of $650,000.

Ingrid Bergman's participation in *Stromboli* resulted in a scandal that made Robert Mitchum's marijuana mistake seem trivial by comparison. The first question one might pose about this production is why Howard Hughes decided to invest RKO's money in it in the first place. He had never expressed any affection for neorealism, the new film style that was being hailed throughout Europe and by influential American film critics as well. Indeed, Hughes's record as a producer suggested that he could not have cared less about the struggles of common people presented in sober, unromantic fashion. And despite the increasing advantages of shooting abroad (cheap labor, frozen funds, quota requirements), RKO's leader did not usually favor

13. The RKO Studio at Melrose and Gower in Hollywood during the Hughes era. Note the poster for *I Married a Communist*. Courtesy of the Academy of Motion Picture Arts and Sciences.

productions made far from the United States, where he and his minions would have little oversight. Nevertheless, in spring 1949 one of Hollywood's biggest stars was on her way to a small island off the coast of Sicily, where she would be making a movie with the patriarch of neorealism, Roberto Rossellini.

From the very beginning production did not go well. Sid Rogell sent Edward Killy, a veteran RKO director, assistant director, and production manager, to the location to watch over RKO's investment. Displeased by the slow pace of shooting and Killy's reports of a burgeoning romance between Bergman and her director, Rogell became even more concerned when he viewed the footage being shipped back to the studio. After looking at a set of dailies, Rogell wrote Killy, "I wonder how anybody can spend the whole day getting so little."[27] The original schedule called for ten weeks of filming, although Rossellini indicated he could wrap things up in six. But by mid-May it appeared that seventeen weeks would be required to complete principal photography. In fact, it would take even longer.

In late August Rossellini refused to turn over the film's climactic footage so that RKO could finish editing the English-language version. A week

14. Roberto Rossellini directs Ingrid Bergman in *Stromboli*. Courtesy of the Academy of Motion Picture Arts and Sciences.

later he demanded more money for all the work he had done. This dustup between the director and Hughes was, however, only a minor tremor compared to the seismic event that shook the country after gossip columnist Louella Parsons revealed that Bergman was pregnant with Rossellini's child.[28] Both were then married to others and already had children with their spouses. Overnight Ingrid Bergman's reputation did a dramatic volte-face. From the beautiful, endearing female who had played a nun in *The Bells of St. Mary's*, as well as Joan of Arc and Ilsa, the noble, conflicted heroine of *Casablanca*, she was transformed by public opinion into a callous, narcissistic fallen woman. Newspapers and magazines reveled in her sin, Hollywood insiders speculated that her career was over, church groups called for *Stromboli* to be banned, and women's groups began organizing a campaign against Bergman and the picture. Dr. Walter W. Van Kirk, executive secretary of the Federal Council of Churches, went even further. He called *Stromboli*, "sex exhibitionism which is a symptom of the moral decay of the West."[29]

Undeterred by the negative publicity, Howard Hughes plowed ahead, figuring this cultural firestorm would make the picture a "must-see."[30] After Rossellini surrendered the crucial footage, Hughes ordered the film to be completed as quickly as possible. A preview in Long Beach in January 1950 resulted in bad reactions from the theater manager, a studio executive, and the patrons who attended.[31] Nevertheless, Hughes did not hesitate.

Stromboli opened widely in February, accompanied by an outrageous advertising campaign intended to foreground the scandal (a graphic depiction of a phallic volcano erupting with the following text: "RAGING ISLAND . . . RAGING PASSIONS! This is IT!"). It was greeted by a lethal combination of societal anger and box-office apathy despite the fact that the company spent almost $50,000 more on its U.S. advertising campaign than on any other 1950 release.[32] Even Rossellini added his voice to those of the detractors. In a particularly infelicitous choice of words, the director told reporters in Rome that he wished "to repudiate the paternity" of the American release version, which he believed RKO editing had mutilated.[33] He also renounced all claims to American earnings generated by the film.[34]

The bottom line: despite the director's objections, the Hughes-approved U.S. release version was much closer to Rossellini's somber vision than to Hughes's risqué preferences. It was slow, prosaic, uninvolving, and not at all sexy. Indeed, *Stromboli* completely failed to deliver the goods promised by its hyperbolic advertising.[35] Foreign audiences were evidently less offended than Americans by Ingrid Bergman's behavior; they contributed nearly twice as much revenue to RKO than it received from the domestic market. Consequently, the film ended up losing only $200,000.

In fact, the Bergman scandal had much more staying power than her movie. It provoked Sen. Edwin C. Johnson of Colorado to label Rossellini "vile and unspeakable" and Bergman a "common mistress," while accusing RKO of an "all-time low in shameless exploitation."[36] He proposed a licensing system that would "prevent immoral actors from acting in films, immoral producers from producing them, and stop immoral films from being shipped across State lines."[37] But Johnson's colleagues in Congress had better things to do than vet Hollywood morals, and the senator's crusade subsided before year's end. The lackluster box-office performance of *Stromboli* probably had something to do with that.

One of Howard Hughes's favorite business strategies was to enter into agreements and then, with the help of his army of lawyers, find ways to negate them. The handling of the requirements of the surprising consent decree with the government and a "secret" arrangement with Floyd Odlum, both involving RKO theaters, are prime examples of his methods.

In July 1949 Shorty Irvine requested that the Department of Justice "postpone from November 8, 1949 until July 15, 1950 the date when the reorganization [of RKO] must be completed in accordance with the [consent decree]," because "it now appears that the future of the RKO company engaged in production and distribution will be seriously jeopardized unless this extension of time is granted." Irvine argued that the company's film production and distribution operations were doing so poorly that it needed to hold onto the theaters longer just to stay afloat. In a memorandum attached to his letter to Philip Marcus of the Department of Justice, he listed picture company losses of "$3,556,140 for 1947, $5,288,750 for 1948, and approximately $1,000,000 for the first six months of 1949."[38]

The government resisted, forcing Irvine to send an even stronger letter to William Amory Underhill, the acting assistant attorney general of the United States, in August. In it, he reminded the Department of Justice that RKO had been the first major movie concern to play ball with the government:

> It must be apparent to you that, had RKO continued the litigation instead of terminating it voluntarily, it would have now ample time in which to effect the contemplated improvement in production. It seems to me that under such circumstances a refusal to grant RKO's request penalizes it and gives an unearned advantage to those defendants who refused to terminate the litigation by consent. . . . I can assure you that the directors responsible for the conduct of this business feel very strongly that they should not be compelled to consummate this reorganization at a time or under circumstances which would penalize this Company vis-à-vis its principal competitors.[39]

Irvine's arguments proved to be persuasive, and the government ultimately gave in, extending the date to May 8, 1950, by which the company had to divorce production from exhibition, but this turned out to be only the first round of a prolonged battle. RKO would soon return to the ring, fighting for further extensions.

The second conflict between Odlum and Hughes involved a confidential arrangement that gave Atlas Corporation an option to match any bona fide offer for the RKO theaters, should the corporation decide to sell them. Shortly before he resigned from the RKO Board in October 1948, Odlum revealed the arrangement to the other board members; this elicited a stinging rebuke from Hughes's lawyer Tom Slack. Slack told the members that "Mr. Hughes considered this contract a private agreement between Atlas

Corporation and himself" and did not want it to affect the board's deliberations about RKO's reorganization in any way.[40]

In August 1949 Hughes declared that the Atlas option had expired. He claimed he had received an offer from a syndicate headed by Cliff Work, Matty Fox, and Stanley Meyer for $5,574,120, which Odlum had declined to match. Odlum considered it a "phoney" offer despite a $1.5 million down payment that had allegedly been placed in escrow with the proviso that Hughes could keep the money if the group failed to come up with the full purchase price.[41] Matty Fox called Odlum's contentions "absurd," but the head of Atlas was right. The deal was never consummated, and, as far as can be determined, Hughes did not pocket the $1.5 million.[42] This was the second time that Howard Hughes had outmaneuvered Floyd Odlum, who was enraged. He sent Hughes the following telegram on August 11:

> We have received . . . your communication of August 10, 1949 protesting how cooperative you have been, as to which we will let the record speak for itself. All the failures on your part to meet the letter and spirit of our contract are or should be even better known to you than to ourselves and we see no point to be served at this time, when you claim our rights have expired, to disclose the support for our claim of breach of contract, particularly in view of the prevalent opinion in your environs and presumably emanating from sources close to you that it was your intention from the start to try to make the option provision in the contract between us ineffectual if you could. Although in your communication of August 10, 1949 you state that you consider we have no further rights under the option clause of the contract, we will have to hold to our own opinion about this and let the contract and circumstances speak for themselves.[43]

Odlum threatened legal action for some time, but ultimately decided not to file suit in the matter.

At the studio Sid Rogell continued to believe filmmaking activities were improving. Even though Hughes had decided to assume the title of "Managing Director–Production" earlier in the year, Rogell was able to operate, for a short time, without too much interference from his boss.[44] On August 15 Rogell informed Ned Depinet that, thanks to the addition of John Houseman, Warren Duff, and Alex Gottlieb, the company now had a "rather imposing group of Producers." He held high hopes for a number of films that were either shooting or nearly finished, particularly *Bed of Roses* (release title: *Born to be Bad*; "a magnificent production from every standpoint"), *The White Tower* ("this picture will make history"), and *Christmas Gift* (release title: *Holiday Affair*; "a wonderfully warm comedy-drama of contemporary life"). "I feel that there is a lot of life in the old place yet," Rogell concluded his report.[45]

In November Depinet raised concerns about the mix of A pictures scheduled for release in 1950—sixteen to be provided by independent producers and fourteen by the studio. This was not the "desired balance." "If the ratio was 10 or 12 from Independents and 18 or 20 from RKO, it would be much better for us," he informed Rogell. Depinet felt the company should not enter into any more independent or participation deals, "otherwise we will find ourselves distributing a lot of pictures and handling a lot of money only to turn it over to Independent producers." As he continued, the corporate president seemed much less upbeat about the future than Sid Rogell. "With theater business so bad, our Foreign market shot and the other ills which have beset our business, it is more necessary than ever, Sid, that we pursue a conservative course if we are to survive. I don't mean to frighten you nor appear to be pessimistic, but if we can check every picture and its box office values very carefully, it can only redound to the benefit of our company," wrote Depinet. He then realized that his letter had become overly gloomy and changed his tune: "In conclusion, Sid, I wish to report that we are beginning to roll. I am confident and optimistic. We have an excellent opportunity. Let's take advantage of it with skillful, sensible and enthusiastic determination."[46]

Howard Hughes loved movies and considered himself an expert filmmaker. He viewed dailies as well as rough cuts in his screening room at the Goldwyn Studio, which had a special sound system designed to compensate for the hearing loss Hughes had suffered during many years spent around airplanes. He also had his own cutting room, where he took films apart and put them back together. William Fadiman remembered his passion for editing, as well as his perfectionism: "He would labour for an untouchable number of hours and days over individual frames or shots to make what *he* thought was right."[47]

Although watching and fiddling with movies was one of his favorite pastimes, the tycoon's complicated business affairs and other pursuits prevented him from spending as many evenings at Goldwyn as he would have liked. This did not, however, lessen his determination that no RKO picture would be released until he was satisfied with it, causing delays in many of RKO's productions. In addition, Hughes liked to tinker with release schedules and final titles as well as final cuts, all of which he considered crucial to a film's success. Unfortunately, he had a penchant for dithering, particularly with respect to titles. He nearly always felt a better one could and should be found for each picture but had a difficult time making up his mind.

By the end of 1949 Ned Depinet was losing patience with Hughes's way of working. President Depinet viewed the business through the prism of distribution and understood that RKO could not compete if it failed to deliver a dependable flow of properly promoted, advertised, commercial pictures. Perhaps believing that Sid Rogell had more access to Hughes than he actually did, Depinet sent Rogell a telegram on December 7, bemoaning the "indefiniteness of release schedule and lack of titles for RKO pictures which we want to release." "It is of vital importance," he continued, "that we definitely decide on release titles and definitely set our release schedule as nearly as we can at this time."[48] Unfortunately, Rogell's hands were tied; "Howard Hughes time" did not mesh with "movie business time," and neither Rogell nor Depinet nor anyone else could force the eccentric millionaire to make prompt decisions.

Indeed, Hughes continued to pay little attention to the suggestions of other RKO executives. At the end of December, for example, RKO cemented a coproduction deal for three pictures with Howard Hawks's company, Winchester Productions, despite the earlier directive from Depinet that the studio should stop making arrangements of this kind with independents.[49]

A new year that ushered in a new decade brought more peculiar decisions by Howard Hughes. On January 4, 1950, Rogell wrote Depinet that Hughes intended to delay the release of *Bed of Roses* (release title: *Born to Be Bad*) until the fall because "he is not particularly interested in whether or not we make a profit in the spring of this year or next year."[50] Hughes had even "written and approved" a new ending for the picture. He also decided that *I Married a Communist* would be released as *The Woman on Pier 13*, despite the fact that there was no Pier 13, much less a woman on it, in the movie. *Weep No More* (release title: *Walk Softly, Stranger*) was finished but remained in limbo awaiting Hughes's arrival at a better title.

But these unorthodox determinations would soon be topped by a memo Hughes sent Rogell on January 10. Despite his thirst for publicity, he had decreed that *Jet Pilot* would be made in secrecy. The film, starring John Wayne and Janet Leigh, was now in production under the direction of Marlene Dietrich's former Svengali, Josef Von Sternberg. Visits from the press were to be kept to an "absolute minimum" and a "firm agreement" was to be signed by any visitor "that no mention will be made of any dialogue, action, or dramatic material which he or she may see or hear while on the set of the picture."[51] Furthermore, the RKO Publicity Department was not to release any material related to *Jet Pilot*, nor was any of the footage to be shown to anyone other than a few people working on it, plus Hughes and Rogell.

One could perceive a rationale for this approach; Hughes wished his pet project to stand out and hoped to build special expectations into its release through a campaign that involved unusual secrecy. But buried in the memo was point number 7, which made no sense at all: "Please request our publicity department, unless there will be a most serious detrimental effect, not to release at any time hereafter any story material, dialogue, or dramatic material from any RKO pictures for publication in any way whatsoever (magazine, book, or otherwise) or for use on radio, recordings, or television."[52] Hughes, inexplicably, had ordered the Publicity Department to stop doing its job, not just for *Jet Pilot* but all other RKO movies as well. This sheer lunacy would have doomed the company to a quick and unseemly death. Fortunately, the mandate never went into effect. Either Rogell ignored it or Hughes himself rescinded it, because RKO pictures would generate more than their fair share of publicity during the next few years.

On March 8, 1950, Hughes attended his first and last meeting of the RKO Board of Directors, which conveniently took place at the Beverly Hills Hotel, where he resided. The meeting was called to abolish the executive committee of the board, a subgroup that had been established years before to deal with pressing matters arising between the board's normal meetings. It was this committee that debated and finally decided the fates of Edward Dmytryk and Adrian Scott back in 1947. Frederick L. Ehrman, whose tenure on the board and the executive committee stretched back to 1939, protested the decision, but the committee was eliminated and then reconstituted with Ned Depinet, Howard Hughes, and Noah Dietrich as its members. Ehrman again objected, believing "that at least a quorum of the Directors serving on the Committee should be domiciled in New York so long as the home offices and the President of the Company are located in New York."[53] But Ehrman's objections were brushed aside in this bald-faced maneuver to consolidate Hughes's power and end any significant oversight of RKO affairs by its board of directors. Ehrman resigned from the board in a huff.

By this time Sid Rogell was having a difficult time maintaining his positive attitude. In March he wrote Ross Hastings, complaining about industry insiders whose "constant criticism, apathy, pessimism and negation" were dragging the movie business down.[54] He was particularly perturbed by the remarks of a "highly paid screenwriter" at a dinner party who stated that he had wanted to take in a movie recently "but couldn't find a good one in the whole town." Rogell then located a newspaper and pointed out twenty-four films, which he considered excellent, playing in the Los Angeles area. Rogell listed the titles in his letter; they included *The Fallen Idol, Twelve O'Clock High, On the Town, Battleground, All the King's Men, The Red Shoes, The Heiress, White Heat, A Letter to Three Wives,* and *Adam's Rib.* Sid Rogell certainly had a point, but he overlooked one salient fact—not one of the twenty-four had been produced by RKO.

While Rogell struggled to push films through the pipeline in Hollywood, and Depinet chaffed in New York over Hughes's reluctance to agree on a definite schedule for upcoming RKO releases, Hughes instructed his lawyers to press the government for more time to divorce the company theaters. They were successful when a three-judge federal court agreed to allow RKO to push back the date for splitting off exhibition from production and distribution until December 31, 1950.[55] The decision suggested that a breach was developing between the Department of Justice, which was continuing to push aggressively for a final resolution of the case, and the courts, which seemed inclined to allow RKO more latitude to hold on to the theaters until its business conditions improved.

Those conditions were not getting better. On April 14 Noah Dietrich, drawing on his training as a certified public accountant, wrote Hughes, stating that "the production company is critically short of working capital" and that, to meet cash requirements for the second quarter, it would be necessary to transfer $1.5 million from the theater arm "by the dividend route and to borrow the remaining million available under the revolving bank credit."[56] Dietrich blamed the situation on independent product (particularly the Disney and Goldwyn pictures), "which produces very little cash for the company." But just as vexing was the tepid performance of most of RKO's recently released films, some produced by the "old management" and some by the "new." Of twenty-five coproductions and straight RKO films distributed in the last six months of 1949 and the first three months of 1950, only six would eventually make a profit, with the biggest profit-maker being *Savage Splendor*, a documentary that finished its run $250,000 in the black. Among the losers: *Mighty Joe Young* ($675,000); *The Judge Steps Out* ($650,000); *Easy Living* ($625,000); *Roughshod* ($550,000); *They Live by Night* ($445,000); *Holiday Affair* ($300,000); and *A Dangerous Profession* ($280,000).

In May Sid Rogell must have felt the walls closing in on him. He was caught between the generally unresponsive, totally unpredictable Hughes and the increasingly frustrated Depinet. On May 3 Rogell received a telegram from RKO's president, containing a tentative release schedule for the rest of the year and requesting confirmation of its contents. Although Rogell did not need to be educated, Depinet lectured him concerning the importance of letting "exhibitors know what they may expect from us so that they will reserve playing time and place reliance in RKO to furnish substantial proportion of their pictures. We need to know what our schedule will be so as to estimate our income and plan our operations." At the end of the message, Depinet again stressed how crucial this information was and then indicated who actually needed to heed his message: "Will you please send this to Howard for his consideration and advise me as promptly as possible if it is safe for us to proceed with our calculations based upon schedule in close conformity with the above."[57]

Sid Rogell probably despaired when this telegram crossed his desk because he knew that Howard Hughes hated to be pressured and was fanatical about controlling everything. Only the day before Rogell had been copied on the latest of his boss's absurd orders. It was from lawyer Gordon Youngman, who had recently been named vice president in charge of the studio and assumed the duties of longtime RKO executive J.J. Nolan after he opted for early retirement: "Mr. Hughes has asked me to send you a memorandum to the effect that in all future distribution deals, even though we do not invest one penny of RKO money, we are to have approval not only of the screen play and star, but all the principal members of the cast and the director and the individual producer."[58] Rogell knew full well that no independent producer of stature would ever agree to such an arrangement.

On May 18 Sid Rogell circulated a memo to the various studio departments, praising producer Lew Rachmil, director George Archainbaud, and cinematographer Nick Musuraca for their work on *Seven Witnesses* (release title: *Hunt the Man Down*), a B picture scheduled for fourteen shooting days that had been completed in eleven. He also complimented all the studio departments that contributed "to the success of this project."[59] It would be his last RKO communique.

Later that day Rogell either quit or was fired. The story in *Daily Variety* claimed Rogell had submitted his resignation to Howard Hughes three weeks earlier "to take effect at the convenience of Hughes."[60] If he did this, he did not mention it to Depinet or anyone else, which seems unlikely. More plausible were the rumors that the nominal production head, tired of Hughes's middle-of-the-night phone calls, told his boss off and was canned as a consequence.[61] Whatever the circumstances, Sid Rogell's fifteen-year sojourn at RKO was over.[62]

Richard Fleischer began his long directing career working for Sid Rogell in the RKO B unit. He described Rogell as tyrannical, tempestuous, and "tough-as-nails," yet considered him to be his mentor and one of the most influential men in his life.[63] Undoubtedly, Rogell was pleased to be placed in charge of all studio production after supervising RKO's cheap pictures for so long. But then to be hamstrung by Hughes—this must have been a maddening experience, considering the relative freedom he enjoyed working for Koerner, Rathvon, and Schary. Like many others, though, Rogell remained a good company man to the end, never saying anything negative about his superior.

Thanks mainly to Howard Hughes, the pace of RKO's postwar decline was accelerating in 1950. Outside the studio gates, industry observers did not seem concerned; Hughes was so rich that he could easily pump fresh capital into the enterprise if things really started to fall apart. But people who worked for the company felt considerably less sanguine about the future. In two years Hughes had purged RKO of executives Peter Rathvon, Dore Schary, J.J. Nolan, Ben Piazza, and Sid Rogell; producers Stephen Ames, Melvin Frank, Norman Panama, Richard Goldstone, Bert Granet, Dudley Nichols, William Pereira, Richard Berger, and Herman Mankiewicz; directors Joseph Losey, Fred Zinnemann, Robert Wise, and Shepard Traube; writers Mel Dinnelli, John Paxton, Robert Pirosh, Martin Rackin, Allen Rivkin, Edith Sommers, and Daniel Mainwaring; actresses Barbara Bel Geddes, Merle Oberon, and Rosalind Russell; actors Albert Sharpe, Lawrence Tierney, Richard Tyler, Bill Williams, and Gabby Hayes; and director of photography Robert De Grasse. Coproduction agreements with Argosy Pictures, Jesse L. Lasky Productions, Independent Artists, the Hakim Brothers, and Frank Ross had also been terminated, and hundreds of other RKO employees, some of long standing, had been cut loose.[64] Most significant, Hughes had sabotaged RKO, as well as the other members of the Big Five, by capitulating to the Department of Justice. Despite the general decline in movie attendance, the vertically integrated companies were still earning most of their revenue from their theaters.[65] Now, the carefully constructed oligarchical system they had developed was about to be dismantled. Paramount's profits, for example, nosedived from $22.6 million in 1948 to $3.3 million in 1949, the year the company divorced its theaters from its production-distribution operations. Making and marketing movies would soon be more challenging than it had been since the earliest days of the business.

Those who continued to draw paychecks with the RKO logo on them could only hope for a dramatic turnaround in the organization's fortunes; in fact, drama at RKO was about to enter hitherto uncharted territory, though the ultimate outcome would not be what company stalwarts desired.

5. "The Predictable Unpredictable"
The Hughes-Depinet Regime (1950–1952)

Not long after Sid Rogell abandoned his office on the Gower Street lot, the Korean War broke out. This civil strife between the Republic of Korea (known as South Korea) and the People's Republic of Korea (North Korea) soon forced American soldiers to return to the battlefield. They made up the largest portion of a United Nations force supportive of South Korea's army. Because the recently formed People's Republic of China and (in more surreptitious fashion) the USSR soon began assisting the North, the conflict ratcheted up Cold War tensions. With China and Russia closing ranks as ideological allies and the Russians having exploded their first nuclear weapon in August 1949, making the possibility of nuclear Armageddon seem very real, another wave of communist paranoia rapidly enveloped America.

The Hughes Aircraft Company became a major supplier of electronic weapons systems to the U.S. military during the Korean War. Consequently, the company enjoyed a spectacular growth spurt in the early 1950s, its earnings rising from $400,000 in 1949 to $5.3 million in 1952.[1] Consequently, Howard Hughes began paying more attention to Aircraft than he had in the past. His dealings with its leaders, as well as the Defense Department, suggested that he might finally be forced to turn RKO operations over to others. But that would not be the case.

Amazingly, Hughes seemed to become even more involved in studio affairs after Rogell left. It didn't take long for him to locate another film industry veteran he could antagonize. On May 31, 1950, the trade papers announced that Samuel Bischoff was joining RKO, though his exact duties were rather muddled in the reports. Hughes stated that Bischoff had been hired as a "producer," then indicated he would be placed in a supervisory capacity over a "certain portion of the RKO production program." *Daily*

Variety interpreted this as an indication the new man would "head up the production organization under the guidance of Hughes."[2] In fact, Howard Hughes would continue to retain final say on all important decisions ... and many that were not so important. Like Sid Rogell, Sam Bischoff would be allowed to make suggestions, not movies. Unfortunately, Bischoff didn't understand the assignment.

Bischoff sported the credentials to be a functioning executive producer. During some twenty-five years in Hollywood, he had worked for several studios in different capacities and produced more than one hundred pictures, including *The Charge of the Light Brigade, Kid Galahad, The Roaring Twenties, You'll Never Get Rich,* and *A Night to Remember.* Initial instructions from C. J. Tevlin ordered him to oversee the physical production of *Jet Pilot* and *Two Tickets to Broadway* and call "Mr. Hughes's attention [to] anything being done wrong or wasteful on the basis of the artistic creation of the pictures which is being assumed by Mr. Hughes."[3] Hughes was particularly concerned about cost overruns on *Jet Pilot.* In short, Hughes seemed to view Bischoff as a glorified production manager.

The energetic Bischoff, however, must have believed his charge was to upgrade the company's entire output, for he immediately began reading scripts and evaluating them.[4] Two projects he dismissed as nonstarters were *The Gaunt Woman* and *The Miami Story;* Hughes evidently disagreed with his assessment because both would eventually be made and released under the titles *Sealed Cargo* and *The Las Vegas Story.* Next Bischoff set to work on the company's B productions. In early July he wrote President Depinet, suggesting a program of twelve Bs per year composed of comedies, musicals, horror films, science fiction pictures, and sports-oriented features.[5] Depinet's reply was generally favorable, though he was adamant that the films had to be made inexpensively (less than $200,000 each), given present market conditions. He was therefore not enthusiastic about musicals, which Bischoff expected to cost between $250,000 and $300,000. He also emphasized that the series Westerns starring Tim Holt should cost "less than $100,000 a piece." RKO had not been able to produce these films at that price since 1943. In a short letter written the next day, Depinet added that "we have released too many cops-and-robbers stories and subjects dealing with violence." He didn't expect these genre pictures to be eliminated entirely, but believed "we should make fewer of them."[6]

Though they did not realize it, both men were engaged in a meaningless exercise. Depinet and Bischoff should have paid more attention to a brief blurb in *Daily Variety* published shortly after Bischoff was hired. It claimed that Howard Hughes held a meeting with the top studio executives, during

15. RKO president Ned Depinet shares a laugh with ventriloquist Edgar Bergen in Depinet's Rockefeller Center office. Courtesy of the Academy of Motion Picture Arts and Sciences.

which he insisted "upon the combination of two themes in RKO films: sex and action."[7] Whether this meeting actually took place remains a matter of conjecture, but the information was accurate. Sex and action were the key ingredients Hughes wanted to see in RKO films, as such previous Hughes's productions as *Hell's Angels, Scarface,* and *The Outlaw* demonstrated, and more recent titles, including *The Woman on Pier 13, Where Danger Lives, His Kind of Woman,* and *Vendetta,* confirmed. There were other subjects of considerable personal fascination to Hughes, and these would also show up in company films, but sex and action always topped the list. He had minimal interest in musicals, sports films, horror pictures, and science fiction, while maintaining only a mild yen for comedies. Sam Bischoff had gotten off on the wrong foot in his new job.

Bischoff soon compounded his blunders. On July 12 he wrote a memo to Tevlin and a letter to Depinet that were both ill-considered. The Tevlin memo proposed that the studio dispose "of our present so-called 'A' Producers," whom he described in the most disparaging terms.[8] Bischoff believed he could replace the current producers with "three or four good writers and make producers out of them. I would come up with much better stories and scripts." The only producers left on the RKO lot were men and one woman (Harriet Parsons) favored by Hughes, so Bischoff was indirectly insulting his boss in the memo. He did it a second time in the Depinet letter, which contained a couple of specific ideas for B comedies, one based on the radio series, *Our Miss Brooks*, starring Eve Arden, and the other a farcical takeoff on Shakespeare's *Hamlet*, to feature the Ritz Brothers. Bischoff admitted pictures of this sort had not been made at RKO in the recent past but emphasized that "you need some comedies in this market." He continued, "I also know that it has been the policy to follow a certain formula that Mr. Hughes has set forth. However, I know that he is too shrewd a businessman to keep to that formula if it is no longer paying off, and it is certainly not paying off from the records that I have seen."[9] Sam Bischoff had badly misjudged the man who had total power over all RKO employees. Hughes did not like anyone to contradict his vision. Consequently, Bischoff quickly receded into the background; he continued to pick up a paycheck until 1952, but his impact on the company's future production activities would be very limited.[10]

Although Ned Depinet was more politically savvy than Bischoff, his relationship with Hughes continued to erode. The source of the friction was Hughes's capricious decision making and its devastating impact on distribution operations. The first explosion took place while Sid Rogell was still working at the studio. Former accountant and Hughes's consigliere, Noah Dietrich, had been assigned to scrutinize RKO's finances and did not like what he discovered. In a letter to Depinet, he pointed out the unprofitable distribution arrangements with Goldwyn and Disney and a loss of "$14,000,000 on [the] program of 56 company pictures released in 1948 and 1949." Then, after making the debatable assertion that "production problems of the Company appear to have been satisfactorily solved," Dietrich informed the corporate president that "management should immediately apply itself to the solution of our problems through drastic economies, elimination of unnecessary functions, a thorough check of all operations and possibly a radical revamping of our distribution system."[11]

Reading this letter in his Rockefeller Center office, Ned Depinet, president of RKO Radio Pictures, was surely infuriated by the presumptuousness of this industry neophyte. He took a month to answer the letter. Dietrich's proposed "radical revamping" of Depinet's personal domain, distribution, particularly galled him. In his reply he countered Dietrich's appraisal, describing RKO's distribution organization as "topnotch" and then pinpointed the true problem as he saw it:

I know that Howard has done a splendid job in reducing studio overhead ... but we have no benefit from this fine job because the pictures have not been available to us for distribution. I wish to reiterate that, unless we secure for distribution a consistent flow of our own produced pictures of very good quality with an occasional smash hit, we will find it difficult to keep our heads above water.... I wish to point out again that we are not in a position where our own produced films can be kept on the shelf for protracted periods of time.[12]

Whether Dietrich ever shared this information with Howard Hughes is impossible to determine, but there was no particular need to do so. Hughes was well aware of Depinet's frustrations, which had been building ever since the "Managing Director–Production" bought control, yet he continued to wreak havoc with the release schedule and mull over the final titles of some films for an excruciating period of time. This not only made it impossible to publicize and advertise the movies properly; it caused many exhibitors to throw up their hands and eliminate RKO as a source of future bookings.

Ned Depinet's growing sense of outrage at Hughes's destructive business practices can be charted from his correspondence during the following year. In July 1950 he wrote Gordon Youngman concerning the importance of films being shipped to New York well in advance of their release so all exploitation angles could be properly explored. "If we do not have the prints to work with until the last minute, we will lose many opportunities for specialized marketing of our product. There isn't any way to estimate what we will lose if our operations are handicapped in such a manner, but it will be a very substantial sum of money," he stated.[13]

Even a story in *Daily Variety* describing Hughes's failure to release films in an orderly, predictable manner as "inexplicable" did not affect his approach.[14] Late in December Depinet wrote Tevlin that "some of our pictures are greatly handicapped as far as publicity is concerned because titles are often determined at the last minute." He mentioned six films scheduled for release during the first half of 1951 whose titles were considered "tentative." In fact, Hughes would change all of them and take his time arriving at the permanent names. They were: *Story of a Divorce* (release title: *Payment on Demand*); *It's Only Money* (*Double Dynamite*); *The Gaunt Woman* (*Sealed Cargo*); *Mad with Much Heart* (*On Dangerous Ground*); *Mother of the Champion* (*Hard, Fast and Beautiful*); and *Sons of the Musketeers* (*At Sword's Point*). In the conclusion to his letter, Depinet emphasized that "every picture should have a final title before photography begins," but, as usual, Howard Hughes was not listening.[15] Pictures such as

Jet Pilot, Two Tickets to Broadway, and *Macao* were true anomalies in that their journey from script to screen actually conformed to Depinet's request; the title of nearly every other Hughes film would be shifted—often several times—before it finally showed up in theaters.

In January 1951 Ned Depinet fired off an anguished telegram to Tevlin that began: "Repeated delays in delivery of pictures is *[sic]* seriously handicapping our operations. We have been disappointed so many times ... that we hardly know how to proceed.... There will be delay in delivery of film or advertising of every RKO picture scheduled during January, February and March. Please wire me revised schedule as of today so that we may try to proceed in orderly manner."[16] His request was disregarded. Depinet's travails were bound to leak out, and in February *Business Week* reported that he "has been ignored by Hughes in setting company policy."[17] This must have been supremely embarrassing to RKO's president and longest-tenured executive.

September found Depinet still attempting to orchestrate a release schedule. A lesser mortal might have simply given up, but, to his credit, the tenacious veteran kept hammering away. "Our schedule is very much shot to pieces," he wired Tevlin, requesting information about the status of seven films.[18] It was also telling that Depinet still had to funnel his correspondence through C.J. Tevlin; even the president of the corporation did not enjoy direct access to Hughes. No wonder RKO's reputation within the industry was sinking to hitherto unexplored depths.

On Gower Street one of the reasons Sam Bischoff quickly retreated into the studio shadows was an unprecedented arrangement that Hughes announced in August 1950.[19] When Sid Rogell departed, it had been rumored that Jerry Wald would replace him as RKO's executive producer. Although this did not pan out, Wald formed a partnership with Norman Krasna in the summer of 1950, and shortly thereafter the two men joined RKO as an independent unit working within the studio structure. Their plans were ambitious: sixty feature films to be made during a five-year period on a total budget of $50 million, with 40 percent of the financing coming from RKO and the rest from bank loans.

This was big news because it suggested that Howard Hughes had finally gotten serious about boosting RKO back to its former position within the industry. None of the creative talent then toiling for the company was in the same league with these two men. W.R. Wilkerson of the *Hollywood Reporter*, ecstatic about "one of the most fabulous production deals in the whole history of this business," prophesied it would "not only benefit RKO, Wald and Krasna, but will greatly accrue to the over-all progress of our business, affording a steady supply of good pictures to a company that has needed such a supply."[20]

Krasna and Wald became acquainted twenty-two years earlier while working on a New York newspaper. After moving to Hollywood in the early 1930s Krasna emerged as a top screenwriter, penning the scripts for such RKO hits as *The Richest Girl in the World*, *Bachelor Mother*, and *The Devil and Miss Jones*. His prolific career included stops at most of the major studios and an Academy Award for his screenplay of *Princess O'Rourke*, which he also directed.

Jerry Wald's scramble up the Hollywood ladder had been even more spectacular. He also started out as a writer, but eventually found his calling as a producer for Warner Bros. Among the many films he nurtured there were *Objective Burma*, *Mildred Pierce*, *Humoresque*, *Key Largo*, *Johnny Belinda*, *Task Force*, *Caged*, and *The Glass Menagerie*. Labeled "a sort of Paul Bunyan of film-making" by the *New York Times*, Wald was a frenetic, exuberant man whose love of the business and, particularly, of good stories fueled his prodigious work habits.[21] It cost Howard Hughes $150,000 to extricate him from his contract with the Warners.

In the press release accompanying the announcement of their new "studio within a studio," Wald and Krasna stated they planned to run the operation like a newspaper city desk, generating ideas for pictures, then researching them thoroughly before moving to the script stage. In this regard, Wald mentioned writer Virginia Kellogg, whom he had "sent" to prison to discover the true nature of women's lives behind bars. She turned her unusual research into the screenplay for *Caged*.[22]

To secure the best talent, Wald and Krasna intended to institute a "Royalty System which will give our creative personnel the incentive to do more and better than they have done before." This also represented a way to control the costs of their pictures. Furthermore, they promised to impose careful production planning on all their projects so that there would be little wasted time and money during principal photography. Though recognizing that their proposals might be interpreted as "unorthodox or excessively dramatic," the partners viewed them as a strategy to lift the industry out of its "quagmire of despondency, indifference and inaction." "We are grateful to Mr. Howard Hughes for having given us this wonderful opportunity to make what we hope will be fine pictures. We are, of course, pleased that he has confidence in us as a team to turn over this exacting assignment of twelve pictures a year for the next five years," they stated.[23]

On August 15, 1950, the Whiz Kids, as they came to be known, held a press conference at RKO. The following excerpt illustrates the deft choreography they employed to dance around questions related to their relationship with Hughes and how much creative freedom he intended to provide them:

MR. WALD: We're going to have the closest thing to a magazine operation we can get. Our relation to Hughes is this: He is the publisher and we are managing editors. He sets the policy. We will discuss it with him. He is putting up the money. We will go overboard in discussing it with him, since we feel we can't have a partnership without that discussion.

QUESTION: What happens if you can't find him?

MR. WALD: We'll find him.

MR. KRASNA: When Hughes agrees to the type of story, then we'll go over the title. Hughes has tremendous outside interests, and has no desire to be involved in minute-to-minute decisions.

MR. WALD: This will be more autonomy than anybody in town has.

QUESTION: Your autonomy ends at $900,000 per picture?

MR. KRASNA: It doesn't end. We go to him for his okay. But his time is so limited. It has to be like this.

MR. WALD: He is mixed up in some top-flight [Korean] war business. He said, "Look, I don't mean to butt in."

MR. KRASNA: He has a big responsibility to the stockholders, which he feels keenly. He met us on a compromise. You might think it ideal for us to have complete authority, but the board of directors and the bank won't allow it. We're grateful that the guy who has enough confidence in us is the same man who has control. The only one we have to please is Hughes.... [Hughes] has no interest in or control of scripts. He believes we will dramatize it in a way satisfactory to him. He is vitally interested in stars. And so is the merchandising department; when they say fine, that is his control. Beyond that, we make the picture. He wants us to operate and get it done. If we had other steps, we couldn't operate easily with the talent we're trying to interest.

QUESTION: Does Hughes have script control?

MR. WALD: No, just the idea. A certain story we've been talking about, very daring and different. He gave us a logical reason why not. He asked "Do you think the public will go for that?" We said "You think it over." Now he's coming around, "If you fellows believe in it so much, do it."[24]

The Predictable Unpredictable / 115

16. The Whiz Kids—Jerry Wald and Norman Krasna—at RKO. Courtesy of the USC Cinematic Arts Library.

This confusing series of questions and answers obscured the fact that Wald and Krasna would have no more authority or opportunity to make pictures without Hughes interference than anyone else at RKO. Perhaps the two men did not understand this fact themselves. The actual contract negotiations cementing them to the company were ongoing and would not be settled for nine months, though both men moved onto the lot and went to work immediately.[25]

In the euphoria that surrounded the initial announcement, Jerry Wald boasted, "We'll have even more autonomy than [Darryl] Zanuck."[26] But less than a month later, he and his partner began to recognize what an impossible position they had placed themselves in. After joining RKO, Wald and Krasna quickly cranked out a number of ideas for films and began assembling talent to work on them but could not secure an audience with

Hughes. They finally wrote him about promises they had made to industry professionals ("which we fear will reflect badly on all of us"), "strained" relations with friends, and the "irreparable harm" being done to the Wald-Krasna operation because of their inability to move forward. Hughes was the only one who could give them approvals and had been unavailable for weeks.[27] They asked for only an hour of the boss's time but were not allowed to see him until three weeks later.

It would take eight months before the first two Wald-Krasna productions *(Behave Yourself* and *The Blue Veil)* began shooting. While the two men continued to develop properties and talk to actors, directors, and others about working on them, Hughes assigned them to doctor a number of pictures that he felt were not turning out well. So, in their "spare time," they labored on such films as *His Kind of Woman, Two Tickets to Broadway,* and *Where Danger Lives* in an effort to make them more palatable to audiences. Their efforts were largely unsuccessful.

If he had had more time, Hughes would have tackled the problems himself. He believed he was a brilliant "fixer" of crippled pictures and spent many hours fiddling with celluloid in his private screening room. When he did proffer instructions concerning how a film might be salvaged or improved, his notes were detailed. Unfortunately, what they reveal is how little he actually understood about filmmaking—especially what makes a movie work or even what a good movie is. Anyone (other than André Bazin) who has ever seen *The Outlaw*, a Western he directed and then edited and reedited for years, will have a good sense of Howard Hughes's deficiencies as a cinematic creator.[28]

Further evidence is provided by *Vendetta*, a film he made independently and then turned over to RKO for distribution at the end of 1950. *Time* magazine offered a concise production history in its review: "*Vendetta* (RKO Radio) began shooting in 1946, ran through three versions, four directors (Max Ophuls, Preston Sturges, Stuart Heisler and, finally, Mel Ferrer) and tireless tinkering by Producer Howard Hughes. Total estimated cost: $3,200,000 which tops what Hollywood's Stanley Kramer (*Champion, The Men*) has spent in all on the five pictures he has produced so far. . . . [*Vendetta*] will make many a moviegoer wonder what all the shooting and reshooting was all about."[29] Indeed, this period drama featured a hopelessly inept performance by Hughes's protégé Faith Domergue and made *The Outlaw* look like Academy Award material by comparison.

A third case in point would be *Target*, an RKO B thriller eventually released under the title, *The Narrow Margin*. In his autobiography, the director of the picture, Richard Fleischer, claimed Hughes liked the film so

17. Howard Hughes in his private editing room at the Goldwyn Studio. Courtesy of University of Southern California, on behalf of the USC Specialized Libraries and Archival Collections.

much he considered scrapping it and shooting it over again as an A with Jane Russell and Robert Mitchum in the lead roles.[30] There is no archival evidence of this, but an extraordinary thirteen-page memo from Hughes to Jim Wilkinson, head of the RKO Editing Department, does exist, detailing the "corrections" that needed to be made in the picture.[31]

First off, no corrections were necessary; the film was just fine as is. Despite its low budget ($230,000), it was taut, suspenseful, well written (by Earl Felton), well directed, and well acted by a cast headed by Charles McGraw, Marie Windsor, and Jacqueline White. Few pictures released by RKO during the Hughes era turned out better. McGraw played a police detective assigned to guard a gangster's widow on a train trip from Chicago to Los Angeles, where she is scheduled to testify before a grand jury. Right away, the cop recognizes that thugs are on board determined to prevent her from ever taking the witness stand. Throughout most of the galvanizing journey, he believes the hard-bitten dame (Windsor) in the compartment next to his is the target. But eventually McGraw discovers she is actually a decoy, a police officer planted by his superiors to throw the killers offtrack. Her identity is discovered and she is murdered, leaving McGraw alone to protect the actual widow (White) and her young son during the remainder of the journey.

The bulk of Hughes's exhaustive instructions concerned the last portion of the picture, which he felt "should be rewritten and shot over" so that "Marie Windsor remains the gangster's wife" and "Jacqueline White remains an innocent bystander ... who happens to be traveling on the train." Thus, Hughes wanted to eliminate the surprising narrative pirouette that was the source of much of the film's originality and power. The rest of the notes include clumsy suggestions about how this could be accomplished while adding a number of illogical scenes in which all three main characters and the boy are placed in jeopardy. For example, Hughes wanted "more hair-raising action in the end of the picture," such as McGraw being chased through and eventually on top of the speeding train, nearly suffering decapitation by an approaching tunnel, and then almost falling off, since the "top of these streamlined trains is not only round but very slippery."[32] Hughes offered no clue how to sort out and successfully resolve the plot strands he had unnecessarily tangled; he expected others to come up with the answers. If they had, a first-rate film noir would have been transformed into a ludicrous version of the perils of Pauline.

Fortunately, most of Howard Hughes's "cutting instructions" were never implemented. Perhaps he became distracted and forgot about the changes he felt were necessary. Or perhaps Richard Fleischer is correct that Hughes allowed the director's version to be released as a sort of quid pro quo for Fleischer handling an extended series of retakes on a picture that meant more to him than *The Narrow Margin: His Kind of Woman*.[33] No matter, this tale offers further proof of how difficult it must have been to make movies while Howard Hughes ran the studio and suggests why most RKO pictures during his regime turned out poorly.

The first two Wald-Krasna pictures offered a small ray of hope. *Behave Yourself*, a tolerable wacky comedy starring Farley Granger and Shelley Winters, brought in more than $1.5 million in film rentals. And *The Blue Veil*, a "weeper" reminiscent of several female melodramas that Jerry Wald had produced at Warner Bros., quickly emerged as the most successful film in the 1951–52 program. The Jane Wyman vehicle generated more than $3.5 million in rentals and a profit of $450,000.

Nevertheless, Howard Hughes continued to give his key producers the run around. In January 1951 an exasperated, insomniac Jerry Wald took to his typewriter at four thirty in the morning to vent his spleen. In a memo to Wald-Krasna junior executive Joe Rivkin, Wald described Hughes's behavior as "discouraging, disconcerting, and just plain bad for our morale." "In my twenty brief, but eventful, years in the film business, I've run against all kinds of problems. This is the first one that has me stumped," he continued. Wald felt particularly betrayed because of all the time he and Krasna had spent attempting to improve RKO product: "We have gone over 16 RKO films, for the third time. We have taken them apart, fixed them, patched them, written scenes, fixed scenes, and all of this for nothing and NOT A WORD OF THANKS or appreciation. Frankly, I didn't expect to get an array of medals, but I did think that they would try to give us what we want, when we wanted it, in return for our efforts."[34]

Wald's lament ran to three and a half single-spaced pages. He and Krasna would continue to pester C. J. Tevlin for approvals, reactions, and responses from Hughes without much success.[35] In a highly competitive business that requires rapid decision making, Howard Hughes continued to take his sweet time. Even worse, when he finally did make up his mind, the answers were often negative, garbled, or contradictory. In July Wald and Krasna asked Hughes for "a little more leeway in production. It seems you love us in bunches or not at all. At one time you will trust us with literally millions of dollars of responsibility, and soon after we are requested not to make tests unless we secure approval. My contention is there are two Hughes', and there's one we're crazy about, and we hope, for God's sake, he's the one reading this letter."[36]

By summer 1951 Wald's staff was keeping a running record of the attempts to reach Hughes for answers in case their disputes ended up in court. In most instances no response would be forthcoming. At the same time, RKO employees had been instructed to document examples of "insubordination" by Wald-Krasna. On several occasions, Wald had begun negotiating with actors without proper authorization, and Hughes didn't like it. In June 1951 their "handling of procedure" was described as "haphazard."[37]

Naturally, after a full year at RKO with only two films to their credit, Wald-Krasna became a ripe subject of investigation by the press. To preempt bad publicity the two men invited Edwin Schallert of the *Los Angeles Times* over for a wide-ranging interview. "Pictures today must compete with circuses, baseball games, ice shows, television, ennui, boredom, installment payments—you can't just turn them out and expect them to sell themselves to the public. You have to sell them with showmanship," asserted

Krasna. Consequently, he claimed he and his partner had decided not to put any movies before the cameras until all the right elements were in place. Wald explained, "We don't buy gimmick pictures. When we get a story we want it to be good not simply today but 10 years from now. We'd rather wait than be wrong about casting. We don't want to come out of a theater after a preview and say, 'That picture would have been better if we'd had so-and-so in the part.' Therefore, you can't rush things." After deftly avoiding the real issue (Howard Hughes), they promised that momentum in their operation was about to accelerate, thanks to fourteen properties nearing production readiness.[38]

Hughes had other ideas. In October C. J. Tevlin ordered his underlings to begin exploring ways to end the Wald-Krasna arrangement that would be least damaging to RKO. The simplest solution seemed to base termination on "default," that is, their failure to deliver the requisite number of movies under the contract. In a classic example of understatement, Ross Hastings, a longtime studio employee now in charge of contracts, commitments, and studio contacts, admitted, "We know, however, that the assertion of this right on our part will result in various claims on their part relating to our interference with their production of pictures."[39] It was no secret that Wald-Krasna had plenty of projects ready to go and would have turned out several more films if Hughes had gotten out of their way.

The Whiz Kids must have become aware that RKO was thinking of cutting them loose, because *Variety* ran a story, appropriately enough on Halloween, presenting their side of the dispute. This time the two men were more candid. The story revealed that Wald and Krasna wanted to wriggle out of their contract due to their "lack of autonomy under the RKO setup" and the "interminable delays in getting answers back from the RKO controlling stockholder and production chief."[40] The uneasy stalemate would linger into the new year.

Meanwhile, Howard Hughes continued to assert his omnipotence concerning every aspect of RKO business. Back in July 1950 he had demanded that he receive a "complete and accurate record" every week of every showing of every RKO film other than regular theatrical presentations. These weekly reports were to include "every trade showing, press preview, showing for important persons, any running for an important person or persons where other parties are invited and both business and pleasure are involved, showings for exhibitors or buyers for circuits, any special showings for conventions, any showings for political or public relations reasons, and extracurricular showings of any kind, etc., etc."[41] Though Hughes blamed this mandate on the Motion Picture Association, which he claimed had "laid down very strict rules with respect to the showing of pictures," this was yet another example of his fanatical determination to control everything.

In September Hughes requested that the Advertising Department in New York obtain a press book "from every 'A' picture to be released by every other company and forward them to the studio" for scrutiny.[42] Hughes was upset because an ad for MGM's Hedy Lamarr picture, *A Lady without Passport*, contained the phrase, "this kind of woman," which he felt infringed on the title of the forthcoming RKO picture, *His Kind of Woman*. Just exactly how this sort of "conflict" would be resolved if it cropped up in the future was left unsaid.

While Hughes tightened his obsessive grip on RKO operations, his company was siphoning down the drain. The division of RKO into two separate companies—RKO Pictures and RKO Theatres—was accomplished at the end of 1950. In all likelihood, RKO's Hollywood employees were unaware of the difficulties that decoupling the theaters from production and distribution would present. For the past three years the corporation's meager profits had all been earned by its theaters, while studio operations and distribution lost millions. Even though production received $10 million from its theater partner in the divorcement, less than a month later treasurer W. H. Clark reported that the financial condition of RKO Pictures was "unsound" because of "the slowing down in releasing our films at the same time that production has been geared to a high level, both in the number of pictures and the production costs."[43] He mentioned that only six A pictures had been made available to theaters in 1950, and "the product generally has not measured up in box-office appeal." Though alarming, his remarks were understated; minus its theaters, the new RKO Pictures Corporation would ultimately report bone-crushing losses of $5,832,000 for 1950.[44]

Clark's concerns may have seemed odd to RKO's board members, since the studio was not making as many pictures as its competitors, nor spending as much on production as they did. The big problem, besides the inferior quality of its major films, had been emphasized over and over again by Ned Depinet: RKO A films were being released in a haphazard, inconsistent manner. The majority of the product funneling through the company's distribution pipeline was composed of B movies, independent pictures, and reissues, none of which generated enough revenue to offset RKO's operating costs. Therefore, it came as no surprise when one of Clark's suggested solutions was "that the release schedule that was developed by Mr. Depinet . . . be followed to the extent that it is at all possible."[45]

Another perplexing fact is related to the company's expenditures for advertising in national magazines. Even though it was not possible to take full advantage of this investment because of RKO's unpredictable schedule of releases, the company sank $1,654,401 into magazine advertising in 1950. All the other companies had recognized that the value of these ads was declining and reduced their outlays. But the studio that could least afford the expense had laid out $1 million more than each of its competitors except MGM (which still fell more than $640,000 behind RKO). Universal, for example, spent only $67,849 on magazine space in 1950; Columbia $100,535; Paramount $214,890; and Warner Bros. $245,390.[46] Ned Depinet finally noticed the problem in May 1951, forwarded the figures to Tevlin, and recommended the obvious: "our large national magazine advertising expenditures are not paying off and should be substantially reduced."[47] Wasteful mistakes like this suggested that some of RKO's employees were not paying attention to recent developments in the business, nor were they in sync with the actual operations of their own company.

By this time the adventures of RKO had become a favorite Hollywood spectator sport. Those fortunate members of the movie colony who did not work for the corporation but paid attention to the machinations of RKO's captain—now an amalgam of Ahab, Bligh, and Queeg—enjoyed nonstop entertainment in 1951 and 1952. Even though total industry revenues were continuing to decline, most of their employers had developed strategies to cope with the challenging economic landscape. At Universal, a new regime headed by Milton Rachmil and Edward Muhl abandoned prestige pictures in favor of popular series aimed at rural audiences *(Francis the Talking Mule, Ma and Pa Kettle)*. And while most of the other companies were slashing their stable of contract actors, Universal signed promising newcomers Tony Curtis, Rock Hudson, Audie Murphy, and Jeff Chandler, who would quickly emerge as bright young stars. At Twentieth Century–Fox Darryl Zanuck reduced average film budgets by more than a million dollars between 1947 and 1952, and the company backed a technological innovation, CinemaScope, that would soon have a very beneficial impact on its bottom line. Paramount managed to cut expenditures but still corralled a dream team of filmmakers, including Hal Wallis, Billy Wilder, Cecil B. DeMille, William Wyler, and George Stevens, to complement its impressive lineup of stars, which now included emerging favorites Audrey Hepburn and the team of Dean Martin and Jerry Lewis. New management, headed by Arthur Krim and Robert Benjamin, gained control of the weakest major studio, United Artists, in 1951. Armed with a brilliant new approach to independent production, they began to attract important producers and slowly rebuilt UA into a powerhouse. Columbia and Warner Bros., two companies that had always been cost-conscious, also developed fruitful relationships with independents in the early 1950s. In addition, those studios became the first to recognize that a lot of money could be made by creating product for television. Only MGM, for years the most successful of Hollywood enterprises, and RKO failed to implement any fresh ideas in response to the postwar decline. Still, MGM's old-fashioned approach continued to make money in the early 1950s; RKO's did not.

Even though production and distribution operations at RKO were spotty, its disputations never flagged. Many found their way to courts of law. Hughes must have employed a strong cadre of lawyers, because he prevailed in many, but not all, of them. The biggest case went all the way to the Supreme Court. Howard Hughes had been jockeying with the government for some time concerning the sale of some 930,000 shares of theater stock he received in the divorcement. After the U.S. District Court in New York City ordered him to unload this stock by February 20, 1955, Hughes decided no time limitation on its disposal should be forced on him. He appealed, stating the court order "would deprive him of 'some millions' of dollars worth of property," and a unanimous Supreme Court reversed the decision.[48] Since Hughes had placed his shares in a trust that afforded him no control over the operation of the theaters, the judges decided that the government could not impose a deadline. Still, RKO's top man did not score an unequivocal victory. The Court affirmed that the government had "power to require some companies to divest themselves of ownership of other companies where necessary to preserve competition and prevent monopoly."[49] Hughes understood this would almost certainly lead to more government pressure, and he closed a deal to sell his theater stock in 1953 anyway, pocketing a nice profit on the transaction (see chapter 7).

Howard Hughes was also successful in fending off a number of lawsuits that developed from his fervent anticommunism. The most notorious involved writer Paul Jarrico, who scripted *Tom, Dick and Harry* and *The White Tower* for RKO in earlier years. Jarrico had been hired to work on a picture, originally titled *The Miami Story*, that eventually switched venues and became *The Las Vegas Story*. When the writer was subpoenaed to testify before the latest incarnation of the House Un-American Activities Committee in 1951, Hughes fired him immediately. Jarrico later refused to answer the committee's big question ("Are you now or have you ever been a member of the Communist Party?"). This prompted Hughes to sue Jarrico, asking the court to affirm "that RKO is not required to pay Jarrico's demands for money for alleged damages, and that RKO is not obligated to Jarrico in any way, either for screen credit or otherwise." Hughes's move against Jarrico represented "the first legal action to be brought by any motion picture studio against any of the men or women who were subpoenaed by the House Un-American Activities Committee, and who, 'on constitutional grounds' refused to answer the question of whether they were Communists."[50]

Howard Hughes had begun "disinfecting" RKO films of red contamination before this, ordering parts of *Slaughter Trail* reshot to eliminate tainted actor Howard DaSilva from the cast, removing the names of composer Hanns Eisler and actor Victor Kilian from the credits of *The Spanish Main* when it was rereleased, and excising screenwriter Josef Michel's credit when *Isle of the Dead* was reissued. Jarrico, as Hughes anticipated, fought back, countersuing RKO for $350,000 in damages and demanding his contributions to *The Las Vegas Story* be recognized. In RKO's suit, Hughes claimed that Jarrico's script had been discarded and completely rewritten by others, but Jarrico recognized a considerable chunk of his work in the finished product.[51]

Disputes over screen credit were commonplace in Hollywood at this time, but Hughes turned this one into a *fracas maximus*. After alleging that he had been under a "great deal" of pressure to settle with Jarrico, Hughes stated that it would be "simpler, easier, and probably cheaper" just to pay Jarrico off. But he would not consider such an action. "As long as I am an officer or director of RKO Pictures, this company will never temporize, conciliate with or yield to Paul Jarrico or anyone guilty of similar conduct," he declared.[52]

The Screen Writers Guild, which arbitrated conflicts of this sort, determined that Jarrico had indeed written the necessary one-third of the script and was entitled to screen credit. This made the guild Hughes's new enemy. He informed the press that he would not abide by the decision, dared the guild to call a strike against RKO, and suggested that it should scrutinize its members to make certain it was not harboring communist sympathizers.[53] Jarrico was appalled. In his counterclaim against RKO, the writer stated that Hughes had blown things out of proportion "to obtain wide-spread publicity with immunity by purporting to pose as a savior of the morals of the American public."[54]

Hughes's war on communism escalated in April 1952. He shut down production, placed one hundred studio workers on "leave of absence status," and declared that all RKO personnel would be carefully screened for subversive tendencies. In an extensive press release that accompanied the layoffs, Hughes claimed that RKO had recently considered 150 screenplays as potential vehicles for two of its stars. After winnowing the pile to 11 possibilities, he had their writers investigated and then "disqualified every one of them because of information concerning one of more persons involved in the past writing of the script or the original story."[55] This outrageous tale seemed to suggest that the only decent writers in Hollywood all espoused the communist party line.

While the latest studio purge certainly took a toll on the people who were laid off, the action was not as dramatic as it seemed because little productive activity was occurring anyway. Six weeks earlier *Variety* ran a story describing Hughes's production policies as "unfathomable" since "neither the studio nor its independent satellites [have] films before the cameras" and "there appears to be little or no production in prospect."[56] Hughes, however, cloaked himself in red, white, and blue and trumpeted his determination "to make RKO one studio where the work of Communist sympathizers will not be used."[57] He even made a rare public appearance to accept a commendation from the American Legion for his adamant denunciation of communism.[58] RKO's commanding officer took advantage of the occasion to claim there were "a substantial number of persons in the motion picture industry who follow the communist party line." He was particularly contemptuous of individuals who considered communism a political party like the Democrats and Republicans. "If you believe that the communist party is in the same category as the Democratic or the Republican Party," he told the legionnaires, "then I think I can answer you in this way: We are not fighting Democrats or Republicans in Korea."[59]

One of the biggest RKO pictures of the year both reinforced and, at the same time, called into question Hughes's patriotism. The air force apparently contacted Hughes and asked him to make a feature film about "the close air support its fighters were supplying troops on the ground" in the Korean conflict. Always anxious to feature aviation in a movie, Hughes responded quickly. *One Minute to Zero* was the result, starring Robert Mitchum and Ann Blyth. Although both the army and the air force cooperated fully in the making of the film, army brass cried foul when they viewed the final product. They were upset by a scene, not included in the original script, that showed artillery fire being directed at "Korean refugees that had been infiltrated by Communist troops." According to Lawrence Suid, an expert on the image of the American military in the cinema, Howard Hughes first ascertained that the Pentagon would take no action against Hughes Aircraft contracts if the scene were retained, then refused to eliminate it. *One Minute to Zero* went into release "without the traditional acknowledgement of armed forces assistance."[60]

Reactions to the Jarrico brouhaha and Hughes's shuttering of the studio were mixed. W. R. Wilkerson, the conservative publisher of the *Hollywood*

Reporter, applauded Hughes: "The Jarrico matter has most definitely developed one big fact—as long as Howard Hughes controls the management of RKO production, the commies, their pals and followers will find no haven on that lot and for this, glory be!" Earlier in the month, Wilkerson had labeled Hughes "one of the great Americans of our day" because of his fight against communism.[61] In Washington Sen. Richard M. Nixon stated, "the demonstrated activity of communists within the motion picture industry is a matter of concern to members of Congress and loyal Americans everywhere."[62] Hughes's stand, he felt, was precisely the sort of response Hollywood needed to make: "Mr. Hughes ... by direct action has moved to rid RKO of any taint of Communism; by court action, he now seeks to establish the principle that no industry need support those whose loyalty to this country is questionable, and by public statement he has rallied the support of right-thinking people across the land behind his campaign to get the Reds out of the motion-picture industry"[63] The Veterans of Foreign Wars, the California Department of the Army and Navy Legion of Honor, the Los Angeles City Council, plus members of the House Un-American Activities Committee, including its chairman, John Stephens Wood of Georgia, also praised Hughes's conduct.

On the other hand, the *Motion Picture Herald* called Hughes's decision concerning RKO workers "ill-advised" because it "unfairly damns by implication the other studios that have not and will not adopt the extraordinary procedure of suspending production."[64] Veteran Disney executive Gunther R. Lessing, then serving as president of the Motion Picture Industry Council (MPIC), concurred, "I believe that Hughes is doing the industry a distinct disservice in spreading the impression that it is infiltrated with Communists. This is just the sort of thing that we seek to combat in the MPIC—the fallacious impression that Communists influence our industry." Even Roy Brewer, the staunchly anticommunist leader of the International Alliance of Theatrical Stage Employees, felt Howard Hughes had gone too far. He asserted that the "action and statement by RKO infers that there are not enough real Americans in the industry to make pictures. This is not true and never was." Others openly questioned Hughes's motives. Mary McCall Jr., president of the Screen Writers Guild, charged that Hughes had used the communist issue as an excuse to suspend production at his troubled studio. "Howard Hughes has thrown a mantle of Americanism over his own ragged production record," she said.[65]

But she and others who complained were swimming against a very powerful current. Hughes's instincts prevailed; the communist issue was so supercharged throughout America that the officials of the Screen Writers

Guild ultimately backed away from the Jarrico case. And Paul Jarrico lost both his suit against RKO and his Hollywood career.[66] But while Hughes undoubtedly enjoyed his role as anticommunist crusader and the plaudits he received for his actions, Mary McCall was right. Paul Jarrico versus Howard Hughes simply diverted attention, for a short time, from the fact that Hughes had transformed RKO into a deplorable mess.

Among the many other lawsuits lodged against RKO during this period, a few stand out. Producer Frank Ross spent much of the 1940s trying to mount his biblical epic, *The Robe*, at the studio. The project encountered many delays and occasioned interminable discussions among the executives concerning its feasibility, but the picture was nearly ready to go before the cameras, with Gregory Peck in the lead role, when Hughes took control of RKO.[67] He had no interest in religious films and immediately canceled it.

Nonetheless, the perverse Hughes instructed RKO's legal staff to file a $1,173,420 lawsuit against Ross in January 1950 for failure to produce the picture.[68] The company had advanced Ross a considerable amount of money for research, office rental, costumes, and other matters during the protracted preproduction period, and Hughes hoped to get some or all of it back. RKO opined that "Ross had abrogated the pact 'in bad faith' leaving his company in debt to the plaintiff for advances made on its preparation." Shortly thereafter, Ross responded with his own million-dollar countersuit against RKO. He claimed that his RKO contract called for production to commence prior to May 15, 1948, but Hughes had prevented that from happening.[69] The struggle continued for two years, until Darryl Zanuck of Twentieth Century–Fox bought the property from Ross and worked out an arrangement to satisfy RKO in the bargain.[70] He introduced his company's new wide-screen process, CinemaScope, in the picture and watched happily as the movie turned into a blockbuster, one of the biggest hits of the 1950s.[71] RKO had been sitting on a goldmine for years and never exploited it.[72]

A lawsuit that particularly rankled Howard Hughes involved Ann Sheridan. RKO signed her to appear in *Carriage Entrance*, a romantic drama set in New Orleans in the 1890s. The studio also gave the actress approval of the script, director, and leading man. The first two approvals did not present a problem, and she accepted Robert Young as her costar, but he turned down the part. Then, the difficulties began, as Sheridan said no to a number of possibilities, insisting that Franchot Tone was the best choice. It appears that RKO did not try very hard to sign Tone for, by that time, Hughes wanted to cast one of his personal favorites—Ava Gardner—in the lead and get rid of Sheridan. She sued and won a $50,000 judgement against RKO. But Sheridan and her lawyer, Martin Gang, considered this insufficient compensation and appealed the decision. To the amazement of Sid Rogell, Gordon Youngman, and casting director Fred Scheussler, all of whom testified that Sheridan had behaved unreasonably in her insistence on Franchot Tone, and to Hughes as well, she won a second time. This forced RKO into a financial settlement that also included employing her for another picture (*Appointment in Honduras*, produced in 1953).

Carriage Entrance popped up on theater screens in 1951 under the title *My Forbidden Past*. It starred Ava Gardner and Robert Mitchum, who, according to Sheridan's testimony, was an actor she had requested, but Hughes told her he was "unavailable" as a possible costar.[73] In a way, Sheridan came out a double winner since she had not been required to perform in the underwhelming picture. Critic John L. Scott, who damned it with faint praise, included a descriptive comment in his review that suggested where Hughes's interests lay: "The plot follows an obvious and familiar line, with no surprises unless one includes the 'battle of the cleavage' staged by [Ava Gardner] and the lovely Janis Carter, who plays Mitchum's straying spouse."[74]

The considerable publicity generated by the Sheridan dispute was dwarfed by another legal proceeding involving actress Jean Simmons and her actor-husband Stewart Granger. Hughes bought Simmons's contract from British producer J. Arthur Rank, giving him the right to make one picture with her *(Androcles and the Lion)*. He wanted more. Negotiations hit a dead end in December 1951, with Hughes claiming he had a firm oral agreement for her services but could not complete the contract because the two actors were insisting, as part of the arrangement, that he buy a house and literary property from them for $100,000 more than they were worth. This was not only an unfair deal, Hughes alleged; it would enable Granger and Simmons to pay taxes at a reduced level because of the capital gains implications and, therefore, represented an illegal maneuver he wanted no part of. Stewart Granger later became so convinced that Hughes's allegations were intended to destroy his marriage, as well as Simmons's career, that he contemplated killing the RKO leader before he could "ruin" their lives.[75] Fortunately, murder would not be necessary.

Simmons brought suit against RKO and the case went to federal court in Los Angeles in June 1952. Martin Gang represented Simmons, as he had Sheridan earlier. After a month of testimony and on the very day that Howard Hughes was supposed to take the stand, a settlement was reached, disappointing the throng of spectators who showed up at the courthouse to get a glimpse of the mysterious Hughes. The timing was not coincidental: Hughes hated to testify in disputes of this kind. As part of the settlement,

RKO agreed to cover all court costs as well as Gang's $35,000 fee and to pay Simmons $66,666 per picture to star in three future films.[76] In announcing the outcome, Judge Ernest A. Tolin chastised RKO for injecting tax fraud charges into the litigation. "I cannot say that the evidence bears out to any degree at all even a suggestion of fraudulent intent or of unclean hands on the part of these plaintiffs," he emphasized.[77]

To those who held on to their RKO jobs during this rocky period, it must have seemed as if their company wanted to fight with everyone.[78] For instance, hostilities between RKO and the industry censors broke out early and continued throughout the Hughes era. Joseph Breen and his coworkers at the Production Code Administration, who had a contentious history with Hughes, shuddered when he took control of RKO. Their fears were well founded. Though less prominent and public than the courtroom skirmishes, the battles between the two combatants were often bruising.

One of the first disputes involved *Born to Be Bad*, whose script the Production Code office found unacceptable, even before Hughes took over RKO, because it contained "the implication of illicit sex which is treated without compensating moral values."[79] Under Hughes, the Nicholas Ray–directed film was shot without any significant accommodations to the PCA. Consequently, Joseph Breen wrote his friend, trade-paper publisher Martin Quigley, "I don't have to tell you that we have had very considerable difficulty with this particular studio in recent months, and I fear that we are gradually heading for a grand crash."[80] Nevertheless, Hughes prevailed in this particular wrangle, setting the stage for more disagreements.

Indeed, it is rare to find an RKO A-budget film made during this period that passed through the industry's censorship apparatus without difficulty. *Vendetta* contained implications of incest as well as other problematic elements. *My Forbidden Past* featured a woman who employed evil means to achieve her goals "without compensating moral values." *His Kind of Woman* contained "sadistic violence," a "flippant attitude toward marriage," and demeaning portrayals of some of its Mexican characters. Likewise, *Macao* offered plenty of material sure to offend the Portuguese and the Chinese, plus an overall "low tone of criminality, excessive brutality and gruesomeness." A "flippant attitude toward marriage" also showed up in *The Las Vegas Story*, and the film strongly suggested an "adulterous sex affair" had taken place between the female lead and her former sweetheart. *Blackbeard the Pirate* included an "excessive number of cold-blooded murders" and an excessive number of shots of Linda Darnell "wearing a costume that unacceptably exposes her breasts." Even *Androcles and the Lion* made it into the Production Code hall of shame after Hughes ordered his favorite "retake man," Nicholas Ray, to shoot a "vestal virgin" sequence. It flaunted a number of beautiful women photographed in a manner to "suggest complete nudity."[81] The latter sequence was eventually excised from the release version, but Hughes triumphed in a surprising number of the other altercations. Looked at individually, however, these squabbles represented mere firecrackers compared to the carpet bombs that would be detonated by *The French Line* in 1954 and *Son of Sinbad* in 1955 (see chapter 7).

Jerry Wald and Norman Krasna worked on many of the controversial films but managed to stay clear of the battles with the PCA. Their primary adversary continued to be Hughes himself. Even though he had allowed them to begin production on two more films—*Clash by Night*, directed by Fritz Lang and starring Barbara Stanwyck and Robert Ryan, and *This Man Is Mine* (release title: *The Lusty Men*), directed by Nicholas Ray and starring Robert Mitchum and Susan Hayward—Hughes continued to avoid, ignore, and hamstring the producers. Toward the end of 1951 negotiations commenced on a "face-saving plan" that might satisfy the two unhappy parties.[82] Suggestions included Wald becoming RKO's executive producer, Krasna writing and directing two pictures a year while, at the same time, being relieved of oversight on other films, and RKO purchasing the common stock in Wald-Krasna Productions, which would enable the partners to realize a capital gain. None of these ideas took root, so RKO informed Wald and Krasna that the company had decided to exercise its right to terminate their contract as of December 31, 1951.[83]

Then, surprisingly, a new deal was signed in January. Among its provisions was one that required RKO (i.e., Hughes) to agree or disagree within one week concerning the characters designated to be the leading roles in proposed Wald-Krasna films. Failure to respond meant that the studio consented to the designation.[84] This provision did not alter the larger issue of final authority over the casting of these roles, which Hughes retained; it simply indicated that, in the past, the two parties had not even been able to agree on which parts were, in fact, the most important ones. This was astounding.

The new arrangement didn't improve relations between RKO and Wald-Krasna. In March Jerry Wald was felled by an ulcer attack. It is easy to understand why working for Howard Hughes would have made him ill. For example, one of Wald's many proposals was to remake the Somerset Maugham story, "Rain," which had boosted Joan Crawford's career in the 1932 United Artists release. Hughes liked the idea of remounting the tale under the title "Sadie Thompson," prompting Wald to discuss it with Ava Gardner, who responded enthusiastically about playing the main character.

When Wald delivered this good news to the boss, Hughes stated that he believed Jane Russell would be a better choice for the role. Wald then reminded Hughes that he had "previously turned down SADIE THOMPSON for Jane Russell."[85] Hughes indicated he would think about it and get back to Wald but did not respond for six weeks. He then called Wald at eleven at night on April 27 to say that "he was positive he could deliver Ava Gardner for MISS SADIE THOMPSON. He [had] discussed this with Miss Gardner and she has now agreed to do it."[86] Wald then reminded Hughes that Gardner was willing to move ahead with the project more than a month earlier. Not surprisingly, the picture never came together at RKO, but Jerry Wald would later produce *Miss Sadie Thompson* at Columbia Pictures, starring Rita Hayworth.

Although Howard Hughes routinely stretched out production deliberations such as those concerning "Sadie Thompson," he responded more quickly whenever budget or casting suggestions were formally presented by Wald-Krasna because the new contract required it. His answers to these requests were almost always negative. On April 1 Milton Pickman, Wald's executive assistant, wrote Norman Krasna, then vacationing in Europe, that Hughes had disapproved the tentative budgets for all their projects. In addition, he had turned down the casting of Marilyn Monroe and Jan Sterling in *High Heels*, Gene Tierney in *Size Twelve*, and James Mason and Linda Darnell in *Strike a Match*.[87]

Once in a while, Jerry Wald would find himself in a position to exact a small measure of revenge for the never-ending roadblocks Hughes flung in his way. Wald wrote Krasna on April 3:

> Last night Tevlin called me and wanted me to do a picture called CASANOVA'S LAST NIGHT with Jean Simmons. I read the script, called him, and told him that I thought it was an excellent vehicle for Sam Katzman at Columbia to do for about $200,000. This, of course, shocked Tevlin because he was under the impression this could be made for around $700,000 in color.... Apparently, acting under Mr. Hughes' instructions, he had called . . . to advise me that Mr. Hughes was prepared to give me Jean Simmons for the picture—that is if I would produce it. My answer to him was as simple as that—why waste money on making a picture which you know is going to be nothing better than AT SWORD'S POINT. The reception of this information was not the most heartening in the world. In fact, as I talked to him I could hear his voice grinding down to a slow, unsteady, unenthusiastic halt. He ended up by saying that—"In other words, you don't want to make this picture." My answer to him was a very powerful and strong—Yes. So much for that end of our business.[88]

When Norman Krasna returned from Europe, he quickly extricated himself from the entire setup. Evidently, friction had been developing between him and Wald for some time and this, combined with the multiple indignities associated with working for Hughes, convinced him to beat a strategic retreat.[89] His employment by Wald-Krasna was terminated at the end of April.[90]

Meanwhile, the indefatigable Jerry Wald soldiered on. Even though he had no more success than before in launching pictures, he wrote Hughes in June, inviting him to open negotiations for a new deal to commence when the Wald-Krasna contract expired at the end of the year.[91] It's quite likely this letter was a bargaining stratagem, since Wald was also spreading the word to the rest of the industry that his services would soon be available if price and conditions were right.

But Jerry Wald also had "Plan C" in mind—a spectacularly ambitious idea that would have rocked Hollywood if he had pulled it off. For the past year, rumors had been circulating that Howard Hughes was fed up with RKO. From time to time Hughes would respond to these rumors in press releases, announcing that he had no intention of selling the studio. On May 21, 1952, for instance, he issued a statement that began: "I am not negotiating, discussing, or considering the sale of my interest in RKO Pictures Corporation to anyone whomsoever."[92]

Later in June Jerry Wald received insider information that contradicted Hughes's statements. Noah Dietrich told Wald that Hughes was ready to get out. This propelled Wald into high gear. Believing he could take over RKO, the brash producer launched a campaign on behalf of his own ascendancy. He began courting powerful individuals who might partner with him and help secure the financing necessary to buy Hughes's stock. His first phone call went to Louis B. Mayer, the famous potentate of MGM who was still smarting because he had been forced out of his beloved company in 1951. Mayer seemed interested, but he was in Hawaii at the time and instructed Wald to wait until he returned to discuss the matter further. Despite the fact that Hughes had made an art form of keeping Jerry Wald in suspended animation, it was not Wald's personality to bide his time, particularly when he was on the trail of something big.[93] So, in the three days following his conversation with Mayer, he called innovative, entertainment-oriented banker Serge Semenenko twice; top independent producer David Selznick twice; and Noah Dietrich about the potential coup, each time embellishing the truth of the situation to make the deal seem more doable and Jerry Wald more indispensable to its success.

In his first call to Semenenko of the First National Bank of Boston, Wald claimed that Dietrich was backing his play, that he intended to tell Hughes he had to sell "because it [RKO] is too much of an anchor around [Hughes's] neck right now," and that he would accompany Wald to a meeting with Hughes the following Friday. Semenenko was insistent that Selznick should become involved, so Wald next phoned him up. After flattering Selznick in every possible way, Wald told him Semenenko headed up an "independent syndicate" that had already put up $1,000,000 to kick-start the deal. Wald then called Semenenko back, informed him that Selznick was definitely on board, and discussed the most strategic way to approach the matter. Semenenko described Hughes as the "predictable unpredictable" and discouraged Wald from naming a specific price per share of RKO stock because this would open the door for Hughes to ratchet up the cost significantly. Semenenko wanted Wald to get Hughes to name a dollar figure at which he would be willing to sell and begin the negotiations there. He also contradicted Wald's perception that Noah Dietrich had some influence over his boss's decisions. Calling Dietrich "nothing but an office boy for Hughes," Semenenko emphasized that Hughes paid attention to no one.[94]

What did Jerry Wald do with this sage advice? He allowed his passion to overpower his reason and discarded it completely. When he spoke to Dietrich in Texas later that same day, Wald alleged that "our new major financial people" were "ready to go forward on this deal" and offered $2.50 per share above market value for Hughes's stock. His stated goal was "to accelerate this thing and really push it forward." The wily Dietrich volunteered little reaction, telling Wald he would be flying to California the next day and requesting that he call him at his office in Hollywood the following afternoon. Wald then quickly contacted Selznick, claiming Dietrich had told him that if their group could put a million dollars in escrow, "we could push the thing right forward."[95] In fact, no one would inflate Jerry Wald's trial balloon; in a flash, the deal that took shape only in Wald's fevered imagination was dead.

Exactly how and why Wald's audacious efforts to take control of RKO came to naught is not possible to determine, though it seems plausible his escalating prevarications were exposed, causing his potential partners to scatter.[96] Given Hughes's personality, it would also have been surprising for him to sell to an ownership group in which Wald was a partner. Considerable enmity existed between the two men, and Hughes knew that Wald was working hard to land a new position with another company if his grandiose RKO scheme did not pan out. Suppose Wald had taken control of RKO and turned the company around. Hughes was not about to allow this embarrassment, which Wald would have trumpeted as the greatest financial reversal in film history. The one fact buried deep within the layers of this short, swirling saga was that Howard Hughes had, indeed, decided to jettison RKO. Despite his protestations to the contrary, he was looking for a buyer.

At the studio C. J. Tevlin continued to ignore all the turmoil and act as if he were superintending a stable operation. In late April he announced completion of filming on "four of the most important pictures in RKO history": *Jet Pilot, The Korean Story* (release title: *One Minute to Zero*), *The Big Sky,* and *Androcles and the Lion.*[97] He promised that these films were already "scheduled for preferred release dates during the 1952 season." True to form, *Jet Pilot* would not debut during the year and *Androcles* would receive only a token release. Tevlin also indicated that studio overhead was running at less than 25 percent, perhaps because so many workers had been laid off in the aftermath of the Jarrico altercation.

In truth, RKO's 1952 pictures would be a patchwork of poor Hughes's movies *(The Las Vegas Story, Macao),* the last of the cheap Tim Holt Westerns *(Road Agent, Desert Passage),* documentaries *(Tembo, Under the Red Sea),* a few mostly embarrassing pickups *(Whispering Smith vs. Scotland Yard, Captive Women),* and other films, some that had been gathering dust for years like *Montana Belle, On Dangerous Ground,* and *The Narrow Margin.* The studio was so desperate for product that it even distributed *Rashomon,* Akira Kurosawa's award-winning exploration of the nature of truth. It was a brilliant film that, unfortunately, had little prospect for commercial success among mainstream American audiences.

While RKO's overall standing within the industry had been reduced to microscopic proportions, it did top its competitors in one category: publicity. Besides all the dubious notoriety it garnered from the lawsuits and Howard Hughes's activist war on communism, the company redefined the art of the press junket under Hughes. A typical example burnished the premiere of *The Las Vegas Story.* Hughes flew more than sixty press people to the gambling capital on a chartered TWA Constellation; surrounded them with stars including Jane Russell, Vincent Price, Lex Barker, Arlene Dahl, Mala Powers, Ursula Theiss, and Jack Buetel; gave each of the writers fifty silver dollars to wager; then wined and dined and dazzled them with fireworks and a parade before presenting the picture. Even the premiere included extra entertainment, with master of ceremonies Jay C. Flippen cracking jokes (he called Hughes a "pair of tennis shoes completely surrounded by money"). If the intention was to squeeze some good reviews out of the journalists, it didn't pay off; most of the critiques were blistering. According to *Newsweek,* the excursion cost RKO $21,000.[98]

An even more bizarre publicity gambit had accompanied the release of *His Kind of Woman* in September 1951. To promote the movie, Hughes ordered the erection of a giant outdoor mural, featuring Jane Russell (in a low-cut outfit, of course) and Robert Mitchum at the intersection of Wilshire Boulevard and Fairfax Avenue in Los Angeles. This provoked an angry backlash among local residents who felt the sign would be unseemly and cause accidents among distracted drivers. Nevertheless, Hughes went ahead, commissioning his favorite graphic artist, Mario Zamparelli, to execute the thirty-five by forty-five–foot painting, with the idea of transporting it on a cross-country tour after its initial installation. A giant party featuring entertainment by Jane Russell, Tony Martin, and Groucho Marx was announced for the unveiling on Saturday, September 22, but Hughes canceled it a couple of days before, ordering the mural's removal. According to the trade press, studio officials were concerned that the stunt might boomerang due to inadequate parking facilities and seating, "causing more disfavor than goodwill."[99] Nonetheless, the hullabaloo received a good deal of breathless coverage in local newspapers and made national news, enabling Hughes to accomplish his primary goal: extra publicity for another of his big-budget pictures. Even Jerry Wald was impressed by the campaign for *His Kind of Woman*.[100]

Wald had attempted to doctor the picture during its extended production and postproduction period, but it's unlikely he felt proud of the final result. Hughes, on the other hand, thought it was "the best picture of my career."[101] Oscar Godbout of the *New York Times* disagreed: "In addition to being one of the worst Hollywood pictures in years, [*His Kind of Woman*] is probably the only one since the advent of Vitaphone that needs sub-titles. One reasonably game spectator is still wondering what it was all about."[102]

While often outrageous, RKO publicity during this period was at least inventive. It sizzled but ultimately failed to sell merchandise, which, for the most part, lacked the qualities promised by the hype. Like *His Kind of Woman*, most of the Hughes's movies cost too much, were poorly written and directed, had little freshness about them, and were uncommercial. The pictures Hughes cared most about turned out to be particularly disappointing; *Two Tickets to Broadway* lost $1,150,000; *His Kind of Woman*, $825,000; *Macao*, $700,000; and *The Las Vegas Story*, $600,000.[103]

Several of the films were weirdly personal—that is, they reflected the head man's own fixations and fetishes. Indeed, if there is an argument to be made for the studio head as "auteur," Howard Hughes would provide a pertinent test case. RKO's problem was that his taste and vision were not markedly superior to that of another dubious cinematic storyteller: Ed Wood. And Wood at least had the excuse of miniscule budgets for his productions.

Exhibit A in this regard was a programmer released in 1951: *The Whip Hand*. Shot under the title, *The Man He Found*, its story proposed that Adolf Hitler did not die in 1945 but somehow survived the war and clandestinely journeyed to a small village in the American heartland. There he and his followers intended to revive National Socialism and take over America as a first step in their second crusade for world domination. A vacationing newspaper reporter (played by Elliott Reid) exposes the führer and his loyal minions to the local militia, who stifle the Nazis' scheme without significant difficulty.

When the film was finished, Howard Hughes decided he didn't like the "Hitler angle" and ordered most of it reshot. The reboot featured a new set of villains much closer to Hughes's purview—a particularly scurvy band of communists performing germ-warfare experiments and plotting the destruction of the U.S. population through biological means. Hughes, of course, not only detested communism; he also had a well-known phobia about germs, which manifested itself in a compulsion to avoid them at all costs. In addition, he gave the main female role to one of the many woman he was pursuing romantically—Carla Balenda. And just as Hughes had done in his previous anticommunist diatribe, *The Woman on Pier 13*, he saddled the movie with a title that had nothing to do with its content. There was no whip, much less a "whip hand," to be found in the picture.

This looney mishmash of personal obsessions evidently contained great significance for Howard Hughes, but ordinary moviegoers had difficulty making sense of it. Was *The Whip Hand* a mystery, a thriller, a horror film, an exploitation picture, an apocalyptic drama? In actuality, it was just another RKO flop that cost $376,000 and finished its run with $225,000 in losses.

Did Hughes feel depressed when films he loved and that sometimes laid bare aspects of his own fevered psyche were roundly dismissed by critics and the public alike? It is difficult to say. The famous tycoon certainly had his sensitivities and did not like to lose—in his business dealings, in his romantic pursuits, in his creative efforts, or in his testosterone-fueled drive to control all the important aspects of his life. But by fall 1952 his life had become uncomfortably unstable, and RKO was one of the principal reasons. While he would never admit that his inept direction of the company was largely responsible for the misery RKO had brought him, he recognized that he could still walk away from the movie business with his Midas touch unblemished if he sold RKO for the right price.

And so he did—after months of denying that RKO was for sale, he turned it over to amateurs. On September 23 at the Beverly Hills Hotel,

Hughes concluded eleven weeks of negotiations with a syndicate composed of Ralph Stolkin, Ray Ryan, Abraham Koolish, Edward "Buzz" Burke, and Sherrill Corwin. They presented Hughes a certified check for $1,250,000 as down payment on a final purchase price of $7,350,000 for his million-plus shares of the production-distribution concern. According to *Time* magazine, Hughes remained "in character" to the very end: "the signing took place around midnight; Hughes in tennis shoes temporarily misplaced the down payment check . . . ; he insisted on a last-minute conference with his lawyer in a clothes closet."[104]

Howard Hughes was to receive $7 a share for stock that had been selling for less than $4 only a week before. This sum, plus the substantial windfall he would reap when he eventually sold his RKO theater company holdings, meant he would score a profit of at least $2 million on his RKO investment.[105] Though Hollywood's elite might scoff at Howard Hughes's creative and managerial skills, no one could deny his success in the business arena. He remained one of the giants of American capitalism.

According to *Daily Variety*, the sale "marked the end of the strangest 53 months in the history of studio operations. It was a period of slackened production, mounting losses and absentee ownership that produced strange new legends around Hollywood."[106] But the trade paper's postmortem was premature. Although Howard Hughes and RKO were about to embark on a trial separation, their marriage was not over—not by a long shot.

6. "The Shortest and Most Bizarre Period of Studio Ownership in Film Industry History"

The Stolkin Interregnum (1952)

Few members of the Hollywood community were familiar with RKO's new leaders. Other than Sherrill Corwin, an exhibitor who owned theaters in the Southern California area, the shadowy owners had no background in the motion picture industry. Evidently, they became enamored of the business after investing in the Dean Martin and Jerry Lewis comedy, *At War with the Army*.

The leader of the "syndicate" that acquired the company was Ralph Stolkin, usually described in the trade papers as a "Chicago businessman." It was erroneously reported that Stolkin; his father-in-law, Abraham Koolish, also from Chicago; and "Texas oilman" Ray Ryan had committed to purchase 90 percent of the Hughes and Depinet stock, with a second oilman from San Antonio, Edward Burke, and Corwin picking up the rest.[1] In fact, each of the partners signed up for an equal number of shares. Stolkin and his associates were contrarians who decided that motion pictures had become a good investment. Stolkin informed *New York Times* reporter Thomas M. Pryor, "I felt the time was ripe. The movie business has been in a lull. Our group believes that the business hasn't even begun to scratch the surface of its future potential and that we can help it to prosper and develop."[2]

The men wasted little time in their makeover of the company. At a meeting held in New York on October 2, all members of the RKO Board of Directors, including Hughes and Dietrich, resigned, except for treasurer W. H. Clark. Replacing them would be Stolkin, Koolish, Corwin, and Burke, plus William Gorman, who represented Ray Ryan's interest. Former RKO vice president Gordon Youngman and attorney Arnold Grant also joined the board. Grant, a prominent West Coast attorney, became chairman as

18. Ralph Stolkin *(center)* prepares to sign papers enabling his syndicate to assume control of RKO. Surrounding him are partners Abraham Koolish, Sherrill Corwin, Edmund Burke, and Ray Ryan. Author's collection.

well as general counsel of the organization. He quickly resigned his membership on the Columbia Pictures Board of Directors after accepting the new position.

Perhaps the biggest surprise was the departure of Ned Depinet as both corporate president and member of the board of directors. Many had expected he would at least retain his seat on the board, but, other than a vague position as "consultant and adviser to the corporation," Depinet was out after some twenty years with RKO. According to the *Motion Picture Daily*, the news was greeted with "widespread regret" throughout the industry.[3] Depinet released a statement expressing his deep appreciation to the "RKO family" and asking its members to show loyalty to the new management. "No finer or more competent group of men and women exists in the motion picture field," he stated."[4]

Ned Depinet had certainly earned a tranquil retirement, having weathered the many storms that cast other RKO executives adrift and, after finally ascending to the corporate presidency, being forced to watch helplessly as his superior, Howard Hughes, steered their ship straight onto the shoals. Ralph Stolkin would replace him as president.

Sherrill Corwin assumed the title of vice president in charge of the studio, but this did not mean he intended to make crucial production decisions for long. The leaders of the "new RKO" promised to bring a top executive producer on board quickly. Among the possibilities mentioned were Sol Siegel, Pandro Berman, William Perlberg, William Dozier, and, of course, Jerry Wald.

Rumors abounded concerning the future of the organization. To quell the most dramatic one—that the new order planned to sell off the library of RKO movies to television and liquidate the studio—the reconstituted board issued the following statement:

> The purchasers of the Hughes interests in RKO and their representatives believe in the principle that a corporation owes an obligation to its employees second only to its stockholders. It is not their intent nor do they believe it the desire of the majority of the stockholders to liquidate or destroy. Rather the objective is to revitalize and build.
>
> A realistic approach must recognize the company's large losses and the urgent need for sure steps to stem and turn the tide. Of necessity, a number of executive changes will be made to bring in and promote youth with its vitality, fresh approach and aggressive thinking. Changes below the executive level will be kept to a minimum....
>
> It is and will be impossible to listen to, deny or comment on all the rumors and gossip that flow from a change such as this. Stockholders, employees, and the public to the extent that it has any proper interest therein, will be promptly notified by the board of directors of the corporation as soon as further changes of policy or personnel are decided upon.[5]

The board largely kept its promise, though it was not able to land a first-rate production topper as quickly as hoped. In short order it did name the New York law firm of Cravath, Swaine, and Moore as RKO's special counsel and lured Arnold Picker away from United Artists as executive vice president, a position described as "active operating head of the company."[6] Given his former job as UA's head of foreign sales, Picker was expected to concentrate on distribution operations. "The move of selecting him, together with all moves being made by the board, is for the purpose of strengthening and revitalizing the affairs of RKO in order to bring it to the position of eminence it once occupied," read another company statement released at the time.[7] Clearly, the new owners felt no need to soft-pedal Hughes's negative impact on the company.

Soon after the Picker hiring, Charles Boasberg was promoted to general sales manager, replacing Robert Mochrie, and Walter Branson to assistant general sales manager. Mochrie quickly resurfaced as vice president of Samuel Goldwyn's company. William Zimmerman took over the New York Legal Department from J. Miller Walker, who resigned, while Richard Condon was named director of advertising, publicity and exploitation. Other resignations accepted during a thorough revamp of the New York office included Don Prince, Terry Turner, Arthur Willi, Leda Bauer, and Harold Hendee, former heads of the Publicity, Exploitation, Talent, Story, and Research Departments. The functions of the last three departments were being reassigned to the Hollywood studio. Kay Norton won the job of new head of publicity. *Daily Variety* reported that she was the "first femme ever to occupy such a publicity top-spot with any major company in show-biz history."[8]

Trade papers predicted that Phil Reisman, who had worked closely with Ned Depinet as head of foreign distribution since the 1930s, would continue in the job, but he, too, cleaned out his desk around the middle of October. Reisman soon grabbed a position with one of RKO's founding fathers, accepting the vice presidency of Joseph P. Kennedy Industries. Replacing him as foreign sales manager would be Alfred Crown, recently an employee of Samuel Goldwyn. Advertising and exploitation expert S. Barret McCormick, another twenty-year RKO veteran, also departed before the beginning of November.

While the frenzied reshuffle took place in New York, the studio resembled a frozen encampment, as its workers awaited the arrival of the next executive producer. But this apparent lack of activity masked a good deal of behind-the-scenes Hollywood scrambling. Desperate to put a picture before the cameras so that the industry would believe RKO was committed to future production, Sherrill Corwin convinced his partners that *Split Second*, an action-thriller written by William Bowers and Irving Wallace, was ready to shoot. Corwin hoped the picture could begin on October 20, but casting proved to be a problem. Robert Mitchum, Robert Ryan, Patricia Neal, and Brad Dexter all rejected parts in the film; still, Corwin managed to get the picture rolling in the Mojave Desert only one week late, with first-time director Dick Powell at the helm. Stephen McNally, Alexis Smith, Keith Andes, and Jan Sterling assumed the main roles.

Most of the other studio activity in October 1952 involved loose ends inherited from Howard Hughes. To comply with promises made to the estate of George Bernard Shaw, *Androcles and the Lion* had to be released by the end of October. It was nip and tuck, but the studio managed to push the picture out before the deadline. This did not mollify its Hungarian producer, Gabriel Pascal, who, instead of promoting the film, griped to the press about Howard Hughes. The RKO potentate, he stated, "had to OK everything on the picture. I was the producer, but I never even met him. On the telephone he talked to me. But how! A man must look a producer or director in the eye if he wants to make a point. He even tried to put certain scenes into the picture while I was away on holiday."[9] Pascal was referring to the infamous "vestal virgin" material, which the new owners had decided to eliminate.

In the personnel arena the company lost the services of director Nicholas Ray, who had a contractual right to depart if Hughes no longer held the title of "Managing Director–Production." Mel Ferrer also requested cancellation of his contract, which was granted. During the two years he worked for the company (and made $120,000), Ferrer did not appear in a single RKO picture, though the Hughes brain trust managed to loan him to three of its competitors for movie roles.[10] RKO also had lingering commitments to William Bendix, Xavier Cugat, Tony Martin, Merle Oberon, Vincent Price, and Alan Young, most of which it would never be able to utilize. Likewise, it owed a picture to director H. C. Potter but failed to mount one, costing the company more than $70,000.

The efforts of Corwin, Ross Hastings, and others to unravel all the tangled strands of RKO's production operations caused them to pass up an opportunity that would have paid handsome dividends. Shortly after taking over RKO, the new owners were offered Arch Oboler's *Bwana Devil*, the film that would kick off the 3-D craze in American cinema, for either outright sale or a releasing arrangement. Sherrill Corwin was intrigued by the prospect, informing Arnold Grant in a telegram that "acquisition of this property might be exciting stimulant to new RKO."[11] But the executives couldn't make up their minds, forcing Oboler to begin distributing the film on his own. It performed so well that he would soon pedal the rights to United Artists for nearly six times what *Bwana Devil* had cost to produce.[12]

Even though purchase of the Hughes's stock had taken eleven weeks of painful negotiations to conclude, the syndicate members apparently never conducted a thorough analysis of what they were buying. On November 1, 1952, Ross Hastings clarified the situation, sending Arnold Grant a report on studio operations. The fact that this document purported only to outline "some of the problems which may occur in November and December of 1952 and January of 1953" and was fifty-four pages in length is a good indication of the magnitude of the mess Hughes had left for the new owners to clean up.[13] While written in a thoughtful, straightforward, unemotional style, its contents were enough to give any executive an ulcer.

Among many ominous matters, Hastings's report stated that RKO had no production program planned for the rest of 1952 or the first half of 1953 and, therefore, no possibility of estimating the studio's cash requirements for the foreseeable future. Consequently, studio overhead, though impossible to calculate, would be high, since many employees under contract had little to do. Nevertheless, Hastings argued that it would be dangerous to furlough staff members since television companies and other film producers were likely to snatch up these veterans quickly, thus making it even more difficult to rekindle RKO production in a timely manner. The report also listed the many claims individuals and organizations had made against RKO, such as MGM's assertion that it was owed approximately $40,000 for Janet Leigh's work on *Holiday Affair, Jet Pilot*, and *Two Tickets to Broadway*. In addition, Hughes had saddled the new owners with all the lawsuits that had yet to be settled from his litigious years, placing the organization at risk for millions of dollars of lawyer fees and potential judgements. Perhaps the most surprising revelation involved the Los Angeles estate RKO had purchased for Peter Rathvon in 1946; although the former corporate president vacated the premises in 1948, the house had remained mostly unoccupied despite an annual cost of approximately $10,000 "which does not include adequate maintenance or any depreciation."[14] Hughes just never bothered to put it up for sale.

Hastings's work demonstrated that the syndicate had bought one massive "lemon," but, by the time the report arrived on Grant's desk, the chairman of the board was facing much bigger difficulties than any of the eye-openers contained within the document. The trouble began on Thursday, October 16, when the *Wall Street Journal* published the first of a series of articles about the men who had taken charge of RKO. After first describing Hughes as "colorful," the anonymous author, his typewriter ribbon oozing with sarcasm, called some members of the syndicate "remarkable men in their own right. They deserve to be much better known than they are." The article proceeded to accuse President Stolkin of building a "little empire of businesses upon the foundation of a yokel gambling device—the punchboard." Stolkin's father-in-law, Abraham Koolish, was characterized as another "punchboard impresario" whose "companies have piled up a bulky record of Better Business Bureau complaints, three Federal Trade Commission cease-and-desist orders, and one grand jury indictment." Ray Ryan evidently had another passion besides hunting for the next oil gusher; he was a "heavy gambler" acquainted with imprisoned racketeer Frank Costello. The two men had also been associates in a business venture. In addition, the article singled out lawyer Sidney Korshak, who had participated in the negotiations with

Hughes and been tapped by management to handle RKO's future labor issues. Korshak's name entered the public consciousness during the Kefauver crime commission hearings in 1951, thanks to his successful campaign to secure an "early parole for 'Cherry Nose' Gioe, the Capone mobster who had been convicted of participating in the million-dollar Browne-Bioff movie industry extortion plot of a decade ago."[15]

Subsequent installments in the series published on October 17, 20, and 28 embellished on the first article, painting a detailed picture of the unsavory backgrounds of Koolish, Stolkin, and Ryan. Not only had Ryan's gambling brought him into Costello's orbit; he had also developed a relationship with racketeer Frank Erickson, who, like Costello, was presently behind bars. Besides punchboards, Stolkin and Koolish's other dubious business ventures included mail-order loans, insurance, and a wide variety of merchandise from auto-seat covers to coonskin caps. Their efforts had provoked a plethora of investigations by the Federal Trade Commission, the U.S. Postal Service, and various branches of the Better Business Bureau. The final story was, arguably, the most devastating. It demonstrated that the National Kids' Day Foundation, a charity supposedly raising money for children suffering from "poverty" or "neglect," had not forwarded "a penny ... to any distressed child or to any children's charity" during its four-year existence.[16] The foundation's campaign had been run by Empire Industries, a direct-mail operation founded by Koolish and run by Stolkin, who served as its president.

W. R. Wilkerson of the *Hollywood Reporter,* smelling some sort of leftwing conspiracy, attempted to defend the Stolkin partners from the "lefty pokes." "It may be good reporting on the part of the *Wall Street Journal,* serving its great list of stock and bond holders, to analyze the personnel and the past activities of the new RKO group. But here in our picture business we are interested in accomplishment. That's what pays off. If this new group can do the job, the nature of their other business interests is of little interest," he wrote. Later, Wilkerson would call the *Wall Street Journal* exposé a "hatchet job."[17] But his was a lonely voice; even the most hardened, mordant denizens of the movie colony were shocked by the revelations. As if the declining box-office revenues, rise of television, and communist paranoia weren't enough to cast a pall over Hollywood, now it appeared that a clutch of mobsters had commandeered a major studio. Only Edward Burke and Sherrill Corwin emerged comparatively unscathed from this public relations catastrophe.

Surprisingly, the *Wall Street Journal's* three "remarkable men" did not cry foul or threaten libel suits. Instead, they meekly rolled over. If they were gangsters, they certainly weren't tough guys. One week after the first article was published, Ralph Stolkin resigned the presidency and he, Koolish, and Ryan's representative, William Gorman, quit the RKO Board. They released a joint statement:

> Our only interest in acquiring stock of RKO Pictures Corp. was our belief that the company can be, under able and independent management, brought to the full realization of its great potential.
>
> We recognize that a mass of unfavorable publicity directed against us as individuals has been or can be damaging. Consistent with our original intent of doing that which is best for the company, and for that reason only, we have submitted our resignation.

Chairman Arnold Grant responded tersely that the board intended "as soon as possible to fill the vacancies with men of outstanding calibre."[18]

Further fallout from the exposé was swift and devastating. Among numerous defections, Sidney Korshak resigned his position as "labor relations consultant" to the studio. Jerry Wald requested cancellation of his contract, received it, and quickly signed on as vice president and executive producer of Columbia Pictures. Less than a month later, head of the RKO Story Department William Fadiman and producer Lew Rachmil followed Wald up Gower Street to the Columbia lot. Reports indicated that RKO was losing $120,000 per week.[19]

Meanwhile, Arnold Grant tried everything he could think of to reinforce the teetering RKO edifice. In New York he announced he would travel to Hollywood "to reorganize the company's studios and get them back into film production."[20] He also asked for exhibitor support during the trying times and assured nervous theater owners that the company "had no plans for a sale of the library to television for the present or in the foreseeable future."[21] Then he switched gears, deciding to emphasize the new executives RKO had hired in foreign and domestic sales, publicity, and advertising. This fresh blood, he forecast, would "cure RKO of its present ills and bring it into the black as a strong, healthy motion picture company."[22] To reassure industry folk that the corporation, despite its stagnant production situation, would not have to curtail distribution operations, Grant listed nine films that RKO intended to release in the near future. None looked particularly exciting, with the exception of Samuel Goldwyn's *Hans Christian Andersen* and Walt Disney's *Peter Pan*. But these longtime suppliers of some of the company's best product would not be members of the RKO family much longer. *Andersen* turned out to be the last of the Goldwyn films marketed by RKO and *Peter Pan* the next-to-last Disney/RKO feature.

Chairman Grant's efforts came to an end in mid-November. Following the withdrawals of Stolkin, Koolish, and Gorman from the board of directors, Grant recommended that new board members be named quickly to fill the vacancies. He also located two promising candidates: Robert Butler, former ambassador to Australia and Cuba, and Lawrence Cowen, president of the Lionel Corporation, maker of toy electric trains.[23] But Edward Burke and Sherrill Corwin believed this was the wrong course of action, since they and the other owners were actively seeking a buyer for the stock formerly owned by Howard Hughes. At a meeting held in New York on November 13, Burke and Corwin refused to second the nominations of the two men Grant proposed as board members or to nominate anyone themselves. Arnold Grant promptly resigned, explaining his actions in this notification to stockholders:

> The action of the Board taken today manacles my hands. It is evidently impossible to reconstitute the Board at this time with persons of sufficient calibre to meet the Corporation's problems. This in turn makes it impossible to have within the corporate structure the atmosphere of strength and integrity which is so necessary to attract and hold employees of outstanding calibre; to interest the investing community in acquiring the stock and participating in the future of your Corporation; to justify banks in extending or enlarging credit to the Corporation, and to obtain and maintain the faith and friendship of the industry in which we work, the theatres that buy our products, and the competitors with whom we are interdependent for friendly business intercourse.[24]

Not long after Grant gave up, Arnold Picker quit and went back to United Artists, and Ernest L. Scanlon, the studio manager for most of the past two years, also resigned.[25] RKO had endured plenty of upheaval in its history, but nothing could compare to the present situation. The company now had a nonfunctional board of directors, no corporate president, and no production chief. This leadership vacuum was, indeed, unprecedented in motion picture annals. If new owners could not be found, and found quickly, RKO appeared to have little hope of survival.

Almost immediately, holders of company securities expressed their dissatisfaction with the extraordinary events of the past month. Two stockholder groups filed suit—one asking that a receiver be appointed by the New York Supreme Court and another requesting the recovery of $3 million from Howard Hughes "for losses sustained while the companies were under his control."[26] The only good news was that production on the one film launched by the Stolkin regime, *Split Second*, continued without interruption.

19. Dick Powell directs Jan Sterling, Keith Andes, and Stephen McNally in *Split Second*. Courtesy of the Academy of Motion Picture Arts and Sciences.

Naturally, the grapevine overflowed with rumors concerning potential new ownership. At one point a syndicate headed by Matty Fox and Elliot Hyman, with financial backing from other unnamed Chicago investors, was expected to purchase the Stolkin holdings.[27] Then former RKO mogul Floyd Odlum and his Atlas Corporation began to purchase RKO stock and were reported to be "studying the situation."[28] Paul White, president of PSI-TV, contemplated buying RKO, then reconfiguring the company for the production and distribution of television product.[29] Other interested parties included groups headed by Louis R. Lurie, described as a "San Francisco capitalist," and Samuel Goldwyn. David J. Greene, a New York investment adviser, also began acquiring blocks of stock in the production company.[30] There were even reports that Howard Hughes "might reassume control temporarily to get the firm operating satisfactorily."[31]

The $64,000 question was how big a loss the shell-shocked members of the Stolkin syndicate would be willing to take on their RKO holdings. They had agreed to pay Hughes $7 per share for stock now selling on the New York Exchange for less than $4. In addition, their bargaining position was extremely weak since recent events had made it impossible for them to run the company. A potential solution blew up in early December:

> It is reported that Stolkin, Burke and Ryan, who have been here [Los Angeles] for the past two weeks trying to effect agreements that would place RKO back in operation, had agreed on Noah Dietrich as president of the company, Ned Depinet as chairman of the board and returning to his duties of directing distribution, and the designation of some new board members. However, it is claimed that Sherrill Corwin, the sole remaining member of the new group on the RKO board, objected to the Dietrich and other appointments and, because of an agreement that Corwin had with his partners earlier, no appointments could be made without his consent. Accordingly the partners are at war and the battle has stalled any new RKO setup.[32]

Clearly, Howard Hughes had been involved in these discussions—the possibility of Noah Dietrich becoming president of RKO was a dead giveaway. And for a few days it looked like this pact might actually happen. On December 5 the *Hollywood Reporter* announced that the other partners had decided to buy out Sherrill Corwin, thus clearing the way for the deal to go through. According to the article, Dietrich would take a year's leave of absence from "Hughes activities to assume the new post."[33]

But this solution came apart within a week. On December 10 negotiations broke off, apparently because of Hughes's "unwillingness to make concessions or deferments to the Stolkin group on their stock purchase agreement with him without Ned E. Depinet returning to the RKO Pictures presidency."[34] Evidently, Hughes had second thoughts about letting Noah Dietrich go to RKO, even for a year, and demanded that Depinet be reinstalled. But Depinet, having suffered so long under the thumb of Hughes, insisted on an "unequivocal guaranty of complete autonomy," which was not forthcoming. Consequently, he declined to return to his former post and the entire arrangement imploded.

The Stolkin syndicate now had few options. Since no one had stepped forward with a bona fide offer for their stock, they reluctantly decided on a different approach, signaled by a release from studio publicity director Perry Lieber on Friday, December 12. It stated that four new directors had been elected to the board of directors: Howard Hughes, Noah Dietrich, J. Miller Walker, and Maurice Bent. While Edward Burke decided to remain on the RKO Board, Sherrill Corwin abandoned the RKO lot and resigned "to devote his time to other business interests."[35] Hughes, who now had control of the RKO Board, agreed to suspend future payments due him by the syndicate for sixty days, thus giving its members two more months to dispose of their stock.

Although the owners hoped they would be able to strike a reasonable deal, their fallback position was now clear. Barring an acceptable offer, they were prepared to return the stock to Hughes. This action would cost them the $1,250,000 down payment but could represent less of a hit than they would absorb from a low-ball sale. It also dragged RKO out of limbo, providing the company with leadership once again. The obvious problem was that Howard Hughes, who had done such a disastrous job of ruling the company the first time around, most likely was going to get a second chance.

The trade press seemed to have already discounted and rationalized Hughes's recent performance. Indeed, it continued to propound the fiction that RKO's difficulties arose because the famous millionaire had been too encumbered by his other business activities to give RKO the necessary attention. When Hughes accepted the chairmanship of the RKO Board, a position he had always rejected in the past, *Daily Variety* read this as a positive move that "augurs renewed personal interest in activities of [the] studio."[36] Hughes quickly reinstalled C. J. Tevlin as vice president in charge of studio operations.

Before the end of the year other familiar assertions began to circulate. Charles Boasberg, RKO general sales manager, flew to Hollywood to meet with Hughes. Upon his return to New York, Boasberg reported that Hughes had told him twenty productions, "the majority of them in color," were planned for 1953. He further reported that "the studio is currently geared for substantial production on . . . properties owned by RKO."[37] In reality, the studio had neither the appropriate scripts nor the requisite personnel to ramp up filmmaking in the near future.

Developments in the initial month of 1953 suggested that no individual or financial entity intended to make an acceptable offer for the syndicate stock. Hughes seemed so sure he would soon be running RKO again that he began pressuring Ned Depinet to return to the corporate presidency. Depinet, however, had had enough; he stated he had made the "considered decision that it would serve no useful purpose."[38] In other words, Depinet felt happy to have rid himself of the frustrations that came with being a toothless CEO.

Hughes then commenced negotiations with Herbert Yates of Republic Pictures to secure the services of James R. Grainger, Republic's vice president in charge of distribution. James Grainger was the father of RKO's most prolific recent producer, Edmund Grainger. In mid-January the elder Grainger was freed by Herbert Yates "in deference to his wishes and out of respect for the excellent job he has done for the Yates organization."[39] Grainger quickly accepted the corporate presidency of RKO, though, of course, he could not assume the post officially until the ownership question was settled.

In February the "shortest and most bizarre period of studio ownership in film industry history" came to an end when the syndicate turned back its stock to Howard Hughes.[40] It was estimated that each partner lost $350,000 in their attempt to command a major motion picture company—approximately "$17,500 per week for each of the 20 weeks the stock was in their possession."[41] Howard Hughes, on the other hand, again lawfully controlled RKO and pocketed a profit of more than $1 million on the fiasco. Studio publicity suggested that Hughes had made a number of concessions to help out the beleaguered group and had ultimately enabled the syndicate to get "off the hook." At least he had the good manners to adopt a magnanimous demeanor as he relieved RKO's short-term owners of more than a million bucks and took back a profoundly broken company.

7. "Incompetence or Indifference"
The Hughes-Grainger Regime (1953–1955)

Like Ned Depinet, James "Jimmy" R. Grainger had enjoyed a long career in the distribution end of the motion picture business. During the silent era, he worked for the Edison Company, the Fox Film Corporation, Marshall Neilan Productions, Goldwyn Pictures, and MGM. In the late 1930s he served as president of Grand National Pictures, a small studio that went bankrupt in 1939. Grainger settled in as executive vice president in charge of sales and distribution at Republic Pictures in the early 1940s and watched with pride as his son Edmund developed into a successful producer there. The two men were primarily responsible for one of the most famous films in the history of Republic: *The Sands of Iwo Jima* (1949). Soon after that film's release Edmund moved to RKO, where he became Howard Hughes's favorite producer. By the time his father arrived, Edmund had supervised *Flying Leathernecks, The Racket, One Minute to Zero, Blackbeard the Pirate,* and the only Stolkin picture, *Split Second*.

President Grainger's first responsibility was unpleasant but predictable. RKO lost a staggering $10,178,003 in 1952. Consequently, like others before him, Grainger was ordered by Hughes to pare company expenses, which meant another round of layoffs. For instance, by the middle of February the Advertising, Publicity, and Exploitation Departments in New York had fired fourteen people, resulting in a savings of $1,895 per week.[1] Similar eliminations in other departments would continue throughout the year. Grainger even decided to cut back the company's venerable house organ, "The RKO Flash," from once a week to twice a month, thus saving $950 per month.[2] Nothing was off limits, as an organization that had already been cut to the bone was sliced down to the marrow.[3]

In his dealings with the press, James R. Grainger appeared jovial and optimistic. During an interview with the *New York Times* in March, he "radiated optimism for the future of the company and the movie business generally."[4] Claiming RKO was "in fine shape," he promised that a "steady stream of motion pictures will be flowing from the studio" in six months. Later in March he said, "There were internal strife and setbacks [at RKO] in the past but look at us now. We'll have 22 new pictures in release from Jan. 1 this year to Aug. 8."[5] Grainger was overly optimistic; RKO would distribute only twenty-four films during the entire year and nearly half of them would be independent productions.

But behind the scenes Grainger was not particularly congenial; he proved to be a gruff, pugnacious executive. When Alfred Crown, the new head of foreign distribution, informed him that he was being hounded by employees in his department about raises, Grainger fired off a memo informing Crown "that under no circumstances will any increases in salary be considered at the present time." Furthermore, he added, "if we have any disgruntled or dissatisfied employes in our organization, the quicker they leave the company the better off the company will be."[6]

A few days later Grainger sent a letter to James Mulvey, president of Samuel Goldwyn Productions, badgering him to "name names." During a meeting Mulvey had told Grainger that "some of the people connected with RKO were in a troubled frame of mind due to the fact that they were not sure of their future status." Grainger then insisted that he reveal who the nervous individuals were, but Mulvey refused to supply their identities. Evidently, Grainger stewed about it for a few days and then decided to write the letter. He again exhorted Mulvey to supply the names of the unhappy souls so he could "meet with them and straighten them out."[7] Whether Mulvey ever complied is unknown, but it seems clear that Grainger expected every RKO worker to whistle the company tune and would tolerate no melancholy versions.

Even some of RKO's famous employees were beginning to grouse. Robert Mitchum, Hughes's most loyal thespian since he had backed him during the marijuana scandal, went public with various gripes. He told columnist Sheila Graham, "I've tried to get hold of people there [RKO] for the past two months, but can't. There've been many good pictures I wanted to do, but I couldn't find anyone to get an okay."[8]

While the new RKO president labored to whip the workforce into shape, reduce overhead, and at the same time turn RKO back into a viable business concern, Howard Hughes was accosted by angry owners of company stock convinced he had wrecked their investments. For the next eighteen months Hughes would be assailed by stockholder suits claiming he had run the company into the ground yet banked significant sums of money for himself

Incompetence or Indifference / 153

in the process. One suit, filed by Eli B. Castleman, Marion V. Castleman, and Louis Feuerman even before Hughes took back the company, demanded that Hughes provide an "accounting for all damages caused by his mismanagement, neglect and reckless disregard of his duties as a fiduciary." It called "for the recovery from him of approximately $3 million, that being the amount of profit realized by him."[9] Feuerman and the Castlemans focused on the employment of Jane Russell as evidence of Hughes's poor management. "It is the consensus of motion-picture critics," the complaint set forth, "that the acting liability [sic] and talent of Jane Russell are of a minor nature and value; [and] that the payment by Radio Pictures of $100,000 to Hughes Tool Co. for her services for a feature picture constituted a waste of its corporate funds."[10]

Another suit filed on behalf of Milton Friedman, who owned a thousand shares of RKO common, stated that the million-plus dollars realized by Hughes and Depinet when the Stolkin syndicate forfeited its deposit should have been turned over to RKO rather than ending up in their pockets.[11] The actions of the two men, according to the complaint, amounted to "complete disregard of their fiduciary duties to RKO."[12] Furthermore, the suit alleged that Hughes and Depinet "'exercised dominion and control' over the corporation's officers, which 'have afforded to defendants for their personal and private gain and advantage on said stock trading and otherwise, inside information relating to the corporate defendant (RKO Corp.) not generally available to other stockholders.'"[13]

A third suit, filed later in the year by minority stockholders Louis Schiff and Jacob Sacks, demanded the appointment of a receiver and contained a number of sensational accusations. It estimated that, as of October 1953, RKO's total losses due to Hughes's "whims, caprices, improvidence, waste and negligence" totaled $38,500,000.[14] Some of the losses stemmed from Hughes's cavalier attitude toward talent contracts, particularly those with actresses. Merle Oberon, Gina Lollobrigida, Ann Sheridan, and French ballerina Renée Jeanmaire "were signed up for film contracts at high compensation but 'no films were made,'" according to the complaint. In addition, it was alleged that some of these signings occurred "solely for the purposes of furthering his personal interests."[15] In other words, Schiff and Sacks were claiming that Hughes had romantic, rather than professional, reasons for adding these women to the RKO payroll. The most outrageous allegation concerned the ballerina. To sign her "it became necessary to engage the services of the entire ballet troupe known as the Ballet de Paris," whereupon the "entire troupe was transported to California at the expense of RKO.... Salaries were paid to all members, including Jeanmarie [sic], but at no time were her services or members of the troupe ever used by RKO. It suffered damages in excess of $250,000."[16]

Perhaps to demonstrate that he really did care about the company and wanted to push it back to prominence, Hughes approved the production of five films shortly after retaking control. The appropriately titled *Second Chance* led the way, followed by *Territorial Prison* (release title: *Devil's Canyon*), *Son of Sinbad*, *The French Line*, and *Thunder in the North* (release title: *Dangerous Mission*). All would be shot in the latest industry craze: 3-D.[17]

One of the intriguing, though perplexing, aspects of the movie business at this juncture was the sudden emergence of 3-D and the parallel development of wide screen. The success of *Bwana Devil* had caused some Hollywood insiders to believe that stereoscopic motion pictures represented a breakthrough capable of prying potential customers away from their new television receivers. Others were more excited by CinemaScope, a widescreen process developed by Twentieth Century–Fox that did not require the cardboard and plastic glasses one slipped on to view a picture in 3-D. Fox planned to showcase CinemaScope in *The Robe* later in 1953. A few naysayers were betting that both 3-D and wide screen would be short-lived fads. Most of the studios had adopted a wait-and-see approach, though several were working on projects that could lend themselves to 3-D filming.

During a meeting on April 16, 1953, Howard Hughes, Noah Dietrich, and C.J. Tevlin debated the pros and cons of the different technological approaches. Despite the efforts of Dietrich and Tevlin to change his mind, Hughes believed 3-D was the answer. He expected most of the studios would opt for wide screen, meaning "we will have clear sailing on the 3-D."[18] James R. Grainger, much to Hughes's chagrin, had already informed the industry trade papers that RKO was fully committed to 3-D.[19] Perversely, Hughes ordered a different approach. Determined to throw off the competition, he did not want "anyone [to] know the extent of our [3-D] operation—let them think we are feeling along like everyone else."

Dietrich viewed the decision to embrace 3-D as a mistake. He argued that the glasses were the problem—"people will go to see such pictures once or twice, but not three times when they have to wear glasses." Tevlin viewed the Hughes subterfuge as impractical. Besides the fact that he expected the "secret" would leak out anyway (it already had, thanks to Grainger), Tev maintained the forthcoming films would be successful only "if they are good pictures and the theatres will play them."[20] In other words, the technological novelty might entice spectators to show up for a *Bwana Devil*, but, subsequently, they would only support superior product (which *Bwana Devil* certainly was not), 3-D or no 3-D.[21] Tevlin also brought up the problem of selling the films to exhibitors, as well as promoting and advertising them, if the company refused to divulge whether they were, or were not, made for 3-D release.

Howard Hughes, however, was "diametrically opposed" to these logical arguments. He did not think the glasses would bother audience members, nor could he see any compelling reason to promote the studio's commitment to the technology. Indeed, he held the opinion that such publicity would only convince other studios to make more 3-D films, resulting in additional competition. The obstinate Hughes declared himself "100% sold on 3-D" but did not want this fact to be made public for one additional reason. Having stuck "his neck out on 3-D . . . if it doesn't go he is going to be charged with the full responsibility."[22] Howard Hughes did not like to be proven wrong, particularly when he was.[23]

In May, as a number of current and former employees of the company prepared to give depositions in the stockholder lawsuits, *Fortune* magazine dropped a journalistic bomb squarely down the RKO chimney. The magazine published a devastating overview of Hughes's RKO tenure, titled "RKO: It's Only Money." Its preface stated, "There are two ways of running a motion picture studio: either you run it yourself or you delegate real authority to someone else. The sad story of RKO is that Howard Hughes, who took over a strong company from Floyd Odlum, has done neither."[24]

After characterizing the RKO potentate as a "$200-million bundle of eccentricities," the unnamed author described Hughes's overall RKO record as "about as dismal as it could possibly be." Among the many questionable business practices enumerated in the article were the bunker mentality that kept Hughes isolated at Goldwyn Studio, making it nearly impossible for his employees to reach him; his consistent inability to execute promised production programs or meet planned release schedules; his thorough domination of the company's board of directors; and his penchant for holding up the distribution of certain films for years—such as *Double Dynamite* (original title, *It's Only Money*, from which the article's title was drawn), *Montana Belle*, and *Jet Pilot*—while he tinkered with them. The short, unhappy efforts of Dore Schary, Peter Rathvon, Sid Rogell, Sam Bischoff, Jerry Wald, and Norman Krasna to work with the boss were recounted, as well as the many professional conflicts that resulted in lawsuits.[25]

One conflict that the writer highlighted pitted Hughes against independent producer Jack Skirball of Gold Seal Productions. Skirball had a deal at RKO to make an adaptation of John O'Hara's novel, *Appointment in Samarra*, starring Gregory Peck, but Hughes reneged, claiming he never agreed to it in the first place. Skirball won the legal skirmish, resulting in a $375,000 judgement, plus damages, against the company.[26] The fact that RKO had advertised *Appointment in Samarra* in *Variety* as one of the big pictures it intended to release in 1951 certainly didn't help Hughes's version of the dispute.[27] The judge in the court action, Joseph W. Vickers, commented on the uniqueness of the case: "Never before has there been a top novel, a screenplay by a top writer, a contract by a major studio with the owner of the property, an announcement, and then a refusal."[28] Once again Howard Hughes was charting new entertainment industry territory.

The *Fortune* article also contained numerous examples of poor planning, squandered talent, and stupefying decision making. For example, instead of simply driving to the RKO lot to inspect a particular set, Hughes had it "dismantled and shipped over to the Goldwyn lot to get his approval." The writer estimated that RKO had piled up some $20 million in losses since Hughes took control.[29]

Not only was Howard Hughes portrayed as an incompetent manager; his questionable business ethics were targeted as well. One of the stockholder suits accused him of selling his personally owned movies, *The Outlaw, Mad Wednesday,* and *Vendetta,* to RKO and thus "sitting on both sides of the negotiating table." The article even suggested that Hughes himself may have leaked the damaging information about Ralph Stolkin and his partners to the *Wall Street Journal*.[30]

Perhaps because the author allowed most of the article's sources to remain anonymous, it did contain a number of juicy quotes. The best of them came from a disgruntled veteran who said "working for Hughes was like taking the ball in a football game and running four feet only to find that the coach was tackling you from behind." Although the writer concluded that it "is almost impossible to estimate the damage done to RKO by Howard Hughes," the article ended on a hopeful note. "RKO, despite its difficulties, could still be pulled together by the right people," wrote the author.[31] This presupposed that the head man was seeking another buyer; unfortunately, Hughes, having finally agreed to serve as RKO's chairman of the board, was not.

Instead, Howard Hughes and his associates were plotting strategy to stem the company's losses. The ongoing cuts had resulted in some savings, but RKO was still hemorrhaging money. One possibility was a sale of the ranch in Encino where most of the company's Westerns had been filmed, along with portions of *The Hunchback of Notre Dame, The Magnificent Ambersons,* and *It's a Wonderful Life*.[32] Hughes didn't see any need to retain the ranch and authorized Noah Dietrich to get the best price he could for its eighty-six acres. Coronet Construction Company, one of the companies taking advantage of the movement to the suburbs by many Americans at the time, bought the land for real estate development in July. They paid $537,500.[33]

Another possibility involved the sale of RKO's old films to television. Because none of the other majors had made this move as yet, RKO stood to profit enormously from such an arrangement. Hughes, Noah Dietrich, and Jimmy Grainger met in April to consider the idea. Grainger was adamantly opposed, believing exhibitors would cut RKO off, refusing to book its product if it pedaled films to the video competition. "No one [can] ride two horses," he said. "If you sell to TV, then you are going out of the picture business." But the pragmatic Dietrich felt the company had no choice, employing a different metaphor to make his point. "A drowning man does not decide what kind of life saver he will use," he remarked. Hughes generally sided with Dietrich. He wasn't convinced theater owners would blackball RKO and, in addition, believed the company was in a uniquely advantageous position because of its poor financial performance. Should the other, more profitable, companies sell their films to television they would incur a substantial tax liability, but RKO could offset the gains with its substantial losses. He figured "RKO could benefit by such a sale 2 or 3 times as much as any other studio."[34] No decision was reached, though it seemed clear when the meeting adjourned that Hughes intended to move forward with the sale. But, as often happened, he proved incapable of making a final decision; no sale of RKO movies to television would take place while he was running the company.

Meanwhile, testimony in the first of the stockholder lawsuits was in the offing, requiring Hughes's lawyers to spend their time coaching the prospective witnesses. They did a good job of it, for when former and current RKO execs were deposed throughout the late spring and summer of 1953 in the Castleman-Feuerman suit, the picture they painted of Howard Hughes was remarkably consistent . . . and remarkably positive.

As might be expected, exhibit A for the prosecution was the *Fortune* article. All the witnesses were asked to address various allegations leveled at Hughes in the article. The phrase "I don't recall" was invoked a great deal, but many of the respondents willingly offered testimony that rebutted the *Fortune* rendition of events. C.J. Tevlin, for example, explained that Hughes's odd decision not to set up an office on the studio lot was made because he didn't want to use the RKO projection rooms and "disturb the other employees." Jerry Wald stated that "if anything was pressing, I could always get in touch with [Hughes]." Noah Dietrich claimed that after

Hughes appeared before the company's board of directors to spell out why he could not devote full time to RKO, the directors "were quite pleased with his explanation."[35]

Even those who might have been expected to hold a grudge against the chairman were restrained in their criticism. Dore Schary admitted having disagreements with Hughes about certain proposed films but said he had also had similar disagreements with previous RKO executives. There are "always differences of opinion," he stated, and felt "no animosity" concerning his abrupt departure from the company. Sid Rogell muttered about Hughes's late night phone calls and mentioned that he and his boss did not see "eye to eye" toward the end of his time at RKO, then proclaimed that the parting was his own fault and that "there was no meanness on either side." Frederick L. Ehrman, who joined the board of directors in 1939 and resigned when the board's executive committee was abolished in 1950, took a few shots at Hughes. He said he disagreed with him on many subjects, including the acquisition of *Montana Belle*, starring Jane Russell, from Fidelity Pictures and *The Outlaw* from Hughes himself. Still, he seemed more interested in defending the board's independence and its actions than attacking Hughes. Although he claimed the board refused to accept a number of Hughes's ideas, he couldn't remember any specific instances of defiance.[36]

The most surprising testimony came from Ned Depinet. Before giving his deposition, Depinet first wrote Tevlin, asking for details of Tevlin's industry background since the lawsuit contended that "Howard placed two inexperiences [sic] people, you and Lockhart, on the management committee, along with Rogell."[37] Evidently, Depinet knew very little about the top studio executive he had worked with for more than four years.

Even more astounding, after the *Fortune* article hit newsstands Depinet called Thomas Slack, Hughes's primary attorney, to inquire about seven different items mentioned in the story: Rathvon's resignation; the delay to the production of *Bed of Roses* (eventually made and released as *Born to be Bad*); the transportation of a set built for *Two Tickets to Broadway* from RKO to Goldwyn Studio at Hughes's request; the delay to the production of *Carriage Entrance* (release title: *My Forbidden Past*) and details concerning the subsequent Ann Sheridan lawsuit; more specific information about the Jack Skirball/Gold Seal suit; the details of Sid Rogell's resignation; and the history of the Wald-Krasna relationship with RKO.[38] Clearly, the corporate president was kept in the dark regarding many important matters while he and Howard Hughes were supposedly working together.

Nevertheless, in his deposition Depinet claimed that he and Hughes were "in daily communication" and that Hughes kept him "fully informed" by telephone or in person. According to Depinet, Hughes also "could not have been more informative to the board" and that it was not a "yes sir" board. Even though Depinet had often railed about Hughes's penchant for changing the titles of company pictures, now he asserted that there was "no more title changing at RKO than at any other studio." Finally, he decided to lay RKO's recent problems at the door of previous management. After stating that Hughes "was positively not responsible for RKO's losses," he used a sports metaphor to make his point: "When you go into a baseball game as a relief pitcher in a bases loaded situation you are not charged with the runs of the fellows already on third base, second base or first base."[39] Exactly how two players (Rathvon and Schary) who had left the team five years earlier could be blamed for RKO's recent tailspin is difficult to fathom.

An even more spirited defense of Hughes's stewardship was mounted in the Schiff-Sacks lawsuit in New York. Joining Tevlin and Depinet in offering depositions were new corporate president James R. Grainger, treasurer W. H. Clark, and comptroller Garrett Van Wagner. All stated that RKO was financially sound and denied the allegations against Hughes. The company's key independent suppliers also submitted affidavits, emphasizing that the demand that RKO be placed in receivership would be a terrible mistake. Roy Disney, representing Walt Disney; James Mulvey, representing Samuel Goldwyn; Sol Lesser, and Frank King "argued that receivership would seriously impair the welfare of RKO and jeopardize the position of indies releasing through the company." In addition, officers of three banks who had loaned money to the company "pressed home the fact that receivership would make it plenty tough on RKO in future financial dealings."[40]

Around the time these gentlemen and others were offering their testimonies, Howard Hughes relocated to Las Vegas. He undoubtedly had several reasons for making the move, but one of them related directly to his RKO legal problems. The stockholder suits had originally been filed in New York and Los Angeles. Then, surprisingly, the Castlemans refiled their plea in Nevada, abandoning the New York and California venues. RKO lawyers promptly filed a motion for a stay of the Schiff-Sacks lawsuit in New York, pending a decision in the Castleman action. This did not sit well with the Schiff-Sacks contingent, who believed some sort of deal had been struck allowing the claim to be adjudicated in Nevada, where Hughes might expect to receive more favorable treatment from the courts. Justice Samuel Di Falco of the New York Supreme Court agreed to review the contention that "the Nevada jurisdiction was selected by defendant Hughes."[41] Even though Bernard Reich, who had originally been retained to bring suit against Hughes and RKO in California by the Castlemans and Louis Feuerman, charged that there had indeed been "collusion" between his clients and the defendants, no hanky-panky was uncovered and Las Vegas became the epicenter of the ongoing litigation.[42] Actor-director Dick Powell summed things up when he quipped, "R.K.O.'s contract list is down to three actors and 127 lawyers."[43]

Consequently, when it came time for Hughes to contribute his own deposition in the Schiff-Sacks stockholder action, he did it in Clark County, Nevada. As expected, Hughes denied all the allegations against him, blaming RKO's poor performance on the postwar slump in the motion picture business. "If the financial result of the operations of RKO and RKO Radio Pictures, Inc., have been disappointing, so also have those of the other companies in the industry," he stated.[44]

A good lawyer with an opportunity to cross-examine Hughes would have feasted on this statement alone. Although Hughes had indeed taken over RKO at a difficult moment in industry history, all the other movie corporations managed to adapt to the continuing decline in box-office revenues. While most could not match their earnings during the war years, they were consistently profitable during the period RKO was losing millions.[45]

A further example of Hughes's obstinate rejection of all charges leveled at him in the lawsuit is contained in paragraph 12 of the deposition:

> This affiant has not had, nor has he ascribed to, any policies of "wanton waste", nor does he believe that RKO or RKO Pictures, Inc., have been managed in accordance with his "whims and caprices". This affiant does not believe it to be true, and affirms that it is not true, that production of motion pictures has ever been "disregarded" or without cause discontinued or slowed down. While acting talent may have been under contract to RKO Radio Pictures, Inc., and not used, such has never been true except where such talent had clearly lost box office appeal. Talent has not been employed at exorbitant prices nor ever at the "whim and caprice or for the purpose of furthering any personal interests" of the affiant.[46]

Clearly, Hughes could not understand, or would not admit, that he was the source of RKO's problems. As Hughes's paragraph suggests, the document was mostly devoid of specific information. But it did contain one interesting revelation. Back in the early 1940s Hughes had placed Jane Russell under contact to the Hughes Tool Company and there she remained; the actress had never received a paycheck from RKO. So each time she starred in an RKO film, Russell had been loaned to the company by Hughes.

Nevertheless, he had not pocketed "one cent" from RKO for her services, even though he testified that Hughes Tool Company had received as much as $200,000 when she appeared in pictures produced by other companies. On the surface, it appeared the crafty Hughes had been careful to insure himself against allegations that he had profited from his unique position vis-à-vis the two entities.

Even though Howard Hughes was now living almost three hundred miles from Hollywood, his interest in RKO did not lessen. He continued to insist on making all important company decisions. Soon enough James R. Grainger found himself dancing to the same frustrating tune Ned Depinet and others had learned so well. Grainger, like Depinet, placed a great deal of importance on distribution planning, a facet of the business that seemed to bore Hughes. In midsummer Grainger felt the RKO lineup for the remainder of 1953 was solid but had concerns about the first six months of 1954. He wrote Noah Dietrich to that effect, requesting a late July meeting with Hughes in Las Vegas and reminding Dietrich that a "steady flow of good product is necessary to maintain weekly gross collections."[47]

Hughes must have been too busy to meet with Grainger because, one month after the proposed meeting, the RKO president sent C.J. Tevlin a memo overflowing with concerns. By this time Hughes had monkeyed around with the release schedule for the rest of the year. It now appeared the company would have only one B film *(Marry Me Again)* for release in September and nothing to distribute in November. In addition to his concerns about what picture(s) would be made available for the vital holiday period, Grainger felt particularly uneasy because there was little activity at the studio, meaning there would be a dearth of product ready for distribution in the coming year. Additionally, Grainger's meetings with members of the RKO sales team and important exhibitors in New York, Chicago, Denver, and San Francisco indicated "that the theatre-going public will not continue to wear glasses and that the novelty of 3-D pictures will cease within the next three months." Noah Dietrich, who was copied on the memo along with Hughes, had been right about 3-D from the beginning. Wide screen, not 3-D, was the way of the future. A frantic Grainger considered it "vitally important" that a meeting with Hughes take place as soon as possible.[48]

No meeting occurred, but Grainger kept trying. He sent Hughes a memo in September, proposing that *Son of Sinbad* be released on December 1, *The French Line* on December 15, and *Jet Pilot* in January. "I would appreciate very much your doing all you can to facilitate meeting these release dates. Your cooperation is requested on approving advertising campaigns so that advertising accessories will be in the branch territories well in advance of release dates," he pleaded.[49] Howard Hughes was not in a cooperative frame of mind; none of these films would be released when Grainger envisioned.

The needle on Grainger's exasperation meter climbed higher after he returned from a tour of the company's European offices in October. By that time RKO's distribution arm was putting out more reissues than new product, and, when a fresh release did appear, its quality rarely exceeded that of *Marry Me Again*. Most ominously, the company still did not have a new film for November, December was looking shaky, and no releases were scheduled after January 16. "You can readily understand this situation has me considerably upset and we must get action," Grainger cabled Tevlin.[50]

Grainger finally scheduled a meeting with Hughes for early November. He reported that *Decameron Nights*, one of two October releases, would be a "colossal flop," and the other, *Appointment in Honduras*, "will give a fair account of itself."[51] The studio had completed four other films—*The French Line, Son of Sinbad, She Had to Say Yes* (release title: *She Couldn't Say No*), and *Rangers of the North* (release title: *Dangerous Mission*)—at least to Grainger's satisfaction. But, thanks to Hughes's inaction, RKO's only new picture that could possibly debut before the end of the year was *The French Line*.

Sensibly, Grainger realized 1953 was now a lost cause, so he began attempting to convince Hughes to rev up filmmaking at the studio right away. He proposed a program of ten movies to be made for a total investment of $9 million. "I understand we own some fine material here that could be put into production as quickly as you give your approval," he stated. "Furthermore, if you approve this program, an announcement can be made which certainly should take off some of the 'heat' that is now being put on RKO by newspapers and trade papers, and should have a very good effect on the stockholders."[52]

Once again, the president would make no headway with the adamantine Mr. Hughes, but his reference to "heat" was on the mark. RKO's staggering loss of $10,178,003 in 1952 was the largest posted by any film corporation since the early years of the Depression; its spasmodic releases were performing poorly; and, despite the efforts of past and present RKO employees to shield Hughes from blame for the company's precipitous decline, the outcome of the shareholder suits did not look promising. Hughes, however, was still counting the profits from his recent sale of the RKO theaters stock for $4,412,845 to a group headed by New York investment counselor David J. Greene and Massachusetts industrialist Albert A. List.[53] Thus, he seemed unfazed.

His attorneys' concerns, on the other hand, were deepening. On November 25, 1953, Raymond A. Cook of the Houston law firm of Andrews, Kurth, Campbell, and Bradley sent Hughes's primary lawyer, Tom Slack, a disquieting letter. Slack had asked Cook to "analyze the present status of the litigation and recommend appropriate courses of action." Although Cook complimented Slack concerning the way the lawsuits had been handled so far, he did discern vulnerabilities that could lead to substantial monetary damages against Hughes.[54]

Cook believed the "most extensive liability would be under a judgment convicting Hughes of general mismanagement with damages allowed by circumstantial comparison of the Hughes record at RKO with (1) comparable prior periods in RKO history and/or (2) with contemporary records of comparable competitors." In addition, Cook felt that Hughes might be "liable for specific losses" such as the transportation of the *Two Tickets to Broadway* set to Goldwyn Studio (approximate cost: $5000), the alleged "examples of new talent expense ... to please his personal whims," and "several examples of 'unnecessary litigation,'" particularly the *Gold Seal* case."

Cook was also concerned about the charges of "self-dealing," particularly the transactions between RKO and the Hughes Tool Company "involving the services of Jane Russell and the distribution of *The Outlaw, Vendetta* and *Mad Wednesday*." While, as Hughes had testified, his Tool Company had never received any compensation for Russell's appearances in RKO films, this did not mean Hughes turned over Jane Russell to RKO free of charge. According to its accounts, RKO owed Hughes Tool Company $450,000 for her performances in *His Kind of Woman, Macao,* and *The Las Vegas Story;* it simply had not collected the money yet. RKO also owed the Tool Company approximately $1 million in unpaid rentals from the distribution of *The Outlaw*. In addition, Cook viewed as problematic RKO's purchase of *Montana Belle*, starring Russell, from Fidelity Pictures, and Hughes's decision to sit on the film for almost four years before releasing it.

Raymond Cook was less worried about the complaint that Hughes had "assumed control of RKO without any actual authority and that later he acted in excess of his actual authority." This argument included the questionable makeup and functioning of the corporation's board of directors, which had allegedly rubber stamped anything Hughes proposed. As Cook explained to Slack, "there is a general principle of agency that an agent who exceeds his actual authority is liable for any loss sustained by the principal for the transaction involved. You will recall that the breadth of this rule initially caused us considerable concern. However, now that the depositions are virtually completed, we find little, if any, evidence which could sustain a judgment on this theory."

But the profit Hughes made from the Stolkin fiasco was another matter. Cook described it as "by far the most likely theory of liability against Hughes." He continued, "the court is going to be confronted with the unfortunate situation of the corporation under Hughes' control losing $30,000,000 while Hughes personally in a few weeks made a profit of $1,250,000.... I would consider that the odds are perhaps three to one that the court will impose liability on Hughes because of this transaction." No wonder Raymond Cook was troubled—it is doubtful that the trade papers or even the plaintiffs, at this moment in time, realized the extent of RKO's failure under Hughes's stewardship. Lawyers could argue endlessly about his policies and decisions, but there was no way to explain away $30 million in losses during a time when every other major movie company was posting profits.

As if this were not enough, Cook found other weaknesses in the Hughes/RKO position. Consequently, he suggested they consider a substantial settlement in two parts: "(a) the amount that should be paid in preference to a trial and (b) the amount we should seek to present to the court with approval of opposing counsel." The figure Cook had in mind for part (a) was "$500,000 by Hughes plus $1,000,000 by Hughes Tool Company" and part (b), "$250,000 by Hughes plus $500,000 by Hughes Tool Company." Cook felt strongly that if they decided to offer a settlement, Hughes should pay part of it rather than having his Tool Company absorb the full cost. "Both in the minds of the court and the stockholders there should be an element of punishment in any judgment in this lawsuit; and to make a settlement acceptable, some substantial amount must be paid by Mr. Hughes," he concluded.[55]

Although Raymond Cook had worked for Hughes in the past, he must not have known RKO's celebrity leader well, for there was no chance this proposed solution would be acceptable to him. Without question, $750,000 was a considerable sum, even to one of the world's richest men, but Hughes did not veto the settlement because of the personal monetary damages. He could never agree to such a solution because it would represent a tacit admission that he had been a shoddy manager of RKO. His colossal ego had gotten him into this mess, and it was not going to help him get out of it. Consequently, the litigation would drag on into 1954.

But before 1953 ended, another sulfuric cloud of Hughes's manufacture enshrouded the studio. The cloud took the shapely form of Jane Russell in one of the company's 3-D releases, *The French Line*. This film, a musical based in part on *The Richest Girl in the World* (1934), did not gain a seal of approval from the Production Code Administration when it was viewed in November.[56] Per industry practice, Joseph Breen and his fellow censors provided the studio with a list of required eliminations for *The French Line* to secure the Code Seal. Hughes, however, ignored the censors and released the film in one theater in Saint Louis just before New Year's Eve.

The French Line was not the first major studio film to enter the marketplace without a Production Code Seal. Earlier in the year United Artists had defied the PCA by distributing *The Moon Is Blue*, a romantic comedy produced and directed by Otto Preminger. That inconsequential movie was denied a seal because of some suggestive dialogue and verboten words (virgin, mistress, seduction) and would almost certainly have quickly disappeared if not for its flouting of industry norms. Instead, the furor surrounding its exhibition, as well as its condemnation by the Catholic Legion of Decency, translated into big bucks at the box office.[57] Hughes clearly noticed. *The French Line* was every bit as forgettable, but it contained footage more disturbing to Breen and the Catholics than anything in *The Moon Is Blue*.

Breen regarded "Lookin' for Trouble," a quasi–strip tease number performed by Jane Russell shimmying about in a skimpy, seven-ounce black satin outfit, as particularly offensive. The 3-D camerawork emphasized Miss Russell's breasts and long legs as well as her bump-and-grind routine, and the lyrics of the song ("I'm gonna find me a lover, one in his prime; one who can show me a real good time") were considerably more suggestive than the chief censor could abide. To make matters worse, Hughes also ignored Breen's ban on certain outlandish advertising devised for the picture. The residents of Saint Louis were treated to ads encouraging them to see "J.R. in 3D—It'll knock *both* your eyes out!" and "Jane Russell in 3 Dimension—and What Dimensions!"

To Hughes's delight, the turn out in Saint Louis was thunderous. The five-thousand-seat Fox Theater attracted standing room–only crowds during the initial days of the engagement. As a new year dawned, *The French Line* was not only the talk of the town; it was occupying space in many of the nation's newspapers. But Howard Hughes's victory would be short-lived. Before long, nearly everyone turned on him . . . and on RKO.

The first naysayers were the critics. Myles Standish of the *St. Louis Post-Dispatch* described the film as "tedious and inept." He couldn't decide if the "Lookin' for Trouble" number was immoral but concluded it was "certainly in bad taste." And he took the Saint Louis police to task for not investigating "the fraud being committed—that of continuing to exploit Miss Russell as an actress."[58] Many of the reviews that followed were similarly merciless.

20. Jane Russell lookin' for trouble in *The French Line*. Courtesy of the USC Cinematic Arts Library.

Next came the Catholic Church. The archbishop of Saint Louis, Joseph E. Ritter, wrote a letter to be read in all diocesan churches, imploring good Catholics to stay away from *The French Line*. He must have quickly concluded that this message was not strong enough, for a few days later he penned a second letter stating that any Catholic who attended a showing at the Fox would do so "under penalty of mortal sin."[59] "The Tidings," a Catholic publication, labeled *The French Line* "foul and nauseous" and Jane Russell's performance, "a spectacle of degradation."[60] The film ultimately received the dreaded "C" ("Condemned") rating from the Legion of Decency.

The bad news continued when several state censor boards, including New York, Ohio, and Pennsylvania, banned *The French Line*. Even Jane Russell piled on, agreeing with the PCA that certain scenes should be cut. "I thoroughly agree with the Breen Office. It's the public's safeguard and the actor's too. I certainly don't want to be associated with any picture that's denied the seal," she stated.[61] "I don't like the accent on sex and never have," she added. "Some of the camera angles are in horrible taste."[62]

A stubborn, unrepentant Howard Hughes continued to hold tight to a conception of himself as the champion of creative freedom and enemy of Breen and all the other small-minded puritans throughout America.[63] Hughes refused to pay a $25,000 fine levied on RKO by the Motion Picture Association for releasing the picture without a Code Seal. He also continued rejecting the many calls for cuts until RKO's principal customers—the largest theater chains—lowered the boom on him.

The Saint Louis premiere had been designed to whet the American public's appetite for *The French Line*. Back in 1943 Hughes used the same approach, opening *The Outlaw* for a short, controversial run at one theater in San Francisco. And it worked; when United Artists distributed the picture three years later, titillated spectators turned out in droves. Plenty more showed up after Hughes cut a "new" version of *The Outlaw*, one that was granted a "B" classification ("Morally Objectionable in Part for All") rather than the original "C" by the Legion of Decency, and released it through RKO in 1950.

But this time the gambit failed because few theaters were willing to book *The French Line* when it was offered for late spring release. The force field of negativity surrounding the movie ultimately compelled Hughes to edit his prize picture more severely than would have been necessary if he had simply agreed to Breen's requested emendations in the first place.[64] This, plus the demise of 3-D, consigned it to RKO's growing roster of celluloid miscarriages.

Early in 1954, as the controversy surrounding *The French Line* continued to swirl, the canny Hughes came up with a unique solution to his vexing legal problems. Perhaps he had been paying attention when one of the suits against him claimed that he operated RKO Pictures Corporation and its subsidiary, RKO Radio Pictures, as if "both corporations . . . are wholly-owned by him."[65] On February 8 Hughes announced his willingness to purchase all the outstanding stock of RKO for $6.00 per share. At that time the shares were selling on the New York Exchange for $2.875 each. Acknowledging "expressions of dissatisfaction among the stockholders," Hughes stated, "I would like to feel that I have given all the stockholders of RKO . . . an opportunity to receive for their stock an amount well in excess of its market value at the time when I first became connected with the company, or at any time since."[66] The *Hollywood Reporter* called it "one of the most astounding moves in the entire annals of the motion picture business."[67] Hughes's offer created pandemonium on the floor of the New York Stock Exchange. A total of 487,200 RKO shares, roughly 23 percent of the entire day's turnover on the Exchange, changed hands on February 8 alone.[68]

Four days later, at a special meeting of the RKO Board of Directors held in Atlanta, Georgia, the offer was approved. Stockholders followed suit at a special meeting in March, voting thirty to one to accept the unexpected offer. Soon after Hughes wrote a check for $23,489,478 to fund the redemption of all the RKO shares. The transaction would make him "the first individual ever to become the sole owner of a major motion picture company."[69]

Only a person of immense wealth could have mounted such an offer. This did not make it any the less amazing. To render the stockholder litigation moot, Hughes agreed to spend an enormous amount of his own money for a studio that had become a rapidly sinking atoll surrounded by an ocean of red ink. Wall Street authorities and industry experts were initially confused—why would Hughes pay so much to rid himself of some legal troubles?[70] After all, he had a battalion of lawyers on call. But a more nuanced picture of the move rapidly emerged, suggesting that the RKO dictator had not lost his financial acumen. *Newsweek* pointed out that a money-losing concern can have latent value, especially to a tycoon whose other enterprises were profitable.[71] If Hughes acquired 95 percent control of RKO, he could then apply the company's losses against the bountiful profits of his other businesses, including Hughes Tool Company, thereby gaining substantial tax advantages.[72]

But a situation as unforeseen as Howard Hughes's initial offer emerged during the redemption period. Stockholders were given until May 17, 1954, to submit the paperwork required to surrender their shares. As that date approached it became clear that the redeemed shares would fall well short of the required number, so the "final" date was extended to June 30. But on June 28 President Grainger reported that only 932,918 shares had been redeemed.[73] Therefore, the company was extending the drop-dead date again, this time to July 31.

By then it should have been obvious that Hughes was never going to corral the stock necessary to pull off his grand scheme. Nevertheless, more extensions of the date-to-tender were offered. September 30 was tried without success, so the "deadline to end all deadlines" became December 31, 1954. This date also would not produce the hoped-for results. Some Wall Street sharpie had decided to frustrate Howard Hughes's plan. The question was who . . . and why?

Well before the end of the year Mr. Who emerged from the shadows. He was none other than former RKO investor and chairman of the board Floyd Odlum of Atlas Corporation, the same man who sold Hughes his controlling position in RKO in the first place. Odlum, through Atlas, began quietly purchasing RKO stock before the "$6 a share" announcement. He continued buying afterward, sometimes paying in excess of $6 on the open market. Thus, by December Atlas held more than a million RKO shares, almost as many as Hughes himself. And Odlum declined to redeem them.

The large acquisition of RKO stock by Atlas kicked off a new round of negotiations between Hughes and Odlum. Only this time the diminutive man from Michigan was holding all the cards. In his public remarks Odlum stated that his renewed interest in the movie company was in line with his long-standing "value" investment philosophy. Claiming the company was worth more than $6 a share, Odlum indicated that Atlas would be willing "to assume the management responsibility but hesitate[s] to do so without assurance of continuity for a period."[74] Whether Odlum was sincere in this offer is impossible to know, but he used it to put additional pressure on Hughes, informing the press that Hughes should agree on December 31 as the "deadline for settling the question of who will manage RKO Pictures Corp." He also stated, "It seems important to me that RKO Pictures Corporation start active employment of its funds in seeking capital profits to offset its capital losses that can be carried forward. Time is running and time elements that seem unimportant now may become critical later."[75] This latest battle of industrial titans churned up Wall Street once again; RKO stock closed at $7.375 per share on December 14.

Although Floyd Odlum had a reputation as a pragmatic, unemotional businessman, it is difficult to believe his reentry into RKO affairs was not personal. After Atlas sold Hughes 929,000 shares of company stock in 1948, the ruthless new company honcho quickly deposed corporate president N. Peter Rathvon, a longtime Odlum associate; found a way to render Atlas's RKO stock options worthless; and reneged on an agreement to give Atlas the opportunity to match any legitimate offer for the RKO theater chain (see chapter 4). While Odlum professed to like Hughes "in spite of and, perhaps, in particular because of his foibles," he must have welcomed the opportunity to pay him back for the events of 1948 and 1949.[76]

At least the Hughes's maneuver did extricate him from his stockholder difficulties. First, Judge Frank McNamee dismissed the suit filed in Nevada. He ruled that RKO's losses during Hughes's stewardship "were the result of 'mistakes of judgment' rather than willful mismanagement, as alleged by the minority groups." He went out of his way to disagree with one of the contentions in the Castleman action. "Jane Russell is not a waste of corporate assets," he stated, adding that her "box office appeal was—and is—large."[77]

A final attempt to frustrate Hughes's efforts legally—an injunction to bar the sale filed by Louis Schiff and Jacob Sacks, who claimed RKO's assets were worth much more than the $23.5 million Hughes had offered—was refused by Judge Collins J. Seitz of the Delaware Court of Chancery in late March 1954. Nevertheless, Judge Seitz arrived at a different conclusion than Judge McNamee concerning Howard Hughes's leadership of the movie concern:

> There is evidence from which it could be reasonably inferred that Hughes was not only unduly wasteful in operating the production end of RKO but because of his position was permitted to remain in control of production long after another person not so situated would probably have been removed. The rather consistent failure of the production department to meet the release dates and to operate even near the picture budgets are strong evidence either of incompetence or indifference. It is noteworthy that other movie producers and distributors were making a profit during the same period.[78]

Indeed they were. In 1953 Paramount posted a profit of $6.7 million; Twentieth Century–Fox, $4.6 million; MGM, $4.5 million; Warner Bros., $2.9 million; Universal, $2.6 million; Columbia, $0.9 million; and United Artists, $0.6 million. Because of the Hughes maneuver, RKO no longer had to divulge its financial results, which must have been ugly.

W.R. Wilkerson of the *Hollywood Reporter*, Hughes's number-one journalistic defender for years, naturally disagreed with Judge Seitz. He seemed to feel that the stockholder suits had been holding RKO back. Now that Hughes was rid of them, happy days were on the horizon: "Our prophecy is that a year from now this production and releasing organization, with its studios and properties, will be pushing all other such companies for top honors.... Eventually under the Hughes operation, it will be one of the most important in its field."[79]

Floyd Odlum also believed that RKO still had potential and was aware that the film industry seemed to be bouncing back from its doldrums. His efforts to regain control of the company from Howard Hughes resulted in protracted negotiations between the two businessmen during the first half of 1955. But Odlum should have realized that he was wasting his time. Hughes would never reopen the RKO door to Odlum, probably because he could not abide the inevitable press coverage that would result. It would claim Odlum had outfoxed Hughes's attempt to take full ownership of the movie outfit, thus ruining his tax-avoidance strategy, and gotten some sweet revenge in the bargain. Odlum should also have learned by this time that Hughes was totally untrustworthy. In addition to his own personal experience dealing with the man, there was further evidence on display in Hughes's recent wheeling and dealing.

William Zeckendorf represented a syndicate that included Lawrence Rockefeller and shipping tycoon Aristotle Onassis. He approached Hughes in fall 1954 with an offer to purchase all his companies. After two months of back and forth, Zeckendorf believed they had a deal. So did *Daily Variety*, which, on November 11, reported that Hughes had agreed to sell.[80] Zeckendorf flew to Los Angeles, where he expected Hughes would turn over Hughes Tool Company, Hughes Aircraft, Trans World Airlines, and his other businesses, minus RKO, to the syndicate for $400 million. The requisite papers were prepared, but Hughes, at the last moment, refused to sign.

An outraged Zeckendorf called the action a "completely unpardonable, unilateral and unconscionable reversal on the part of Howard Hughes." Hughes responded as if Zeckendorf had lost his mind: "I have denied this rumor in the past. Let me say once and for all this rumor is totally and utterly untrue. I have no intention of selling anything to Mr. Zeckendorf."[81] Evidently, William Zeckendorf had been ensnared by a favorite Hughes subterfuge. Although he had no interest in letting go of his companies, Hughes dangled them in front of Zeckendorf and his partners to find out what they were worth without having to cough up any appraisal fees.[82] Floyd Odlum should have paid rapt attention to this sorry episode.

If the Zeckendorf version of events was accurate, it is interesting that the one piece of the Hughes empire he removed from the negotiating table was RKO. Some optimists probably read this as a sign that Hughes still hoped to turn the company around. But his ongoing inaction concerning the studio did not support this interpretation. About the only noteworthy event that took place in Hollywood following the $6 per share announcement was another round of studio layoffs in September 1954. Included in this set of dismissals were five people who had worked more than twenty years for RKO, including Claire Cramer, the head of the Wardrobe Department, and Harold Barry, the head of the Construction Department. "Informed sources predicted that the wholesale firings may mean that the company will fold up its cinema shop as a producing company, but continue to exist as a releasing and distribution company—in the same manner as United Artists operates," reported the *Los Angeles Times*.[83] Others speculated that trimming the workforce meant Hughes was getting ready to sell the company again.

Consequently, RKO's status continued to plummet, though one wondered how much lower it could sink. In February 1955 industry expert Edwin Schallert reported that in the six and a half years Hughes had "headed the organization there has probably been a 90% reduction in studio personnel. Many of the heads of departments have disappeared from the lot. A skeleton crew is maintained today at best, while very few pictures are being made directly under Hughes supervision, and there remain hardly any producers working directly for the establishment."[84]

Nevertheless, two months following the publication of Schallert's article, President Grainger informed the world that the company's future looked bright. RKO had abandoned 3-D but embraced "Superscope," a wide-screen process invented by Joseph and Irving Tushinsky.[85] Not only would most of its forthcoming productions be in Superscope, but all would be in color. According to Grainger, nine films were ready for release, including two "of the greatest productions ever turned out of Hollywood": the long-gestating *Jet Pilot* and a historical epic titled *The Conqueror*, starring John Wayne and Susan Hayward. "We are hopeful Mr. Hughes will give us release dates on both these tremendous films soon," said Grainger. He also promised "additional good tidings" in the near future. The press release containing this cheery information was dated April 1, 1955.[86]

In fact, it was déjà vu all over again at RKO. Despite Grainger's claim that "we have been very busy at the studio," Schallert's version of RKO activities was much closer to the truth than the RKO president's.[87] Only one film was started by the company in 1954—*The Conqueror*, which was largely photographed in the Saint George, Utah, area.[88] Walt Disney finally gave up during the year, abandoning RKO and creating his own Buena Vista Film Distribution Company. *Daily Variety* estimated the absence of the Disney product would mean "an annual loss to RKO of distribution

21. John Wayne and director Dick Powell watch an action scene unfold in *The Conqueror*. Courtesy of the USC Cinematic Arts Library.

income running upwards of at least several million dollars."[89] Samuel Goldwyn also bailed out. And the studio now had one solitary producer under contract, Harriet Parsons.[90]

Parsons's sojourn at the company reveals a good deal about Howard Hughes's character. She had been hired during World War II by Charles Koerner, after producing and directing many short subjects. Her first feature for RKO was the wonderful *Enchanted Cottage* in 1945, to be followed by *Night Song* and *I Remember Mama* in 1948. When Hughes's took over, she was one of the few producers he retained. Parsons continued on the payroll during his entire RKO stewardship, though he allowed her to make only three pictures in seven years. As one might imagine, her frustrations multiplied over time and occasionally reached the boiling point.

In March 1953 Harriet Parsons learned that RKO was moving forward with *The French Line* even though *Size 12*, a project she had been developing for more than a year, had similar characters, themes, and background. Angry and heartsick, she typed out a four-page, single-spaced letter to the boss, which included the following:

> Since it seems to be impossible for me to see you or talk to you on the phone, and since there is no one else in authority at RKO to whom I can talk ... and since my repeated attempts to talk to you through [lawyer] Greg Bautzer during the past three months have resulted only in repeated assurances from you that "SIZE 12" would be made and repeated promises that you would discuss casting with me (none of these promises ever fulfilled) I have come to the conclusion that my only recourse is to state my case in a letter. If this does not bring any concrete results I have come to the reluctant conclusion that I will have to leave RKO before Harriet Parsons and "SIZE 12" become the laughing stock of the industry (if they are not already).[91]

Parsons's letter did not achieve the hoped-for results—*Size 12* would never be made—though she stayed on at RKO and produced *Susan Slept Here* in 1954. The pertinent question is why Hughes retained her services for so long. Had he decided to take a leadership role in correcting one of the obvious inequities in the film business—the shocking absence of women in top Hollywood jobs? Although females were fixtures in the acting and writing areas, precious few worked as studio executives, producers, or directors. Not only was Hughes employing Parsons; he also supported the only woman director in Hollywood, Ida Lupino, whose recent films had been financed and released by RKO.

But Hughes was no premature feminist; as usual, he had a hidden agenda. One year before Harriet Parsons wrote her anguished letter, Mervin Houser of the RKO Publicity Department came up with an idea he thought would help promote *Clash by Night*, which Parsons had produced for Wald-Krasna and RKO. Before a screening of the film for the Hollywood Women's Press Club, he envisioned, there would be "a stage ceremony at which Harriet Parsons, producer of CLASH BY NIGHT and the only active woman producer in pictures, would be honored with the presentation of a scroll by a group of celebrities."[92] Houser discussed his brainstorm with Parsons; she, naturally, loved the idea. But he did this without first getting approval from Hughes, who was plenty upset. His assistant Nadine Henley transcribed his reaction as follows:

I think it would be a mistake. In the first place I don't think we want to accentuate and publicize Harriet Parsons's connection with any picture. I don't think it helps sell the picture.

I don't think we want to publicize that any picture is made by a woman producer or director because this immediately places the picture in some kind of freak classification and leads the audience to believe that it probably is not as good or as strong as a picture made by a man.

The problem now is to get out of this publicity stunt if possible without making Harriet Parsons unhappy. If that is impossible then we will have to go ahead with it. I don't want Harriet Parsons to be upset at this point.[93]

"Freak classification"? Howard Hughes clearly had no interest in supporting the rights of women; indeed, he was a major-league chauvinist. But then why did he soften his usually hard-hearted stance out of fear of upsetting Harriet Parsons when the Houser idea spun out of control? The answer is likely contained in another section of Parsons's March 1953 letter to him: "Your treatment of me has been pretty shabby, Howard, in many ways. You persist in discussing my projects with my mother, instead of me, despite the fact that I have been making pictures for 20 years, am the only active woman producer in Hollywood and the only woman member of the Screen Producers' Guild, and despite the fact that it was not my mother who produced 'THE ENCHANTED COTTAGE', 'I REMEMBER MAMA', 'CLASH BY NIGHT', etc."[94] Harriet was the daughter of Louella Parsons, the powerful gossip maven who described Hughes as "one of the most glamorous men in the world" and frequently featured him in her columns.[95] While one cannot be sure, it seems likely that Hughes kept Harriet Parsons around the RKO lot all those years to bolster his relationship with her mother.

The only area where RKO continued to excel in 1955 was promotion. In January the company pulled off another outlandish publicity stunt. Some 165 members of the press were flown (on TWA planes, of course) to Ocala, Florida, then ferried to Silver Springs resort, where they joined Jane Russell, Richard Egan, Gordon Scott, Jayne Mansfield, Barbara Darrow, and other Hollywood personalities. There they were invited to don bathing suits, aqualungs, masks, and flippers. So equipped, they could then dive approximately twenty feet below the surface of the clear spring and view a preview of the latest Jane Russell film, *Underwater!*. A majority of the writers and actors opted to watch the footage from the resort's submarine boats, but about twenty-five were game for the skin-diving experience, including Russell, Egan, Mansfield, Scott, Lori Nelson, and Rosemarie Bowe. RKO called it "the first underwater premiere in film history."[96]

The junket, organized by head of publicity Perry Lieber, was a big success. It even merited a tongue-in-cheek photo spread in *Life* magazine.[97] Unfortunately, the sort of ingenuity on display at the premiere of *Underwater!* was absent in the pedestrian film and in the remainder of the company's other 1955 releases as well. Most, such as *Escape to Burma*, *Rage at Dawn*, *Wakamba!*, and *Texas Lady*, would be drive-in–quality product made by independent producers. However, the worst of the lot was another full-fledged RKO production that had received a good deal of attention from Hughes himself. But when Howard Hughes took special interest in a production, tribulation often followed. Such was the case with *Son of Sinbad*.

Shot on the Gower Street lot in 1953, this quasi sequel to *Sinbad the Sailor* (1947) featured Dale Robertson plus a bevy of beautiful women, including striptease superstar Lili St. Cyr, Sally Forrest, Marie Blanchard, and more than a hundred eager starlets. Many of these women had been offered RKO contracts by Hughes's minions and promised they would appear in at least one RKO production. Unfortunately, this was it.[98]

Given the subject matter, one might have expected a rollicking action-adventure. Instead, this Baghdad hodgepodge contained a ludicrous plot whose only apparent raison d'être was to display a lot of attractive female flesh, swaddled in skimpy costumes and often jiggling away in provocative belly-dance numbers. It did not take long for another clash between the studio and the Production Code Administration to break out.

This time RKO mounted the offensive. In late January 1954 various newspaper columnists, including Louella Parsons and Bob Thomas, quoted an unnamed source from the industry censorship office to the effect that *Son of Sinbad* would make *The French Line* "look anemic by comparison." An infuriated James Grainger wrote Joseph Breen, describing such remarks as "untrue and libelous" . . . and also completely unfounded, since no one in the Breen office had even seen the picture. Grainger defended the movie, calling it a "Class 'A' picture of the highest quality, produced with an all-star cast and photographed in Technicolor." Furthermore, according to Grainger, it "contains nothing offensive or censorable and is entirely suitable for all audiences in the best theatres of this country and the rest of the world." He continued his tirade by asserting that the alleged remarks "were made maliciously and for the purpose of harassing and injuring RKO."[99]

Joe Breen was highly offended by Grainger's letter. He responded that none of the PCA employees had leaked any information about the picture to the gossips and that he was "greatly surprised that [Grainger] would write to me the kind of letter you have written."[100] Shortly thereafter, a cut

22. Lili St. Cyr puts on a show in *Son of Sinbad*. Courtesy of the Academy of Motion Picture Arts and Sciences.

of the picture was viewed by the PCA staff. Evidently, the gossip writers had a more accurate take on it than President Grainger because Breen quickly fired off a letter to C. J. Tevlin, informing him that many changes would have to be made for *Son of Sinbad* to gain a Production Code Seal. He included a three-page list of required emendations.[101]

As usual, Howard Hughes dithered. By the time a new cut of the movie was ready for presentation to the PCA staff, nearly a year had elapsed and Breen had retired. Whether the prospect of another ugly battle with Hughes hastened his departure is hard to say. Breen's replacement, Geoffrey M. Shurlock, viewed the new version and was pleased that "one objectionable dance" and "some particularly upsetting shots" had been removed. Still, he had issues. A dance featuring Sally Forrest had been trimmed considerably, but Shurlock would not approve what remained "because of the girl's costume." He told Jim Wilkinson, head of the studio Editing Department, that if RKO eliminated the dance entirely, the film would receive a seal. Two months later Shurlock and Wilkinson worked together on another cut of the problematic dance, which Shurlock finally okayed, since most of the dance was now presented in long shot.[102] This was much the same strategy employed to gain belated approval for the notorious "Lookin' for Trouble" number in *The French Line*. Perhaps because of the fiasco that accompanied the release of that picture, Hughes gave in and a Production Code Seal was issued on March 24, 1955. It didn't help much. The Catholic Legion of Decency condemned *Son of Sinbad* anyway, labeling it a "serious affront to Christian and traditional standards of morality and decency" and an "incitement to juvenile delinquency."[103] And critics engaged in another blood feast, ripping the picture apart. Jack Moffitt's review in the *Hollywood Reporter* was typical. He deemed it "made for (and by) adolescents of all ages" and "an affront to the public intelligence." If it is financially successful, he added, "bad taste all over the world will have been given encouragement."[104] A review in the *Los Angeles Times* was simply titled, "Sinbad Son Falls Flat on His Fez."[105] The independently made films that RKO was pushing through its distribution pipeline at this juncture were rank enough, but the biggest stinkers were the ones that bore an unmistakable Howard Hughes watermark.

Son of Sinbad opened in early June 1955. Around the middle of that month James Grainger's efforts to work with Howard Hughes had become so exasperating that he begged Noah Dietrich for help. In a letter to Dietrich describing "a very serious situation which should be discussed with Mr. Hughes at the earliest possible moment," Grainger lamented the toll that Hughes's lack of attention to RKO matters was taking on its employees: "We have a worldwide organization depending on the product which RKO Radio Pictures, Inc. releases, and the morale, as well as the effectiveness, of our organization is going to be badly shattered within a very short period unless we are going to be able to announce a program of pictures for 1956." Grainger then outlined some possible productions that excited him, but he might as well have been talking to his office wall, for the boss was finished with the movie business.[106]

It now seems clear that the major reason Howard Hughes remained interested in RKO during the preceding sixteen months was its potential value to his relations with the Internal Revenue Service. Floyd Odlum had sabotaged his grand scheme, so Hughes began trolling for someone else to take the movie company off his hands—someone who would pay his price and not embarrass him in the process.[107] He found his quarry in an unlikely place: the automobile-tire business.

On July 15, 1955, after three days and nights of nonstop negotiations, Howard Hughes sold RKO to Thomas F. O'Neil, president of General Teleradio, a subsidiary of the General Tire and Rubber Company.[108] The purchase price: $25 million. President Grainger, perhaps greatly relieved, proclaimed that the deal represented "the largest single financial transaction in the motion picture industry and one of the largest cash sales by an individual in the history of American finance."[109] According to *Daily Variety*, Hughes strolled away from RKO with a paper profit of more than $6.5 million.[110]

8. "He Had a Great Sense of Entitlement, Mr. Hughes"

The Six-Foot-Four Enigma (1948–1955)

There is one aspect of RKO's history that everyone—company employees, journalists, Hollywood historians, film scholars, Hughes biographers—seems to agree about: Howard Hughes was primarily responsible for the ruination of the company.[1] As should be clear by this stage, his erratic, incomprehensible approach to management brought RKO tumbling down to the brink of extinction. Yet more should be said. The following is an attempt to drill a bit deeper, to gain greater understanding of his behavior between 1948 and 1955, when, except for approximately three months, he maintained a steely grip on the organization.

Today people's memories of this renowned man are colored by the final years of his life. Those years were spent cut off from the flow of humanity by his overpowering paranoia. He moved from one foreign hotel to another, bed-ridden, addicted to narcotics, watching old movies over and over. He supposedly viewed his favorite—*Ice Station Zebra*—at least 150 times.[2]

Once in a great while Hughes would surprise the world, such as his famous telephone call to journalists that short-circuited Clifford Irving's attempt to pedal a fraudulent book about him. But, for the most part, he maintained a hermetic existence in the twilight years, surrounded by a phalanx of Mormons who nursed him and barred access to all those intent on invading his precious privacy. Then came frantic efforts to rush this very sick old man back from Mexico to Houston before it was too late. He didn't make it, but it was somehow fitting that he died thousands of feet above the earth in a jet airplane. The year was 1976 and seventy-year-old Howard Hughes, the madman with the Midas touch, was gone.

But back in 1948, when he purchased the Atlas Company's stake in RKO, most of the public held a very different image of Hughes. Viewed as a dashing, heroic figure, Hughes epitomized both the American dream and the

American spirit. Yes, he was fortunate to inherit a great deal of money at a young age, but look what he had done with it. Instead of lazing about clipping bond coupons, he rolled up his sleeves and worked tirelessly, becoming a pioneer in one of the most exciting new industries of the twentieth century: aviation. Even though he never attended college, Hughes focused his gifted brain on the physics of flight, learning everything there was to know about it and becoming a brilliant aeronautical engineer. He built aircraft that could fly higher, faster, and farther, and he tested those aircraft himself, despite the inherent dangers. In the 1930s the swashbuckling Hughes set a number of speed and flight-endurance records, including besting the previous around-the-world mark by four days. Celebrated for his achievements, he became the honoree at ticker-tape parades and multiple awards ceremonies.[3] With the exception of Charles Lindbergh, the pilot who first soloed across the Atlantic, no one was considered a greater aviator.

Hughes's reputation was burnished by his height (six foot four), good looks, and magnetism. Long before Hugh Hefner created his famous magazine, Hughes patented the playboy lifestyle, enjoying well-publicized romantic relationships with such famous actresses as Billie Dove, Carole Lombard, Katharine Hepburn, Ginger Rogers, Olivia de Havilland, Lana Turner, and Ava Gardner. Hughes had once been married—to Houston socialite Ella Rice in 1925. But they divorced after four years, and he immediately became one of the world's most eligible bachelors, the object of constant speculation concerning which of the favored beauties would eventually land him.

Hughes was also considered a great patriot who marshaled all his available resources in support of the American war effort. He designed improved machine guns for B-17 bombers and received government contracts to develop the Hercules, the largest "flying boat" ever built, and the XF-11, a photo-reconnaissance plane. Neither was finished before V-J day, a failure that greatly embarrassed him. Even worse, the Hercules, known derisively as the "Spruce Goose," entered the public consciousness as a boondoggle, an enormous waste of precious taxpayer dollars, since it had never lifted off the water and, according to many experts, would never fly. This prompted a congressional investigation of Hughes's government contracts in 1947. Thanks to his own masterful testimony in Washington, Hughes survived the inquisition with his patriotic reputation intact and, later that year, proved the naysayers wrong by piloting the behemoth Hercules on a short flight in Long Beach harbor. The man's firm stance against communism magnified his heroic stature.

Hughes's bravery also contributed to the growing legend. Despite several crashes, he kept flying experimental aircraft until he cracked up the

XF-11 in Beverly Hills in 1946. He was pulled from the wreckage in the nick of time, but doctors still expected he would die from his injuries. Soon enough, however, Hughes was out of the hospital and flying again.

And then there was his fantastic wealth. The key to his fortune was, unquestionably, an oil-well drill bit invented by his father, which became the cornerstone of the highly successful Hughes Tool Company. But on the back of that drill bit, Howard Hughes Jr. built an empire that included such enterprises as the Hughes Aircraft Company, Trans World Airlines (TWA), and Grand Prize, the largest brewery in Texas. Everything he touched seemed to throw off greenbacks. No one (not even Hughes himself) knew how much money he had, but the quintessential pilot was, without question, one of the richest men in the world. Yet, despite his enormous bankroll and myriad accomplishments, Hughes projected the pleasing image of a down-to-earth human being. A shy man without pretensions, he wore old clothes and tennis shoes, ate his lunch out of a brown paper bag, and tooled around Los Angeles in beat-up Chevrolets.

In sum, Howard Hughes exemplified the greatness of America, a country that cherished individualism, hard work, courage, patriotism, intelligence, humility, vision, and achievement. By the 1940s Hughes was as close to royalty as a democratic, capitalistic nation could manage. And he had ascended to that glorified position by force of will, not divine right.

Thus, few people around the country and throughout the world would have bet against Hughes as he embarked on the next exhilarating chapter of his life—running a global movie corporation. He was no Hollywood neophyte, either, having produced a number of movies and directed a couple of them himself. From all accounts, those movies had been financial successes, like his other moneymaking ventures. Although there were certainly rumblings within the Hollywood community because of Hughes's previous penchant for meddling in the work of seasoned filmmakers, most believed he would be far too busy to do much of that at RKO.

Equally well known were the man's "peculiarities," especially his passion for privacy and his phobias concerning dust and germs and disease, but these eccentricities had never seemed to hinder him, business-wise, in the past. No wonder astute businessman Floyd Odlum sold Hughes the Atlas stock despite a better offer from another interested party; like so many, Odlum was seduced by the myth of Howard Hughes.

But myth and reality rarely sync up, and Howard Hughes in 1948 was not the same man who had accomplished so much earlier in life. Perhaps because of the pills he gobbled to deaden the pain from his flying accidents, especially the XF-11 crash, he had become disorganized, forgetful, obsessive, and distrustful of everyone except his closest associates. He had also reached a point in his life when he was afraid to fail, to commit mistakes that would make him appear fallible. Consequently, decision making became difficult for him, even when his inability to act meant guaranteed convulsions in his enterprises.

A man able to recognize even a few of these character flaws might have stepped back from the fray, perhaps assuming the chairmanship of his companies and then hiring the best managerial talent available to run them. But Hughes was incapable of critical self-analysis. In fact, he was not as down-to-earth as people believed. As Ava Gardner later remarked, "He had a great sense of entitlement, Mr. Hughes."[4] The quiet, bashful boy-from-Texas facade masked an ego that had grown to massive proportions and stifled his ability to recognize his own limitations. Consequently, Hughes turned into the micromanager from hell, insisting that he have the final say on all important matters, even though he never seemed able to make up his mind.

There is no need to reiterate the damaging effects of Hughes's procrastination at this point, but more should be said about other aspects of his destructive approach to leadership—for example, the oft-repeated excuse that the demands of his other enterprises kept him from devoting sufficient time to RKO. On the contrary, he devoted too much time to RKO.

Without question, Howard Hughes proved hard to reach during his RKO years. But this appears to have been a calculated strategy related to his indecisiveness. Ned Depinet, Jerry Wald, Norman Krasna, Jimmy Grainger, and myriad producers, writers, and directors were not alone in their frustration; key employees of Hughes's other companies found contacting him just as difficult, especially when key decisions needed to be made. Ironically, there is evidence that most of the tycoon's professional efforts were devoted to RKO in the early 1950s, a fact that frustrated Tool Company, Aircraft, and TWA executives no end.[5]

Hughes's tenacious pursuit of beautiful women may be another reason he was so often incommunicado. If there is even a smidgen of truth to the multiple accounts of Hughes's romantic activities during this period, it is no wonder he was difficult to contact. On numerous occasions, he would invite a woman to lunch or dinner, then take her to a nearly airport and fly off to some romantic spot to impress, and perhaps seduce, her. Sometimes, he was shamefully sneaky; Janet Leigh's date to go sailing with her agent morphed into a Hughes-orchestrated odyssey to the Grand Canyon and Las Vegas. Leigh, who was frightened of Hughes and considered his actions a "kidnapping," was hysterical by the time she finally returned home.[6]

Norman Krasna indelicately maintained that "Hughes was using RKO as a whorehouse."[7] Although Howard Hughes was obsessed with a seemingly endless assortment of women, on the surface Krasna's remark seems patently ridiculous. Why would one of the world's most famous, wealthy men need a studio to gain access to beautiful females? And yet many of the women who appeared in his RKO films were objects of Hughes's desire: Jane Russell, Ava Gardner, Ingrid Bergman, Linda Darnell, Janet Leigh, Faith Domergue, Joan Fontaine, Terry Moore, Susan Hayward, Jean Simmons, Yvonne De Carlo, Marie Windsor, Virginia Mayo, Carla Balenda, Ida Lupino, Jane Greer, Marilyn Monroe, Ursula Theiss. Whether Hughes bought RKO to barter movie roles for female companionship must remain a matter of gossip-sheet speculation, but, without question, his Don Juan proclivities took time and affected his ability to respond quickly and thoughtfully whenever decisions at RKO and the other businesses needed to be made. So did his rampant paranoia and its corollary—his fanatical privacy. Hughes apparently never set foot on the Gower Street lot, and most of RKO's workers never met their boss. Nonetheless, they knew, from early on, that they couldn't trust him.

As previously mentioned, Hughes was required to testify before the Senate Special Committee Investigating the National Defense Program in 1947, accused of squandering more than forty million taxpayer dollars during the war and failing to deliver, in a timely fashion, military hardware contracted by the government. The Hercules was the major agenda item. During his testimony, Hughes bellowed, "I'm supposed to be capricious, a playboy, eccentric, but I don't believe I have the reputation of a liar. For twenty-three years no one has questioned my word"[8]

The rhetoric carried plenty of dramatic weight at the time, but it was just that—pure rhetoric. Hughes lied often and without compunction. The assurances he gave Peter Rathvon and Dore Schary after buying control of RKO and the pledge to his new employees that their jobs were safe represented the first big whoppers. Soon enough Rathvon and Schary were jettisoned and pink slips began appearing on RKO desks like flies at a Labor Day picnic. At least, Hughes was an equal-opportunity prevaricator; he was just as likely to behave falsely in his dealings with financial titans like Floyd Odlum and William Zeckendorf as with producers Jerry Wald and Norman Krasna and lesser figures in the RKO organization.

Howard Hughes's impersonal, secretive, untrustworthy, and illogical management style poisoned the atmosphere at the studio. Albert E. Van Schmus landed an entry-level job at RKO in 1941, remaining on the Gower Street lot for several years before moving to a position with the Production

Code Administration. "It was a nice studio to work for, *really* nice," he said. "All the people were nice. And they were kind of proud of that fact, they thought they had kind of a family group there. They liked each other and were happy to work there."[9] Laraine Day, an MGM contract actress who made six pictures for RKO in the 1940s, also remembered the studio fondly: "The fact that they didn't have the tremendous star system like MGM made it a warm family.... You knew everybody; you knew all the crews from other pictures, even from several stages down the way. It was more fun."[10] John Cromwell directed pictures for RKO, off and on, from the early thirties to the early fifties. He concurred, "It [RKO] seemed to be full of free souls who felt that at least they were doing what they wanted to do. In that respect it was *very* pleasant to be there. I enjoyed every minute of it. I didn't care about the work. There wasn't any politics. You didn't have the feeling of somebody in some position trying to get the better of you or anything of that kind."[11]

But after he took control, Hughes had the offices bugged so he could spy on his workers and hired an army of private detectives to surveil the ones who interested him most. Producer John Houseman described Hughes's influence as "pervasive and sinister" and claimed he fostered "a distasteful and unproductive atmosphere—one to which I developed an intense and debilitating allergy."[12] Houseman wasn't alone. RKO became the least desirable site of employment in Hollywood, and the toxic atmosphere that enveloped the studio soon spread to the New York headquarters, the domestic branches, and the foreign offices of the company.

Despite his manifold deficiencies, Hughes might be remembered as a tolerable leader if he had demonstrated any aptitude for the job of production chief. But this, arguably, was his greatest shortcoming. Once again, his ego-soaked approach got in the way. Hughes believed that the pictures he wanted to see and the public would pay to see were one and the same.[13] He couldn't have been more wrong—he had neither commercial sense nor artistic taste. In addition, he considered himself a brilliant filmmaker who could look at a script, a reel of dailies, an edited sequence, or a rough cut of an entire movie and quickly discern how to make them better. But Hughes's capabilities in this regard were dubious at best, disastrous at worst, as the parade of dreadful movies that marched out of RKO during his time amply illustrates. Exhibit A is composed of his favorite films, the expensive Jane Russell–vehicles that received the lion's share of his attention. *Double Dynamite, His Kind of Woman, The Las Vegas Story, Macao, The French Line, Underwater!*—no wonder one of the stockholder suits claimed Russell was a waste of corporate assets. Thankfully, some of her performances in non-RKO movies, such as *Gentlemen Prefer Blondes* (Twentieth Century–Fox, 1953), demonstrated that she had genuine talent. Even the grateful and obedient Robert Mitchum, who costarred in two pictures with Russell and always maintained a certain affection for Hughes, could restrain himself no longer after his studio contract ended. In 1955 he said, "RKO made the same film with me in it for ten years. They were so alike I wore the same suit in six of them and the same Burberry trench coat. They made a male Jane Russell out of me.... Only two pictures I made in that time made any sense whatever. I complained and they told me frankly that they had a certain amount of baloney to sell and I was the boy to do it."[14]

One of the quirks of the capitalist system is that corporate leaders sometimes prove to be ongoing disasters, yet emerge from their deficient stewardship much richer than they were before. Obviously, Hughes managed this sleight of hand at RKO. But, during the period when he was driving the movie company along the fast track to perdition, he was also mismanaging Hughes Aircraft and Trans World Airlines to his enormous financial advantage.

The most brilliant scientists of Hughes Aircraft, including Simon Ramo and Dean Wooldridge, grew so exasperated with their employer that they quit and formed a new electronics firm in 1953. "The Ramo-Wooldridge Corporation, financed by Thompson Products, Inc., of Cleveland, went on to supervise the development of intercontinental ballistic missiles for the air force, and eventually became TRW, Inc., one of the giants of the space and technology industry, with revenues surpassing those of Hughes Aircraft itself." Undaunted by their departure and by threats from secretary of the air force Harold E. Talbott to cut off all military contracts with Hughes Aircraft, which Talbott called a "hell of a mess," Hughes and his lawyers came up with a brilliant scheme to save face and money at the same time. They created the Hughes Medical Institute later in 1953, then turned Hughes Aircraft over to the new institute. Thereafter, Hughes would receive millions in interest payments and save even more in taxes. According to Donald L. Bartlett and James B. Steele, "Hughes had created the ultimate charity: the American taxpayer was to pick up the entire bill for the Howard Hughes Medical Institute, while Hughes basked in the warm glow of testimonials to his philanthropy and quietly collected money from his own charity."[15]

The TWA Board of Directors and its banking lenders, fearing Hughes's ruinous oversight was about to throw the company into bankruptcy, wrested control of the airline from him in 1960. This resulted in the longest legal battle in the history of American business and, eventually, the forced sale of Hughes's TWA stock. But in the greatest irony of them all, the men who ran TWA after Hughes could no longer interfere with them had increased the value of his stock more than sixfold by the time he unloaded his shares in 1966. Howard Hughes loved his pet airline more than all his other enterprises combined and was devastated after losing his grip on the TWA throttle. "It's not mine any more," he wailed. "I can't run my hands over it any more."[16] He exited with a check of $546,549,771 to assuage his grief.[17]

Thus, even though he made mountains of money before, during, and after his misadventure at RKO, Hughes's management of the movie outfit was no anomaly. He was an equally incompetent commander of companies much larger and more financially significant than RKO. Others have suspected there was method to Hughes's madness. Joseph Losey, for example, believed he "wanted to run [RKO] into the ground so he could take a huge tax loss."[18] Hughes hated taxes and was continually hatching schemes to avoid paying them, but this explanation is blind to the man's character.

Howard Hughes cared deeply about his honor, his reputation, and his image. He was also hypercompetitive, a prideful person who never set out intentionally to fail. The sad fact is simply this—Howard Hughes had become a psychological mess when he took over RKO, a ticking time bomb of Napoleonic hubris, personal obsessions, physical torments, and mental neuroses that rendered him incapable of running any complicated organization. RKO had suffered at the hands of some of its past lackluster leaders, but no former company CEO could compete with Mr. Hughes; he was a one-man wrecking crew.

9. "An Untoward Turn of Events"
The O'Neil-O'Shea-Dozier Regime (1955–1957)

Why would a tire company purchase a movie studio? In truth, General Tire was much more than a rubber manufacturer—a fledgling conglomerate, the organization had begun expanding its commercial horizons before its leaders ever thought about RKO. During World War II General Tire jumped into the radio business, gaining control of the Yankee Network of New England. Afterward it continued along an acquisitive path, adding the Don Lee network on the Pacific Coast, as well as 58 percent of the nationwide Mutual network, to its holdings. The company also started to purchase television stations and, by the end of 1955, controlled outlets in New York (WOR), Los Angeles (KHJ), Boston (WNAC), Memphis (WHBQ), and West Palm Beach (WEAT). General Teleradio was the name of the subsidiary created to manage the radio and television businesses of General Tire.

William F. O'Neil, the founder of General Tire, scoffed at the belief that his family should confine itself to manufacturing tires: "Who says we should stick to the rubber business? Our business is to *make money!*"[1] Thomas F. O'Neil, anointed president of General Teleradio by his father, stood six foot four and weighed 215 pounds. A former football player, Tom was a big man with big ideas. Early in the game he hatched a brilliant one to please his television customers—bring quality Hollywood product to the masses. He created *Million Dollar Movie*, a program that became extraordinarily popular on his stations. Audience members wanted to see feature films on their home screens, a desire exacerbated by the heads of the major studios, who had agreed to withhold thousands of old films from the networks and independent stations after television emerged as a serious competitor to their industry. O'Neil negotiated a four-year lease, at fire sale prices, for thirty pictures from the Bank of America. The bank had foreclosed on them when their producers failed to pay off the loans used to

23. Thomas F. O'Neil *(left)* presents a check for $25 million to Hughes's lawyer Thomas B. Slack, cementing the purchase of RKO by General Teleradio. Courtesy of University of Southern California, on behalf of the USC Specialized Libraries and Archival Collections.

finance the productions. Among the films were *Arch of Triumph, Body and Soul, Letter from an Unknown Woman, The Dark Mirror, One Touch of Venus, A Double Life,* and two RKO releases: *Miracle of the Bells* and *Magic Town.* O'Neil then showcased one of these "million dollar movies" every night for a week on his stations, earning excellent ratings in the process. After they had played out on the General Teleradio channels, the films were offered for presentation on other independent stations, adding to the revenues. *Time* magazine reported that General Teleradio made "more than $600,000 profit on the overall deal."[2]

Thus, insiders quickly recognized why General Teleradio paid $25 million to gain control of RKO. The studio had more than seven hundred old films gathering dust in its vaults—films that could be repurposed for the company's television viewers. Residents of Hollywood also realized that the release of the RKO library would spell the end of the industry-wide holdout. The big losers would be theater owners, who had exerted considerable pressure on their suppliers to withstand the entreaties of the television companies. But once one company broke ranks, which RKO was about to do, all the others would soon follow. A lot of capital could be realized from those old releases, most of which had not seen daylight in many years, and no studio chief wanted to start negotiating after his competitors flooded the market with their pictures.

Even though Tom O'Neil's entry into the motion picture business promised to shake up the status quo, he was welcomed by most members of the show business community who had had their fill of Howard Hughes. Martin Quigley, publisher of *Motion Picture Daily*, editorialized,

> The O'Neil interests bring to the industry a measure of character, intelligence and experience that will have a deep and far-reaching effect. They bring a sense of public and private responsibility that will enhance and embellish the industry. Their arrival should be accorded a solid and hearty welcome.
>
> It is well known that the O'Neils were primarily attracted to RKO Radio Pictures as a source of library material, consisting of older pictures, which could immediately be made available for purposes of programs for the extensive television facilities which they operate. Less well known is the fact that they have equally been attracted by the prospects of rehabilitation of a ranking major film company out of what has been the neglected and semi-dormant film interest under the capricious control of Howard Hughes.[3]

In short, even a complete neophyte looked promising after Hughes's devastating RKO performance.

When the deal was announced, the press reported that Tom O'Neil initially wanted to buy only RKO's completed films, not the company. But Hughes insisted on an all-or-nothing transaction. Thus, some expected O'Neil to turn around and sell the studios and the distribution operation quickly, holding on to the library of old pictures for broad-based television sales, as well as broadcasting on his own stations. But Martin Quigley was right; Tom O'Neil aspired to be a movie mogul. At a press conference on July 26, 1955, he stated, "Teleradio regards acquisition of RKO Radio Pictures . . . as a great opportunity to continue and increase the company's role in production and distribution of films for theatrical release and intends to vigorously pursue such a policy." He also told the reporters he expected RKO to be a "successful business venture."[4] A few months later he folded RKO into a new organization titled RKO Teleradio Pictures and assumed the chairmanship of its board of directors.[5]

O'Neil did not waste any time backing up his words. Within a week of the initial press conference, he hired Daniel T. O'Shea to replace James R.

Grainger as corporate president of RKO. Chester B. Bahn of *Film Daily* saluted Grainger for keeping the organization afloat during the twilight of the Hughes's era: "Herculean is the only way to describe the accomplishment of James R. Grainger, RKO's extremely able president, in the last few years. He held together and inspired a domestic and foreign sales organization in the face of all obstacles. You hear much about the value of morale in selling; well, it was Grainger who saw to it that RKO morale was sustained."[6] Jimmy Grainger set off on the same path as his predecessor, Ned Depinet; he continued to serve RKO in an "advisory capacity" for a few months and then resigned.[7]

The new president's RKO roots stretched back to the early 1930s, when he emerged as one of the organization's most important attorneys. Dan O'Shea departed the company in the midthirties to become David Selznick's chief adjutant in his newly formed independent venture. There O'Shea's hard-nosed negotiating skills often impressed and frustrated various industry executives, including RKO's leaders. O'Shea's association with Selznick lasted almost fifteen years, after which he accepted the position of senior vice president of the Columbia Broadcasting System (CBS) radio and television networks in 1950. There he supervised the organization's business affairs. A savvy professional, O'Shea appeared to be a fine choice to guide the "new RKO." One of his first moves was to cement a long-term production agreement with the Selznick Company.[8]

In his early remarks as corporate president, O'Shea underlined Tom O'Neil's commitment to making RKO a force in Hollywood once again. "The new regime is completely dedicated to the job of reconstructing the RKO trade-mark ... so that it will come to mean the great things that the organization stood for in the past," said O'Shea. He continued, "It is the firm intention of the new management to utilize the world's foremost talents insofar as these may be acquired and to allow such talents to function with independence of thought and action."[9]

It took O'Neil and O'Shea a bit longer to find a production head, but in November the new president announced that William Dozier was taking over at the studio. Dozier also had an RKO pedigree, having served as Charles Koerner's assistant, starting in 1944. Following Koerner's death, Dozier worked for Peter Rathvon for a few months in 1946, then moved to Universal-International, where he was associate head of production. After his stint at Universal he joined Samuel Goldwyn for a time before accepting the position of executive producer of dramatic programs and later director of network programs for CBS Television. Tom O'Neil must have been impressed that CBS veterans O'Shea and Dozier understood the brave new

24. RKO president Daniel T. O'Shea with Ginger Rogers. Courtesy of the Academy of Motion Picture Arts and Sciences.

world of television as well as the feature film business. O'Neil expected RKO to be originating video fare as well as theatrical films in the near future.

Early in 1956 publicity chief Perry Lieber, who had spent twenty-five years at RKO, quit the company, presumably because he did not want to relocate to New York from Los Angeles.[10] Lieber had been one of the stars of the Hughes era, masterminding the *Underwater!* junket and other zesty RKO premieres for such films as *Hard, Fast and Beautiful; Two Tickets to Broadway;* and *The Las Vegas Story*. The latter title proved prophetic—Lieber soon landed a job with Howard Hughes in the gambling mecca.

Lieber's departure enabled his assistant, Mervin Houser, to take over as RKO's national director of publicity. Even before ascending to the top position, Houser had become an indefatigable company cheerleader, who considered a day without a publicity release akin to a day without food and drink. In early December he let the world know that RKO would make "12 to 15 top-budget pictures in 1956" and also enter into "various package deals with independents to insure a steady flow of quality product . . . at the rate of at least two pictures a month." According to Houser's release, the determined Dozier promised, "RKO will release pictures and not announcements"—a direct swipe at the previous management.[11] Later Dozier would fire another potshot at Hughes, when he decided to place *Son of Sinbad* on the shelf. "It cost us a million dollars to take that picture out of circulation," he said, "but we consider it a good investment. We have to begin some place and we are not interested in making only disgraceful pictures."[12]

Bill Dozier's ambitious production pledge was reinforced in December 1955, when President O'Shea traveled to Los Angeles to discuss future pictures with him and Charles Glett, the studio's new executive vice president. They kicked around more than thirty possible stories and considered a wide range of talent, including Ginger Rogers, John Farrow, Fritz Lang, Dana Andrews, Robert Ryan, Dick Powell, Red Skelton, James Arness, Bing Crosby, Deborah Kerr, Cary Grant, Sam Fuller, Eddie Fisher, and Debbie Reynolds. Although they spent nearly all their time on the topic of future theatrical filmmaking, the men paid some attention to possible television activities. The most promising idea involved setting up three units "to produce 1-hour and 1 1/2-hour subjects at a cost from $100,000 to $150,000."[13]

On December 19 O'Shea was back in New York, where he announced that Eddie Fisher and Debbie Reynolds, "the brightest young twosome in show business, will be brought together by RKO to co-star in a top budget comedy-musical"[14] In addition, he revealed that the initial "new RKO picture" would be *The First Traveling Saleslady*, starring former Gower Street queen Ginger Rogers. It would be followed by *Back from Eternity*, to be directed by John Farrow, who had just signed a three-picture pact with the company. The RKO leaders also purchased a best-selling novel, *Cash McCall*, for production and expected David Selznick to begin shooting Ernest Hemingway's *A Farewell to Arms* with Jennifer Jones in June. "It is our intention," said O'Shea, "to create an atmosphere at RKO where talented and gifted men and women can function in a creative climate to produce outstanding entertainment."[15]

Meanwhile, Tom O'Neil had been busy negotiating a deal that would substantially mitigate the cost of the RKO purchase. Just before the end of 1955 O'Neil made his move—the move that would lead to a floodtide of movie presentations on television.[16] For $15.2 million, he sold the worldwide television rights to 740 RKO features and 1,000 shorts to Matty Fox, who represented the C&C Super Corporation.[17] RKO Teleradio, naturally, retained broadcasting rights to all the films in the cities where it owned stations, meaning *Million Dollar Movie* would be supplied for years to come. Plus, the company held on to the right to cherry-pick 150 films from the library "and sell the first TV showing of those films to a nationally advertised sponsor."[18] It appeared to be a brilliant transaction. Early in 1956 Howard Hughes agreed to purchase *The Conqueror* and *Jet Pilot* for $8 million, which meant O'Neil was now within $2 million of recouping his company's entire RKO investment. Plus, in addition to acquiring the features O'Neil needed for his own stations, he still owned two Hollywood studios, the theatrical negatives and release prints, plus reissue and remake rights to all the vintage movies and a global distribution setup. Trade-paper writers trundled out the superlatives. *Daily Variety* described O'Neil's purchase of RKO and subsequent dealings as the "most amazing financial coup in the history of the film business," and the *Hollywood Reporter* chimed in, calling the C&C sale, "one of the most fantastic transactions the picture business has ever known."[19] The *Daily Variety* story claimed O'Neil had already banked an "assured profit of $2,200,000" on his RKO investment.[20] And a *Business Week* article quoted a "West Coast industry observer" who labeled Tom O'Neil's handling of his RKO purchase, a "monument in the industry."[21]

Alas, the C&C deal, in retrospect, turned out to be less than brilliant; indeed, it was, arguably, one of the worst in show business history. Two words were key: "in perpetuity." O'Neil sold off television rights to *Cimarron*, *King Kong*, the Astaire-Rogers musicals (except *Roberta*), *Bringing Up Baby*, *Gunga Din*, *The Hunchback of Notre Dame*, *Citizen Kane*, *Cat People*, *Out of the Past*, *Crossfire*, *The Set-Up*, and hundreds of other valuable pictures FOREVER. More sensible studio heads followed his lead by packaging and syndicating their old films in much more inventive and financially lucrative ways. The licensing of movies to television ultimately turned into a bonanza, and, soon enough, it became obvious that O'Neil had been snookered; the RKO library was worth much, much more than $15.2 million.

Throughout 1956 RKO appeared to be the phoenix of movie studios, springing back to life from the ashes left behind by the Hughes bonfire. Mervin Houser's releases proclaimed boundless good news:

> Acquisition of *Cash McCall* signals the company's intent to compete for the top story material. The story department, headed by William Nutt, has doubled in size, with more story analysts to be hired and the "long-inactive New York story department" to be reactivated. (January 4)

President O'Shea announces he has allocated $22,500,000 "as the overall budget for the first eleven pictures which will be produced by RKO Studio within the first six months of 1956." (January 13)

Four new features—*The First Traveling Saleslady, Tension at Table Rock, Back from Eternity,* and *Beyond a Reasonable Doubt*—will be shooting at RKO's Hollywood studios by March 14. (February 13)

RKO engages J. Walter Thompson as its advertising agency "in line with [its] policy of aligning itself with the top creative talent in every area of RKO's operation." (March 7)

RKO establishes a major film service unit to serve the television industry. According to executive vice-president Charles Glett, the bicoastal operation "will service the wants and requirements of television producers, advertising agencies, sponsors . . . with our unexcelled service facilities and the aggregate of our resources in both man-power and material." Fred Ahern, formerly RKO studio production coordinator who had also worked for five years as director of operations for CBS Television in Hollywood, is named Supervisor of Television Operations for the company. (April 12)[22]

For the most part, journalists (particularly trade-paper writers) swallowed and then coughed up Houser's flack in unadulterated form. There was ample evidence to back him up; the Gower Street Personnel Department had been hiring at a rapid clip, and a studio that had often resembled a morgue under Hughes was now brimming with vitality and optimism.

But behind the scenes small tensions began to develop. The executive alignment at the studio was a throwback to RKO's early years, when the production head reported to another studio executive. For example, David O. Selznick had worked under the aegis of B. B. Kahane when he supervised moviemaking for RKO between 1931 and 1933. In this case Bill Dozier appeared on the company org chart beneath Charlie Glett, who had been associate producer of a couple of early 1940s RKO pictures, *Syncopation* and *All That Money Can Buy,* and then worked with Dan O'Shea for Selznick later in the decade. In all likelihood, O'Shea, who also worked with Glett at CBS, had recommended he be hired in the new "executive VP" position.

After working with Dozier for a few months, Glett began to feel the production chief did not respect him and was trying to schedule regular studio planning meetings at times when he could not attend. This occasioned a long, somewhat testy memo from Dozier, in which he called the situation a simple misunderstanding and stated, "I have no sinister motive in allowing these meetings to be held in your absence any more than I would suspect your having a sinister motive if they were held in my absence." After reminding Glett that "the task facing us all, that of getting out a program of pictures, is sufficiently difficult, without looking for additional aggravations," he ended the memo with a couple of humorous postscripts, most likely to lighten the tone.[23]

One day after sending the memo to Glett, Dozier forwarded one to Dan O'Shea complaining about constant demands from Merv Houser to accommodate press interviewers. Some of the interviews were not turning out to Dozier's liking, but, more important, they were taking too much of his time. Although Houser had emphasized that he could not do his job without Dozier's cooperation, the executive producer told O'Shea, "I would be most happy to conserve *all* my time and energy for the somewhat sizable task at hand." He asked the boss to instruct the irrepressible Houser to back off.[24]

Bill Dozier's dustups with Glett and Houser did not escalate, but his developing relationship with Dan O'Shea soon began to take a familiar, rather disturbing, turn. As corporate president, O'Shea assumed he had the final word whenever major production decisions needed to be made. Unlike George Schaefer or Howard Hughes, he was neither dictatorial nor dogmatic, but when he and Dozier disagreed about a potential production, O'Shea's point of view generally prevailed. And the two men often had different ideas about the sorts of films their company should be making.

For instance, Dozier wired O'Shea in late March, recommending the studio strike a deal with producer Bert Friedlob to make *Powder Keg*, a "far above average western of [the] intimate variety." He also mentioned that he had sent a script of *Run of the Arrow*, another Western from writer-director Sam Fuller, to Van Johnson in hopes he would accept the main role.[25] O'Shea responded that he didn't like *Powder Keg* "for reasons have already told you," which suggests that Dozier had previously done his best to change the president's mind.[26] Obviously, his efforts failed. O'Shea was quite excited about *Run of the Arrow*, calling its script "splendid," but not about Van Johnson, a choice he described as "poor physical casting [that] would be limiting at the box office." Dozier gave way on *Power Keg* but challenged O'Shea on Johnson; clearly, he felt it would be a coup to cast him in the Fuller picture.[27] But again the president's dictum prevailed—Rod Steiger ended up playing the protagonist in *Run of the Arrow*.

The O'Shea-Dozier disagreements had all the earmarks of the latest chapter in the long, lamentable history of RKO New York executives interfering in the studio's creative affairs. But, in time, O'Shea became less intrusive in Dozier's domain, and the two men started working together in a mostly collegial manner. Still, Bill Dozier must often have reflected on the war years with considerable nostalgia. Back then, Dozier's mentor, Charles Koerner, enjoyed total freedom to make all of the studio's important creative decisions.

In late June RKO was the most active studio in Hollywood. Principal photography on five pictures had been completed and three more were before the cameras, with at least nine films scheduled to begin shooting by early 1957. Among the latter were "three big RKO productions to be filmed abroad": *Escapade in Japan*, to be shot in Tokyo; *Bangkok*, to be filmed in the Thai city; and *Pakistan*, to be made in Lahore and star John Wayne.[28] Indeed, the company's ambitions seemed boundless. Following the adaptation of MGM's *Ninotchka* into the successful Broadway musical comedy *Silk Stockings*, Bill Dozier started to believe that some of RKO's old pictures might be vehicles for similar treatment. His first thought was *Alice Adams* (1935), and he began talks with writer-director Moss Hart and lyricist Alan Jay Lerner about transforming the Katharine Hepburn picture for the stage. Dozier also believed musical versions of *Stage Door* (1937) and *Kitty Foyle* (1940) had Broadway potential.[29]

Both within and without the movie colony, people viewed the resurrection of RKO with considerable amazement. On July 16 *Newsweek* published a cover story that called it "one of the fastest and most supercolossal comebacks in Hollywood history." "Hughes' onetime 'white elephant,' in fact, has become a bellwether of its industry overnight," wrote the magazine's associate editor Sandford Brown. The author gave full credit to Tom O'Neil for recognizing a world of increasing leisure time and deciding, in O'Neil's own words, to create "a sort of General Motors of entertainment." Besides RKO, O'Neil now presided over an empire of nearly six hundred radio stations, six television stations estimated to be worth "about $10 million," two music publishing companies, and a recording company. To Brown, O'Neil had already established himself as an industry pacemaker, for "it was only a matter of weeks after RKO sold its movies to television that Twentieth Century–Fox, Warner Bros., [and] Metro-Goldwyn-Mayer began to follow suit."[30] New blood was needed to revitalize the movie industry, and Tom O'Neil appeared to be supplying it.

This laudatory article in a national newsmagazine was followed a month later by similar praise in *Variety*. Frank Scully wrote, "The spectacle of one man's junk heap becoming another man's Comstock Load is what makes the capitalist system an unpredictable mystery."[31] Scully made Hughes look like a chump and O'Neil a genius. The journalistic approbation surely pleased O'Neil and all the members of the RKO family. But, lamentably, these assessments were premature. None of the pictures produced by the new regime had hit theaters as yet. The euphoria that accompanied the return of more than 1,500 workers to the Hollywood studios had apparently blinded nearly everyone to a simple fact: the commercial and artistic quality of these ballyhooed films remained a question mark, and they would determine RKO's future.

Even though he knew that his first movie, *The First Traveling Saleslady*, had not turned out well, an emboldened Bill Dozier charged forward. In mid-August he sent O'Shea a seven-page memo outlining a highly ambitious array of potential "blockbusters" to be produced in 1957 and the early part of 1958.[32] The list began with *The Naked and the Dead*, Norman Mailer's best-selling novel, which Dozier figured would cost between $2.5 to $3 million with a top cast or around $1.6 million "utilizing stars of the caliber of Rod Steiger." Other properties owned by the studio with their probable budgets included *Cash McCall* ($1.75–2.5 million); *Bangkok* ($2.5–2.85 million); a musical version of the 1937 RKO picture *Stage Door* ($2–2.5 million); *On My Honor* ($1.25–1.3 million); *Pakistan* ($1.5–2.75 million); *Galveston* ($1.75–2.25 million); *Rachel Cade* ($2+ million); and *The Cid* (no estimate).[33] Dozier foresaw the top actors in the business being cast in these pictures, everyone from John Wayne and Marlon Brando to Doris Day and Deborah Kerr. He also added eight smaller projects to the list, pictures that could be made for less than a million and a half.

Shortly afterward O'Shea and Dozier met to discuss all the properties. For the most part, the president agreed with his production chief about the upcoming program. The only eliminations from Dozier's original lineup were *Stage Door* and *The Cid*. The final proposal, which O'Shea forwarded to Tom O'Neil for his approval, retained the other potential blockbusters, plus some of the smaller pictures and a few independent films, bringing the 1957 program total to twenty-four films at a cost of $22,800,000.[34] Interestingly, Dan O'Shea scaled back Dozier's original budget estimate for nearly every production before submitting the proposition to O'Neil. For instance, he reported that *The Naked and the Dead* would cost only $2 million with a top cast.

In seeking O'Neil's support, O'Shea informed him that, even though the producing arm of RKO had to be rebuilt "virtually from scratch," the bustling studio would complete thirteen pictures by the end of November. "We feel that if we do not move aggressively on these [proposed] projects, or at least on the best five or six of them, soon, we will not only lose momentum, endangering some of the projects, but will seriously damage our producing organization which is as good as any in town and better than many," argued the president.[35] Clearly, O'Shea was hoping for a quick green light from the big boss.

Tom O'Neil was disinclined to rush ahead, though he did not express any initial reservations about the 1957 program. In late September Dozier and O'Shea met with him in New York, and the sessions went well. Several productions were approved, and Dozier believed he would soon receive the go-ahead on six other future films, including a remake of *Vivacious Lady* (1938), titled *Bigger Than Both of Us;* an Audie Murphy–project set in the Ozark Mountains; and another Sam Fuller picture, *China Gate*.[36] Before returning to the West Coast, Dozier appeared on national television, where he predicted the best days lay ahead: "I look at the future with eagerness and optimism, and I think I speak for a whole new generation of creative and technical workers in Hollywood. We have a big stake in the future of the picture business, a big personal stake, and that matters very much to us."[37] Shortly thereafter Merv Houser spit out another publicity missive, announcing that RKO was readying fifteen features for filming in late 1956 and 1957.[38]

William Dozier felt so confident about the smooth functioning of his studio that he undertook a trip to Asia later in October. After spending time in Japan, where *Escapade in Japan* was filming, he continued on to Hong Kong. There he received the bad news that a number of lead actors—including Cary Grant, Burt Lancaster, William Holden, Tyrone Power, and James Cagney—had turned down roles in future RKO productions.[39] This was not a good omen.

Other alarming portents had already appeared. *The First Traveling Saleslady*, the initial offering from the new RKO, which had premiered in August, was the first of these. Even Ginger Rogers and Carol Channing (in her motion picture debut) could not breathe any life into Stephen Longstreet and Devery Freeman's humdrum script. James Arness, then one of television's biggest stars, and future luminary Clint Eastwood, cast in a small part, also languished in uninteresting roles, and the picture quickly faded into oblivion. RKO Teleradio needed a box-office rocket to blast off its first program of movies; instead, it tossed out a fizzling cherry bomb.

No studio is ever judged on one picture, so there was still plenty of reason for hope. But the movies that followed in fall 1956—*Back from Eternity, Beyond a Reasonable Doubt*, and *Tension at Table Rock*—were no better. *Back from Eternity* proved to be a disappointing remake of the 1939 B-disaster film, *Five Came Back*. Despite wide screen, a longer running time, and a hefty budget to work with, John Farrow, who certainly knew the material since he also directed *Five Came Back*, fashioned a pallid facsimile of the original. After Terry Turner of the Sales Department viewed *Beyond a Reasonable Doubt*, he bluntly told Dozier he did not think there was any way to market the picture to the public.[40] He was correct; an anticapital punishment treatise wrapped up in a contrived thriller package, it created barely a ripple at the box office, despite the participation of stars Joan Fontaine and Dana Andrews and director Fritz Lang. It would be Lang's last American picture. Likewise, potential spectators gave the cold shoulder to *Tension at Table Rock*, a moody, laconic Western only a notch above the cowboy fare that glutted television channels at this time. The shadows were beginning to lengthen on Gower Street.

Undeterred, the zealous Mervin Houser launched another Icarian press release on November 19. This one promised that RKO would distribute "fourteen film productions, representing a total expenditure of $33,000,000 ... during the first six months of 1957." Among them would be *Jet Pilot*, which Houser described as "one of the costliest pictures ever filmed."[41] For so many reasons, it seemed appropriate that this pet project of Howard Hughes, which had been seven years in the making, would finally arrive in theaters after he was no longer associated with the company. Of course, the debut of *Jet Pilot* had been announced by RKO on several previous occasions, only to be aborted by Hughes before prints were struck. But this time the film would be released as promised—just not by RKO.

Back in December 1955 *Life* magazine published a flattering article about the O'Neils, which contained the following statement from Tom: "Look ... the situation is fundamentally the same as in the rubber business. A rubber factory will turn out various kinds of tires, tubes, all sorts of rubber products, depending on what it can sell. RKO is just a factory, a film factory. TV films, features, industrial films, commercials, educational films, cartoons, it's all the same raw material, film, something happening on the screen. Sure, whatever it is has to be good. You can't sell bum tires and stay in business either."[42] Although one might argue with O'Neil's belief that rubber factories and film studios were "fundamentally the same," he was correct about the importance of quality merchandise. RKO was turning out nothing but "bum" movies and, consequently, would not remain "in business" much longer.

Intimations of the company's demise were contained in a four-page memo written by Tom O'Neil one week after Houser's November 19 press release began to circulate. The document did not mention the poor pictures produced by the new RKO up to that point. Instead, it contained the sort of cost-benefit analysis often generated in business schools and corporate accounting departments. After toting up the noncreative costs of operating the studio ($2.5 million per year) and the costs of maintaining the domestic and foreign distribution operation ($13 million) and adding those costs to interest charges of $700,000 to $800,000 a year, O'Neil took a step back and examined the movie industry as a whole. He was impressed by the economic models adopted by independent companies that released their product through established distributors and by the one major that did not operate a studio:

> Are both fixed production costs and fixed distribution costs necessary? I would say no because there are outfits who are in the production business without any fixed distribution organization such as Goldwyn, Hecht-Lancaster and any number of independent producers who seek distribution through other than their own outlets. There is also one major distributor who has no fixed non-creative production cost or facility, namely, United Artists. It is, therefore, de facto possible for a producer to operate without a fixed distribution facility and a distributor to operate without production facilities.[43]

O'Neil's calculations indicated RKO would require approximately $42 million per year in film rentals just to break even, given the present setup.[44] And since movies were a much less predictable business than automobile tires or even radio and television broadcasting, where advertising brought in a fairly dependable amount of revenue, the numbers made no sense to him. But he had concocted a solution—*eliminate* the distribution network, including its heavy costs. "The entire industry is suffering from an oversupply of distribution facilities and the reduction of one operating unit should not result in any lessening of the total amount of film rentals available to all producers in the aggregate. It is further felt that a further reduction by other members of the industry may result in an increase in efficiency between the producer and the ultimate consumer so that the film business may be able to survive its present-day problems by a simple application of some of the rudimentary principles of business," he reasoned. O'Neil continued, "I am confident that we can produce more pictures with more money concentrated on the quality aspect of production as opposed to the hitchhiker type of unnecessary, inflexible fixed charge that burdens the selling price of our product."[45]

On the surface Tom O'Neil's idea made a lot of sense. The major studios operated distribution exchanges in the same cities throughout the United States and, for the most part, had set up offices or entered into relationships with local suppliers in the same foreign countries. Clearly, a reasonable amount of consolidation could save a great deal of money.

And, thus, Tom O'Neil arrived at the conclusion that he had not only figured out a way to make the movie business work for his RKO Teleradio conglomerate but also unearthed a flaw in the studio system that had eluded most industry leaders, some of whom had been running successful companies since the silent era. O'Neil did not hold much respect for these men, and he didn't expect them to be overly impressed by his insight, since "any status quo in current operating procedure is always the sentimental favorite as to the way in which a business should be operated."[46]

Tom O'Neil's memo was addressed to Dan O'Shea. There is no record of his response, if indeed the RKO president ever committed one to paper. Even if he argued against O'Neil's breakthrough idea, it wouldn't have mattered. The chairman of the board had made up his mind.

O'Neil conveyed the news to company leaders during a meeting in Palm Beach, Florida, in early December. O'Shea; Dozier; executive vice-president Edward L. Walton; studio manager Ray Klune; and Walter Branson, the head of distribution who would soon be out of a job, attended the conclave. Although O'Neil's decision meant RKO was about to forfeit its status as a major studio, the men must have been relieved that the company leader still appeared committed to making movies. On December 5 he announced that RKO would produce at least fourteen "features budgeted at more than $15,000,000 in 1957."[47]

Shortly thereafter the trade papers learned of the company's radical new direction. President O'Shea issued a statement on December 10 that RKO was considering "reshaping its entire production and distribution structure to meet changing trends and conditions in the foreign and domestic markets." A front-page article in *Daily Variety* reported that RKO leaders had held discussions with executives at Universal-International and other companies "looking for some merger of distribution interests for purposes of economy." O'Shea also indicated that RKO would concentrate on four "top budget" productions in early 1957, with five more scheduled to begin shooting later in the year and in 1958—this totaled only nine films.[48] The remainder of the fourteen-film program, as promised by O'Neil on December 5, would evidently be supplied by independents.

A new conception of RKO's place in Hollywood began to emerge after these startling announcements. It appeared the company had decided to reshape itself into the most formidable "independent" in town, concentrating on the making rather than the marketing of A-level movies.[49] But, almost immediately, this image became muddied by activity on Gower Street. Before the end of the year, scores of employees began receiving termination notices.[50] Even heads of some departments were being let go.[51] If the organization was really committed to future production, why was it slashing its studio workforce?

In early 1957 it became apparent that RKO would not be producing many future movies. Both of the company's Story Departments were closed down, and the sacking of studio personnel continued without letup. In his "personal and confidential" memo to Don Moore, the head of the New York Story Department, a downtrodden Bill Dozier instructed Moore to get rid of all his staff because of "our wide-spread curtailment program." That department had, only recently, been resurrected after Howard Hughes originally eliminated it. The last line of Dozier's memo read, "I could go on making long speeches about what an untoward turn of events this is, but that would not be helpful, so I shall refrain from making them."[52]

Why did Tom O'Neil abruptly change his mind and decide to abandon the filmmaking business? It is difficult to say, though the company's desultory productions, most especially its last release of 1956, must have been a contributing factor. *Bundle of Joy*, an expensive musical remake of *Bachelor Mother* (1939), starring the nation's favorite newlyweds, Eddie Fisher and Debbie Reynolds, arrived in theaters just before Christmas. Rushed into production in early summer because of Reynolds's pregnancy, this Norman Taurog–directed confection exceeded its ample budget estimate but still turned out disappointingly. The film completely failed to replicate the charm and wit of the original, which had been a giant hit for the company. Without question, Chairman O'Neil noticed that Dan O'Shea and Bill Dozier were batting zero after their first five productions; amazingly, these pictures were no better than the ones produced under the aegis of Howard Hughes. And he must also have been aware that RKO's share of North American film rentals, which stood at 9 percent in 1949, had fallen to 4 percent in 1956.[53]

News- and trade papers were soon filled with stories concerning the death throes of RKO. *Daily Variety*, for example, ran an article that began: "The fade of RKO as a major entity in the film business became reality today with the official confirmation that the company's domestic distribution will be taken over by [Universal-International], the axing of 800 employees in its 32 exchanges and the virtual shuttering of its studio publicity department."[54] In his mournful obituary for the organization, published by the *Los Angeles Mirror–News*, Dick Williams stated that General Tire intended to "move one of its tire company auxiliaries" onto the Gower Street lot, whose fifteen sound stages were now empty.[55] "The RKO debacle again proves that inexperience and bad management in the production and distribution of motion pictures are more conducive to a quicker death than in any other business," wrote W. R. Wilkerson of the *Hollywood Reporter*. He continued, "The O'Neils have been a great business success in American industry, BUT they didn't know anything about the picture business and this lack of knowledge sank a company that, with proper experience and

25. Director Norman Taurog *(left)* and producer Edmund Grainger *(right)* watch Eddie Fisher and Debbie Reynolds record songs for *Bundle of Joy*. Courtesy of the USC Cinematic Arts Library.

good management . . . could have [been] . . . profitable . . . instead of an outright failure." The blustery Wilkerson ascribed none of the blame to Howard Hughes, whom he had been defending for years.[56]

Surprisingly, Tom O'Neil denied the rumors that RKO was headed for liquidation. At a press conference on January 24, O'Neil revealed that RKO Teleradio had lost $4.5 million in 1955 and $1.5 million in 1956 but stated "emphatically that RKO would continue to produce features."[57] After explaining how much the company would save by contracting with Universal to handle distribution of its product, O'Neil explained, "we are actually freeing more money for investment in the direct creative costs of RKO film production."[58] The company even took out a full-page ad in *Daily Variety* on January 28, explaining that the new approach could, potentially, "reduce . . . fixed domestic overhead by 53% for any given picture." It also maintained, "Our decisions on distribution and production are made with one goal in mind—to make better motion pictures more efficiently. This will benefit the public and the motion picture exhibitor as well as ourselves."[59]

Balderdash. O'Neil had no intention of redirecting the savings realized by closing down RKO distribution into the making of better and more expensive future movies, though he did need to keep alive the pretense that RKO would continue to be an operating motion picture production company. There were a number of reasons for this, including the momentum built up by the O'Shea-Dozier combo—the corporation had several films in postproduction, others about to roll, and commitments to produce more. And, for various technical reasons, it would require about three years to close down its foreign operations. In addition, to take full advantage of its substantial tax losses, RKO had to continue putting out movies for at least three more years.

Behind the scenes the executives were not spending much time planning future pictures. Rather, they were mostly concerned with how to handle severance for all the pink-slipped employees and what to do about two obvious white elephants: RKO's Gower Street and Culver City studios. With respect to the former issue, workers received at least two weeks' severance pay and an additional vacation allowance of one to two weeks' salary when they were let go. It wasn't much, especially for those who had toiled at RKO for many years, but studio manager Ray Klune told Dan O'Shea that "we have had practically no cases of individual employees complaining that they have been unsatisfactorily treated in the matter of termination procedure."[60]

Klune was also tasked with analyzing the studio situation. Initially, he recommended that the company "dispose of the Culver City property at the earliest possible moment" and "operate the Gower Street studio as a servicing studio." In other words, Ray Klune felt that RKO Pathe should be sold right away, with Gower Street transformed into a rental plant, where RKO would retain only sufficient staff to make it attractive to prospective users. Tom O'Neil, however, seemed determined to get both studios off his books. Klune's notion of operating Gower Street as a rental facility did not appeal to him, even though 1957 did not look like a good year to dispose of it. As Klune suggested, "a seller's market for motion picture producing facilities might be much more attractive 3 to 5 years hence than it is today." Consequently, O'Neil began to think about some sort of "4-wall deal."[61] In this scenario RKO would eliminate all its Gower Street personnel and then rent the studio to a single operator, whose staff would run it, most likely, as a "servicing studio."[62] At some future and, presumably, more propitious date, the company would then sell it.

But no matter which way O'Neil turned, collateral problems popped up. His determination to eliminate workers as rapidly as possible took its toll on the uncompleted pictures. In mid-February *Run of the Arrow, The Unholy Wife, I Married a Woman, The Girl Most Likely, Escapade in Japan,* and *Jet Pilot* were in various stages of postproduction, while *Stage Struck* was still shooting. But every studio department was now either severely understaffed or closed altogether—no one was home at the Property, Drapery, Wardrobe, or Construction Departments, for instance, which literally had padlocks on their doors. The few workers left in the Accounting and Insurance Departments were drowning in paperwork.[63] Thus, finishing Dozier's movies had become an ordeal.

Eventually they were completed, and most distributed during the year by Universal. There wasn't a winner among them. They ran the gamut from the dreadful Red Skelton comedy, *Public Pigeon No. 1*, to the offbeat Sam Fuller Western, *Run of the Arrow*, which, unfortunately, had little popular appeal. Ironically, the one picture that actually paid off at the box office was the seven-year wonder, *Jet Pilot*. A nutty mishmash of Howard Hughes obsessions (aviation, communism, brainwashing, Palm Springs, large-breasted women), it demonstrated how important a top star could be to a movie's commercial appeal. Box-office champion John Wayne, with assistance from Janet Leigh, carried this turkey to profitability on his broad shoulders, as he had Hughes's other laughable epic, *The Conqueror*.[64]

That picture, one of RKO's final releases before distribution migrated to Universal, was considerably worse than *Jet Pilot*. A Chicago critic branded *The Conqueror* a "plotless, pointless, utterly boring 12th century tale of conquest by rape and murder" and a "monstrous waste of money and talent."[65] The film's reputation has not improved with time; it merits a prime spot in books listing the worst movies ever made.[66] While this level of opprobrium may have bothered Hughes, he was undoubtedly comforted by the revenue that came rolling in, since he had purchased both films from RKO before disappearing from the Hollywood scene.

Although no one should have expected the mediocre 1957 releases to be highly successful, Tom O'Neil began to believe that Universal-International's handling of them had a lot to do with their weak performances. At some point he must have realized why the other studio heads scoffed when he decided his distribution arm was dispensable. Naturally, a company was going to favor its homegrown product over the films it was marketing for other organizations. RKO had done that with all the independent films it distributed through the years. The only indie producers accorded special treatment were Sam Goldwyn and Walt Disney, and even they (particularly the hard-to-please Goldwyn) often felt their pictures were treated as second-class merchandise. Eventually, RKO sued Universal, their agreement ended after eleven releases, and the few remaining pictures that dribbled out between 1958 and 1960 were distributed by several different organizations, including Warner Bros., Columbia, and Disney's new setup, Buena Vista. The company's last major production would be *The Naked and the Dead*, which Warner Bros. marketed in August 1958.

Tom O'Neil's determination to rid himself of the studios did not go well either. No one expressed any serious interest in operating the Gower Street lot on a "4-wall" basis. There were some feelers concerning outright purchase. The audacious writer-director Sam Fuller, who claimed to be in league with Twentieth Century–Fox president Spyros Skouras, contacted Ray Klune to find out how much RKO Teleradio would require for Gower Street.[67] Klune reckoned $12 million would be acceptable, though this was just to kick off negotiations; he knew full well that no one was going to pay that much for a movie studio that had been allowed to deteriorate for years.[68] A more bizarre inquiry came from one Michael Conrad, who visited Klune in his studio office, along with attorney Charles L. Nichols and Virginia Doak of the Virginia Doak Agency. Conrad purported to represent "Detroit automobile people . . . anxious and determined to get into the picture business." The discussions were going fine until Conrad announced that his backers "wanted to make 300 films in the period of 18 months." Ray Klune then pointed out "that such activity as this would require all of the facilities in Hollywood, not just our own Gower Street or our Gower Street and Culver City plants."[69] The session ended with promises of a meeting within a week with President O'Shea in New York, but nothing ever developed.

While a buyer was sought, Klune continued to eliminate personnel until only a skeleton crew remained on Gower Street. By early fall 1957 the Sound, Music, Camera, Art, and Publicity Departments, among others, had all been shuttered. Indeed, the only significant department left was editing, now composed of three people: department head Jim Wilkinson, his secretary and file clerk Helen Seitz, and Kenny Kling, who had charge of the vaults and film handling.[70] Domestic and foreign distribution of RKO pictures, as well as the demands of the C&C deal, meant their services would be needed until the company disposed of the studios.

That finally happened in November, when Desilu, the successful television company owned by Desi Arnaz and Lucille Ball, bought both studios. Several layers of ironic varnish coated the final sale documents. RKO motion picture stages would soon be used to shoot television series; the rapid growth of television, unquestionably, had played a role in the company's decline. And Ball, who made more than twenty features for RKO in the 1930s and

1940s without ever approaching the upper reaches of fan popularity, was now one of the biggest stars in the world, able to purchase her old lot and move into the dressing room once occupied by her idol, Ginger Rogers. Even though Lucy may have resented the inability of RKO's former leaders to turn her into a "picture personality" during her younger days, she and husband Desi still felt nostalgic about the Gower Street facility—they met there on the set of the studio's musical film, *Too Many Girls* (1940).

Lucy and Desi's homecoming took place on January 27, 1958, when escrow closed and Desilu took possession of the lots. They had paid $6,150,000 for the two properties (plus the "Forty Acres" back lot in Culver City), a bargain price that reflected Tom O'Neil's stony determination to put his Hollywood escapade behind him. Arnaz and Ball would have to spend a good deal more money to refurbish both studios, but, soon enough, more than twenty-five Desilu programs would begin taking shape in RKO's old bungalows and on its sets.[71] Less than a year later Cecil Smith of the *Los Angeles Times* called Desilu a "colossus" and described the studios as throbbing with activity.[72]

Where had Tom O'Neil and his associates gone wrong in their effort to revitalize RKO? Perhaps their biggest mistake was undue haste. One can certainly understand why they felt compelled to move rapidly—RKO's status as a major studio had been so decimated by the Hughes regime that immediate action seemed obligatory to rebuild its standing in Hollywood. In addition, everyone knew that O'Neil's primary interest in the company had been its backlog of completed motion pictures, not its potential as a production outfit going forward. Thus, to demonstrate his commitment to future RKO product, O'Neil decided his new organization had best begin turning out features right away.

But given the sad state of affairs at 780 Gower Street, the men handed the job had little to work with. Consequently, O'Shea, Glett, and Dozier made a number of rapid, questionable decisions. The first was to rush bad scripts into production, including several remakes of earlier RKO productions. Most of these added color and wide screen, plus other new elements, to the original narratives in an attempt to disguise the fact they were actually retreads. *Bundle of Joy* and *The Girl Most Likely* turned out to be indifferent musical versions of *Bachelor Mother* (1939) and *Tom, Dick, and Harry* (1941). *Back from Eternity* and *Stage Struck* attempted to update *Five Came Back* (1939) and *Morning Glory* (1933) without much success. And *The Unholy Wife*, inspired by *They Knew What They Wanted* (1940), quickly soured into rotten fruit, despite the presence of Diana Dors and a risqué advertising campaign that must have brought a smile to Howard

Hughes's face. The new RKO's original films weren't any better, particularly its embarrassing comedies: *The First Traveling Saleslady, Public Pigeon No. 1,* and *I Married a Woman.*

Although the poor scripts combined with less-than-scintillating direction meant these pictures had little chance of success, the studio's casting choices contributed to their failures. Most of the "stars" of the RKO Teleradio productions were either past their prime (Ginger Rogers, Joan Fontaine, Dana Andrews, Jane Powell, Henry Fonda) or would never develop into box-office luminaries (Rod Steiger, Red Skelton, Barry Nelson, James MacArthur, Glynnis Johns, Cameron Mitchell, Susan Strasberg, George Gobel). The studio had high hopes for pop music star Eddie Fisher, who made his movie debut in *Bundle of Joy* opposite his wife, Debbie Reynolds; unfortunately, the film demonstrated that acting was not his forte.

In short, it would have been more sensible to rebuild RKO movie production slowly and thoughtfully, relying on the acquisition of independent product to keep the wheels of distribution revolving while stronger in-house pictures were developed. The company's headlong plunge back into the always-hazardous waters of studio filmmaking garnered a great deal of publicity but ultimately capsized the vessel. O'Shea, Glett, and Dozier must shoulder a good deal of the responsibility for this, but the captain who abandoned his ship was Tom O'Neil.

O'Neil learned the principles of business at his father's hip and at Holy Cross College, where he majored in economics. He had demonstrated solid leadership skills during the period when he broadened the General Tire empire into the radio and television arenas. O'Neil seemed initially intoxicated by the glamorous world of moviemaking, entertaining visions of becoming one of the trendsetters in "new Hollywood," and he must have enjoyed all the adulation he received when it appeared he had miraculously resuscitated RKO. But then both his financial projections and his initial movies began to look inauspicious, and he quickly threw in the towel. O'Neil failed, not because he didn't know anything about the motion picture business, as W.R. Wilkerson contended. He failed because he was too impatient, too unwilling to ride out RKO Teleradio's initial difficulties. Given reasonable recovery time and enlightened management, the company might have survived and even flourished. United Artists, which had been close to collapse in the late 1940s, was now one of the best organizations in the business, thanks to the leadership of Arthur Krim and Robert Benjamin. If they had merged their company with RKO at some point in the 1950s, as some observers suggested could happen, this corporate history might have a very different ending.

After RKO surrendered the old studio to Desi Arnaz and Lucille Ball, a number of RKO's former personnel were hired by the new proprietors. Still, it was surely a sad day for many when the RKO sign on the old water tower, with its distinctive lightning bolt trademark, was replaced by a sparkling new one that read: DESILU!

With the exception of the war years, RKO had never been a stable company, particularly at the executive level, but a surprising number of loyal employees did spend most of their lives working for the organization. The aforementioned Jim Wilkinson and Helen Seitz of the Editing Department first reported for duty at 780 Gower Street in 1920 and 1924, respectively, when the studio was known as Robertson-Cole and then FBO. Others who put in more than twenty-five years there included Bill Eglinton, head of the Camera Department; John Aalberg, head of the Sound Department, Linwood Dunn, the camera-effects magician; Roy Webb, who wrote more musical scores for RKO films than any other composer; Ben Bender of accounting, who worked his way up to the position of studio comptroller; and Harry J. Wild and Nicholas Musuraca, two of the best cinematographers in Hollywood. They were among a sizable group of talented people who held on tenaciously during RKO's many tempestuous days, always doing their best to make the company a first-rate purveyor of celluloid entertainment. But now the dazzling RKO achievements of Katharine Hepburn, Fred Astaire, Ginger Rogers, Victor McLaglen, Charles Laughton, Cary Grant, Irene Dunne, Orson Welles, Maureen O'Hara, Joan Fontaine, Robert Mitchum, Robert Ryan, David Selznick, Pandro Berman, Merian C. Cooper, John Ford, George Stevens, Mark Sandrich, Gregory La Cava, Alfred Hitchcock, Val Lewton, Leo McCarey, Jacques Tourneur, Frank Capra, Robert Wise, Nicholas Ray, and so many others were past history, and no one would ever have an opportunity to contribute to the RKO legacy. One of the most captivating dream factories in motion picture history expired in 1957.

Epilogue

In 1952 RKO bought the rights to produce a movie based on Agatha Christie's *The Mousetrap*. Christie's play had recently opened on the British stage, and the contract stipulated that a film version could be made as soon as it ended its run. A landmark murder mystery, *The Mousetrap* has played continuously in the West End of London ever since, racking up more than twenty-five thousand performances. One is tempted to invoke this story as a prime example of the bad luck that dogged RKO throughout its existence. There are plenty of other examples, such as the untimely death of Charles Koerner in 1946. But, in truth, RKO's disappearance as a major movie company after twenty-nine years in the business was not the result of bad luck or bad timing. As my research demonstrates, RKO expired because of bad management.

Although I have concentrated on the often disappointing performances of the corporate presidents and production heads of the organization, the ultimate blame for RKO's failure rests with the five businessmen who placed these individuals in their positions. In a chronicle replete with many ironies, perhaps the most surprising is that these five tycoons were highly successful in their other money-producing endeavors yet fumbled their attempts to build RKO into a leading motion picture company. As James MacGregor Burns states in his classic study, *Leadership:* "All leaders are actual or potential power holders, but not all power holders are leaders."[1] The failed five all held the power over RKO at different times, but none wielded it wisely; they never provided the supervision that RKO required.

David Sarnoff, the dynamic president of Radio Corporation of America, made the deals that brought RKO into existence in 1928. But it was a bad portent that his initial motivation was to sell RCA sound equipment, not create successful movies. Nevertheless, Sarnoff expected the new company to become a profit center and made sure it had distribution and exhibition capabilities as well as a production plant. Unfortunately, he never conducted a careful study of the motion picture business. If he had, he would have known better than to hire Hiram Brown as RKO's first corporate president. Brown's background was in the leather trade, and he soon discovered that pedaling movies was quite different than pedaling shoes. At least Brown and Sarnoff chose an industry veteran, writer-producer William LeBaron, and put him in charge of the studio. But LeBaron had great difficulty pulling free of the protocols of silent filmmaking and recognizing and hiring the talent necessary to prosper in talking pictures. When the Depression started to hammer Hollywood in late 1930, RKO had already fallen far behind most of its competitors in the quality of its product.

Sarnoff recognized his initial errors and forced Brown out in 1932. But then he made another mistake, which turned out to be just as grave. He placed one of his close associates, Merlin "Deac" Aylesworth, in charge of RKO. Sarnoff did not ask Aylesworth to give up his position as head of the National Broadcasting Company and its two nationwide radio networks, which RCA controlled. Rather, he expected the new RKO president to handle the job on a part-time basis during one of the most challenging periods in American movie history. Is it any wonder that RKO would soon be bankrupt?

Aylesworth had nothing to do with the hiring of David O. Selznick, who replaced William LeBaron at the Gower Street studio. Sarnoff made this brilliant decision, which quickly led to better pictures and the beginnings of a formidable stock company, featuring Katharine Hepburn, Fred Astaire, and others. But then David Sarnoff negated his master stroke, backing Aylesworth's successful effort to get rid of Selznick after he had been RKO's executive producer for only a year and a half. Before the end of the decade, Selznick would make *Gone with the Wind* and be recognized as one of the greatest producers in Hollywood history.

Sarnoff's growing discontent with the movie business and with RKO, which went into receivership in 1933, was signaled by his decision to sell a substantial portion of RKO stock to **Floyd Odlum** in 1935. A value investor whose Atlas Corporation had acquired large stock positions in a number of different business concerns, Odlum recognized that, even though RKO showed no signs of emerging from receivership, its fortunes were rising. A strict cost-cutting campaign had pared company expenses, its popular Astaire-Rogers musicals were the envy of Hollywood, and the corporation was beginning to post profits again.

Odlum soon asserted himself, booting Aylesworth upstairs and replacing him with lawyer Leo Spitz. Odlum and Spitz then chose Sam Briskin of

Columbia Pictures to take over the studio. A pattern had now emerged—for the third consecutive time, RKO placed a person (Spitz) who had no significant industry experience in the top company job and hired another (Briskin) who had never been a creative executive to head up its film production operations. Soon enough, the abrasive Briskin allowed the popularity of RKO's pictures to deteriorate, and the company's financial performance started to slide.

Briskin gave up and returned to Columbia in 1937, whereupon Spitz and Odlum made a more enlightened move. They placed RKO's top producer, Pandro Berman, in charge of the Gower Street operations. Berman, who had piloted most of the Astaire-Rogers and Hepburn pictures and preferred making one film at a time, liked and respected Leo Spitz and reluctantly agreed to take on the formidable task of running the entire studio. Like Selznick before him, Berman's efforts soon resulted in higher-quality RKO movies.

Unfortunately, another famous man now injected himself into the RKO narrative. The Rockefellers held a substantial block of RKO stock and were poised to acquire even more when the receivership period finally came to an end. Most of the family members expressed little interest in the Hollywood company, but **Nelson Rockefeller** was a patron of the arts, fascinated by the latest developments in several different art forms. Perhaps believing he could help the cinema take its place beside painting, sculpture, music, and literature as a recognized conduit of distinctive aesthetic expression, Nelson decided to push RKO in a new direction.

With the backing of David Sarnoff and to the chagrin of Floyd Odlum, Rockefeller brushed aside Leo Spitz and replaced him with George J. Schaefer, the energetic head of distribution at United Artists. Schaefer arrived in late 1938, just as Pandro Berman's efforts were beginning to bear fruit. The following year—one of the best in RKO history—would feature *Gunga Din, Love Affair, Bachelor Mother,* and *The Hunchback of Notre Dame,* among other fine pictures. Nevertheless, Schaefer decided he should make all important production decisions, as well as oversee distribution and exhibition, and his intrusion into Pandro Berman's bailiwick rankled the studio chief. He quit in 1939.

Soon after Berman left for MGM, RKO pulled out of receivership, but the celebrations were short-lived. Once again the company's fortunes began to tumble. Partially to please his patron Nelson Rockefeller but mostly because he wanted RKO to become known for high-quality product, Schaefer invested large sums in prestigious literary properties and hired a number of new producers, several of whom had never made Hollywood pictures before. The resultant movies did not turn out well. Film rentals declined precipitously and even the president's most famous protégé, Orson Welles, whose initial film was the renowned *Citizen Kane*, proved to be a liability rather than an asset. Consequently, six months after America's entry into World War II, RKO was again close to bankruptcy.

By this time David Sarnoff and the Rockefellers were fed up with RKO. Floyd Odlum, however, was not. He reasserted himself, replacing Schaefer with his longtime associate N. Peter Rathvon, who partnered with new production chief, Charles Koerner, to form the best team of executives in RKO history. To the surprise of many, these two men turned the organization around quickly; by the end of 1943 RKO's pictures had been embraced by thousands of spectators, it was making eye-popping profits, and its stock was a Wall Street darling.

One of the company's deficiencies had always been its limited roster of contract acting talent. Though Koerner never managed to pull together a cadre of stars that could equal those of MGM, Paramount, Warner Bros., or Twentieth Century–Fox, he took advantage of changing industry conditions to stud company releases with such figures as Cary Grant, Jean Arthur, John Wayne, and Olivia de Havilland. He also fostered harmonious working conditions at the studio. When the war ended, RKO was riding high, now considered one of the best places to work in the movie capital.

Sadly, less than six months later, Charles Koerner died suddenly. Peter Rathvon then decided to move to the West Coast and take over the studio duties; this decision was the most consequential slip-up made by an otherwise superior corporate president. In less than a year, Rathvon realized that superintending a full slate of productions was not his forte and, with Odlum's approval, hired Dore Schary as executive producer.

Schary had a solid record as a writer and producer and relished the opportunity to head up a major studio. He believed that the right movies could have a salutary effect on American society, as well as yield profits, so he set about making the sort of progressive films that he favored. But Schary began his new job in a most unfortunate year. The war-fueled boom in moviegoing ended in 1947, and, suddenly, many of RKO's large-budget films began to lose alarming amounts of money. In addition, the House Un-American Activities Committee investigation into communist infiltration of Hollywood that year tainted the entire industry and forced RKO to dismiss Edward Dmytryk and Adrian Scott, two of its most talented personnel. It also made the liberal Schary, who had opposed the subsequent blacklisting of suspected communists, a lightning rod of controversy.

Unsentimental businessman Floyd Odlum did not like any of this, but he was especially upset by RKO's stock price, which had been sliding for more than a year. Thus, it came as no surprise when he sold Atlas's controlling position in RKO in May 1948. In many ways, Odlum was the best of RKO's behind-the-scenes powers. His initial management team of Leo Spitz and Sam Briskin had been a dud, but he did better with Spitz-Berman and hit a home run the third time, when he paired Rathvon and Koerner. Nevertheless, Odlum's contributions to the betterment of RKO will always be overshadowed by his decision to sell the Atlas stock to Howard Hughes. Both Rathvon and Schary attempted to convince him that turning RKO over to this peculiar millionaire would be a mistake. But, despite a better offer he received at the time, Floyd Odlum ceded the power to the famous aviator, thereby making the biggest blunder in the history of RKO.

There is no need to spend additional space ruminating on the disastrous stewardship of **Howard Hughes.** His lethal management style was composed of indecisiveness, procrastination, bad ideas, terrible taste, and an inability to trust the competency of others. Isolated from the day-to-day activities of his studio, surrounded by yes men, the solipsistic Hughes carried on as if he were one of the true visionaries in cinema history. Instead, he will be remembered as the only man who single-handedly destroyed a major motion picture company.

Tom O'Neil could have prevented RKO's demise. He had good intentions but lacked the expertise and the patience to resurrect the studio. O'Neil placed well-qualified men in the top jobs at the company and supported their efforts . . . for a year and a half. But when he finally realized how badly damaged the company was and suffered through the initial slate of poor films turned out by his handpicked executives, O'Neil washed his hands of Hollywood, selling the studios for a bargain price. Although hardly an incompetent, as his success at building General (later RKO) Teleradio attests, O'Neil's résumé contained the same hole as the four other men who controlled the corporation over time. He was an outsider in an industry run by men who grew up with the movies and built them into a successful business. Their specialized knowledge acquired through many years of the industry's evolution was something O'Neil could not duplicate, and he had neither the temperament nor the stamina for on-the-job training.

Although RKO died in 1957, it lives on in the minds of many who treasure the films of Hollywood's golden era. Few mourn other important twentieth-century companies that also have vanished, such as General Foods, Montgomery-Ward, American Motors, and Hughes's Trans World Airlines. But the studio that manufactured *King Kong, Top Hat, Citizen Kane,* and *It's a Wonderful Life* occupies a special place in the collective memory of

Americans, as well as many foreign lovers of the cinema. The nostalgic resurrection of RKO in such postmodern films as *The Rocky Horror Picture Show* (1975) and *The Purple Rose of Cairo* (1985) verifies that the company with the boisterous logo—a mighty radio tower straddling the globe—will never disappear. RKO continues to stand as tall as that tower—a symbol of a time when cinematic creativity was at its peak, and the entire world embraced Hollywood movies.

Notes

PREFACE

1. Richard B. Jewell, *RKO Radio Pictures: A Titan Is Born* (Berkeley: University of California Press, 2012), 4–6.
2. Bernard Eisenschitz, *Nicholas Ray: An American Journey* (London: Faber and Faber, 1993), 165.

CHAPTER 1

1. Andrew Roberts, *The Storm of War: A New History of the Second World War* (New York: HarperCollins, 2011), 200.
2. George Schaefer to Charles Koerner, 4 June 1942. All unsourced references are to letters and other documents found in the RKO Corporate Archive. See the preface to this text.
3. N. Peter Rathvon to Charles Koerner, 10 July 1942.
4. "Floyd Odlum Takes Over," *Time*, 22 June 1942, 78–79.
5. "Rathvon, Depinet, Koerner Head RKO; Smith Resigns," *Motion Picture Herald*, 4 July 1942, 23.
6. In October one trade paper described Koerner's job as the "hottest spot . . . in the industry." "RKO Gets New Deal," *Daily Variety*, ninth anniversary ed., October 1942.
7. Charles Koerner, "Address to Studio Employees," ca. June 1942.
8. Rathvon to Koerner, 27 June 1942.
9. "Matters to Be Discussed at Department Heads Meeting," 5 November 1942.
10. Jack Moss, telegram to George Schaefer, 2 June 1942.
11. The Mexican Spitfire comedies, starring Lupe Velez, were a farcical series of slapstick movies produced by RKO between 1939 and 1943.
12. These figures and all unsourced financial data of this kind are taken from the C. J. Tevlin Ledger—see the preface.

13. Joseph McBride, *Orson Welles* (New York: Viking, 1972), 55.
14. Sid Rogell, memorandum to Jim Wilkinson, 10 December 1942.
15. Dannis Peary, "Mark Robson Remembers RKO," *Velvet Light Trap* 10 (Fall 1973): 34.
16. Earl Rettig to George Schaefer, 14 May 1942.
17. Lynn Shores to Walter Daniels, 26 June 1942, 11 July 1942.
18. Gordon Youngman, telegram to Ross R. Hastings, 25 June 1942.
19. Ross R. Hastings, memorandum to Charles Koerner, 11 July 1942. Nine days earlier studio lawyer Gordon Youngman had recommended a countersuit against Welles if he did decide to sue, because "the damage he has caused us is greater than any possible damage we could have caused him." Youngman, memorandum to N. Peter Rathvon, 2 July 1942.
20. "The Gate," *Time*, 20 July 1942, 44.
21. Thomas F. Brady, "Welles versus Hollywood Again," *New York Times*, 12 July 1942, sec. 8, p. 3.
22. T. Latta McCray, memorandum to N. Peter Rathvon, 23 October 1946.
23. Charles Koerner to Pare Lorentz, 3 July 1942.
24. Edwin Schallert, "R.K.O. May Brush Off Another 'Revolutionist,'" *Los Angeles Times*, 14 July 1942, 13.
25. "Supreme Court Rejects Effort to Remove Bilbo," *Los Angeles Times*, 15 October 1946, 7.
26. Pare Lorentz, *FDR's Moviemaker: Memoirs and Scripts* (Reno: University of Nevada Press, 1992); Robert L. Snyder, *Pare Lorentz and the Documentary Film* (Reno: University of Nevada Press, 1994).
27. Aljean Harmetz, "Hollywood Hails Lorentz, Documentary Pioneer," *New York Times*, 22 October 1981, C22.
28. Philip K. Scheuer, for example, labeled Lorentz "one of those whose heads were lopped off shortly after Charles Koerner, veteran theater man, took over the reins of R.K.O. Another was Orson Welles." "R.K.O. Arranging to 'Save' Lorentz Picture," *Los Angeles Times*, 6 October 1942, 15. Later, Scheuer would add, "Shabbiest treatment [of 1942] was accorded Orson Welles and Pare Lorentz, producer-directors, who were broken, as it were, on the wheel of Hollywood—and, more specifically, R.K.O.'s—intolerance." "Town Called Hollywood," *Los Angeles Times*, 27 December 1942, 5.
29. Thomas F. Brady, "Late Summer House-Cleaning in Hollywood," *New York Times*, 30 August 1942, sec. 8, p. 3.
30. Terry Ramsaye, "Miracle Man," *Motion Picture Herald*, 21 November 1942, 7.
31. Brady, "House-Cleaning in Hollywood."
32. Charles Koerner to Edwin L. Weisl, 21 September 1942.
33. "New $3,000,000 Loan for RKO," *Variety*, 29 July 1942, 5.
34. "Aid from Britain," *Motion Picture Herald*, 22 August 1942, 8.
35. Rathvon to Koerner, 22 October 1942.
36. Charles Koerner to N. Peter Rathvon, 26 October 1942.

37. Ned Depinet to Hugh L. Ducker, 19 July 1943. Floyd Odlum had recommended taking the large write-off in 1942 because that would enable the corporation to report much higher earnings in the following year if business remained strong. Koerner to Rathvon, 22 December 1942.

38. "War Restrictions Reshape Trade Economy in Year," *Motion Picture Herald*, 2 January 1943, 26.

39. Floyd Odlum to Charles Koerner, 17 August 1942.

40. Floyd Odlum, memorandum to Charles Koerner, 30 September 1942.

41. David Hempstead, memorandum to Charles Koerner, 6 October 1942.

42. By the end of the war, it was estimated that U.S. productivity was almost half that of the rest of the world combined. Thomas Schatz, *Boom and Bust: American Cinema in the 1940s* (Berkeley: University of California Press, 1997), 286.

43. "First of RKO's 'America' Shorts Ready October 23rd," *Motion Picture Herald*, 3 October 1942, 51; "RKO Shows John Smith, Soldier, in First 'This Is America' Short," *Motion Picture Herald*, 17 October 1942, 15. After RKO stopped distributing the *March of Time*, Twentieth Century–Fox began releasing the documentary series.

44. Ned Depinet to Charles Koerner, 21 December 1941.

45. "Koerner Says Pix 'Indestructible' Despite War, Etc.," *Variety*, 13 January 1943, 5.

46. Koerner to Rathvon, 5 March 1943.

47. Charles Koerner to Harry Warner, 4 February 1943.

48. In the five years leading up to America's entry into the war, the Big Five companies averaged fifty releases per year; from 1942 to 1946 they averaged thirty. Schatz, *Boom and Bust*, 170.

49. Rathvon to Koerner, 19 March 1943.

50. Koerner to Rathvon, 24 March 1943.

51. Ibid., 20 October 1942.

52. "Cinema," *Time*, 9 August 1943, 94.

53. Clayton R. Koppes and Gregory D. Black, *Hollywood Goes to War* (New York: Free Press, 1987), 130.

54. Hedda Hopper, Looking at Hollywood, *Los Angeles Times*, 4 October 1943, A8.

55. "R.K.O. Security Offering Made," *Los Angeles Times*, 16 April 1943, 20.

56. Russ Merritt, "R.K.O. Radio: The Little Studio That Couldn't," *Marquee Theatre* (Madison, WI: WHA-TV, 1973), 19.

57. Philip K. Scheuer, "Director, Freed from Snake Pit, Takes Talent on Trip to Fame," *Los Angeles Times*, 10 June 1951, D1.

58. Edmund Bansak, *Fearing the Dark: The Val Lewton Career* (Jefferson, NC: McFarland, 2003), 68; Chris Fugiwara, *Jacques Tourneur: The Cinema of Nightfall* (Jefferson, NC: McFarland, 2001), 72; Joel E. Siegel, *Val Lewton: The Reality of Terror* (New York: Viking, 1972), 38.

59. Bansak, *Fearing the Dark*, 129.

60. "Odlum Named Chairman of R.K.O. Board," *Los Angeles Times*, 3 June 1943, 18.
61. "Six Tinters in RKO '43–'44 Lineup of Forty Features," *Variety*, 14 July 1943, 12.
62. Koerner to Rathvon, 8 October 1943.
63. "Film Costs Up 25% Says RKO Head," *Variety*, 29 October 1943, 5.
64. "Radio-Keith-Orpheum Corporation Annual Report for 1943," 25 May 1944.
65. Rathvon to Koerner, 30 December 1943.
66. "RKO Ratifies 7-Year Deal for C.W. Koerner," *Variety*, 28 April 1943, 5.
67. Koerner also hired Odets's partner from the Group Theatre days, Harold Clurman. They collaborated on *Deadline at Dawn*, a 1946 release written by Odets and directed by Clurman.
68. "R.K.O. Builds London Inside," *Los Angeles Times*, 31 October 1944, 11.
69. Cary Grant never won an Oscar.
70. Koerner to Rathvon, 21 January 1944, 21 March 1944.
71. Ibid., 21 March 1944. RKO later had to write off, as a dead loss, $136,666.66 it paid Ginger Rogers to star in *The Gibson Girl*. Norman Freeman to Ned Depinet, 1 April 1946.
72. Edwin Schallert, "Betty Hutton, Bracken Comedy-Musical Team," *Los Angeles Times*, 16 February 1944, A10. *Mama's Bank Account* would instead be mounted as a Broadway play titled *I Remember Mama*, before finally reaching the screen in 1948.
73. Koerner to Rathvon, 7 April 1944, 20 September 1944. Koerner's efforts were only temporarily effective. Greer and Vallee divorced later in 1944, Grant and Hutton split up in 1945, and Lamarr's marriage to Loder ended in 1947.
74. "Chest Drive Tops Goal in Los Angeles," *Los Angeles Times*, 15 November 1944, 1.
75. Charles Koerner, memorandum to William Dozier, 6 September 1944.
76. Koerner to Rathvon, 7 April 1944. In September, Koerner called Dozier "by far the most valuable asset we could possibly get." Koerner to Rathvon, 20 September 1944.
77. Bansak, *Fearing the Dark*, 253.
78. Koppes and Black, *Hollywood Goes to War*, 165.
79. Unfortunately, *Tender Comrade* would take on a sinister coloration in the postwar era, as discussed in chapter 3.
80. Koerner to Rathvon, 6 May 1943.
81. Gary Fishgall, *Gregory Peck: A Biography* (New York: Scribner, 2002), 90.
82. Koerner to Rathvon, 22 December 1944.
83. "Radio-Keith-Orpheum Corporation Annual Report for 1944," 24 May 1945.
84. "'Goon Squad' Tactics Reported in Film Strike," *Los Angeles Times*, 30 March 1945, A2.
85. B.D. Bender to W.H. Clark, 23 October 1945; William Dozier, telegram to Charles Koerner, 23 October 1945.

86. Ralph Roddy, "After a Costly Film Studio Snarl H'wood Faces Still Further Labor Strife in '46 with 20,000 Workers," *Variety*, 9 January 1946, 79. For a succinct overview of the strike of 1945, see Schatz, *Boom and Bust*, 164–68.

87. Koerner to Rathvon, 2 May 1945.

88. Edwin Schallert, "Capra, Wyler Company Aligned with R.K.O.," *Los Angeles Times*, 23 August 1945, A3.

89. RKO had already used the story as the basis for *The Falcon Takes Over* in 1942.

90. The title of the film was changed from *Farewell, My Lovely* to *Murder, My Sweet* because company officials feared the original title would suggest the picture was just another frothy Dick Powell musical rather than an expressionistic crime drama.

91. Koerner to Rathvon, 25 July 1945.

92. Charles Koerner, "Agenda," 11 August 1945.

93. Ibid.

94. Koerner to Rathvon, 24 August 1945.

95. Charles Koerner, cablegram to William Dozier, 18 September 1945.

96. William Dozier to Charles Koerner, 23 October 1945.

97. The official name of the complex was Estudios Churubusco Azteca.

98. One report indicated that "RKO is understood to have put $1,500,000 of its own money into the project and borrowed an equal amount from a Mexican bank for the enterprise." Hollywood Inside, *Daily Variety*, 17 August 1944, 2.

99. Koerner to Rathvon, 19 December 1945.

100. "Picture Industry in Koerner Tribute; RKO Veepee Dies in Hollywood at 49," *Variety*, 6 February 1946, 4.

101. Rathvon to Koerner, 11 October 1943.

102. Hopper, Looking at Hollywood, 19 February 1946, A2.

103. Arthur Ungar, "Let's Stand United," *Daily Variety*, 7 February 1946, 3.

104. Edward Dmytryk, *It's a Hell of a Life but Not a Bad Living* (New York: Times Books, 1978), 58.

105. Jacques Rivette and Francois Truffaut, "Renoir in America," *Sight and Sound* 24, no. 1 (1954): 14.

106. Pat O'Brien, *The Wind at My Back: The Life and Times of Pat O'Brien* (Garden City, NY: Doubleday, 1964), 261–62.

CHAPTER 2

1. "N. Peter Rathvon Assumes Permanent Charge of RKO Production Following Death of Charles W. Koerner," RKO press release, 7 February 1946.

2. Hollywood Inside, 13 February 1946, 2.

3. John L. Scott, "Hollywood Boom Year Anticipated," *Los Angeles Times*, 23 December 1945, B2.

4. William Dozier would return to RKO in 1955, accepting the job of production head that he coveted in 1946. See chapter 8 of this text.

5. Floyd Odlum, telegram to N. Peter Rathvon, 8 April 1946.

6. Paramount would finally purchase the old RKO lot and incorporate it into its own facilities in 1967.

7. Norman Freeman, memorandum to N. Peter Rathvon, 16 April 1946.

8. Jeffrey Richards, *Hollywood's Ancient Worlds* (London: Continuum, 2008), 66.

9. Norman Freeman to Ned E. Depinet, 30 April 1946.

10. N. Peter Rathvon to Ned E. Depinet, 3 September 1946.

11. The bonanza from abroad was especially thrilling. "In late 1945, reports of foreign revenues from Europe and the Far East indicated that in the three-month period following V-J Day, Hollywood distributors' overseas revenues exceeded those of the entire year of 1941." Schatz, *Boom and Bust*, 160.

12. Rathvon to Depinet, 20 May 1946.

13. Ned E. Depinet to N. Peter Rathvon, 3 June 1946.

14. Norman Freeman, "Analysis of Results of Program Pictures," 29 October 1946.

15. Rathvon did float the idea of producing some experimental films containing themes rarely treated in B pictures. As an example, he cited Paramount's *The Lost Weekend*, though he readily acknowledged that that film was not a B. Rathvon referred to this notion, somewhat pompously, as "Operation Pegasus." Ned Depinet had no faith in the plan, and it was never implemented.

16. Bansak, *Fearing the Dark*, 161, 218. See also "Court Affirms Plagiarism Case Award," *Los Angeles Times*, 28 April 1948, 2.

17. Depinet to Rathvon, 23 April 1946.

18. "Transcript of Conference between Executives, Producers, and Joseph Breen, RKO Studios," 11 April 1946.

19. Ibid.

20. Rathvon to Depinet, 25 April 1946. The properties mentioned, with the exception of "If This Be Known," would ultimately be filmed and released under the following titles: *Out of the Past*, *Riff-Raff*, and *They Won't Believe Me*.

21. Edwin Schallert, "'Electra' Goes to R.K.O.; Male Stars Well Cast," *Los Angeles Times*, 19 April 1946, A3.

22. See Schatz, *Boom and Bust*, 181–83.

23. "Film Companies Face New Federal Action," *Los Angeles Times*, 8 August 1944, 9.

24. Schatz, *Boom and Bust*, 324.

25. A typical RKO block of five, which the company had offered exhibitors since 1941, was composed of two A pictures and three Bs. Most interested theater owners grudgingly accepted the Bs in order to book the two As.

26. Malcolm Kingsberg to N. Peter Rathvon, 14 June 1946.

27. Leon Goldberg to N. Peter Rathvon, 14 October 1946.

28. Ibid., 25 October 1946.

29. John M. Whitaker to N. Peter Rathvon, 28 October 1946.

30. Ned Depinet, telegram to N. Peter Rathvon, 19 September 1946. Rank would soon redirect his professional interests to Universal, investing heavily in that company and releasing such films as *Black Narcissus*, *Odd Man Out*, and

the Academy Award–winning *Hamlet* through Universal's distribution channels in the United States. See Clive Hirschhorn, *The Universal Story* (New York: Crown, 1983), 156.

31. N. Peter Rathvon to Edward Dmytryk, 20 September 1946.
32. Edward Dmytryk to N. Peter Rathvon, 2 October 1946. This comment would take on special poignancy one year later, when Dmytryk was accused of "un-American activities."
33. Ned E. Depinet, cablegram to N. Peter Rathvon, 1 October 1946.
34. Charles Koerner to N. Peter Rathvon, 15 November 1943.
35. Rathvon to Depinet, 11 November 1946.
36. Depinet to Rathvon, 30 November 1946.
37. "Statement by N. Peter Rathvon," 30 December 1946.
38. "Statement by Mr. Dore Schary," 30 December 1946.
39. "RKO 1946 Net $12,187,805," *Daily Variety*, 25 April 1947, 1. It was also the greatest year in industry history, with total gross revenues of $1.7 billion. See Schatz, *Boom and Bust*, 290.
40. While 25 percent was the standard distribution fee for many of the top independent producers, and some had recently agreed to pay a higher percentage, RKO distributed the Goldwyn films on a 17 percent flat deal. See Ernest Borneman, "Rebellion in Hollywood: A Study in Motion Picture Finance," *Harper's Magazine*, October 1946, 340.
41. Samuel J. Briskin to Peter Rathvon, 6 May 1946.
42. Rathvon to Depinet, 7 May 1946.
43. Depinet to Rathvon, 23 May 1946.
44. Beverly Jones, memorandum to N. Peter Rathvon, 4 November 1946.
45. Samuel J. Briskin, telegram to Ned Depinet, 13 January 1947.
46. Ned Depinet, telegram to Samuel J. Briskin, 16 January 1947.
47. The film's reputation as a "dud" persisted for many years. At some point, its owner failed to renew the copyright, and the picture fell into the public domain for a time. This led to holiday screenings by every American television station that could get hold of a print and, ironically, to the rediscovery of *It's a Wonderful Life* as a classic. It is now, arguably, the most beloved of Christmas movies.
48. Joseph I. Breen to David O. Selznick, 25 May 1945.
49. G. M. Shurlock, "Memo to the PCA Files," 15 June 1945, *Notorious* file, Production Code Administration (PCA) Collection, Margaret Herrick Library, Academy of Motion Picture Arts and Sciences (hereafter cited as MHL, AMPAS), Beverly Hills.
50. William Gordon, memorandum to Alfred Hitchcock, 15 April 1946.
51. William Gordon to Joseph I. Breen, 28 June 1946.

CHAPTER 3

1. N. Peter Rathvon to Ned E. Depinet, 3 February 1947.
2. Norman Freeman to Ned E. Depinet, 5 February 1947.

3. "Confidential Minutes of a Meeting in Mr. Rathvon's Office on February 19th," 1947.

4. "Confidential Minutes of a Meeting in Mr. Rathvon's Office on February 25th," 1947.

5. Freeman to Depinet, 5 February 1947.

6. The steady decline in motion picture attendance would continue throughout the rest of the 1940s and the 1950s. In 1946 America's motion picture theaters were welcoming 90 million people every week; by 1956 that number had been reduced to 46.5 million. See Drew Casper, *Postwar Hollywood, 1946–1962* (Malden, MA: Blackwell, 2007), 43.

7. Freeman to Depinet, 23 January 1947.

8. Floyd Odlum to N. Peter Rathvon, 23 April 1947.

9. *Mystery in Mexico* ended up costing much more than the company expected ($306,000) and lost $140,000. *The Fugitive*, a coproduction between RKO and Argosy Pictures, was partially shot at Churubusco and released in 1948. No more RKO pictures would be made at the Mexican studio.

10. Advertisement, *Fortune*, February 1947.

11. Phillips Brooks Nichols to N. Peter Rathvon, 7 March 1947.

12. J. Miller Walker to the Directors, 13 August 1947. See also "Pathe News Acquired by Warner Bros.," *Los Angeles Times*, 28 July 1947, A1.

13. Harry J. Michalson, memorandum to Ned E. Depinet, 21 October 1947.

14. "Minutes of a Meeting of the Executive Committee of Radio-Keith-Orpheum Corporation," 23 November 1947.

15. William L. Pereira to RKO Radio Pictures, 1 October 1947. Pereira's career as a producer ended less than a year later, when Howard Hughes took control of the company. Although his time in Hollywood was short, he did win an Academy Award for contributions to the special effects of *Reap the Wild Wind* (Paramount, 1942). After his sojourn at RKO, he returned to architecture, designing such iconic structures as CBS Television City in Los Angeles, the Disneyland Hotel, and the Transamerica Pyramid in San Francisco, among many others.

16. "Meeting of the Executive Committee," 23 November 1947.

17. "Direct Expenses 'A' Releases Advertising, Publicity, Exploitation and Sales Promotion Based on Picture Budgets," 8 October 1947.

18. David Goldman, memorandum to N. Peter Rathvon, 25 November 1947.

19. "Hollywood Hit Hard by British Tax on Imports," *Los Angeles Times*, 9 August 1947, 1.

20. Adrian Scott to Dore Schary, 9 June 1947, folder 8, box 113, Dore Schary Collection, Wisconsin Center for Film and Theatre Research (hereafter cited as WCFTR), Madison.

21. Nancy Lynne Schwartz, *The Hollywood Writers War* (New York: Knopf, 1982), 254.

22. The "unfriendlies" had been accompanied to Washington by members of the Committee for the First Amendment, including such notables as Humphrey Bogart, Lauren Bacall, Danny Kaye, Dorothy McGuire, Paul

Henreid, and John Huston. They dispersed and voiced only lukewarm criticisms of HUAC after the hearings ended.

23. Edward Dmytryk, *Odd Man Out: A Memoir of the Hollywood Ten* (Carbondale, IL: Southern Illinois Press, 1996), 73.

24. Testifying during one of the residual lawsuits in 1952, Schary stated that he "tried to get Scott to sign a statement that he was not a Communist to show the board of directors," but Scott refused. See "Scott's Failure to Deny Red Party Tie Cost Him Film Job, Schary Testifies," *Los Angeles Times*, 13 February 1952, 5.

25. "Meeting of the Executive Committee," 12 November 1947.

26. Ibid., 13 November 1947, 22 November 1947.

27. Eric Johnston, formerly president of the national Chamber of Commerce, had replaced Will H. Hays as head of the Motion Picture Association of America in 1946.

28. "Johnston Gives Industry Policy on Commie Jobs," *Daily Variety*, 26 November 1947, 1.

29. Dore Schary, *Heyday: An Autobiography* (Boston: Little, Brown, 1979), 166.

30. "Two Discharged by R.K.O. after Contempt Count," *Los Angeles Times*, 27 November 1947, 2.

31. In 1952 Adrian Scott was awarded $84,000 in his civil suit against RKO, but Judge Ben Harrison overturned the verdict and ordered a new trial. Scott would never collect a cent. See Jennifer E. Langdon, *Caught in the Crossfire: Adrian Scott and the Politics of Americanism in 1940s Hollywood* (New York: Columbia University Press, 2008), 386. Dmytryk became the first member of the Hollywood Ten to break ranks. In 1951 he went to the FBI office in Los Angeles, answered all questions posed, and named many of his former left-wing associates, including Scott. Consequently, he was able to resume his American directing career in 1952. Dmytryk's justification of his actions is contained in *Odd Man Out*.

32. Dore Schary, transcript of testimony before the House Un-American Activities Committee, 29 October 1947, folder 8, box 94, Schary Collection, WCFTR.

33. "Meeting of the Executive Committee," 12 November 1947.

34. "RKO Execs Back Up Schary's Red Hearing Statements," *Daily Variety*, 14 November 1947, 1, 10.

35. "Confidential Minutes . . . February 19th," 1947.

36. N. Peter Rathvon, memorandum to Dore Schary, 12 February 1947, folder 13, box 111, Schary Collection, WCFTR. In the original novel, the man is murdered because he is homosexual.

37. Cecil Brown, "Excerpt from Broadcast of March 18, 1947," Mutual Broadcasting System.

38. Joseph M. Proskauer to Ralstone R. Irvine, 4 April 1947, folder 16, box 126, Schary Collection, WCFTR.

39. The film did not win any Oscars, perhaps because of the dark shadow cast on it by HUAC. Ironically, *Gentleman's Agreement*, a Twentieth Century–Fox

production dealing with the same subject matter, took Best Picture. Its director, Elia Kazan, would eventually also be sucked into the McCarthyist vortex.

40. Seymour Peck, "There's New Hope for Hollywood in Dore Schary of 'Crossfire,'" *PM*, 22 July 1947.

41. Jacques F. Ferrand to Dore Schary, 15 August 1947, folder 16, box 126, Schary Collection, WCFTR.

42. Dore Schary, "The Screen and Society," *National Jewish Monthly*, October 1947, 60.

43. "Meeting of the Executive Committee," 23 November 1947.

44. Ned E. Depinet, memorandum to Members of the Executive Committee, 30 October 1947.

45. For detailed information on the problems of United Artists, see Tino Balio, *United Artists: The Company Built by the Stars* (Madison: University of Wisconsin Press, 1976), 186–229.

46. Grad Sears, telegram to Peter Rathvon, 10 November 1947.

47. "Contract Dated January 1, 1947 between RKO Radio Pictures, Inc. and Dore Schary," 4 March 1947.

48. Odlum to Rathvon, 13 December 1947; N. Peter Rathvon to Floyd Odlum, 16 December 1947.

49. Rathvon, memorandum to Schary, 3 November 1947.

50. Floyd Odlum to Dore Schary, 1 December 1947.

51. Hedda Hopper, "Roz Russell Sees O'Neill's 'Electra' as Real Thriller," *Los Angeles Times*, 30 November 1947, A1.

52. Dore Schary to Ned E. Depinet, 4 August 1947, folder 6, box 94, Schary Collection, WCFTR.

53. Rosalind Russell and Chris Chase, *Life Is a Banquet* (New York: Random House, 1977), 147–48.

54. For Edward Dmytryk's assessment of Nichols's failure as a director, see *Hell of a Life*, 76.

55. Edwin Schallert, "Rosalind Russell Wearies of Roles as Career Girl," *Los Angeles Times*, 10 March 1946, B1.

56. Bill Koenig, memorandum to Manny Wolfe, 20 September 1945.

57. Val Lewton, memorandum to Manny Wolfe, 26 September 1945.

58. Ben Goldman, memorandum to J.J. Nolan, 25 September 1945.

59. Joseph I. Breen to William Gordon, 12 June 1946.

60. Before he left RKO, a prophetic William Dozier had recommended Mitchum for the part: "I think the company has an enormous property in Mitchum, and a project like BUILD MY GALLOWS HIGH can do for him exactly what HIGH SIERRA did for Humphrey Bogart." William Dozier, memorandum to N. Peter Rathvon, 16 May 1946.

61. According to writer Daniel Mainwaring, Dore Schary "didn't like OUT OF THE PAST because it had been bought before he came. He didn't like anything that was in progress at the studio when he got there. He just threw them out without any decent publicity." Tom Flinn, "Screenwriter Daniel Mainwaring Discusses 'Out of the Past,'" *Velvet Light Trap* 10 (Fall 1973): 45.

62. Dore Schary, "Speech to the American Jewish Congress," 15 December 1947, folder 1, box 26, Schary Collection, WCFTR.

63. Dore Schary to Ned E. Depinet, 17 November 1947.

64. Dore Schary, memorandum to Ned Depinet, 26 January 1948. During the Depression Nicholas Schenck told *Film Daily Year Book* readers much the same thing: "There is nothing in this business which good pictures cannot cure." Quoted in Ross Melnick, *American Showman: Samuel "Roxy" Rothafel and the Birth of the Entertainment Industry* (New York: Columbia University Press, 2012), 355.

65. In May 1948 the British repealed the 75 percent tax, ending the embargo. The tax was replaced by an agreement to remit an annual maximum of $17 million, "plus an amount equal to the combined earnings of all British product released in the United States." Additional revenues earned by the U.S. companies could be used to set up production facilities and make pictures in England, precipitating "runaway production" and the development of "Hollywood, U.K." See Schatz, *Boom and Bust*, 300.

66. Ralph B. Austrian to Stephen Dunn, 7 January 1944.

67. "The Assessor vs. Industry," *Los Angeles Times*, 9 June 1947, A4.

68. Schatz, *Boom and Bust*, 326. Before he became Roosevelt's vice president, Harry Truman had led a Senate committee in 1943 that investigated various alleged improprieties by the motion picture industry in its war-related activities. See Betty Lasky, *RKO, the Biggest Little Major of Them All* (Englewood Cliffs, NJ: Prentice-Hall, 1984), 182–83.

69. Jack Sher and Louis Berg, "The Wolf at Hollywood's Door," *Los Angeles Times*, 29 February 1948, G4.

70. Dore Schary, "Top Industry Leaders Stress Need for More Creative Films, 'Back to Work–Attitude for All,'" *Variety*, 7 January 1948, 5–6.

71. Doremus and Company, "News Item," 24 May 1948.

72. Ralstone R. Irving, memorandum attached to letter to Philip Marcus, 28 July 1949.

73. Atlas had already sold enough of its RKO stock holdings, at prices between twenty-one and twenty-eight dollars per share, to cover its initial investment in the corporation, but it still owned 929,000 shares of RKO common. "Rathvon Out to 'Buy' RKO," *Daily Variety*, 15 July 1947, 1, 12.

74. "Hughes RKO Deal Off," *Daily Variety*, 8 April 1948, 1.

75. Rathvon to Odlum, 8 April 1948.

76. "Meeting of the Executive Committee," 16 January 1948.

77. Depinet, memorandum to Members, 5 March 1948; "Meeting of the Executive Committee," 15 April 1948.

78. "Minutes of a Special Meeting of the Board of Directors of RKO Radio Pictures, Inc.," 6 April 1948.

79. "Meeting of the Executive Committee," 13 January 1948. RKO would sell its stake in Churubusco to the Mexican government in 1950.

80. "Minutes of a Special Meeting of the Board of Directors of Radio-Keith-Orpheum Corporation," 8 June 1948.

81. "Confidential Meeting in Mr. Rathvon's office," 19 February 1947.

82. Odlum's wife, Jacqueline Cochran, was amazed by Hughes's tenacious haggling. He "must have been to our house sixty times.... He just loved to deal," she said. Donald L. Bartlett and James B. Steele, *Empire: The Life, Legend, and Madness of Howard Hughes* (New York: Norton, 1979), 164.

83. Rathvon did his best to stop the Hughes takeover. Odlum evidently agreed that if the RKO president could raise $5 million he would sell him half of the Atlas RKO holdings. But Rathvon failed to come up with the money. "Two Bids for RKO Go in Discard," *Daily Variety*, 7 May 1948, 1.

84. Hopper, Looking at Hollywood, 14 May 1948, 21.

85. Schary, *Heyday*, 169.

86. "Hughes with $16 Million Films Biggest Investor," *Daily Variety*, 12 May 1948, 8.

87. N. Peter Rathvon, memorandum to Studio Department Heads, 12 May 1948.

88. Schary, *Heyday*, 170.

89. "Schary Will Stick at RKO, He Sez after Hughes Talks," *Daily Variety*, 9 June 1948, 1.

90. "Ned Depinet Beams Optimism after RKO Parlay Here," *Daily Variety*, 26 May 1948, 6.

91. Ross Hastings to Joe Nolan, 25 June 1948. Nolan would join the ranks of departing RKO executives within a year.

92. Ross Hastings, memorandum to Messrs. Lockhart, Rogell, and Tevlin, 3 September 1948. Schary's severance package was minimal, but Hughes did allow him to purchase the *Battleground* project and take it with him.

93. "Dore Schary Quits at RKO after Halting of Pictures," *Los Angeles Times*, 1 July 1948, 2.

94. Back in January Rathvon had confidently declared that if Atlas sold its controlling interest in RKO, top management would not be affected. Clearly, he had been assured by Floyd Odlum that he would not sell the Atlas stock to any individual or group that planned to get rid of Rathvon, Depinet, or Schary. And Howard Hughes honored the agreement ... for a couple of months. "No Change in RKO Tops if Control Sold—Rathvon," *Daily Variety*, 28 January 1948, 9.

95. "Statement by N. Peter Rathvon," 26 July 1948.

96. William J. Fadiman to Leda Bauer, 23 July 1948; Leda Bauer to William J. Fadiman, 26 July 1948.

97. "Trio Named to Rule RKO," *Daily Variety*, 26 July 1948, 1, 3.

98. Bauer to Fadiman, 26 July 1948.

99. Schary, *Heyday*, 173. The general belief that Schary had been a success at RKO still pertains. Neal Gabler remarks that Schary did "particularly well for RKO" in *An Empire of Their Own: How the Jews Invented Hollywood* (New York: Crown, 1988), 396.

100. Sergio Leemann, *Robert Wise on His Films* (Los Angeles: Silman-James, 1995), 84.

101. For the resilient Schary, RKO proved to be just a stopover en route to a more appealing destination—two weeks after departing he landed the job of MGM production head at a salary of $6,000 per week. There he reactivated *Battleground*, which became one of the biggest hits of 1949. After surviving an intense conflict with MGM patriarch Louis B. Mayer, Schary continued to function as studio leader until 1956. See Thomas Schatz, *The Genius of the System: Hollywood Filmmaking in the Studio Era* (New York: Holt, 1988), 446.

102. Anonymous memorandum, ca. early July 1948.

CHAPTER 4

1. One of the primary challenges presented by the next four chapters is navigating through the fogbank of gossip, misinformation, innuendo, speculation, and complete fantasy that enshrouds the personage of Howard Hughes. While I cannot ignore this material, I attempt to stick to facts as much as possible and include less-than-verifiable information only when it rings true because of related factual material or jibes with my own efforts to understand the events described. A typical example of this problem may be found in director Mervyn LeRoy's autobiography. He claims that after making *Without Reservations* for RKO he was glad to return to his home studio, MGM, because working "around Hughes was too nerve-wracking; you never knew when he would call up, at any hour, with some minor problem to discuss at major length." *Without Reservations* was released in 1946, more than two years before Hughes bought control of RKO. See LeRoy, *Take One* (New York: Hawthorn Books, 1974), 164–65.

2. Many claimed Howard Hughes never set foot on the Gower Street lot. One tale, repeated by director Fritz Lang and others, had Hughes showing up unannounced one day, touring the facility with his flunkies, and then uttering two words: "Paint it." Hughes later denied the story. See Tony Thomas, *Howard Hughes in Hollywood* (Secaucus, NJ: Citadel, 1985), 104.

3. Hughes's "fortress" at 7000 Romaine was essentially a communications center with a large switchboard and staff who received, routed, and responded to telephonic and paper messages. The building also functioned as Hughes's primary storage facility.

4. During the first two years of Hughes's management, a number of directives were issued, tightening access to Hughes until it was practically impossible to reach him without using Tevlin as the conduit.

5. Norman Freeman, memorandum to William Fadiman, 20 May 1948.

6. "Crisis in Hollywood," *Time*, 13 September 1948, 100.

7. Workers in Hughes headquarters on Romaine Street had orders to locate him immediately if either Louella Parsons or Hedda Hopper, the gossip queens of Hollywood, called. He was more responsive to them than to key figures in his organization. See Bartlett and Steele, *Empire*, 213.

8. Ned E. Depinet to Dore Schary, 3 September 1948, folder 6, box 94, Schary Collection, WCFTR.

9. "Mitchum Gets 60-Day Jail Sentence," *Los Angeles Times*, 10 February 1949, A1.

10. Hedda Hopper, "Mitchum's 'Nos' Don't Come Easy," *Los Angeles Times*, 6 November 1949, E1. Hughes also loaned the actor $50,000 to buy a house after he completed his jail term.

11. "Government Approves R-K-O Plan to Divorce Film Holdings: Court to Be Asked for Consent Decree," *Wall Street Journal*, 2 November 1948, 2.

12. Michael Conant, *Antitrust in the Motion Picture Industry* (New York: Arno, 1979), 101–2.

13. Robert Sklar, *Movie-Made America* (New York: Random House, 1975), 273.

14. "Minutes of an Adjourned Special Meeting of the Board of Directors of Radio-Keith-Orpheum Corporation," 15 October 1948.

15. "Minutes of a Special Meeting of the Board of Directors of Radio-Keith-Orpheum Corporation," 28 October 1948, 29 October 1948.

16. "Adjourned Special Meeting," 30 October 1948.

17. Herman A. Lowe, "RKO Divorcement OKed," *Daily Variety*, 2 November 1948, 1, 3.

18. Although Hughes often promised options to Noah Dietrich, his most important business associate for many years, he never honored his promise. Dietrich quit in 1957 over this and other issues. See Noah Dietrich, *Howard: The Amazing Mr. Hughes* (Greenwich, CT: Fawcett, 1972), 294.

19. "Adjourned Special Meeting," 30 October 1948.

20. Sid Rogell to Ned Depinet, 19 November 1948.

21. Aubrey Solomon, *Twentieth Century–Fox: A Corporate and Financial History* (Metuchen, NJ: Scarecrow, 1988), 67.

22. Rogell to Depinet, 4 January 1949, 8 February 1949.

23. Director Joseph Losey was one of several people who made this claim. See Tom Milne, ed., *Losey on Losey* (Garden City, NY: Doubleday, 1968), 76.

24. Nicholas Ray believed Howard Hughes actually prevented him from being blacklisted. He expressed his gratitude to Hughes on several occasions. See Eisenschitz, *Nicholas Ray*, 123–24.

25. Complicating these tangled personal relationships even further, Robert Ryan was loaned by RKO to Enterprise Pictures in 1948 to play a character clearly based on Hughes. Given that Smith Ohlrig (note character's name) in the melodrama *Caught* is presented as rich, cold, manipulative, controlling, and borderline insane, it is difficult to believe screenwriter Arthur Laurents's contention that Hughes knew the film was a roman à clef about him, read the script before production, and still allowed Ryan to play the part. The fact that Max Ophuls, who had been abused, insulted, and fired by Hughes during the making of *Vendetta*, was directing, and Barbara Bel Geddes, the actress Hughes had publicly disdained, was playing the principal female role, causes one to be even more skeptical of the Laurents tale. See Arthur Laurents, *Original Story By: A Memoir of Broadway and Hollywood* (New York: Knopf, 2000), 140–43.

26. Sid Rogell to Edward Killy, 17 May 1949.

27. Ibid.
28. Louella O. Parsons, "Ingrid Bergman Expecting Baby," *Los Angeles Examiner*, 12 December 1949, 1.
29. "Moral Decay Exhibited, Cleric Says," *Los Angeles Times*, 16 February 1950, 26.
30. There were reports that Hughes himself was the source of the Parsons story. See Samantha Barbas, *The First Lady of Hollywood: A Biography of Louella Parsons* (Berkeley: University of California Press, 2005), 292–93; and Richard Hack, *Hughes: The Private Diaries, Memos and Letters* (Beverly Hills, CA: New Millennium, 2001), 193–94.
31. Patricia Clary, "Ingrid's New Film," *Los Angeles Evening Herald and Express*, 25 January 1950, A-20.
32. "1950 National Campaigns," 28 November 1950.
33. Barrett McGurn, "'Stromboli' Altered, Rossellini Charges," *Los Angeles Times*, 16 February 1950, 26.
34. "Rossellini in Huff Gives Up U.S. Earnings of 'Stromboli'," *Los Angeles Evening Herald and Express*, 21 February 1950, A-14.
35. *Stromboli* and the ensuing scandal effectively derailed Ingrid Bergman's career. She would not work in the United States again for almost ten years.
36. "Hollywood Lashes Back at Senate Morals Blast," *New York World Telegram and Sun*, 15 March 1950, 23.
37. "Movie Morals: Whose Business?" *U.S. News and World Report*, 21 April 1950, 21.
38. Ralstone R. Irvine, letter and attached memorandum to Philip Marcus, 28 July 1949. These losses were racked up by the production division, not the corporation as a whole.
39. Ralstone R. Irvine to William Amory Underhill, 17 August 1949.
40. "Adjourned Special Meeting," 30 October 1948.
41. "Odlum's Option Lapses; Court Action Is Seen," *Daily Variety*, 5 August 1949, 1, 6.
42. "Odlum Threatens Hughes Suit," *Hollywood Reporter*, 5 August 1949, 1, 4.
43. Floyd B. Odlum, telegram to Howard R. Hughes, 11 August 1949, Howard Hughes Collection, 1991/039-87, Texas State Archives, Austin (hereafter cited as TSA).
44. "Hughes Named Prod. Director," *Daily Variety*, 12 July 1949, 1.
45. Rogell to Depinet, 15 August 1949.
46. Ned Depinet to Sid Rogell, 3 November 1949.
47. Eisenschitz, *Nicholas Ray*, 166.
48. Ned Depinet, telegram to Sid Rogell, 7 December 1949.
49. Gordon Youngman, telegram to Ned Depinet, 29 December 1949. Only two pictures would result: *The Thing* (1951) and *The Big Sky* (1952).
50. Rogell to Depinet, 4 January 1950.
51. Howard Hughes to Sid Rogell, 10 January 1950.
52. Ibid.

53. "Memorandum of Action Taken at a Meeting of the Board of Directors of Radio-Keith-Orpheum Corporation," 8 March 1950.
54. Sid Rogell to Ross Hastings, 21 March 1950.
55. "RKO Postponement Indicates Gov't Disinclined to Harry Film Majors into Any Hasty Divorcement Decrees," *Variety*, 26 April 1950, 5.
56. Noah Dietrich, memorandum to Howard Hughes, 14 April 1950, Hughes Collection, 1991/039-26, TSA.
57. Depinet, telegram to Rogell, 3 May 1950.
58. Gordon E. Youngman to Sidney Lipsitch, 2 May 1950.
59. Sid Rogell, memorandum to All Departments, 18 May 1950.
60. "Rogell Tendered RKO Resignation 3 Wks. Ago," *Daily Variety*, 22 May 1950, 1.
61. Director Richard Fleischer claims this is what happened. See Richard Fleischer, *Just Tell Me When to Cry: A Memoir* (New York: Carroll and Graf, 1993), 41.
62. In 1952 Sid Rogell went to work as a production executive at Twentieth Century–Fox. He remained at that studio until 1963, when he joined Pacific Title as its president.
63. Fleischer, *Just Tell Me*, 27.
64. Hughes evidently did feel compassion toward some of the people he fired. For example, after Ben Piazza, longtime studio casting director, was let go in the late 1940s, Hughes agreed to pay him a pension of $300 per month out of company funds (Gordon Youngman to Jack Poor, 20 July 1955). Indeed, William Fadiman marveled at Hughes's unpublicized kindnesses: "You may or may not know that he helped a great many people, in private. He did so many wonderful things. But he would always remember that he was a businessman first. Then a human being." Quoted in Peter Harry Brown and Pat H. Broeske, *Howard Hughes: The Untold Story* (Cambridge, MA: Da Capo, 2004), 239.
65. Schatz, *Boom and Bust*, 329.

CHAPTER 5

1. Bartlett and Steele, *Empire*, 172.
2. "Bischoff RKO Prod'n Chief," *Daily Variety*, 31 May 1950, 1, 11.
3. C. J. Tevlin, memorandum to Samuel Bischoff, 10 June 1950.
4. Samuel Bischoff, memorandum to Gordon Youngman, C. J. Tevlin, and William Fadiman, 5 June 1950.
5. Samuel Bischoff to Ned Depinet, 3 July 1950.
6. Ned Depinet to Samuel Bischoff, 31 July 1950, 1 August 1950.
7. Hollywood Inside, 6 June 1950, 2.
8. Samuel Bischoff, memorandum to C. J. Tevlin, 12 July 1950.
9. Bischoff to Depinet, 12 July 1950.
10. After his sojourn at RKO, Samuel Bischoff quickly caught on as a producer with other studios, making such films as *The Phenix City Story*,

Screaming Eagles, and *Bullet for Joey,* before moving into television, where he supervised the *George Sanders Mystery Theatre* and *The Fox* for NBC.

11. Noah Dietrich to Ned Depinet, 13 April 1950.
12. Ned Depinet to Noah Dietrich, 15 May 1950.
13. Ned Depinet to G. E. Youngman, 26 July 1950
14. "Hughes Hugs Backlog, Loses 100G Monthly, Biz Baffled," *Daily Variety,* 11 October 1950, 3.
15. Ned Depinet to C. J. Tevlin, 21 December 1950.
16. Ned Depinet, telegram to C. J. Tevlin, 18 January 1951.
17. "Who'll Get Hughes' Stock?" *Business Week,* 17 February 1951, 123.
18. Depinet, telegram to Tevlin, 25 September 1951.
19. The press called it "the largest independent film production deal in Hollywood history." See "$50,000,000 Film Production Deal Completed Here," *Los Angeles Times,* 14 August 1950, 1.
20. W. R. Wilkerson, Trade Views, *Hollywood Reporter,* 14 August 1950, 1.
21. Gladwin Hill, "On the Planning Stages with Wald and Krasna," *New York Times,* 4 March 1951, X5.
22. "Press Announcement from Wald-Krasna Productions," August 1950. Later Wald would send Horace McCoy out on the rodeo circuit for five months before McCoy wrote the keenly observed screenplay for *The Lusty Men.*
23. Ibid.
24. "Transcript of Conference on Wald-Krasna Independent Production Set-Up," 15 August 1950.
25. The final contract apparently ran 250 pages in length. See "Depinet, RKO Execs to Hollywood for Workout on Wald-Krasna Snag," *Variety,* 14 November 1951, 3.
26. "Big Deal," *Time,* 28 August 1950, 72.
27. Jerry Wald and Norman Krasna to Howard Hughes, 13 September 1950, "Hughes, Howard," file, box 2, Correspondence 1952, Jerry Wald Collection, School of Cinematic Arts Library, University of Southern California (hereafter cited as USC), Los Angeles.
28. After RKO rereleased *The Outlaw* in 1950, syndicated columnist Jimmie Fidler labeled the picture, "one of the most ludicrously inept pieces of cinematic trash ever screened." "News and Views of Hollywood," *Valley Times,* 13 February 1951, 13.
29. "The New Pictures," *Time,* 22 January 1951, 92–94.
30. Fleischer, *Just Tell Me,* 45.
31. Howard Hughes, "Cutting Instructions—'Target,'" memorandum to Jim Wilkinson, 29 November 1950, box 1:16, Richard Fleischer Collection, USC.
32. Ibid.
33. Fleischer, *Just Tell Me,* 49. For a hilarious account of Fleischer's efforts to implement Hughes's reclamation ideas on *His Kind of Woman,* see pages 49–77.
34. Jerry Wald, memorandum to Joe Rivkin, 17 January 1951.

35. "Gordon E. Youngman Resigned as Vice-President in Charge of RKO Studio; C.J. Tevlin as Successor," RKO News Service release, 13 December 1950.

36. Wald and Krasna to Hughes, 3 July 1951.

37. Leonard S. Picker, memorandum to C.J. Tevlin, 14 June 1951.

38. Edwin Schallert, "Pair Cite Need for Film Flair," *Los Angeles Times*, 23 September 1951, D1.

39. Ross Hastings, memorandum to C.J. Tevlin, 30 October 1951.

40. "Report Wald-Krasna Seeking Exit from Their Hughes-RKO Contract," *Variety*, 31 October 1951, 3.

41. Bill Gay, memorandum to Gordon Youngman, 7 July 1950.

42. Gordon Youngman to S. Barret McCormick, 16 September 1950.

43. W.H. Clark to the Directors, 24 January 1951.

44. "$5,832,000 Loss for RKO Pix during Last Year," *Variety*, 19 May 1951, 3. With the exception of United Artists, which reported a small loss in 1950, all the other major companies racked up solid profits for the year.

45. Clark to the Directors, 24 January 1951.

46. "Total Amount of Advertising Magazine Space for Year 1950," dictated by Mr. Depinet's secretary over telephone, 8 May 1951.

47. Depinet to Tevlin, 22 May 1951.

48. "High Court Backs Hughes' Film Deal," *Los Angeles Times*, 5 February, 1952, 7.

49. "Hughes Wins 7–0 Supreme Ct. Victory over Right to Kill Sale Deadline," *Variety*, 6 February 1952, 7, 21.

50. "Paul Jarrico Is Sued by RKO," *Hollywood Reporter*, 18 March 1952, 1, 8.

51. One has to wonder why Jarrico wanted his name to appear in *The Las Vegas Story* credits. Richard L. Coe was one of a number of critics who slammed the picture; he called it an "amateurish charade" that "makes for shatteringly dreary entertainment." "Las Vegas Must Be a Terrible Dive," *Washington Post*, 13 March 1952, 10B.

52. "Suit Filed by RKO Studio over Screen Credit," *Los Angeles Times*, 18 March 1952, 1, 4.

53. "Hughes Gets Reply from Writers," *Los Angeles Times*, 31 March 1952, 1.

54. "Paul Jarrico Sues, Hughes Hits Back," *Los Angeles Times*, 29 March 1952, 1, 3.

55. "Hughes Cuts RKO Personnel 25%," *Daily Variety*, 7 April 1952, 11.

56. "Films' Biggest Mystery—RKO," *Variety*, 20 February 1952, 3, 12.

57. "Red Situation Forces RKO Payroll Cut," *Los Angeles Times*, 6 April 1952, 1, 16.

58. Film company executives were intimidated by the American Legion during this period. The legion had approximately three thousand branches and threatened to picket theaters showing films it considered subversive. Legion members were particularly successful in their efforts to suppress Charlie Chaplin's *Limelight*, a campaign that Howard Hughes happily supported. See Peter Lev, *The Fifties* (Berkeley: University of California Press, 2003), 10.

59. "Hughes Opines Red Influence in H'w'd Is 'Substantial,'" *Daily Variety*, 2 April 1952, 3, 11.

60. Lawrence H. Suid, *Guts and Glory: The Making of the American Military Image in Film*, rev. ed. (Lexington: University Press of Kentucky, 2002), 137–38.

61. Wilkerson, Trade Views, 31 March 1952, 1; 18 March 1952, 1.

62. "Hughes Studio Closing Rouses Hollywood Ire," *Motion Picture Herald*, 12 April 1952, 19.

63. "Nixon Lauds Hughes for Jarrico Case," *Los Angeles Times*, 4 April 1952, 29.

64. "Hughes Studio Closing."

65. "Hughes' Commie Blast," *Variety*, 9 April 1952, 29. Later, during the Jarrico trial, Hughes denied that he filed suit against Jarrico as an excuse "to close down RKO studio." See "Hughes Testifies on Firing Jarrico," *Los Angeles Times*, 21 November 1952, 1, 2.

66. According to Jarrico biographer Larry Ceplair, Paul Jarrico "researched and drafted a fairly convincing dossier proving that Hughes had broken every one of the Ten Commandments. 'Since the issue was his right to take my name off a film under a morality clause . . . , I did think his morality was pertinent; after all, his name was on the film too—and remained on.' But Jarrico's lawyer assured him that Hughes's morality was irrelevant 'under the rules of the legal game we were playing.'" *The Marxist and the Movies: A Biography of Paul Jarrico* (Lexington: University Press of Kentucky, 2007), 286–87.

67. Edwin Schallert, "'Robe' Finally Seems Set with Peck Likely Star," *Los Angeles Times*, 8 June 1948, 20.

68. "RKO Sues Ross for Million Plus," *Hollywood Reporter*, 13 January 1950, 1, 3.

69. "Frank Ross Heaves $1 Million 'Robe' Rebuttal at Hughes," *Daily Variety*, 11 April 1950, 1, 7.

70. "20th Buys 'Robe' from Ross, RKO," *Daily Variety*, 8 May 1952, 3.

71. *The Robe*, which cost $4.1 million to produce (less than RKO projected), generated $17.5 million in domestic rentals and a $7.5 million more overseas. By the end of 1954 it had become the top-grossing film in Fox's history. Solomon, *Twentieth Century–Fox*, 88, 248.

72. Foolishly, RKO agreed to accept only the money it had spent developing *The Robe* ($819,000) in the settlement with Ross and Twentieth Century–Fox. Some sort of percentage of profits arrangement would have brought in much more, but general counsel J. Miller Walker affirmed that "we cannot receive back more than our investment." J. Miller Walker to Noah Dietrich, 9 October 1953, Howard Hughes Collection, 1991/039–88, TSA.

73. "Anne [sic] Sheridan Asks Court to Summon Hughes," *Los Angeles Times*, 1 February 1951, 31.

74. John L. Scott, "Revenge Not So Sweet in 'My Forbidden Past,'" *Los Angeles Times*, 12 May 1951, 14.

75. Stewart Granger, *Sparks Fly Upward* (New York: Putnam's Sons, 1981), 270–72.

76. Howard Hughes, miffed that journalistic accounts indicated he lost this legal dispute, had his acolyte Walter Kane contact Dan Lundberg of KNXT Radio News. Lundberg reported on July 18 that Hughes himself had written "and dictated the terms of the settlement" because he did "not want to put the State to any further expense on this issue." "Radio Reports, Inc.," prepared for Carl Byoir Associates, 18 July 1952.

77. "Settlement via 'Negotiable Pact' Ends Simmons-Granger-RKO Suit," *Daily Variety*, 18 July 1952, 1, 9.

78. Hughes's many legal battles at RKO would ultimately pale compared to the titanic war of litigation that erupted a few years later over his leadership of Trans World Airlines. See David B. Tinnin, *Just About Everybody vs. Howard Hughes* (Garden City, NY: Doubleday, 1973).

79. Stephen Jackson to Harold Melniker, 5 April 1948, *Born to Be Bad* file, PCA Collection, MHL, AMPAS.

80. Joseph I. Breen to Martin Quigley, 25 September 1950, *Born to Be Bad* file, AMPAS.

81. The information in this paragraph is taken from the PCA, AMPAS, files on the individual films mentioned.

82. Joe Rivkin, "Confidential Memorandum," 5 November 1951.

83. Hastings, memorandum to Tevlin, 27 December 1951.

84. Picker, memorandum to Tevlin, 29 February 1952.

85. Jerry Wald, memorandum to Milton Pickman, 28 March 1952, box 2, Correspondence 1952, Wald Collection, USC.

86. Jerry Wald, memorandum to files, 27 April 1952, box 2, Correspondence 1952, Wald Collection, USC.

87. Milton Pickman to Norman Krasna, 1 April 1952, "Krasna, Norman" file, box 2, Correspondence 1952, Wald Collection, USC. None of these projects would ever be produced at RKO.

88. Jerry Wald to Norman Krasna, 3 April 1952, "Krasna, Norman" file, box 2, Correspondence 1952, Wald Collection, USC. Katzman was a producer of low-budget fare for Columbia at this time.

89. Toward the end of April, C.J. Tevlin told Howard Hughes that Wald wanted "to get rid of Krasna." Hughes voiced no objections. "File Memorandum: Conversation with Tevlin re: Wald," 24 April 1952, Hughes Collection, 1991/039–88, TSA.

90. Ross Hastings, memorandum to Sidney Lipsitch, 5 May 1952.

91. Jerry Wald to Howard Hughes, 9 June 1952.

92. Nadine Henley, memorandum, with statement from Howard Hughes attached, to C.J. Tevlin, 22 May 1952.

93. "Transcript of Telephone Conversation between Jerry Wald and Louis B. Mayer," 28 June 1952, "RKO" file, box 4, Correspondence 1952, Wald Collection, USC.

94. "Transcript of Telephone Conversation between Jerry Wald and Serge Semenenko," 30 June 1952; "Transcript of Telephone Conversation between Jerry Wald and David Selznick," 30 June 1952; "Jerry Wald and Serge Semenenko," 1 July 1952, all in "RKO" file, box 4, Wald Collection, USC.

95. "Transcript of Telephone Conversation between Jerry Wald and Noah Dietrich," 1 July 1952; "Jerry Wald and David Selznick," 1 July 1952, both in "RKO" file, box 4, Wald Collection, USC.

96. Selznick and Semenenko were good friends and talked regularly. They must have realized that Wald's renditions of his conversations with each of them were larded with distortions and exaggerations.

97. C. J. Tevlin, telegram to J. Miller Walker, 30 April 1952.

98. "Las Vegas Junket," *Newsweek*, 25 February 1952, 86.

99. Hollywood Inside, 20 September 1951, 4.

100. Jerry Wald to Howard Hughes, 4 September 1951, box 2, Correspondence 1952, Wald Collection, USC.

101. Louella O. Parsons, "In Hollywood," *Los Angeles Examiner*, 8 April 1951, sec. 7, p. 15.

102. O.A.G. [Oscar Godbout], "At the Paramount," *New York Times*, 30 August 1951, 20.

103. These films were among the last entries in the Tevlin Ledger, which covered the company's release years through the 1951–52 season. Subsequent financial information (with the exception of *The Whip Hand* figures) will be based on (or inferred from) other sources.

104. "Midnight Sale," *Time*, 6 October 1952, 100.

105. "A Passing Fancy Looks Like a $2,000,000 Profit," *Daily Variety*, 24 September 1952, 6.

106. Ibid.

CHAPTER 6

1. "New Regime Mapping RKO Policy Today," *Daily Variety*, 30 September 1952, 3.

2. Thomas M. Pryor, "Hollywood Report; Head of New Group Now Controlling R.K.O. Speaks Up," *New York Times*, 28 September 1952, X5.

3. "Depinet Resignation Stirs Widespread Regret in Industry," *Motion Picture Daily*, 3 October 1952, 1.

4. Ned E. Depinet, "To the RKO Family," *RKO Flash*, 4 October 1952, 1.

5. "New RKO Group's First Job Is Screening of All Execs," *Hollywood Reporter*, 3 October 1952, 4.

6. "Picker to RKO Radio as Exec. Vice-Prexy," *Film Daily*, 8 October 1952, 1, 8.

7. "Picker Named Vice-President of RKO Studios," *Los Angeles Times*, 8 October 1952, 2.

8. "RKO Femme Touch," *Daily Variety*, 17 October 1952, 1.

9. Marie Torre, "Hollywood's a Lost Soul, Pascal Wails," *New York World-Telegram and Sun*, 15 November 1952, 6.

10. Ross Hastings, telegram to Arnold Grant, 20 October 1952.

11. Sherrill Corwin, telegram to Arnold Grant, 13 October 1952.

12. Tino Balio, *United Artists: The Company That Changed the Film Industry* (Madison: University of Wisconsin Press, 1987), 49–50.

13. Ross R. Hastings, "Studio Report" to Arnold Grant, 1 November 1952, 1.

14. Ibid., 51–52.

15. "RKO's New Owners," *Wall Street Journal*, 16 October 1952, 1.

16. "Common Interest in Philanthropic Venture Maintains Ex-RKO Officers Stolkin, Koolish Tie with Hollywood," *Wall Street Journal*, 28 October 1952, 10.

17. Wilkerson, Trade Views, 17 October 1952, 1; 28 October 1952, 1.

18. "Stolkin Quits as RKO President; He and 2 Others Leave Board," *Wall Street Journal*, 23 October 1952, 1.

19. "RKO Chairman Coming Here to Revamp Studio," *Los Angeles Times*, 29 October 1952, A2.

20. Ibid.

21. "No RKO Pix Going to TV, Says Grant," *Daily Variety*, 31 October 1952, 1.

22. "RKO Team Now 'Ready': Sets 9 Release Dates," *Motion Picture Herald*, 1 November 1952, 16.

23. "Suit Asks RKO Receivership," *Daily Variety*, 14 November 1952, 1, 3.

24. "Press Release from Arnold M. Grant to the Shareholders of RKO Pictures Corporation," 13 November 1952.

25. "Uncertainty Remains on RKO Owners," *Boxoffice*, 29 November 1952, 39.

26. "Grant Resigns from RKO; Corwin Is Acting Head," *Boxoffice*, 15 November 1952, 39.

27. "Matty Fox, Hyman Deal Again Delays RKO Board Action," *Hollywood Reporter*, 12 November 1952, 1.

28. "Atlas Studying, Following RKO Situation," *Film Daily*, 21 November 1952, 1.

29. "Paul White Envisions Turning RKO into Combo TV-Theatrical Pix Plant," *Daily Variety*, 19 November 1952, 1, 11.

30. "Who'll Gain Control of RKO Still an Unanswered Question," *Boxoffice*, 29 November 1952, 9. Greene spearheaded a group that would purchase the RKO theater chain in 1953.

31. "RKO Future a Jigsaw Puzzle," *Daily Variety*, 19 November 1952, 1, 11.

32. "Row within Group Stymies RKO Move," *Hollywood Reporter*, 2 December 1952, 1.

33. "Sherrill Corwin Exiting RKO," *Hollywood Reporter*, 5 December 1952, 1, 4.

34. "Hughes-Stolkin Talks on RKO Future Collapse," *Motion Picture Daily*, 11 December 1952, 1, 3.

35. Perry Lieber, "Press Release," 12 December 1952. The announced appointment of Bent, described by Lieber as a "senior partner of the investment firm of Merrill Lynch, Pierce, Fenner and Beane," was a mistake. A few days later his place was taken by A. D. Simpson, vice chairman of the National Bank of Commerce in Houston, Texas.

36. "Hughes RKO Board Chairman," *Daily Variety*, 18 December 1952, 1.

37. "RKO Operation Takes Shape," *Motion Picture Herald*, 27 December 1952, 26.

38. "Hughes Regains Control of RKO; Apparently Didn't Put Up a Cent," *Wall Street Journal*, 15 December 1952, 2.

39. "Hughes Gets Grainger for RKO," *Hollywood Reporter*, 15 January 1953, 1.

40. "RKO 'Ownership' Back to Hughes," *Daily Variety*, 9 February, 1953, 1.

41. "Stolkin Throws in Sponge," *Daily Variety*, 13 February 1953, 7.

CHAPTER 7

1. Perry Lieber, memorandum to James R. Grainger, 10 February 1953.

2. J. R. Grainger, memorandum to Perry Lieber, 24 February 1953.

3. In June Grainger announced that company expenses had been cut "about $1,000,000 per annum." He seemed particularly proud that a crackdown on long-distance phone calls by employees would save $10,000 a year. "RKO Sales Okay but Studio Hustle Still No. 1 'Must,'" *Variety*, 10 June 1953, 3, 20.

4. Thomas M. Pryor, "Diverse Hollywood; Warners Order a Slowdown as R.K.O.'s New President Views a Rosy Future," *New York Times*, 8 March 1953, X5.

5. "Grainger's New Setup for RKO," *Variety*, 25 March 1953, 5.

6. J. R. Grainger, memorandum to Alfred Crown, 14 April 1953.

7. J. R. Grainger to James Mulvey, 20 April 1953.

8. Sheila Graham, "Hollywood," *New York Mirror*, 25 January 1953, 46.

9. "Hughes Regains Control," 2.

10. "Hughes Sued on His RKO Operations," *Los Angeles Times*, 16 December 1952, 14.

11. "$1,000,000 RKO Suit Names Howard Hughes," *Los Angeles Times*, 7 April 1953, 2.

12. "RKO Minority Stockholder Charges Hughes and Depinet with 'Disregard of Duties,'" *Daily Variety*, 15 April 1953, 18.

13. "1,000,000 RKO Suit."

14. "Two Stockholders Ask RKO Receiver," *Los Angeles Times*, 14 October 1953, 29.

15. "Charge Hughes Put Stars on Payroll for Own Interest," *Los Angeles Herald Express*, 14 October 1953, 1.

16. "Two Stockholders."

17. Unlike the other films, *Son of Sinbad* would not be released in 3-D.

18. "File Memo—3-D Films and Publicity," 16 April 1953, Howard Hughes Collection, 1991/039-88, TSA.
19. "RKO Plans All Future Pix in 3-D," *Daily Variety*, 25 March 1953, 1.
20. "3-D Films and Publicity," TSA.
21. The *Variety* review of *Bwana Devil* described Arch Oboler's script and direction as "extremely poor" and also criticized the 3-D technique (still in the "gimmick stage") and glasses ("uncomfortable and annoying to the wearer"). "Bwana Devil," *Variety*, 28 November 1952, 3.
22. "3-D Films and Publicity," TSA.
23. Harry Warner also believed in the "3-D revolution." He predicted all movies would be 3-D within two years. His brother Jack held a different (and correct) opinion: "It's a novelty good for a fast buck at the box office." See Tino Balio, ed., *The American Film Industry*, rev. ed. (Madison: University of Wisconsin Press, 1985), 430.
24. "RKO: It's Only Money," *Fortune*, May 1953, 123.
25. Ibid., 123–27, 206–15.
26. RKO appealed the judgement, which was later reduced to $279,497.51. See "Judgment for $279,000 Given in RKO Film Suit," *Los Angeles Times*, 12 August 1955, 12.
27. Advertisement for *Appointment in Samarra*, *Variety*, 14 June 1950, 15.
28. "Film Producers Win $375,000 in RKO Suit," *Los Angeles Times*, 16 February 1953, 2.
29. "RKO: It's Only Money," 206. The set had been constructed for the musical *Two Tickets to Broadway*.
30. This evidently was not the case. A file memo dictated to Hughes's personal assistant, Nadine Henley, on 22 October 1952 contains speculation about who might have been the main source of the *Wall Street Journal* articles. The principal suspect was New York investment adviser David J. Greene, who would spearhead the purchase of Hughes's RKO Theaters stock later in the year. Hughes Collection, 1991/039-88, TSA.
31. "RKO: It's Only Money," 215.
32. "File Memo: Sale of RKO Ranch," 16 April 1953, Hughes Collection, 1991/039-88, TSA.
33. "RKO Ranch Goes Thataway," *Daily Variety*, 10 July 1953, 1. Today one of the houses subsequently built on the tract is worth more than the entire purchase price.
34. "File Memo: Sale of Film Library to TV," 16 April 1953, Hughes Collection, 1991/039-88, TSA.
35. C. J. Tevlin, "Outline of Testimony," 16 July 1953; Jerry Wald, "Outline of Testimony," 9 July 1953; Noah Dietrich, "Outline of Testimony," 14 July 1953, all in Hughes Collection, 1991/039-88, TSA.
36. Dore Schary, "Outline of Testimony," 8 July 1953; Sid Rogell, "Outline of Testimony," 13 July 1953; Frederick L. Ehrman, "Outline of Testimony," 27 May 1953, all in Hughes Collection, 1991/039-88, TSA.
37. Ned Depinet to C. J. Tevlin, 27 May 1953.

38. "Questions Raised by Ned Depinet, as Submitted over the Telephone to Mr. Slack by Manly Fleischman," 5 May 1953, Hughes Collection, 1991/039–45, TSA.
39. Ned Depinet, "Outline of Testimony," n.d., Hughes Collection, 1991/039–88, TSA.
40. "RKO Execs Gang Up to Nip Dissident Stockholders' Suit," *Daily Variety*, 16 September 1953, 11.
41. "RKO Receivership Plea Probe," *Hollywood Reporter*, 11 November 1953, 1.
42. "Renews Demand Court Probe Hughes' 'Collusion' in Stockholder Suit Mess," *Daily Variety*, 17 November 1953, 10.
43. Thomas M. Pryor, "R.K.O. Is More Involved with Lawsuits Than with Film Production—Addendum," *New York Times*, 22 November 1953, X5.
44. Howard R. Hughes, draft deposition in Louis J. Schiff and Jacob Sacks, plaintiffs, against RKO Radio Pictures, Hughes Tool Company, etc., n.d., Hughes Collection, 1991/039–88, TSA.
45. See Joel W. Finler, *The Hollywood Story* (New York: Crown, 1988), 286–87.
46. Hughes, draft deposition, Hughes Collection, TSA.
47. J. R. Grainger, memorandum to Noah Dietrich, 14 July 1953.
48. J. R. Grainger, memorandum to C. J. Tevlin, 25 August 1953.
49. J. R. Grainger, memorandum to Howard Hughes, 9 September 1953.
50. J. R. Grainger, telegram to C. J. Tevlin, 6 October 1953.
51. Grainger, memorandum to Dietrich, 28 October 1953.
52. Grainger, memorandum to Hughes, 24 November 1953.
53. "Hughes Sells Theater Stock for 4 Million," *Los Angeles Times*, 9 November 1953, 17.
54. Raymond A. Cook to T. A. Slack, 25 November 1953, Hughes Collection, 1991/039–88, TSA.
55. Ibid.
56. Joseph I. Breen, memo to files, 17 February 1954, *The French Line* file, PCA Collection, MHL, AMPAS.
57. Many theaters refused to book *The Moon Is Blue*, "but where it did play it broke box-office records." Balio, *United Artists* (1987), 70.
58. Quoted in "Cops Find Jane Film Just So-So," *Long Beach Independent*, 31 December 1953, 9.
59. Leonard J. Leff and Jerold L. Simmons, *The Dame in the Kimono: Hollywood, Censorship, and the Production Code from the 1920s to the 1960s* (New York: Weidenfeld, 1990), 207.
60. Quoted in "Catholics Blast New Russell Film," *Los Angeles Mirror*, 8 January 1954, 8.
61. "Jane Russell Backs Censor in Film Row," *Los Angeles Times*, 28 December 1953, 2.
62. "Hughes Defies Censors (Even Jane Blushes)," *New York Post*, 28 December 1953, 4.

63. Later, in a thoughtful article, influential film critic Bosley Crowther lamented the fact that RKO had chosen *The French Line* to challenge the hegemony of the Hollywood censors: "The patent cheapness of this picture makes it hard for an idealist to feel anything of a liberalizing nature has been achieved by the move of Mr. Hughes." "Looking for Trouble," *New York Times*, 23 May 1954, sec. 2, p. 1.

64. Leff and Simmons, *Dame in the Kimono*, 211.

65. "RKO Pictures Holders Blame Howard Hughes for $38.5 Million Loss," *Wall Street Journal*, 14 October 1953, 24.

66. "Hughes Bids 23 Million to Buy RKO," *Los Angeles Times*, 8 February 1954, 2.

67. "Hughes Bids for All RKO Stock," *Hollywood Reporter*, 8 February 1954, 1.

68. Harold Walsh, "RKO Steals Mart Show as Thousands Rush in to Buy," *Los Angeles Times*, 9 February 1954, 18.

69. "H. Hughes' Check for $23 1/2 Million Buys RKO Assets," press release from Carl Byoir and Associates, 31 March 1954.

70. Gene Arneel, "Legalistics, Taxes, 'Pride,' 'Privacy' Cue $23,489,478 Bid by Hughes," *Variety*, 10 February 1954, 4, 10.

71. "First Round Is Hughes's," *Newsweek*, 22 February 1954, 81.

72. Later reports suggest that Hughes needed to acquire only 80 percent of the stock to realize the tax advantages.

73. J. R. Grainger, "Announcement to the Stockholders," 28 June 1954.

74. Associated Press story, 30 November 1954.

75. Floyd B. Odlum to J. Miller Walker, 13 December 1954.

76. Associated Press story.

77. "Nevada Judge Quashes Suits against Hughes," *Los Angeles Times*, 31 March 1954, 1.

78. "Incompetence or Indifference," *Variety*, 31 March, 1954, 20.

79. Wilkerson, Trade Views, 1 April 1954, 1.

80. "Draw Papers for Hughes to Sell Entire Empire—Except RKO—for $400,000,000," *Daily Variety*, 11 November 1954, 1, 4.

81. "Zeckendorf Blasts Hughes' 'Unconscionable' Nix on Deal," *Daily Variety*, 12 November 1954, 1.

82. Bartlett and Steele, *Empire*, 209.

83. "Filmland Buzzes over RKO Rumors," *Los Angeles Times*, 24 September 1954, 29.

84. Edwin Schallert, "RKO's Future Analyzed by Times Critic," *Los Angeles Times*, 6 February 1955, D1.

85. RKO adopted Superscope to avoid paying the steep fees charged by Twentieth Century–Fox for leasing CinemaScope, which had become the dominant wide-screen process by that time.

86. Perry Lieber, "President J. R. Grainger Sees RKO in High Gear; Record Year Sighted," RKO News Service release, 1 April 1955.

87. Ibid.

88. *The Conqueror* locations were close to an area where the United States had tested atomic bombs. In later years many members of the cast and crew developed cancer, leading some to speculate that their disease resulted from exposure to nuclear radiation left behind as a residue in the soil.

89. "RKO Loss in Millions Due to Disney Bowout," *Daily Variety*, 23 September 1954, 1.

90. "RKO Shakes Down to Indy Lot," *Daily Variety*, 23 September 1954, 1, 3.

91. Harriet Parsons to Howard Hughes, 26 March 1953, Hughes Collection, 1991/039-45, TSA.

92. Mervin Houser, memorandum to Perry Lieber, 28 April 1952, Hughes Collection, 1991/039-88, TSA.

93. "File Memorandum: RKO Publicity," 2 May 1952, Hughes Collection, 1991/039-88, TSA.

94. Parsons to Hughes, Hughes Collection, TSA.

95. Brown and Broeske, *Howard Hughes*, 215.

96. John L. Scott, "Stars, Press Go Overboard for 'Underwater!' Premiere," *Los Angeles Times*, 11 January 1955, B7.

97. "Movies Are Wetter Than Ever," *Life*, 10 January 1955, 67–68.

98. Victoria Price, *Vincent Price: A Daughter's Biography* (New York: St. Martin's Press, 1999), 171. Dale Robertson later recalled that *Son of Sinbad* began shooting with only four pages of script: "Nobody knew what the story was going to be about.... At the end of the day you'd get a couple of pages for the next day. We'd shoot and laugh and have water fights; there was no need in being serious." This description suggests that the movie was rushed into production, in all likelihood, to satisfy those contractual obligations. It also helps us understand why it turned out so poorly. Ronald L. Davis, *The Glamour Factory: Inside Hollywood's Big Studio System* (Dallas: Southern Methodist University Press, 1993), 175.

99. J.R. Grainger to Joseph I. Breen, 26 January 1955, *Son of Sinbad* file, PCA Collection, MHL, AMPAS.

100. Joseph I. Breen to J.R. Grainger, 27 January 1955, *Son of Sinbad* file, PCA Collection, MHL, AMPAS.

101. Joseph I. Breen to C.J. Tevlin, 11 February 1954, *Son of Sinbad* file, PCA Collection, MHL, AMPAS.

102. Geoffrey M. Shurlock, "Memo for the Files," 13 January 1955, 8 March 1955, *Son of Sinbad* file, PCA Collection, MHL, AMPAS.

103. "Trend Toward Laxity?" *Time*, 30 May 1955, 84; Helen Dudar and Peter J. McElroy, "Hollywood and the Legion of Decency: Censored Movies," *New York Post*, 24 May 1955, 4.

104. Jack Moffitt, "Sex Is Flaunted in Oriental Concoction," *Hollywood Reporter*, 31 May 1955, 3.

105. Philip K. Scheuer, "Sinbad Son Falls Flat on His Fez," *Los Angeles Times*, 2 June 1955, B9.

106. J.R. Grainger to Noah Dietrich, 16 June 1955.

107. Amazingly, Floyd Odlum and Howard Hughes did later make another deal. In September 1955 they agreed to merge Atlas Corporation and RKO

Pictures Corporation. RKO Pictures, which Hughes still controlled, was a corporate shell containing some $15 million that Hughes had deposited for redemption of the RKO shares when he tried to purchase the entire company. But it also included a $30 million capital loss carryover, which could "be applied against Atlas Profits over a five-year period." This factor provoked Odlum's interest in the merger. See "Hughes Agrees to Sell RKO Pictures to Atlas," *New York Herald Tribune*, 24 September 1955, 3.

108. "Closing with Hughes," *Variety*, 20 July 1955, 3.

109. J. R. Grainger, telegram to R. S. Wolff et al., 18 July 1955.

110. "Hughes' RKO Profit, $6,539,969," *Daily Variety*, 19 July 1955, 1. An anonymous, undated document, most likely written by one of Hughes's employees, calculated Hughes's final profit at $7.7 million, plus "Hughes Tool Co. has received $2 million for the rights to certain of his pictures." "RKO Chronology," box 93, Hughes Collection, Lied Library, University of Nevada at Las Vegas.

CHAPTER 8

1. Even Tony Thomas, in his generally positive book about Hughes, calls his leadership of RKO "disastrous." Thomas, *Howard Hughes in Hollywood*, 147.

2. "The Secret Life of Howard Hughes," *Time*, 3 December 1976, 23.

3. Hughes was given the Harmon Trophy as the outstanding aviator of 1936 and 1938; the Collier Trophy in 1939 for his successful around-the-world flight; the Octave Chanute Award in 1940 for advancing the arts, sciences, and technology of aviation; and the Congressional Gold Medal in 1941 for his achievements in advancing the science of aviation.

4. Peter Evans and Ava Gardner, *Ava Gardner: The Secret Conversations* (New York: Simon and Schuster, 2013), 91.

5. In his deposition during the Castleman lawsuit, Noah Dietrich stated that Hughes's interest in RKO operations was "active and vital" and estimated that he "devoted about 50% of his time to RKO." Noah Dietrich, "Outline of Testimony," 14 July 1953, Howard Hughes Collection, 1991/039–88, TSA. C.J. Tevlin went even further in his deposition in the Schiff-Sacks suit: "Mr. Hughes does spend a substantial amount of time on the affairs of Radio. Indeed I believe that he frequently devotes more hours during a day to studio matters than are devoted by some executives in this industry and many business men in commercial fields outside this industry." Affidavit of C.J. Tevlin, 11 September 1953, Hughes Collection, 1991/039–91, TSA.

6. Janet Leigh, *There Really Was a Hollywood* (Garden City, NY: Doubleday, 1984), 91–93.

7. Brown and Broeske, *Howard Hughes*, 241.

8. Hack, *Hughes*, 176.

9. Barbara Hall, "Oral History with Albert E. Van Schmus," MHL, AMPAS.

10. Davis, *Glamour Factory*, 5.

11. Susan Dalton and John Davis, eds., "John Cromwell," *Velvet Light Trap* 10 (Fall 1973): 23.

12. John Houseman, *Front and Center* (New York: Simon and Schuster, 1979), 317.
13. RKO Story Department head William Fadiman ruminated on Hughes's inability to empathize with audience members: "Howard, since he had little contact with human beings except on brief occasions, was never able to arrive at an area where he could understand completely what Mr Smith and Mr Jones wanted in Oklahoma City. And that's what made him a failure." Eisenschitz, *Nicholas Ray*, 166.
14. Jerry Roberts, ed., *Mitchum in His Own Words* (New York: Limelight, 2000), 168.
15. Bartlett and Steele, *Empire*, 192, 193, 200.
16. "Secret Life," 24.
17. Tinnin, *Just About Everybody*, 356.
18. Michel Ciment, *Conversations with Losey* (London: Methuen, 1985), 79.

CHAPTER 9

1. Robert Coughlan, "The O'Neil's Money Machine," *Life*, 5 December 1955, 187.
2. "Free Movies Every Night," *Time*, 1 August 1955, 55.
3. Martin Quigley, "Hail and Farewell!," *Motion Picture Daily*, 20 July 1955, 1, 6.
4. "O'Neil Putting Film Biz First," *Hollywood Reporter*, 27 July 1955, 1, 4.
5. "RKO-Teleradio Firm Organization Voted," *Los Angeles Times*, 22 November 1955, 31.
6. Chester B. Bahn, "RKO Radio to GT & R," *Film Daily*, 20 July 1955, 4.
7. Perhaps weakened by two and a half years of wearing a Howard Hughes's straitjacket, Grainger settled into semiretirement after leaving RKO. In 1959 he formed Inter-Continental Films and Inter-Continental Releasing Organization with Benedict Bogeaus, an independent producer who supplied several films to RKO during the Hughes period. I have been unable to find a record of any movies made or released by Inter-Continental.
8. "Selznick Sets RKO Prod'n Deal," *Daily Variety*, 2 September 1955, 1, 3.
9. Edwin Schallert, "RKO Aims to Recapture Former Glory," *Los Angeles Times*, 11 September 1955, D1, D3.
10. Edwin Schallert, "'Trumpet Unknown' Will Glorify Battle Medic; RKO Key Man Resigns," *Los Angeles Times*, 10 January 1956, B7.
11. Mervin Houser, "William Dozier Announces That RKO Radio Will Produce 12 to 15 Pictures during Coming Year," RKO News Service release, 6 December 1955.
12. "Dozier De-Emphasizes RKO's Girls," *New York Herald Tribune*, 18 June 1956.
13. "Production Meeting, Attended by Messrs. O'Shea, Dozier, Glett," 15 December 1955.

14. Mervin Houser, "Daniel T. O'Shea, RKO President, Announces Eddie Fisher–Debbie Reynolds Film for RKO; Purchase of Best Seller Novel, 'Cash McCall' with All-Star Cast for Early Production," RKO News Service release, 19 December 1955.

15. The deal O'Shea negotiated with David Selznick fell apart early in 1956. *A Farewell to Arms*, Selznick's last production, would be released by Twentieth Century–Fox in 1957.

16. The sale of the RKO library did indeed lead to a floodtide of motion pictures for television presentation: "In 1956 alone, as a direct result of the major studios finally releasing product to television, almost three thousand features entered television distribution." William Lafferty, "Feature Films on Prime-Time Television," in Tino Balio, ed., *Hollywood in the Age of Television* (Boston: Hyman, 1990), 242.

17. Matty Fox was an aggressive show business entrepreneur who had been circling RKO for years. Groups he claimed to represent had made offers for the theaters, the entire corporation, and television rights to RKO's films at various times during the Hughes administration.

18. "RKO Radio Pictures Leases 740 Feature, Other Films for TV Use to C&C Super Corp. for $15 Million," *Wall Street Journal*, 27 December 1955, 7.

19. Quoted in "Hughes-O'Neil Deal Called Amazing Coup," *Los Angeles Times*, 7 January 1956, A1.

20. "O'Neil's $2,200,000 RKO Profit," *Daily Variety*, 6 January 1956, 1.

21. "Quick Turnaround on RKO Fills Everybody's Pockets," *Business Week*, 14 January 1956, 52.

22. This information has been gleaned from press releases written by Mervin Houser and disseminated by the RKO News Service on the dates indicated.

23. William Dozier, memorandum to Charles Glett, 26 March 1956.

24. William Dozier, memorandum to Daniel T. O'Shea, 27 March 1956.

25. William Dozier, telegram to Daniel T. O'Shea, 28 March 1956.

26. Daniel T. O'Shea, telegram to William Dozier, 29 March 1956.

27. Dozier, memorandum to O'Shea, 2 April 1956.

28. Mervin Houser, "Arthur Siteman Leaves for Orient to Scout Locations for Three Big RKO Productions," RKO News Service release, 25 June 1956.

29. "O'Neil's RKO Pix-TV-Legit Parlay," *Daily Variety*, 7 June 1956, 1, 11.

30. Sandford Brown, "Lights, Camera, Profits," *Newsweek*, 16 July 1956, 73–76.

31. Frank Scully, "Lull (Meaning Howard Hughes) Now a Hum as RKO Plant Jumps," *Variety*, 15 August 1956, 8.

32. Dozier, memorandum to O'Shea, 14 August 1956.

33. *Galveston* was to be based on a story RKO purchased back in 1944 that had never been mounted as a feature production. See Edwin Schallert, "New Picture Planned with Galveston Locale," *Los Angeles Times*, 29 June 1944, A10.

34. Daniel T. O'Shea, memorandum to Thomas F. O'Neil, 21 August 1956.

35. Ibid.

36. Dozier, memorandum to O'Shea, 2 October 1956.
37. Mervin Houser, "Dozier Expresses Optimism in National Television Talk," RKO News Service release, 1 October, 1956.
38. Mervin Houser, "RKO Has in Preparation 15 Projects to Start Filming Late 1956 and 1957," RKO News Service release, 4 October 1956.
39. D.W. [Dan Winkler] to William Dozier, 23 October 1956.
40. Dozier, memorandum to O'Shea, 22 August 1956. After Terry Turner resigned as director of exploitation for RKO during the Stolkin period, he accepted a position with General Teleradio. Now he was back figuring ways to sell RKO product again.
41. Mervin Houser, "RKO Announces $33,000,000 in Pictures to Be Released within Next Six Months," RKO News Service release, 19 November 1956.
42. Coughlan, "O'Neil's Money Machine," 200.
43. Thomas F. O'Neil, memorandum to Daniel T. O'Shea, 26 November 1956.
44. This figure represented another indicator of how far RKO's business had declined over the past ten years: in 1946 the company raked in $72,966,727 in film rentals. See "RKO's $12,187,805 Record Net Places It No. 5 in '46 Film Profit Sweepstakes," *Variety*, 30 April 1947, 6.
45. O'Neil, memorandum to O'Shea, 26 November 1956.
46. Ibid.
47. Mervin Houser, telegram to William Dozier, 5 December 1956.
48. "RKO Asks UI to Merge Distribution," *Daily Variety*, 10 December 1956, 1, 4.
49. As late as the end of February 1957, William Dozier was still claiming that RKO would "emulate Goldwyn." See "Dozier Champions RKO's 'Individual' Policy as 'Lifesaver, Not Executioner' of Pix Biz," *Daily Variety*, 26 February 1957, 1, 4.
50. "Confidential Meeting Notes—Messrs. Bender, Berry, Daniels, Figueroa, Klune," 14 December 1956.
51. "RKO Studio to Be Very Quiet," *Variety*, 19 December 1956, 4.
52. William Dozier, memorandum to Don Moore, 3 January 1957.
53. Finler, *Hollywood Story*, 35.
54. "RKO Washing Up as Film Co.?," *Daily Variety*, 23 January 1957, 1.
55. Dick Williams, "End of an Era Nears for RKO Gower St. Studio," *Los Angeles Mirror–News*, 24 January 1957, pt. 1, p. 14. Williams was wrong—thankfully, the studio never became a tire-processing plant.
56. Wilkerson, Trade Views, 24 January 1957, 1.
57. Thomas M. Pryor, "Hollywood Views; Film Future of R.K.O. in the Balance," *New York Times*, 27 January 1957, X5.
58. Al Steen, "Goodbye to RKO Exchanges; Universal to Handle Pictures," *Boxoffice*, 26 January 1957.
59. "What's Happening at RKO," *Daily Variety*, 28 January, 1957, 23.
60. R.A. Klune, memorandum to Daniel T. O'Shea, 7 February 1957.

61. Klune, memorandum to O'Shea, 21 January 1957, 14 February, 1957.

62. In Hollywood parlance, a "4-wall" deal is when a distributor rents a theater for a defined period to showcase a film and, as a consequence, is able to keep all the box-office revenue from its showings.

63. Klune, memorandum to O'Shea, 14 February, 1957.

64. John Wayne biographer Scott Eyman has called *The Conqueror* and *Jet Pilot*, along with a third film Wayne made for Hughes, *Flying Leathernecks*, "among the most bizarre [pictures] in the annals of Hollywood." Scott Eyman, *John Wayne: The Life and Legend* (New York: Simon and Schuster, 2014), 199.

65. S.L., "The Conqueror," *Chicago Daily News*, 5 March 1956, 25.

66. See, for example, Harry Medved, *The Fifty Worst Films of All Time*, with Randy Dreyfuss (New York: Popular Library, 1978); and Michael Sauter, *The Worst Movies of All Time* (Secaucus, NJ: Citadel, 1999).

67. Klune, memorandum to O'Shea, 11 June 1957.

68. The dilapidated RKO Pathe plant in Culver City was in even worse physical condition. After Desilu bought the studios, Lucille Ball's brother Fred took charge of the renovation. "The offices at RKO were a disaster," he recalled. "Every office needed refurbishing—every stairway, every parking lot, everything in the studio needed work." Coyne Steven Sanders and Tom Gilbert, *Desilu: The Story of Lucille Ball and Desi Arnaz* (New York: Morrow, 1993), 146.

69. R.A. Klune, "File Memo—Gower Street Studio," 20 June 1957.

70. R.A. Klune, memorandum to Edward L. Walton, 6 November 1957.

71. "The New Tycoon," *Time*, 7 April 1958, 69.

72. Cecil Smith, "Desilu Colossus Pouring Money, Talent into New Television Film Play Series," *Los Angeles Times*, 10 August 1958, G5.

EPILOGUE

1. James MacGregor Burns, *Leadership* (New York: Harper and Row, 1978), 18.

Selected Bibliography

Balio, Tino, ed. *The American Film Industry.* Rev. ed. Madison: University of Wisconsin Press, 1985.
———. *Grand Design: Hollywood as a Modern Business Enterprise, 1930–1939.* New York: Scribner's, 1993.
———, ed. *Hollywood in the Age of Television.* Boston: Hyman, 1990.
———. *United Artists: The Company Built by the Stars.* Madison: University of Wisconsin Press, 1976.
———. *United Artists: The Company That Changed the Film Industry.* Madison: University of Wisconsin Press, 1987.
Bansak, Edmund. *Fearing the Dark: The Val Lewton Career.* Jefferson, NC: McFarland, 2003.
Barbas, Samantha. *The First Lady of Hollywood: A Biography of Louella Parsons.* Berkeley: University of California Press, 2005.
Bartlett, Donald L., and James B. Steele. *Empire: The Life, Legend, and Madness of Howard Hughes.* New York: Norton, 1979.
Belton, John. *Widescreen Cinema.* Cambridge, MA: Harvard University Press, 1992.
Benamou, Catherine L. *It's All True: Orson Welles's Pan-American Odyssey.* Berkeley: University of California Press, 2007.
Berg, A. Scott. *Goldwyn: A Biography.* New York: Knopf, 1989.
Bergan. Ronald. *The United Artists Story.* New York: Crown, 1986.
Blum, John Morton. *V Was for Victory: Politics and American Culture during World War II.* San Diego: Harcourt Brace Jovanovich, 1976.
Bordwell, David, Janet Staiger, and Kristin Thompson. *The Classical Hollywood Cinema: Film Style and Mode of Production to 1960.* New York: Columbia University Press, 1985.
Brown, Peter Harry, and Pat H. Broeske. *Howard Hughes: The Untold Story.* Cambridge, MA: Da Capo, 2004.
Burns, James MacGregor. *Leadership.* New York: Harper and Row, 1978.

Carringer, Robert L. *The Magnificent Ambersons: A Reconstruction.* Berkeley: University of California Press, 1993.
Casper, Drew. *Postwar Hollywood, 1946–1962.* Malden, MA: Blackwell, 2007.
Ceplair, Larry. *The Marxist and the Movies: A Biography of Paul Jarrico.* Lexington: University Press of Kentucky, 2007.
Chambers, John Whiteclay, and David Culbert. *World War II, Film, and History.* New York: Oxford University Press, 1996.
Chandler, Alfred, Jr. *The Visible Hand: The Managerial Revolution in American Business.* Cambridge, MA: Harvard University Press, 1977.
Ciment, Michel. *Conversations with Losey.* London: Methuen, 1985.
Conant, Michael. *Antitrust in the Motion Picture Industry.* New York: Arno, 1979.
Davis, Ronald L. *The Glamour Factory: Inside Hollywood's Big Studio System.* Dallas: Southern Methodist University Press, 1993.
Dick, Bernard. *City of Dreams: The Making and Remaking of Universal Pictures.* Lexington: University Press of Kentucky, 1997.
———. *Columbia Pictures: Portrait of a Studio.* Lexington: University Press of Kentucky, 1992.
———. *Engulfed: The Death of Paramount Pictures and the Birth of Corporate Hollywood.* Lexington: University Press of Kentucky, 2001.
Dietrich, Noah. *Howard: The Amazing Mr. Hughes.* Greenwich, CT: Fawcett, 1972.
Dmytryk, Edward. *It's a Hell of a Life but Not a Bad Living.* New York: Times Books, 1978.
———. *Odd Man Out: A Memoir of the Hollywood Ten.* Carbondale, IL: Southern Illinois Press, 1996.
Doherty, Thomas. *Hollywood's Censor: Joseph I. Breen and the Production Code Administration.* New York: Columbia University Press, 2007.
———. *Projections of War: Hollywood, American Culture, and World War II.* New York: Columbia University Press, 1993.
Donati, William. *Ida Lupino: A Biography.* Lexington: University Press of Kentucky, 1996.
Eames, John Douglas. *The MGM Story.* London: Octopus Books, 1977.
———. *The Paramount Story.* New York: Crown, 1985.
Eisenschitz, Bernard. *Nicholas Ray: An American Journey.* London: Faber and Faber, 1993.
Eliot, Marc. *Cary Grant: A Biography.* New York: Harmony Books, 2004.
Evans, Peter, and Ava Gardner. *Ava Gardner: The Secret Conversations.* New York: Simon and Schuster, 2013.
Eyman, Scott. *John Wayne: The Life and Legend.* New York: Simon and Schuster, 2014.
———. *Print the Legend: The Life and Times of John Ford.* New York: Simon and Schuster, 1999.
Finler, Joel W. *The Hollywood Story.* New York: Crown, 1988.
Fishgall, Gary. *Gregory Peck: A Biography.* New York: Scribner, 2002.

Fleischer, Richard. *Just Tell Me When to Cry: A Memoir.* New York: Carroll and Graf, 1993.
Fowler, Roy Alexander. *Orson Welles.* London: Pendulum, 1946.
French, Philip. *The Movie Moguls.* London: Weidenfeld and Nicholson, 1969.
Fugiwara, Chris. *Jacques Tourneur: The Cinema of Nightfall.* Jefferson, NC: McFarland, 2001.
Gabler, Neal. *An Empire of Their Own: How the Jews Invented Hollywood.* New York: Crown, 1988.
Gardner, Ava. *My Story.* New York: Bantam Books, 1990.
Gladstone, B. James. *The Man Who Seduced Hollywood: The Life and Loves of Greg Bautzer, Tinseltown's Most Powerful Lawyer.* Chicago: Chicago Review, 2013.
Gomery, Douglas. *The Hollywood Studio System: A History.* London: British Film Institute, 2005.
———. *Shared Pleasures: A History of Movie Presentation in the United States.* Madison: University of Wisconsin Press, 1992.
Granger, Stewart. *Sparks Fly Upward.* New York: Putnam's Sons, 1981.
Hack, Richard. *Hughes: The Private Diaries, Memos and Letters.* Beverly Hills, CA: New Millennium, 2001.
Heylin, Clinton. *Orson Welles versus the Hollywood Studios.* Chicago: Chicago Review, 2005.
Hirschhorn, Clive. *The Columbia Story.* New York: Crown, 1990.
———. *The Universal Story.* New York: Crown, 1983.
———. *The Warner Bros. Story.* New York: Crown, 1979.
Hodgson, Godfrey. *America in Our Time: From World War II to Nixon—What Happened and Why.* New York: Random House, 1976.
Hollis, Richard, and Brian Sibley. *The Disney Studio Story.* New York: Crown, 1988.
Holston, Kim R. *Susan Hayward: Her Films and Life.* Jefferson, NC: McFarland, 2002.
Hopper, Hedda. *From under My Hat.* Garden City, NY: Doubleday, 1952.
Houseman, John. *Front and Center.* New York: Simon and Schuster, 1979.
———. *Run-Through: A Memoir.* New York: Simon and Schuster, 1972.
Hoyt, Eric. *Hollywood Vault: Film Libraries before Home Video.* Berkeley: University of California Press, 2014.
Hurst, Richard Maurice. *Republic Studios: Between Poverty Row and the Majors.* Metuchen, NJ: Scarecrow, 1979.
Izod, John. *Hollywood and the Box Office, 1895–1986.* New York: Columbia University Press, 1988.
Jarlett, Franklin. *Robert Ryan: A Biography and Critical Filmography.* Jefferson, NC: McFarland, 1990.
Jewell, Richard B. *The Golden Age of Cinema: Hollywood 1929–1945.* Malden, MA: Blackwell, 2007.
———. *RKO Radio Pictures: A Titan Is Born.* Berkeley: University of California Press, 2012.

———. *The RKO Story.* With Vernon Harbin. London: Octopus Books, 1982.
Jobes, Gertrude. *Motion Picture Empire.* Hamden, CT: Archon Books, 1966.
Jones, J. R. *The Lives of Robert Ryan.* Middletown, CT: Wesleyan University Press, 2015.
Kemper, Tom. *Hidden Talent: The Emergence of the Hollywood Agents.* Berkeley: University of California Press, 2010.
Kerr, Paul, ed. *The Hollywood Film Industry.* London: Routledge and Kegan Paul, 1986.
Kindem, Gorham, ed. *The American Movie Industry: The Business of Motion Pictures.* Carbondale: Southern Illinois University Press, 1982.
Koppes, Clayton R., and Gregory D. Black. *Hollywood Goes to War.* New York: Free Press, 1987.
Langdon, Jennifer E. *Caught in the Crossfire: Adrian Scott and the Politics of Americanism in 1940s Hollywood.* New York: Columbia University Press, 2008.
Lasky, Betty. *RKO, the Biggest Little Major of Them All.* Englewood Cliffs, NJ: Prentice-Hall, 1984.
Laurents, Arthur. *Original Story By: A Memoir of Broadway and Hollywood.* New York: Knopf, 2000.
Leemann, Sergio. *Robert Wise on His Films.* Los Angeles: Silman-James, 1995.
Leff, Leonard J., and Jerold L. Simmons. *The Dame in the Kimono: Hollywood, Censorship, and the Production Code from the 1920s to the 1960s.* New York: Weidenfeld, 1990.
Leigh, Janet. *There Really Was a Hollywood.* Garden City, NY: Doubleday, 1984.
LeRoy, Mervyn. *Take One.* New York: Hawthorn Books, 1974.
Lev, Peter. *The Fifties.* Berkeley: University of California Press, 2003.
———. *Twentieth Century–Fox: The Zanuck-Skouras Years, 1935–1965.* Austin: University of Texas Press, 2013.
Linet, Beverly. *Susan Hayward: Portrait of a Survivor.* New York: Athenium, 1980.
Litman, Barry R. *The Motion Picture Mega-Industry.* Boston: Allyn and Bacon, 1998.
Lorentz, Pare. *FDR's Moviemaker: Memoirs and Scripts.* Reno: University of Nevada Press, 1992.
Maltby, Richard. *Hollywood Cinema.* 2nd ed. Malden, MA: Blackwell, 2003.
Mast, Gerald, ed. *The Movies in Our Midst: Documents in the Cultural History of Film in America.* Chicago: University of Chicago Press, 1982.
McBride, Joseph. *Orson Welles.* New York: Viking, 1972.
———. *Whatever Happened to Orson Welles?* Lexington: University Press of Kentucky, 2006.
McCarthy, Todd. *Howard Hawks.* New York: Grove, 1997.
McCarthy, Todd, and Charles Flynn. *Kings of the Bs.* New York: Dutton, 1975.
McGilligan, Patrick, and Paul Buhle. *Tender Comrades: A Backstory of the Hollywood Blacklist.* New York: St. Martin's Press, 1997.

Medved, Harry. *The Fifty Worst Films of All Time*. With Randy Dreyfuss. New York: Popular Library, 1978.
Melnick, Ross. *American Showman: Samuel "Roxy" Rothafel and the Birth of the Entertainment Industry*. New York: Columbia University Press, 2012.
Miller, Don. *B Movies*. New York: Ballantine Books, 1973.
Miller, Gabriel. *Clifford Odets*. New York: Continuum, 1989.
Milne, Tom, ed. *Losey on Losey*. Garden City, NY: Doubleday, 1968.
O'Brien, Pat. *The Wind at My Back: The Life and Times of Pat O'Brien*. Garden City, NY: Doubleday, 1964.
Ohmer, Susan. *George Gallup in Hollywood*. New York: Columbia University Press, 2006.
Parsons, Louella O. *Tell It to Louella*. New York: Putnam's Sons, 1961.
Powdermaker, Hortense. *Hollywood, the Dream Factory*. Boston: Little, Brown, 1951.
Price, Victoria. *Vincent Price: A Daughter's Biography*. New York: St. Martin's Press, 1999.
Richards, Jeffrey. *Hollywood's Ancient Worlds*. London: Continuum, 2008.
Roberts, Andrew. *The Storm of War: A New History of the Second World War*. New York: HarperCollins, 2011.
Roberts, Jerry, ed. *Mitchum in His Own Words*. New York: Limelight, 2000.
———. *Robert Mitchum: A Bio-Bibliography*. Westport, CT: Greenwood, 1992.
Rogers, Ginger. *Ginger: My Story*. New York: HarperCollins, 1991.
Russell, Jane. *Jane Russell: My Path and My Detours, an Autobiography*. New York: Watts, 1985.
Russell, Rosalind, and Chris Chase. *Life Is a Banquet*. New York: Random House, 1977.
Sanders, Coyne Steven, and Tom Gilbert. *Desilu: The Story of Lucille Ball and Desi Arnaz*. New York: William Morrow, 1993.
Sauter, Michael. *The Worst Movies of All Time*. Secaucus, NJ: Citadel, 1999.
Sbardellati, John. *J. Edgar Hoover Goes to the Movies: The FBI and the Origins of Hollywood's Cold War*. Ithaca, NY: Cornell University Press, 2012.
Schary, Dore. *Heyday: An Autobiography*. Boston: Little, Brown, 1979.
Schatz, Thomas. *Boom and Bust: American Cinema in the 1940s*. Berkeley: University of California Press, 1997.
———. *The Genius of the System: Hollywood Filmmaking in the Studio Era*. New York: Holt, 1988.
Schwartz, Nancy Lynne. *The Hollywood Writers War*. New York: Knopf, 1982.
Server, Lee. *Ava Gardner: "Love Is Nothing."* New York: St. Martin's Press, 2006.
———. *Robert Mitchum: "Baby, I Don't Care."* New York: St. Martin's Press, 2001.
Siegel, Joel E. *Val Lewton: The Reality of Terror*. New York: Viking, 1972.
Silverman, Stephen M. *The Fox That Got Away: The Last Days of the Zanuck Dynasty at Twentieth Century–Fox*. Secaucus, NJ: Stuart, 1988.
Sklar, Robert. *Movie-Made America*. New York: Random House, 1975.

Slide, Anthony. *The American Film Industry: A Historical Dictionary.* New York: Limelight, 1990.

Snyder, Robert L. *Pare Lorentz and the Documentary Film.* Reno: University of Nevada Press, 1994.

Solomon, Aubrey. *Twentieth Century–Fox: A Corporate and Financial History.* Metuchen, NJ: Scarecrow, 1988.

Staiger, Janet, ed. *The Studio System.* New Brunswick, NJ: Rutgers University Press, 1995.

Stanley, Robert. *The Celluloid Empire: A History of the American Motion Picture Industry.* New York: Hastings House, 1978.

Suid, Lawrence H. *Guts and Glory: The Making of the American Military Image in Film.* Rev. ed. Lexington: University Press of Kentucky, 2002.

Telotte, J. P. *Dreams of Darkness: Fantasy and the Films of Val Lewton.* Urbana: University of Illinois Press, 1985.

Thomas, Tony. *Howard Hughes in Hollywood.* Secaucus, NJ: Citadel, 1985.

Thompson, Frank. *Robert Wise: A Bio-Bibliography.* Westport, CT: Greenwood, 1995.

Tinnin, David B. *Just About Everybody vs. Howard Hughes.* Garden City, NY: Doubleday, 1973.

Vaz, Mark Cotta. *Living Dangerously: The Adventures of Merian C. Cooper.* New York: Villard, 2005.

Von Sternberg, Josef. *Fun in a Chinese Laundry.* New York: Macmillan, 1965.

Wasko, Janet. *Movies and Money: Financing the American Film Industry.* Norwood, NJ: Ablex, 1982.

Zierold, Norman. *The Moguls.* New York: Coward-McCann, 1969.

Zollo, Paul. *Hollywood Remembered: An Oral History of Its Golden Age.* Lanham, MD: Taylor Trade, 2002.

Index

3-D, 142, 154–5, 161, 165

A pictures, 3, 25, 42, 101, 222n25
Aalberg, John, 210
Action in Arabia, 22
Adventure in Baltimore, 79
advertising, 53, 63, 121–22, 165. See also promotion; publicity
Agee, James, 43
Ahern, Fred, 195
American Legion, 125, 234n58
Ames, Stephen, 106
Andes, Keith, 141, 147
Androcles and the Lion, 129–30, 134, 141
anti-Semitism, 68–69
antitrust, 13, 47
Appointment in Honduras, 128, 162
Appointment in Samarra, 155–56
Archainbaud, George, 105
Argosy Pictures, 46, 94, 106, 224n9
Arnaz, Desi, 207–8, 210
Arthur, Jean, 18, 41, 214
Astaire, Fred, 17, 210
At Sword's Point, 111, 131
Atlas Corporation, 18, 78, 82, 93, 99–100, 169–70, 244n107
attendance, 60, 106
Audience Research, 53
Austrian, Ralph, 76
Aylesworth, Merlin "Deac", 39, 212

B pictures, 15–16, 25, 42–43, 47, 59, 61, 108, 222n25
baby boom, 60
The Bachelor and the Bobby-Soxer, 50, 60, 72
Back from Eternity, 193, 195, 199, 208
Back to Bataan, 79
Badman's Territory, 51
Balenda, Carla, 136, 184
Ball, Lucille, 207–8, 210
Barry, Harold, 172
Bartlett, Donald L., 186
Battleground, 79, 83, 228n92, 229n101
Bauer, Leda, 84, 141
Bed of Roses (Born to be Bad), 79, 83, 100, 102, 158
Bedlam, 43, 44
Behave Yourself, 116, 118
Behind the Rising Sun, 17, 22
Bel Geddes, Barbara, 59, 83, 106, 230n25
Bell, Ulric, 17, 25
Belle of the Yukon, 25
The Bells of St. Mary's, 28, 32, 51
Bender, Ben, 210
Bendix, William, 142
Bent, Maurice, 148, 239n35
Bergen, Edgar, 109
Berger, Richard, 59, 106
Bergman, Ingrid, 28, 30, 54–55, 95–98, 184, 231n35
Berlin Express, 41, 79

Berman, Pandro, 140, 213
The Best Years of Our Lives, 51, 63
Beyond a Reasonable Doubt, 195, 199
The Big Sky, 134
The Big Steal, 90–91
Bischoff, Samuel, 107–10, 112, 232n10
Blackbeard the Pirate, 129, 151
blacklist, 66
block booking, 34, 47, 222n25
Blood on the Moon, 76, 79, 89
The Blue Veil, 116, 118
board of directors. *See* RKO Board of Directors
Boasberg, Charles, 141, 149
Bodyguard, 79
Bombardier, 17
Bonestell, Chesley, 15
Born to be Bad, 100, 102, 129, 158
Born to Kill, 72
The Boy with Green Hair, 76, 79, 85, 89
Branson, Walter, 141, 202
Breen, Joseph, 3, 44, 54, 73–74, 129, 165, 176–77
Brewer, Roy, 48, 126
Bride By Mistake, 21, 23, 26
Bringing Up Baby, 194
Briskin, Sam, 29–30, 37, 46, 51–53, 212–13
Brisson, Frederick, 46
British tax, 63, 76, 77, 227n65
Brown, Hiram, 212
Brown, Wally, 25
budgets, 1, 20, 42, 60–61
Build My Gallows High (*Out of the Past*), 45
Bundle of Joy, 203, 204, 208, 209
Burke, Edward "Buzz", 137–39, 144, 146, 148
Bwana Devil, 142, 154–55

California Pictures, 81
Cantor, Eddie, 25, 26, 30
Capra, Frank, 29, 46, 51, 52, 210
Carney, Alan, 25
Carriage Entrance (*My Forbidden Past*), 127–28, 158

Casanova Brown, 25
casting, 18, 34, 59, 130, 209
Castleman, Eli B. and Marion V., 153, 159–60
Cat People, 9, 18, 19–20, 194
Catholic Legion of Decency, 165, 167
Caught, 230n25
censorship, 54–55, 91, 129–30, 165–67. *See also* Production Code Administration
Channing, Carol, 199
China Sky, 16
Churubusco, 31, 62, 78, 221n97, 224n9, 227n79
CinemaScope, 122, 127, 154
Citizen Kane, xii, 4, 194
Clair, Rene, 41, 49
Clark, W.H., 121, 138, 159
Clash by Night, 130, 174–75
Clurman, Harold, 220n67
Cochran, Jacqueline, 12–13
Cohn, Harry, 37, 66
color, 149, 172, 208. *See also* Technicolor
Columbia, 33, 122, 123–24, 145, 170
Columbia Broadcasting System (CBS), 191
combat films, 13, 79
communism, 64–68, 95, 123–27, 214
Condon, Richard, 141
Conference of Studio Unions (CSU), 28, 48
The Conqueror, 172, 173, 194, 206, 243n88
Conway, Tom, 25
Cook, Raymond, 163–64
Cooper, Gary, 25
Cooper, Merian C., 46, 210
coproductions, 106; RKO-Argosy, 224n9; RKO-Rainbow Productions, 28; RKO-Rank, 31, 49; RKO-Vanguard, 29, 50, 54, 58–59; RKO-Winchester Productions, 102
Cornered, 30, 51
corporate profits. *See* profits
Corwin, Sherrill, 137–42, 144, 146–48
Crack-Up, 38, 44

Cramer, Claire, 172
Cromwell, John, 95, 185
Crosby, Bing, 28, 30
Crosby, Floyd, 7
Crossfire, 65, 68–70, 72, 85, 194
Crown, Alfred, 141, 152
Cugat, Xavier, 142
Culver City studio. *See* RKO Pathe
Curse of the Cat People, 25
Cyr, Lili St., 176, 177

Dangerous Mission, 154, 162
A Dangerous Profession, 104
Darnell, Linda, 129, 184
DaSilva, Howard, 124
Day, Laraine, 18, 23, 34, 185
Days of Glory, 16, 22, 26–27
Decameron Nights, 162
De Grasse, Robert, 106
de Havilland, Olivia, 16, 18, 181
Depinet, Ned: in Europe, 49; frustration with Howard Hughes, 101–2, 110–12, 148, 149; *It's a Wonderful Life*, 53; lawsuits, 158–59; resignation, 139; RKO executive, 2, 37, 59, 84, 109
Desilu, 207–8, 210
The Devil and Miss Jones, 41
The Devil Thumbs a Ride, 60
Devil's Canyon, 154
Di Falco, Samuel, 159
Dick Tracy Meets Gruesome, 43
Dietrich, Noah, 92, 103, 104, 110, 132–33, 138, 148, 157, 161, 178, 230n18
Dinnelli, Mel, 106
Disney, Roy, 159
Disney, Walt, 25, 37, 145, 172, 206
distribution, 15, 102, 110, 161, 201–3
divestiture, 91, 93, 104, 121. *See also* theaters
Dmytryk, Edward, 16, 43, 49, 65–68, 70, 89, 225n31
documentaries, 13, 134
Domergue, Faith, 116, 184
Double Dynamite, 94, 111, 155
Douglas, Kirk, 74

Dozier, William, 31, 39, 140, 191, 195–99, 208
Duff, Warren, 24, 74, 100
Dunn, Linwood, 210
Dunne, Irene, 59, 210
Durning, Harry M., 89, 92

Earhart, Amelia, 11–12
Easy Living, 79, 104
Eglinton, Bill, 210
Ehrman, Frederick L., 65, 103, 158
Eisler, Hanns, 124
The Enchanted Cottage, 32, 173, 175
Escapade in Japan, 197, 199, 206
Escape to Burma, 176
exhibition, 47, 91–93
Experiment Perilous, 23
exploitation. *See* advertising

Fadiman, William, xiv, 84, 94, 145, 245n13
Falcon series, 25
The Falcon's Brother, 9, 11
The Fallen Sparrow, 17
Farber, Manny, 43
The Farmer's Daughter, 50, 57, 60
Farrow, John, 193, 199
Fellows, Robert, 24
Ferrer, Mel, 142
Feuerman, Louis, 153, 160
Fighting Father Dunne, 89
film laboratories, 48
film noir, 30, 44–45, 74
first-run theaters. *See* theaters
The First Traveling Saleslady, 193, 195, 199
Fisher, Eddie, 193, 203–04, 209
Fleischer, Richard, 105, 116–18
Flight for Freedom, 11–13
Flippen, Jay C., 134
Fontaine, Joan, 30, 34, 184, 210
Ford, John, 46, 94, 210
foreign markets, 63, 71, 77
Forrest, Sally, 176, 177
Foster, Norman, 9
Fox, Matty, 100, 147, 193, 246n17
Freeman, Norman, 38, 42–43, 70

Freeman, Y. Frank, 39
The French Line, 154, 161, 162, 164–68
Friedlob, Bert, 196
Friedman, Milton, 153
From This Day Forward, 38, 51
The Fugitive, 224n9
Fuller, Sam, 196, 199, 206, 207

Gang, Martin, 127, 128–29
Gardner, Ava, 127, 130–31, 181, 183, 184
Garfield, John, 18, 38, 74
The Gaunt Woman (Sealed Cargo), 108, 111
General Teleradio, 178, 188–89
General Tire, 178, 188, 209
The Ghost Ship, 43
Giesler, Jerry, 89, 90
Gilroy, Bert, 15, 16
The Girl Most Likely, 206, 208
Girl Rush, 25
Glett, Charles, 193, 195–96, 208
Goetz, William, 25
Goldberg, Leon, 48
Golden, Edward, 16
Goldman, David, 63
Goldwyn, Samuel, 17, 37, 51, 66, 77, 147, 173, 206
Gordon, William, 55
Gorman, William, 138, 145, 146
Government Girl, 16, 17
Gower Street studio, 40–41, 63, 205, 207–8
Grainger, Edmund, 149, 151, 204
Grainger, James R., 149, 151–52, 154, 157, 159, 161–62, 169, 176, 179, 191, 245n7
Granet, Bert, 43, 59, 106
Granger, Farley, 118
Granger, Stewart, 128
Grant, Arnold, 138–39, 143, 145–46
Grant, Cary, 17, 18, 22, 23, 25, 38, 54–55, 58–59, 210
Great Day, 72
Green, L. Lawrence, 65
Greene, David J., 147, 162, 240n30
Greer, Jane, 23, 40, 59, 74–75, 184

Gross, Jack, 24, 43, 59, 90
Gunga Din, xii, 194

Hakim Brothers, 106
Hale, Barbara, 40, 59
Hans Christian Anderson, 145
Hard, Fast and Beautiful, 111, 192
Hastings, Ross, 103, 120, 142–43
Hatch, L. Boyd, 89, 92
Hawks, Howard, 81, 102
Hays, Will, 37
Hayward, Susan, 30, 130, 184
Hearst, William Randolph, xii
Heartbeat, 38
Heavenly Days, 22
Hempstead, David, 12–13, 16, 24
Hendee, Harold, 141
Henley, Nadine, 174
Henreid, Paul, 30, 38, 225n22
Hepburn, Katharine, 40, 181, 197, 210
Here We Go Again, 11
Higher and Higher, 16, 26
His Kind of Woman, 109, 116, 118, 121, 129, 134–35
Hitchcock, Alfred, 54–55, 210
Hitler's Children, 16, 22
Holiday Affair, 100, 104, 143
Hollywood Ten, 64–65
Holt, Tim, 61, 108, 134
Honeymoon, 60, 72
Hopper, Hedda, 67, 229n7
horror films, 18, 20, 43–44
House Un-American Activities Committee (HUAC), 64–65, 123–24, 214
Houseman, John, 57, 100, 185
Houser, Mervin, 174–75, 192, 196, 200
Hughes, Howard, 80–81, 180–82; anticommunist, 81, 95, 123–27, 136; "auteur", 135–6; board of directors, 92, 103, 138, 148; broken promises, 83, 99–100, 171, 184, 228n94, 230n18; businessman, 87, 92, 168–69, 181, 186–87, 243n107; censorship, 91, 129–30, 165–67, 176–78; changes in RKO culture, 87, 88, 106, 178, 184–85; delays, 102, 111–12,

116, 119, 155, 161, 200; executive practices, 85, 99–100, 120–21, 155, 182–83, 187, 229n4; lawsuits, 123–24, 127–29, 143, 146, 152–53, 155, 157–60, 170, 236n78; playboy, 181, 183–84; production decisions, 109, 112, 154, 185; profits, 137, 150, 162, 164, 179, 186, 206, 244n110; publicity, 102–3, 134–35, 175–76, 229n7; questionable ethics, 156, 163; reputation, 81, 89, 133, 136, 180–84, 187; RKO purchase, 79–82, 150, 215; RKO sale, 136–37, 178–79, 190; scandal, 89–90, 95–98; taste, 109, 135, 185; tinkerer, 83, 101, 111, 116–18
Hughes Aircraft Company, 107, 125, 171, 182, 186
Hughes Medical Institute, 186
Hughes Tool Company, 87, 160–61, 163, 171
The Hunchback of Notre Dame, 156, 194
Hunt, Marsha, 34
Hunt the Man Down, 105

I Married a Communist (The Woman on Pier 13), 94, 95, 102
I Married a Woman, 206, 209
I Married the Navy (Bride by Mistake), 23
I Remember Mama, 76, 79, 175
If You Knew Susie, 79
income tax, 38, 46
Independent Artists, 46, 106
independent production companies, 40, 46–7, 101, 122–23, 201
independent theater owners, 34, 47
Indian Summer, 71, 89
International Alliance of Theatrical Stage Employees (IATSE), 28, 48
International Pictures, 25, 29
Irvine, Ralstone E. "Shorty", 91–92, 93, 99
Isle of the Dead, 124
It's A Wonderful Life, 51–53, 223n47
It's All True, 4–7, 35

It's Only Money (Double Dynamite), 94, 111, 155

Jarrico, Paul, 123–24, 125–26, 127, 235n66
Jeanmaire, Renée, 153–54
Jeffries, Anne, 40, 59
Jet Pilot, 94, 102–3, 108, 112, 134, 143, 161, 172, 194, 200, 206
Johnny Angel, 32
Johnson, Edwin C., 98
Johnson, Van, 196
Johnston, Eric, 28, 37, 66
Journey into Fear, 9–10, 17
The Judge Steps Out, 104

Kahane, B.B., 37
Karloff, Boris, 24–25, 43
Kenny, Elizabeth, 23, 45
Kilian, Victor, 124
Killy, Edward, 96
King Kong, 194
Kingsberg, Malcolm, 37, 47–48
Klune, Ray, 202, 205, 207
Koerner, Charles W., 3–37, 49–50, 214; cleaning up after George Schaefer, 4–9; illness and death, 32–33, 37; leadership, 24, 31; production decisions, 8–9, 11, 16–17, 18, 21–22, 28–30, 34; profits, 17–18, 26, 33–34; relationship with Peter Rathvon, 9–10, 39, 214; reputation, 7, 34–35; scorecard, 11, 14, 16–17, 21, 25, 33, 35; wartime challenges, 14–15
Koolish, Abraham, 137–39, 143, 144, 146
Korshak, Sidney, 143–44, 145
Krasna, Norman, 112–16, 119–20, 130, 132
Kurosawa, Akira, 134

Ladies Day, 9
A Lady Takes a Chance, 17, 41
Lamarr, Hedy, 23, 25, 34
Lang, Fritz, 200
Larrinaga, John, 15
Larrinaga, Mario, 15

The Las Vegas Story, 108, 123, 124, 129, 134, 135
lawsuits, 8, 43, 67, 87, 123–29, 157–60, 163–64
layoffs, 124, 151, 172
LeBaron, William, 212
Leeds, Lila, 89
Leigh, Janet, 143, 183, 184
The Leopard Man, 18, 19
Lesser, Sol, 20, 40, 159
Lessing, Gunther R., 126
Lewton, Val, 18–20, 24–25, 43–44, 210
Liberty Films, 29–30, 46, 51, 53
Lieber, Perry, 176, 192
A Likely Story, 72
List, Albert A., 162
Lockhart, Bicknell, 83, 88
The Long Night, 60, 72
Lorentz, Pare, 7–8
Losey, Joseph, 57, 106
losses: 1941–42, 33; 1942–43, 10, 17; 1944, 26; 1947–48, 72, 77, 99; 1948–49, 79; 1949–50, 121; Goldwyn deal, 17, 110; industry-wide, 94; under Howard Hughes, 153, 156, 162, 164, 170
Loy, Myrna, 30, 58–59
Luce, Henry, 13
Lupino, Ida, 174, 184
Lurie, Louis R., 147
The Lusty Men, 130

Macao, 112, 129, 135, 163
MacMurray, Fred, 18
Mad Wednesday, 81, 156, 163
Mad with Much Heart (On Dangerous Ground), 111
Magic Town, 72, 189
The Magnificent Ambersons, 4–5, 17, 35
Mainwaring, Daniel, 73, 106, 226n61
Man About Town, 41, 49
The Man He Found (The Whip Hand), 136
Mannix, Eddie, 66
March of Time, xiii, 13
Marcus, Philip, 99

Marine Raiders, 22
Marry Me Again, 161, 162
Marshal, Alan, 23, 34
Martin, Tony, 142
Marx, Groucho, 94
The Master Race, 22
Mayer, Louis B., 37, 132
McCall, Mary Jr., 126–27
McCarey, Leo, 24, 28, 210
McCormick, S. Barret, 10, 141
McGraw, Charles, 117–18
McGuire, Dorothy, 23, 30
McNally, Stephen, 141, 147
McNamee, Frank, 170
Mendes, Lothar, 13
Menjou, Adolphe, 64
Mercury Productions, 7, 9, 35
Metro-Goldwyn-Mayer (MGM), 21, 33, 34, 94, 123, 143, 170, 197
Mexican Spitfire Sees an Elephant, 9
Meyer, Stanley, 100
The Miami Story (The Las Vegas Story), 108, 123
Michalson, Harry, 62
Michel, Josef, 124
Mighty Joe Young, 104
Million Dollar Movie, 188–89, 194
The Miracle of the Bells, 76, 79, 189
Miss Sadie Thompson, 130–31
Mitchum, Robert, 18, 40, 59, 70, 74–75, 89–91, 152, 186, 210, 226n60
Mochrie, Robert, 141
Monroe, Marilyn, 131, 184
Montana Belle, 134, 155, 158, 163
The Moon is Blue, 165
Moore, Don, 203
Mother of the Champion (Hard, Fast and Beautiful), 111
Motion Picture Association of America (MPAA), 66, 120, 167
Mourning Becomes Electra, 45, 46, 72–73
Mr. Blandings Builds His Dream House, 58, 59, 79
Mr. Lucky, 17
Mulvey, James, 152, 159
Murder My Sweet, 30, 32, 35

Music in Manhattan, 22
Musuraca, Nicholas, 74, 105, 210
My Forbidden Past, 128, 129, 158
My Pal Wolf, 22
Mystery in Mexico, 62, 224n9

The Naked and the Dead, 198, 207
Name, Age and Occupation, 7–8
The Narrow Margin, 116–18, 134
National Broadcasting Company (NBC), 78
The Navy Comes Through, 9, 10
neorealism, 95–96
Nevada, 22
newsreel. *See* RKO Pathe Newsreel
Nichols, Dudley, 16, 24, 45, 46, 72–73, 106
Night Song, 79, 173
Nixon, Richard M., 126
Nocturne, 38, 72
Nolan, J.J., 4, 83, 105
None but the Lonely Heart, 22, 64
Norton, Kay, 141
Notorious, 38, 53–55

oaters, 61
Oberon, Merle, 59, 142, 153
Oboler, Arch, 142
O'Brien, Pat, 18, 25, 34, 35, 38
Odets, Clifford, 22, 64
Odlum, Floyd, 2, 18, 178, 212–15; Chairman of the Board, 20, 88–89; and Dore Schary, 50, 67–68, 72; interest in *Flight for Freedom*, 12–13; RKO Board resignation, 92–94; RKO theaters, 99–100; stock purchase, 147, 169; stock sale to Hughes, 78, 79–81, 182. *See also* Atlas Corporation
O'Donnell, Cathy, 59
Office of War Information, 17, 25
On Dangerous Ground, 111, 134
Once Upon a Honeymoon, 9, 10
One Minute to Zero, 125, 134, 151
O'Neil, Thomas F., 178, 188–92, 197–209; distribution deal, 201–2, 204–5, 206–7; RKO sale, 207–8; television

rights sale, 193–94. *See also* RKO Teleradio Pictures
O'Neil, William F., 188
O'Neill, Eugene, 45
Ophuls, Max, 81, 230n25
O'Shea, Daniel T., 29, 190–93, 195–96, 198–99, 202, 208
Ostrow, Lou, 15–16
Out of the Past, 60, 71, 73–74, 75, 194, 226n61
The Outlaw, 44, 81, 116, 156, 163, 167
overhead, 62, 94, 143, 204

Paley, William, 78
Paramount, 21, 33, 40, 48, 106, 170, 222n6
Paramount case, 47, 77, 91–93
Parsons, Harriet, 59, 110, 173–75
Parsons, Louella, 97, 175, 229n7
Pascal, Gabriel, 142
Passport to Destiny, 22
Pathe. *See* RKO Pathe
Pathe newsreel. *See* RKO Pathe Newsreel
Paxinou, Katina, 73
Paxton, John, 57, 69, 106
Payment on Demand, 111
Peck, Gregory, 27, 127, 155
Pegler, Westbrook, 67
Pereira, William, 40, 59, 63, 224n15
Peter Pan, 145
Petticoat Larceny, 15
Piazza, Ben, 106, 232n64
Picker, Arnold, 140, 146
picket lines, 28, 29, 48
Pickman, Milton, 131
Pirosh, Robert, 79, 106
Porter, Jean 70
Portrait of Jenny, 62
Potter, H.C., 58, 142
Powell, Dick, 30, 38, 59, 74, 141, 147, 160, 173
prestige films, 8, 22, 45
Price, Vincent, 134, 142
Pride of the Yankees, 17
Prince, Don, 141

Production Code Administration, 16, 44, 54–55, 73, 129, 165–67, 176–78
profits, 15, 21, 33, 56, 106, 170, 214; 1929–30, xi; 1942–43, 10–11, 16–17, 20; 1943–44, 25–26, 27; 1945–46, 32, 51; 1946–47, 53–54, 56; 1947–48, 69, 72, 74, 77; 1948–49, 90, 94; 1949–50, 104; 1951–52, 118
promotion, 175. See also advertising; publicity
Public Pigeon No. 1, 206, 209
publicity, 53, 63, 89, 102–3, 134–35, 175–76

Quigley, Martin, 190

Race Street, 79, 89
Rachel and the Stranger, 79, 89–90
Rachmil, Lew, 105, 145
The Racket, 95, 151
Radio Corporation of America (RCA), xi, 2, 18, 211
Raft, George, 38, 90, 94
Rage at Dawn, 176
Rainbow Productions, 28, 32
Ramo, Simon, 186
Rangers of the North (Dangerous Mission), 162
Rank, J. Arthur, 31, 49, 60, 128, 222n30
Rashomon, 134
Rathvon, N. Peter: Churubusco, 31, 62, 84; corporate presidency, 2, 48, 56, 84, 214; contracts, 71; and Dore Schary, 49–51, 58, 59; foreign productions, 41–42; Head of production, 37–39, 41–45, 51, 56, 60, 72, 214; and Howard Hughes, 78, 82, 85, 170, 228n83; HUAC fallout, 67, 68; and independent producers, 45–47; relationship with Charles Koerner, 9–10, 20–21, 27, 39; resignation, 83–84
rationing, 15
Ray, Nicholas, 57, 95, 130, 142, 210, 230n24
receivership, 1, 159, 212
Redgrave, Michael, 73

Reich, Bernard, 159
Reis, Irving, 16
Reisman, Phil, 141
Renoir, Jean, 35
Republic Pictures, 34, 151
Return of the Badmen, 71, 89
Reynolds, Debbie, 193, 203–04
Riff-Raff, 45
Riskin, Robert, 46–47
Ritter, Joseph E., 167
Rivkin, Joe, 119
RKO Board of Directors, 20, 50, 88–89, 92, 99, 103, 138, 145–46, 148, 169
RKO film library, 189–90, 193–94
RKO Pathe, 22, 40, 48, 62, 78, 205
RKO Pathe Newsreel, xiii, 13, 62, 77
RKO Pictures Corporation, 121–22, 146, 168; executive restructuring, 141, 145; performance, 134, 141, 143, 172; sale, 137, 178–79
RKO Radio Pictures: antitrust negotiations, 47, 77, 91–92, 99, 104, 106; casting, 18, 34, 59; contributions to war effort, 4, 13, 20; corporate profits, 20, 27, 56; cost-cutting, 70–72, 77, 78; escalating costs, 20, 42, 60–61, 63, 76; executive instability, xii, 2, 86–87; expansion plans, 38; fiscal concerns, 3–4, 76–77, 79, 94, 99, 104; fiscal health, 9, 10–11, 32, 33–34, 51; HUAC fallout, 65–68; personnel problems, 14–15, 43; reputation, 17–18, 34, 35–36, 86; sale, 79–82; stars, 4, 18, 25, 30, 34, 38, 39–40, 59; stock performance, 18, 78; studio facilities, 40–41, 62–63, 78. *See also* coproductions; divestiture; Gower Street studio; losses; profits; RKO Board of Directors; RKO film library; RKO Pathe; RKO Pictures Corporation; RKO stock; RKO Teleradio Pictures; RKO Theaters
RKO ranch, 40, 156-7
RKO stock, 18, 72, 78, 80, 123, 137, 147–50, 168–70

RKO Teleradio Pictures, 190, 194, 204, 209
RKO Theaters, 93, 99, 121, 137
The Robe, 41, 60, 127, 154, 235n71, 72
Robinson, Casey, 26, 27
Robinson, Edward G., 25
Robson, Mark, 5, 19, 43
Rockefeller, Nelson, 5, 213
The Rockefeller family, 2, 18, 213–14
Rogell, Sid: B unit, 16, 42, 59; studio manager, 4; under Howard Hughes, 88, 90, 94, 100, 102–5, 158
Rogers, Ginger, 25, 30, 181, 199, 209, 210, 220n71
Rogers, Lela, 64
Roosevelt, Franklin D., 13, 27
Ross, Frank, 41, 106, 127
Rossellini, Roberto, 96–98
Roughshod, 79, 89, 104
Run of the Arrow, 196, 206
Russell, Jane, 131, 135, 153, 160–61, 163, 165–67, 184, 185–86
Russell, Rosalind, 18, 23, 30, 45, 73, 106
Ryan, Ray, 137–39, 143–44
Ryan, Robert, 8, 18, 25, 40, 70, 75, 95, 210, 230n25

Sacks, Jacob, 153, 159–60, 170
Sam Wynne (Strange Bargain), 94
Sarnoff, David, xi, 18, 211–12, 214
Savage Splendor, 104
Scanlon, Ernest L., 146
Schaefer, George J., xii, 1–2, 4, 5, 9, 47, 213–14
Schary, Dore, 49–51, 57–60, 65–77, 81–85, 158, 214–15; contract, 71–72, 79; defense of *Crossfire*, 68–69, 76; HUAC fallout, 65–68; liberal, 57, 81; production decisions, 59–60, 76–77, 79; resignation, 83, 84; scorecard, 79, 85
Schenck, Joseph, 37
Schiff, Louis, 153, 159–60, 170
Schwartz, Sol, 37
Scott, Adrian, 43, 49, 64, 65–67, 68, 89
Scott, Randolph, 38

Screen Actors Guild, 48
Screen Writers Guild, 124, 126–27
Sealed Cargo, 108, 111
Seitz, Collins J., 170
Seitz, Helen, 207, 210
Selznick, David O., 27, 28–29, 50, 54, 58–59, 132–33, 191, 210, 212
Semenenko, Serge, 132–33
The Set Up, 83, 194
Seven Days Ashore, 22, 25
Seven Days Leave, 9, 11
Seven Miles From Alcatraz, 9
Seven Witnesses (Hunt the Man Down), 105
The Seventh Victim, 18
She Couldn't Say No, 162
She Had to Say Yes (She Couldn't Say No), 162
She Wore a Yellow Ribbon, 94
Sheridan, Ann, 127–28, 153
Shores, Lynn, 5–6
Show Business, 26
Shurlock, Geoffrey M., 177
Siegel, Don, 90–91
Silberberg, Mendel, 65
Simmons, Jean, 128–29, 184
The Sin of Harold Diddlebock (Mad Wednesday), 81
Sinatra, Frank, 18, 23, 25, 38, 94
Sinbad the Sailor, 38, 48, 52–53
Sister Kenny, 22–23, 38, 45
Size Twelve, 131, 174
Skirball, Jack, 155–56
The Sky's the Limit, 17
Slack, Thomas, 99, 158, 163, 189
Slaughter Trail, 124
Smith, Alexis, 141
So Well Remembered, 31, 41, 49, 79
social-issue films, 57, 68
Sokolsky, George, 67
Son of Sinbad, 154, 161, 162, 176–78, 193, 243n98
Sons of the Musketeers (At Sword's Point), 111
Sorrell, Herbert, 28, 48
Sothern, Ann, 59
The Spanish Main, 32, 51, 124

Sparks, Robert, 59, 74
The Spiral Staircase, 38, 45, 50, 51
Spitz, Leo, 25, 37, 212–13
Split Second, 141, 146–47, 151
Stage Struck, 206, 208
Stanwyck, Barbara, 130
stars, 4, 18, 25, 30, 34, 40, 122, 185, 209
Station West, 71, 89
Steele, James B., 186
Steiger, Rod, 196, 209
Step Lively, 21
Sterling, Jan, 141, 147
Stevens, George, 29–30, 46, 122, 210
Stevenson, Robert, 95
Stewart, James, 51, 52
stock. *See* RKO stock
Stolkin, Ralph, 137–140, 143–45, 146, 156
The Stolkin syndicate, 137, 147–49. *See also* Burke, Edward; Corwin, Sherrill; Koolish, Abraham; Ryan, Ray; Stolkin, Ralph
Story of a Divorce (Payment on Demand), 111
Strange Bargain, 94
Strike a Match, 131
strikes, 28, 31, 48, 53, 60
Stromboli, 95–98
Sturges, Preston, 81
Suid, Lawrence, 125
Superscope, 172, 242n85
Susan Slept Here, 174

Talbot, Harold E., 186
Tall in the Saddle, 22, 26
Target (The Narrow Margin), 116
Tarzan Triumphs, 20
Taurog, Norman, 204
taxes. *See* British tax; income tax
Technicolor, 32, 48, 53
television, 76, 123, 157, 188, 193–94, 197, 207
Tender Comrade, 16, 22, 25, 26, 64
Tension at Table Rock, 195, 199, 200
Territorial Prison (Devil's Canyon), 154

Tevlin, C.J., xiv, 83, 88, 112, 119, 134, 149, 157, 158, 177
Texas Lady, 176
theaters, 13, 33, 47–48, 91–93, 99, 104, 106, 121, 189–90; drive-in theaters, 60; first-run theaters, 60; foreign theaters, 31, 42. *See also* divestiture, Paramount case, RKO Theaters
They Got Me Covered, 17
They Live by Night, 76, 89, 104
They Won't Believe Me, 45, 60
This is America, 13
This Land Is Mine, 35
This Man is Mine (The Lusty Men), 130
Thomas, J. Parnell, 67
Those Endearing Young Charms, 32
Thunder in the North (Dangerous Mission), 154
Thunder Mountain, 61
Tierney, Lawrence, 40, 106
Till the End of Time, 38, 50, 51
Tom, Dick and Harry 123, 208
Tone, Franchot, 127–8
Tourneur, Jacques, 19, 26, 74–75, 210
Trail Street, 60, 72
Trans World Airlines, 171, 182, 186, 236n78
Truman, Harry S., 27, 77, 227n68
Trumbo, Dalton, 64
Turner, Terry, 141, 199
Twentieth Century-Fox, 21, 33, 122, 127, 170
Two Tickets to Broadway, 108, 112, 116, 135, 163
Tycoon, 72

Underhill, William Amory, 99
Underwater!, 175–76
Ungar, Arthur, 34
The Unholy Wife, 206, 208
unions, 28, 48
United Artists, 33, 71, 122, 165, 170, 209
Universal Pictures, 33, 94, 122, 170, 202–4, 206

Valli, Alida, 59
Van Kirk, Walter W., 97
Van Schmus, Albert E., 184
Van Wagner, Garrett, 159
Vanguard Films, 29, 54. *See also* Selznick, David O.
Velez, Lupe, 217n11
The Velvet Touch, 79
Vendetta, 109, 116, 129, 156
vertical integration, 47, 77, 91–93
Vickers, Joseph W., 156

Wakamba!, 176
Wald, Jerry, 112–16, 119–20, 130, 132–33, 140, 145, 157
Wald-Krasna Productions, 112–16, 118–20, 130–32
The Waldorf Declaration, 66
Walk Softly, Stranger, 79, 89, 102
Walker, J. Miller, 141, 148
Walton, Edward L., 202
Wanger, Walter, 66
war bonds, 13
War Chest, 24
Warner, Harry, 15, 37, 240n23
Warner, Jack, 37, 240n23
Warner Bros., 15, 21, 33, 122–23, 170, 207
Wayne, John, 18, 25, 38, 172–73, 206
Webb, Roy, 54, 210
Weep No More (Walk Softly, Stranger), 102
Weisl, Ed, 9
Welles, Orson, 4–7, 9–10, 35, 210
westerns, 22, 61, 134
Where Danger Lives, 109, 116
White, Jacqueline, 117–18
White, Paul, 147
The White Tower, 41, 49, 100, 123
The Whip Hand, 136
widescreen, 154. *See also* CinemaScope; Superscope

Wild, Harry J., 210
Wilkerson, W. R., 112, 125–26, 144, 170, 203–04, 209
Wilkinson, Jim, 117, 177, 207, 210
Willi, Arthur, 141
Winchester Productions, 102
The Window, 62, 89
Windsor, Marie, 117–18, 184
Winters, Shelley, 118
Wise, Robert, 4–5, 19, 43, 106, 210
Without Reservations, 38, 51, 229n1
Wolfe, Manny, 73
The Woman in the Window, 25
The Woman on Pier 13, 95, 102, 109
Woman on the Beach, 35, 38, 60, 72
A Woman's Secret, 76, 79, 89
Wooldridge, Dean, 186
Work, Cliff, 100
World War II, 1, 11, 21, 27; studio contributions to war effort, 4, 13, 20; war-themed films, 11, 16–17, 22, 51, 79; wartime filmmaking, 13–15; wartime profits, 15, 20–21, 33; wartime prosperity, 11, 33; wartime shortages, 14–15. *See also* rationing; war bonds
Wright, Robert, 92
Wyler, William, 29, 46, 51
Wyman, Jane, 118

Yates, Herbert, 149
Young, Alan, 142
Young, Loretta, 59
Young, Robert, 38, 69, 70, 127
Youngman, Gordon, 92, 105, 111, 138
Youth Runs Wild, 21, 25

Zamparelli, Mario, 135
Zanuck, Darryl, 37, 94, 115, 122, 127
Zeckendorf, William, 171
Zimmerman, William, 141
Zinnemann, Fred, 106

www.ingramcontent.com/pod-product-compliance
Lightning Source LLC
Chambersburg PA
CBHW020642230426
43665CB00008B/286